YUMEKUI KENBUN

NIGHTMARE INSPECTOR

STORY AND ART BY SHIN MASHIBA

1

LOST THINGS

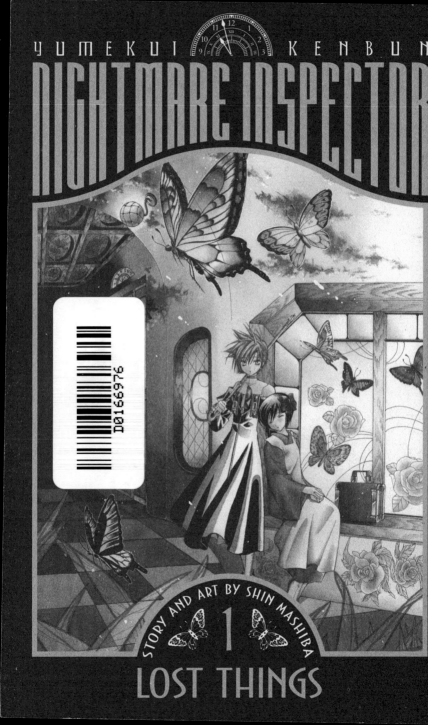

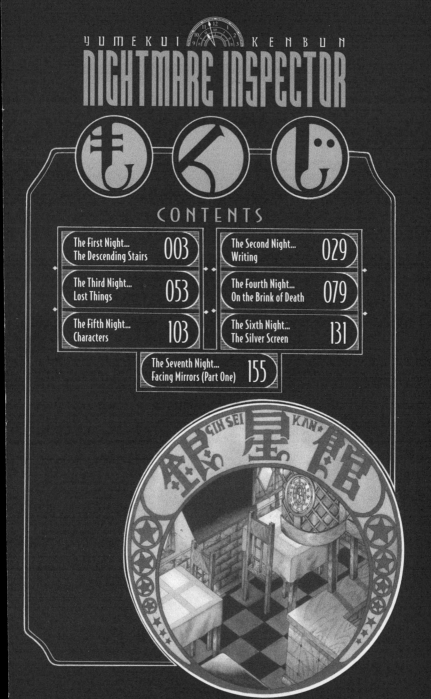

YUMEKUI KENBUN
NIGHTMARE INSPECTOR

CONTENTS

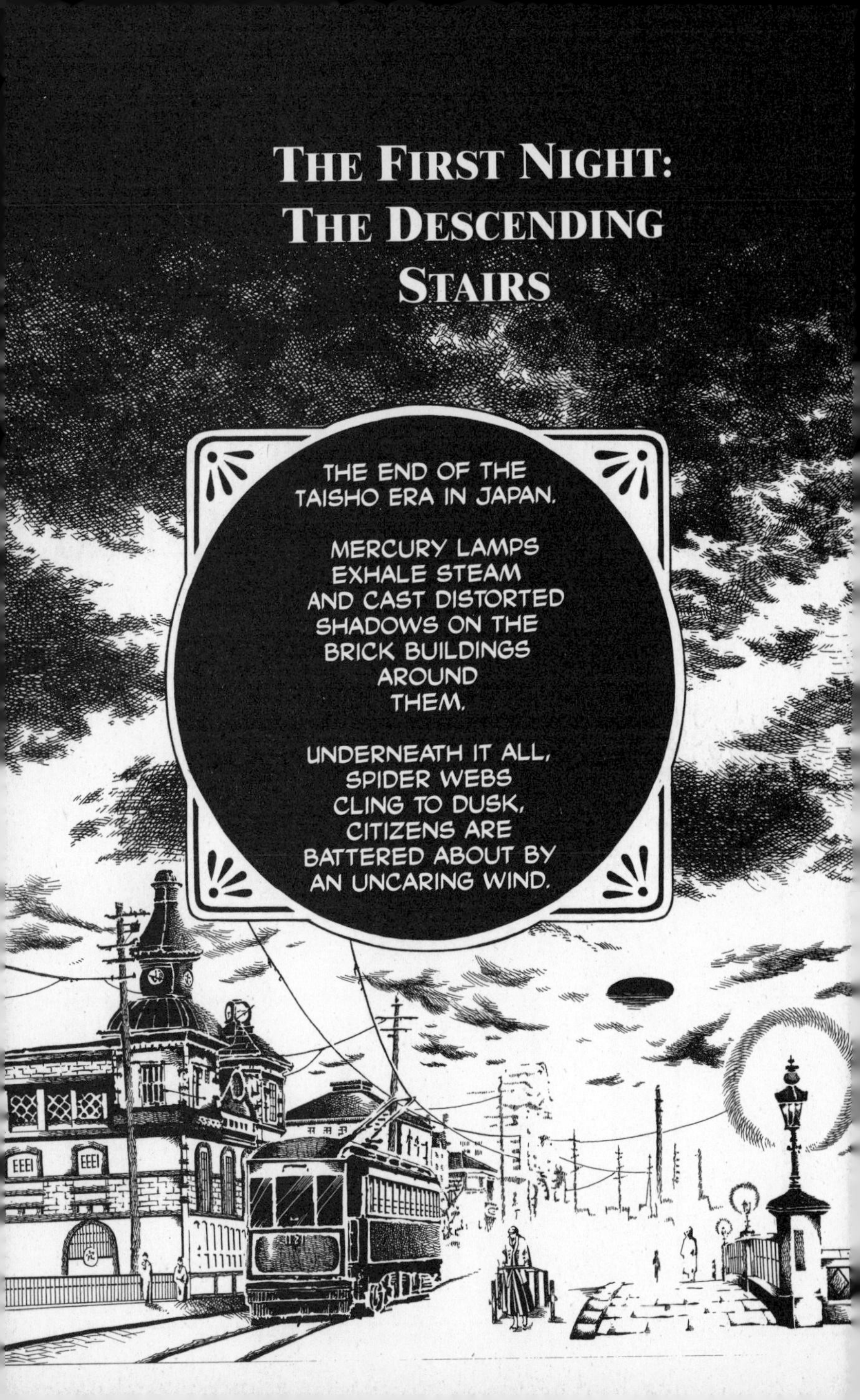
THE FIRST NIGHT: THE DESCENDING STAIRS
THE END OF THE TAISHO ERA IN JAPAN.
MERCURY LAMPS EXHALE STEAM AND CAST DISTORTED SHADOWS ON THE BRICK BUILDINGS AROUND THEM.
UNDERNEATH IT ALL, SPIDER WEBS CLING TO DUSK, CITIZENS ARE BATTERED ABOUT BY AN UNCARING WIND.

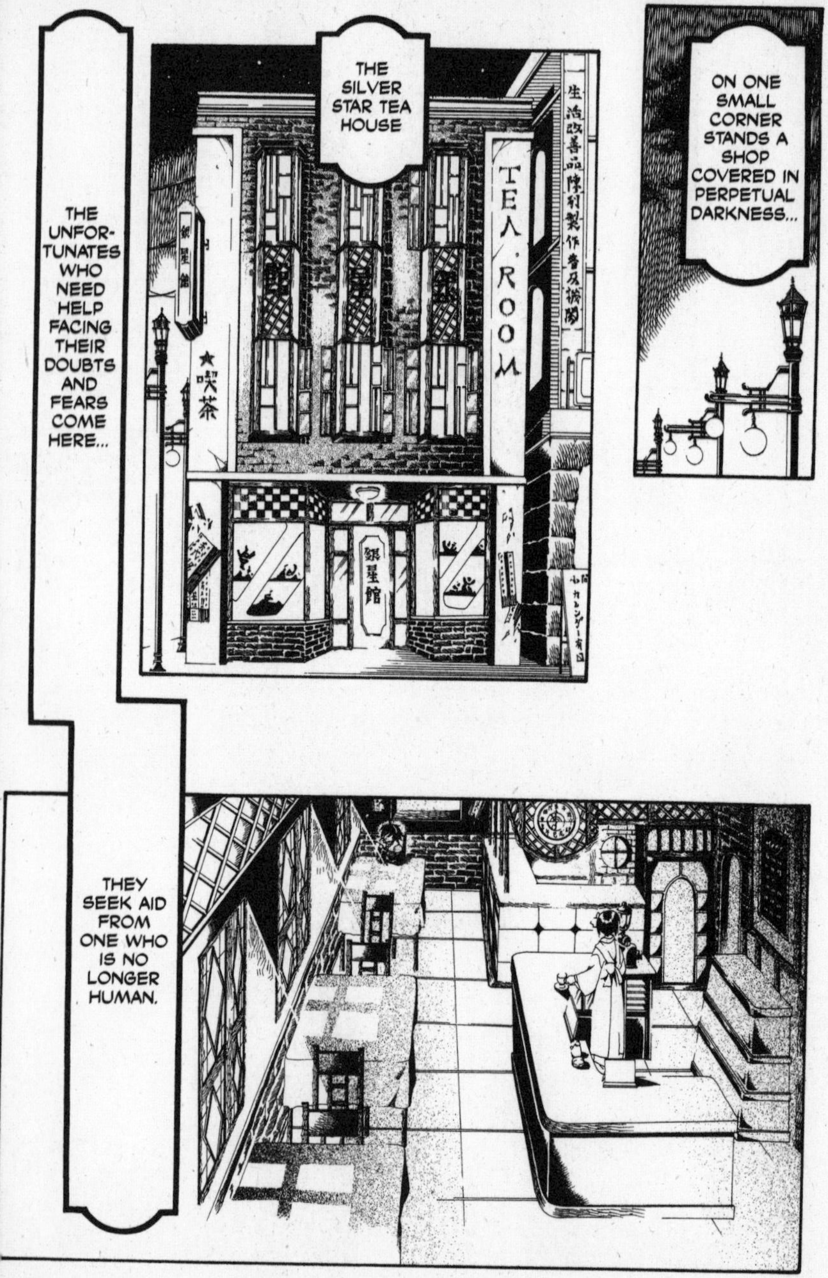
ON ONE SMALL CORNER STANDS A SHOP COVERED IN PERPETUAL DARKNESS...
THE SILVER STAR TEA HOUSE
TEA ROOM
銀星館
喫茶
THE UNFORTUNATES WHO NEED HELP FACING THEIR DOUBTS AND FEARS COME HERE...
THEY SEEK AID FROM ONE WHO IS NO LONGER HUMAN.

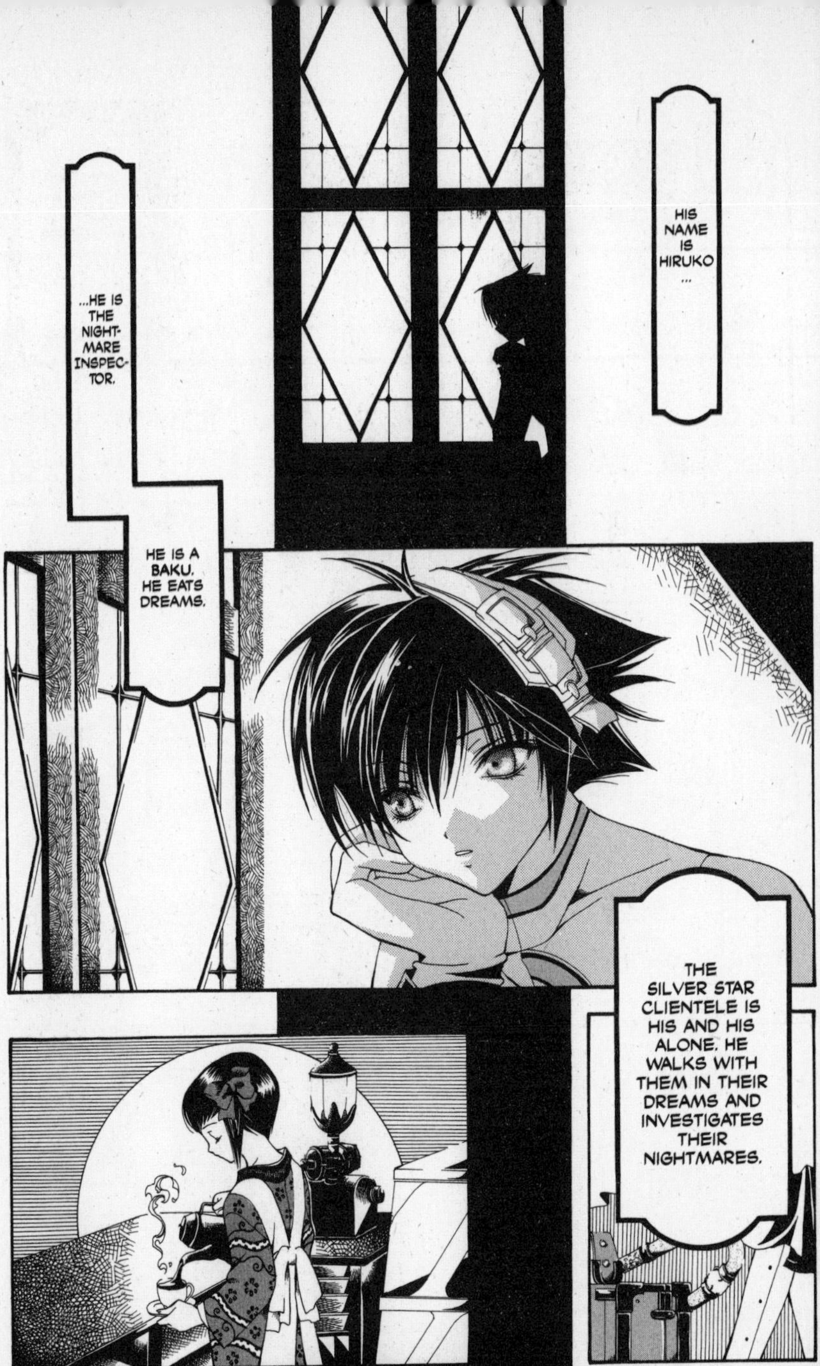
HIS NAME IS HIRUKO...
...HE IS THE NIGHT-MARE INSPEC-TOR.
HE IS A BAKU. HE EATS DREAMS.
THE SILVER STAR CLIENTELE IS HIS AND HIS ALONE. HE WALKS WITH THEM IN THEIR DREAMS AND INVESTIGATES THEIR NIGHTMARES.

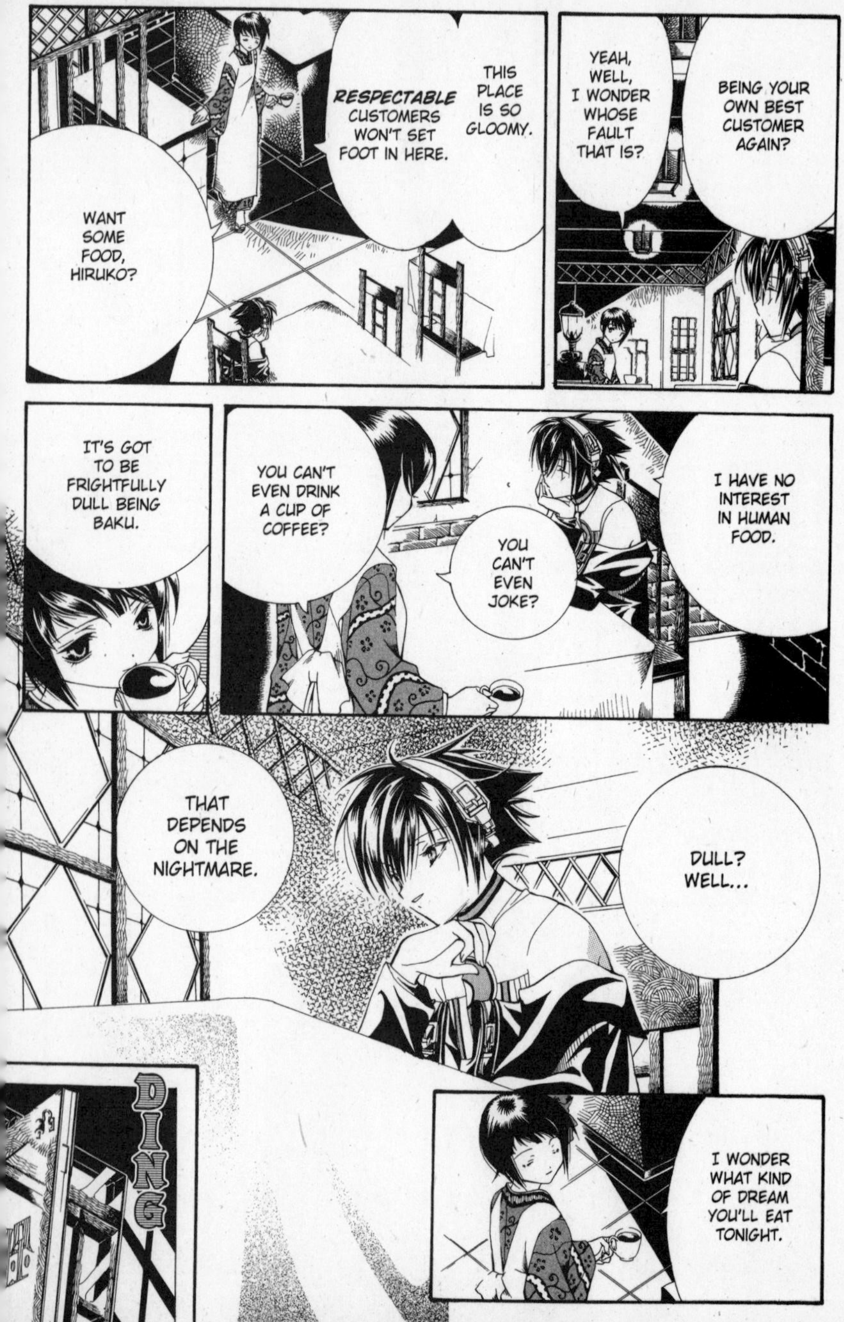
BEING YOUR OWN BEST CUSTOMER AGAIN?
YEAH, WELL, I WONDER WHOSE FAULT THAT IS?
THIS PLACE IS SO GLOOMY.
RESPECTABLE CUSTOMERS WON'T SET FOOT IN HERE.
WANT SOME FOOD, HIRUKO?
I HAVE NO INTEREST IN HUMAN FOOD.
YOU CAN'T EVEN JOKE?
YOU CAN'T EVEN DRINK A CUP OF COFFEE?
IT'S GOT TO BE FRIGHTFULLY DULL BEING BAKU.
DULL? WELL...
THAT DEPENDS ON THE NIGHTMARE.
I WONDER WHAT KIND OF DREAM YOU'LL EAT TONIGHT.
DING

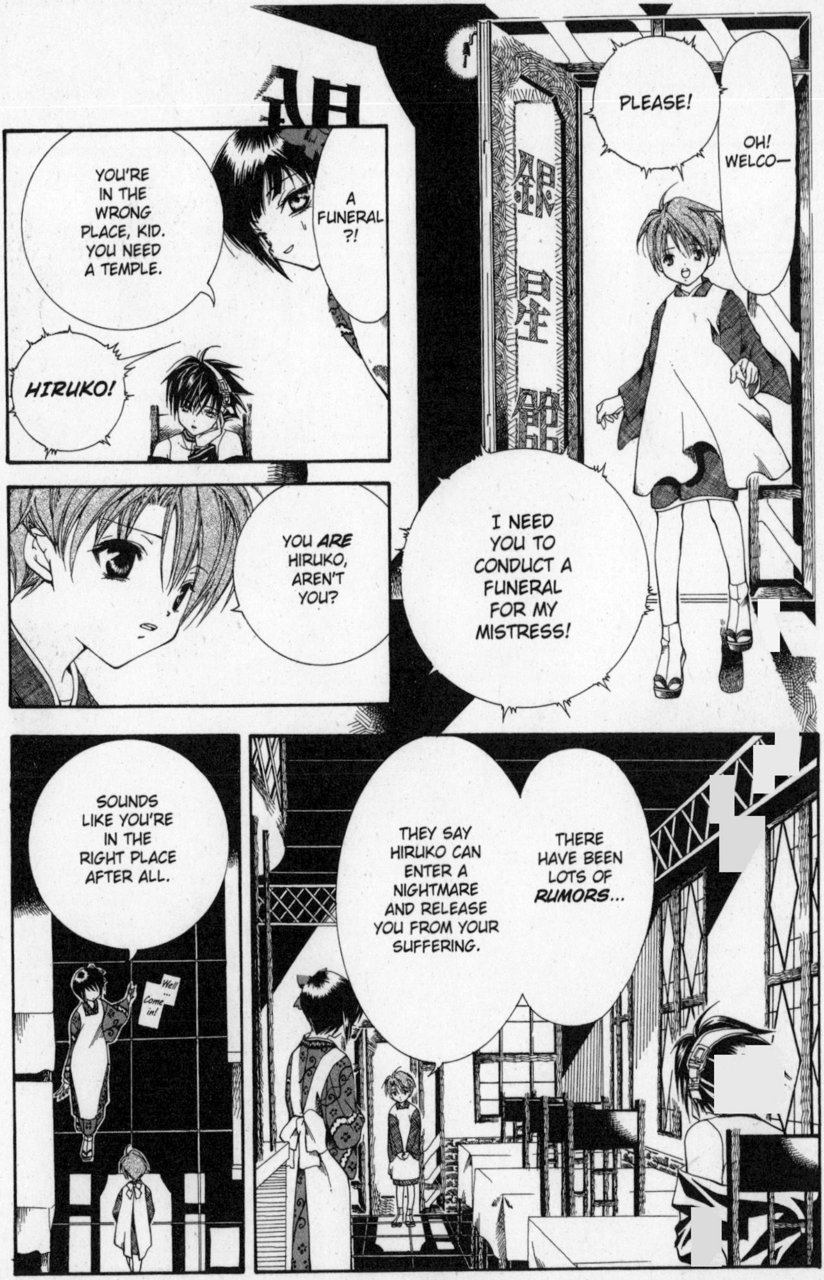
OH! WELCO—
PLEASE!
I NEED YOU TO CONDUCT A FUNERAL FOR MY MISTRESS!
A FUNERAL ?!
YOU'RE IN THE WRONG PLACE, KID. YOU NEED A TEMPLE.
HIRUKO!
YOU ARE HIRUKO, AREN'T YOU?
THERE HAVE BEEN LOTS OF RUMORS...
THEY SAY HIRUKO CAN ENTER A NIGHTMARE AND RELEASE YOU FROM YOUR SUFFERING.
SOUNDS LIKE YOU'RE IN THE RIGHT PLACE AFTER ALL.
Well... Come in!

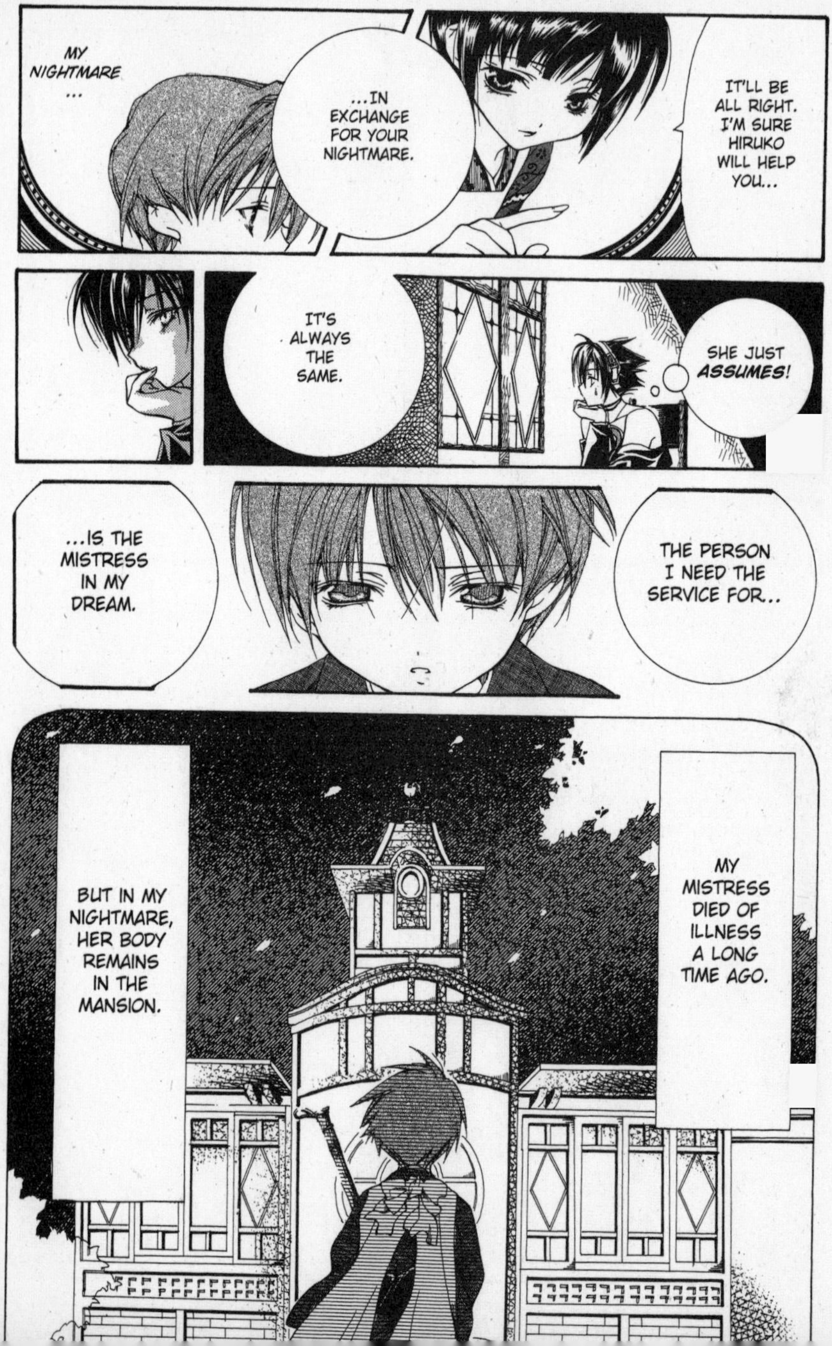
IT'LL BE ALL RIGHT. I'M SURE HIRUKO WILL HELP YOU...
...IN EXCHANGE FOR YOUR NIGHTMARE.
MY NIGHTMARE ...
SHE JUST *ASSUMES*!
IT'S ALWAYS THE SAME.
THE PERSON I NEED THE SERVICE FOR...
...IS THE MISTRESS IN MY DREAM.
MY MISTRESS DIED OF ILLNESS A LONG TIME AGO.
BUT IN MY NIGHTMARE, HER BODY REMAINS IN THE MANSION.

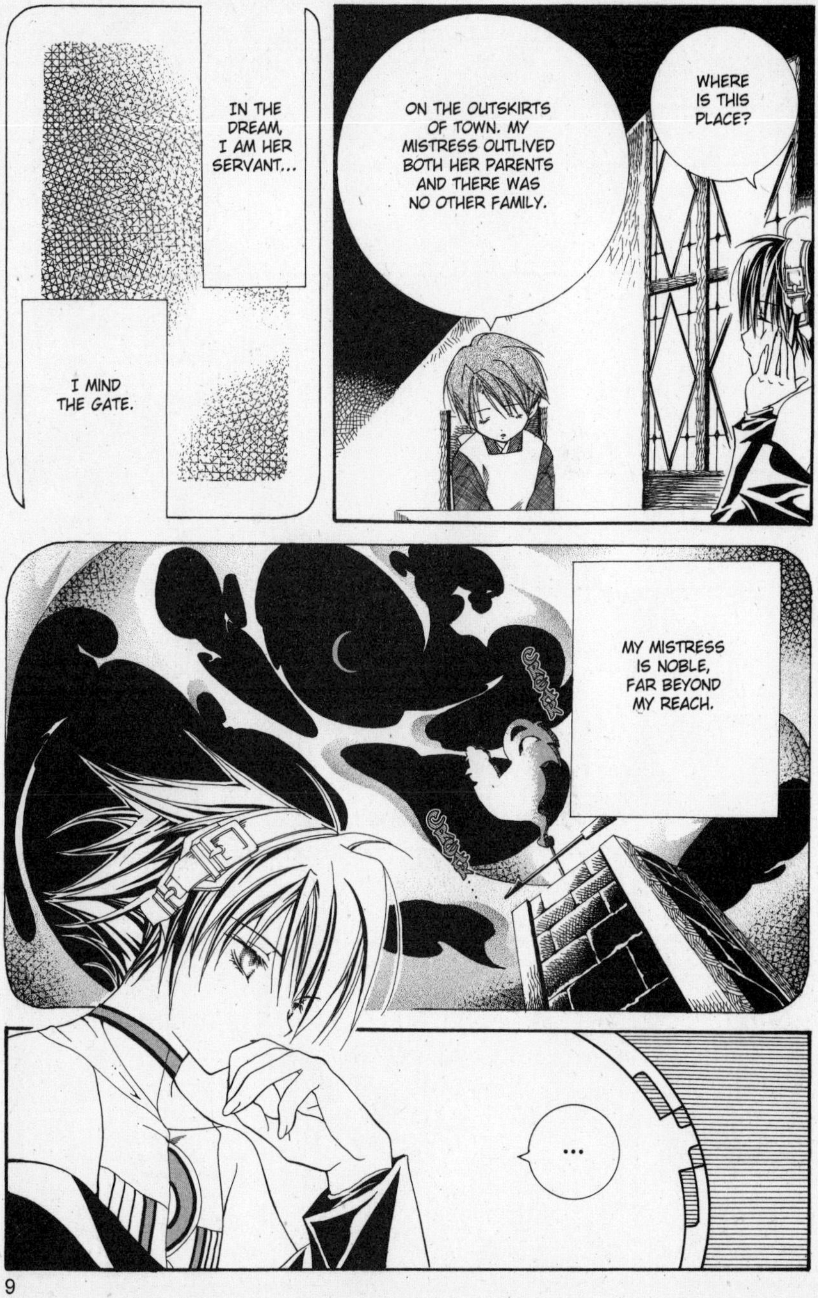
WHERE IS THIS PLACE?
ON THE OUTSKIRTS OF TOWN. MY MISTRESS OUTLIVED BOTH HER PARENTS AND THERE WAS NO OTHER FAMILY.
IN THE DREAM, I AM HER SERVANT...
I MIND THE GATE.
MY MISTRESS IS NOBLE, FAR BEYOND MY REACH.
...

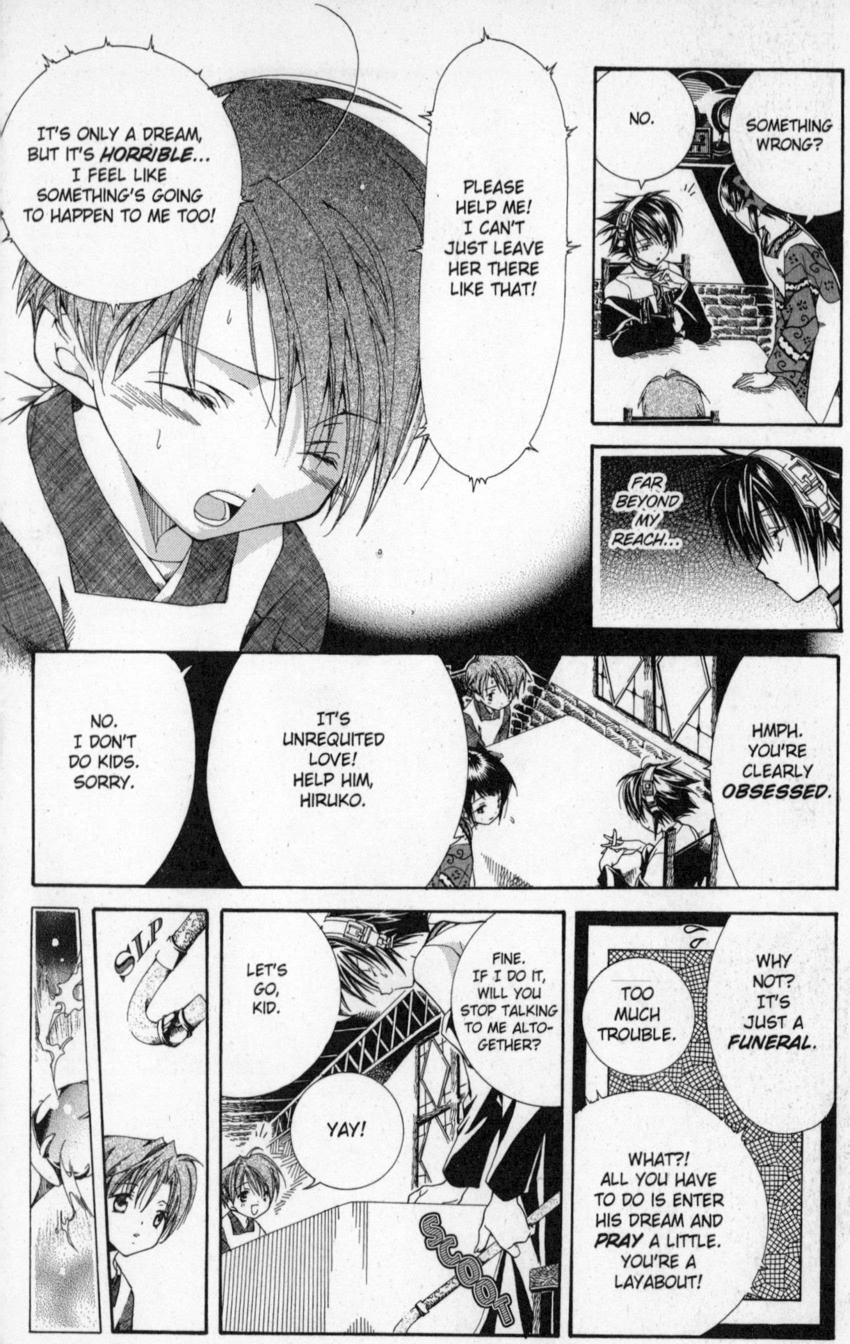
SOMETHING WRONG?
NO.
FAR BEYOND MY REACH...
PLEASE HELP ME! I CAN'T JUST LEAVE HER THERE LIKE THAT!
IT'S ONLY A DREAM, BUT IT'S HORRIBLE... I FEEL LIKE SOMETHING'S GOING TO HAPPEN TO ME TOO!
HMPH. YOU'RE CLEARLY OBSESSED.
IT'S UNREQUITED LOVE! HELP HIM, HIRUKO.
NO. I DON'T DO KIDS. SORRY.
WHY NOT? IT'S JUST A FUNERAL.
TOO MUCH TROUBLE.
WHAT?! ALL YOU HAVE TO DO IS ENTER HIS DREAM AND PRAY A LITTLE. YOU'RE A LAYABOUT!
FINE. IF I DO IT, WILL YOU STOP TALKING TO ME ALTO-GETHER?
LET'S GO, KID.
YAY!
SCOOT
SLP

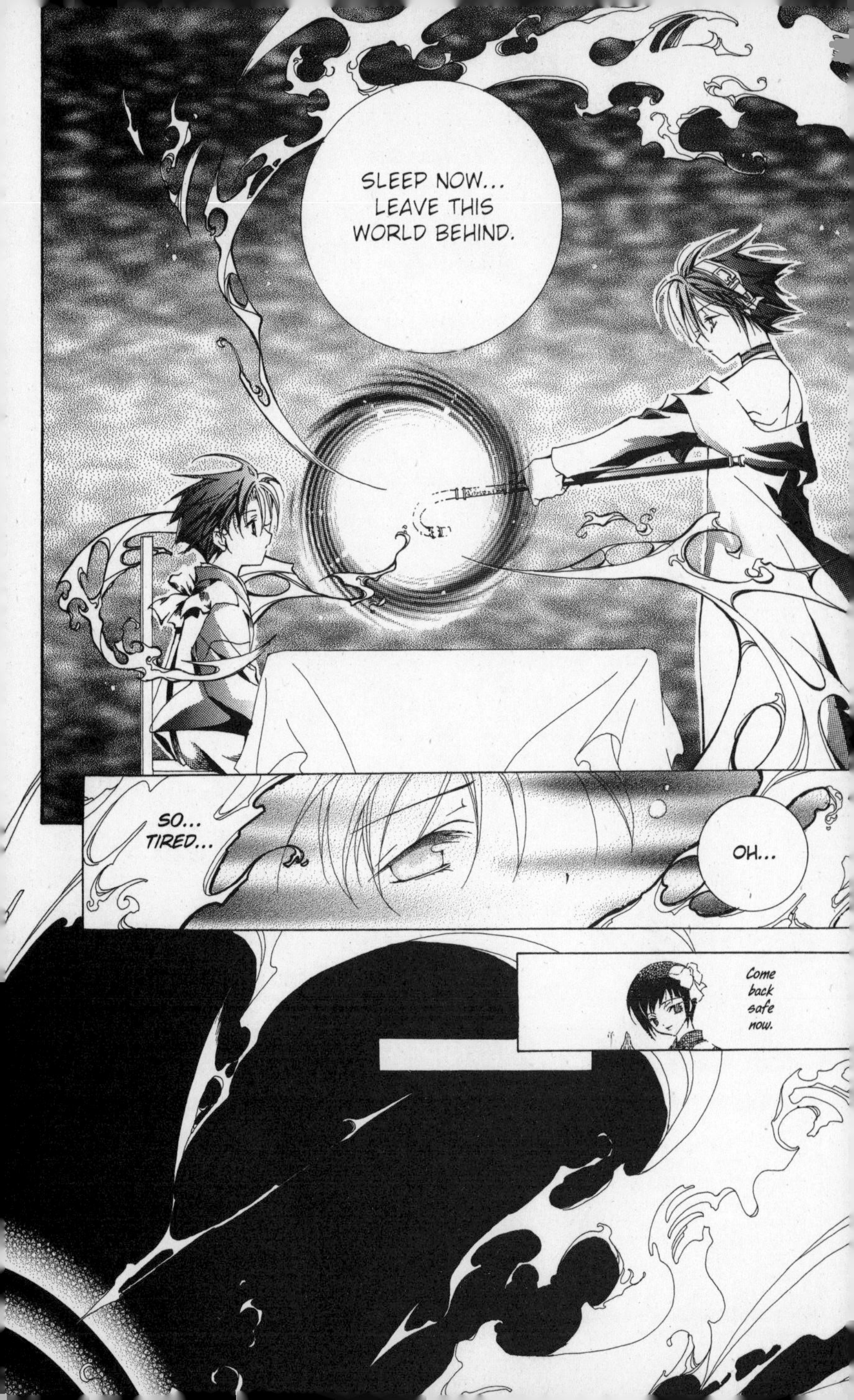
SLEEP NOW... LEAVE THIS WORLD BEHIND.
OH...
SO... TIRED...
Come back safe now.

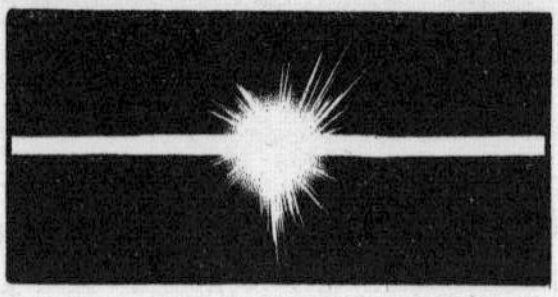

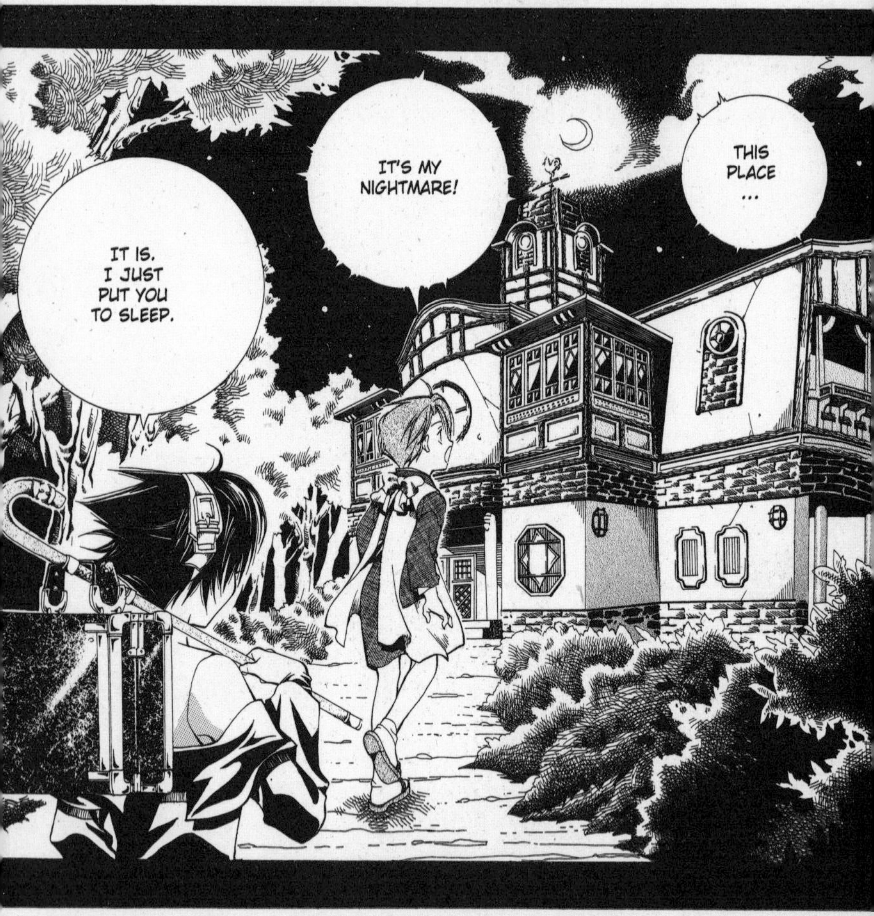
THIS PLACE ...
IT'S MY NIGHTMARE!
IT IS. I JUST PUT YOU TO SLEEP.

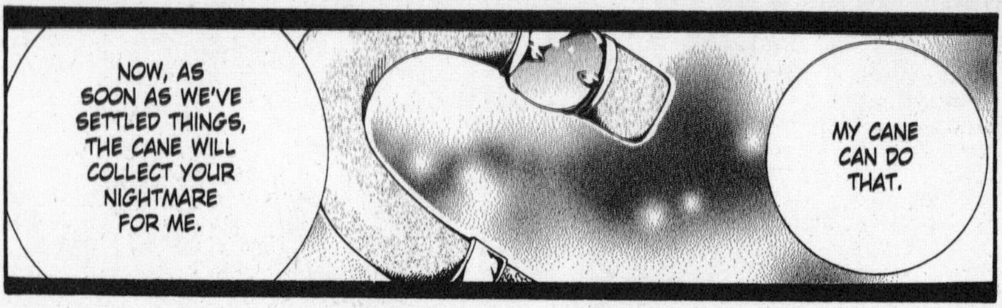
MY CANE CAN DO THAT.
NOW, AS SOON AS WE'VE SETTLED THINGS, THE CANE WILL COLLECT YOUR NIGHTMARE FOR ME.

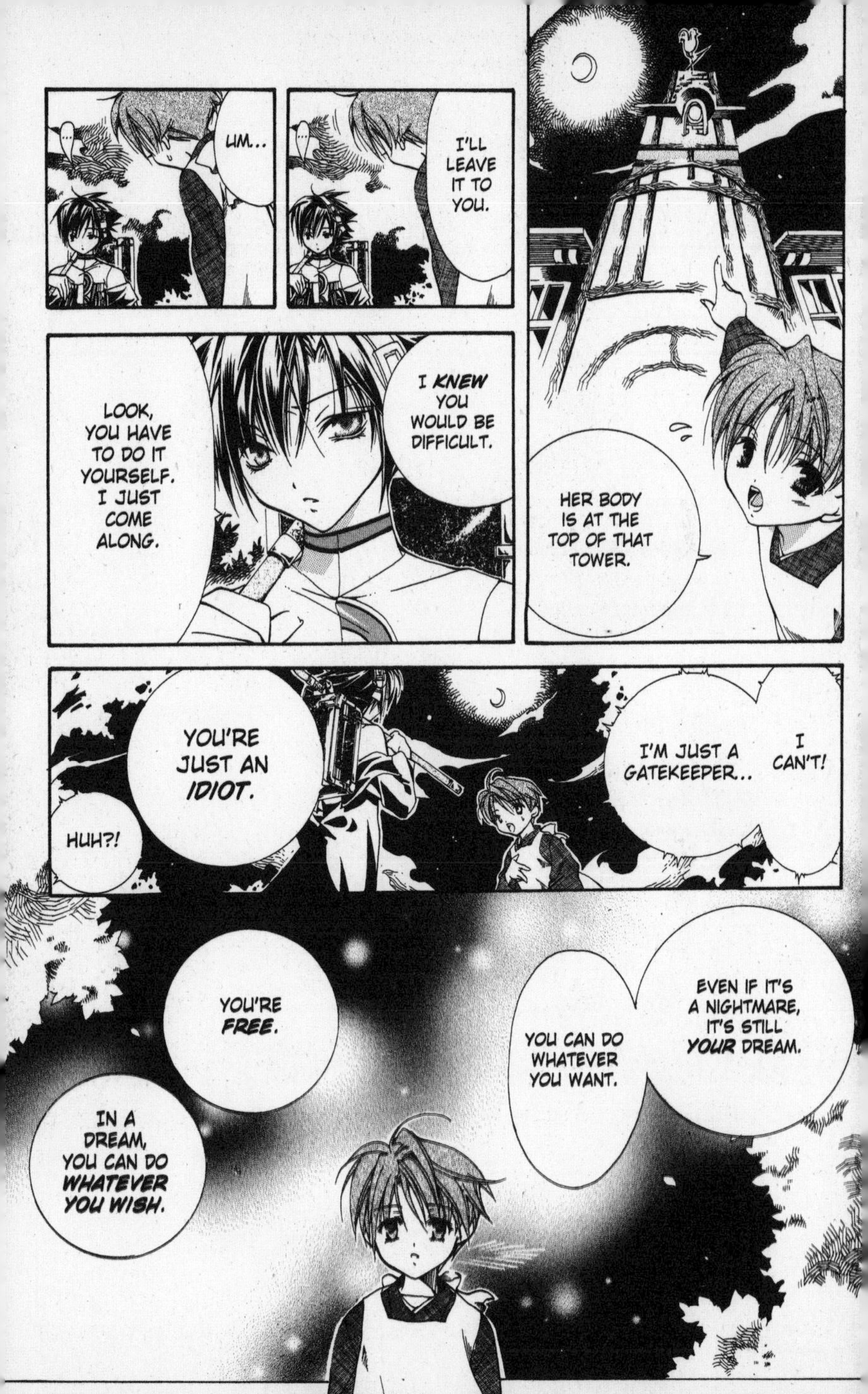
HER BODY IS AT THE TOP OF THAT TOWER.
I'LL LEAVE IT TO YOU.
...
UM...
...
I *KNEW* YOU WOULD BE DIFFICULT.
LOOK, YOU HAVE TO DO IT YOURSELF. I JUST COME ALONG.
I CAN'T!
I'M JUST A GATEKEEPER...
YOU'RE JUST AN *IDIOT*.
HUH?!
EVEN IF IT'S A NIGHTMARE, IT'S STILL *YOUR* DREAM.
YOU CAN DO WHATEVER YOU WANT.
YOU'RE *FREE*.
IN A DREAM, YOU CAN DO *WHATEVER YOU WISH*.

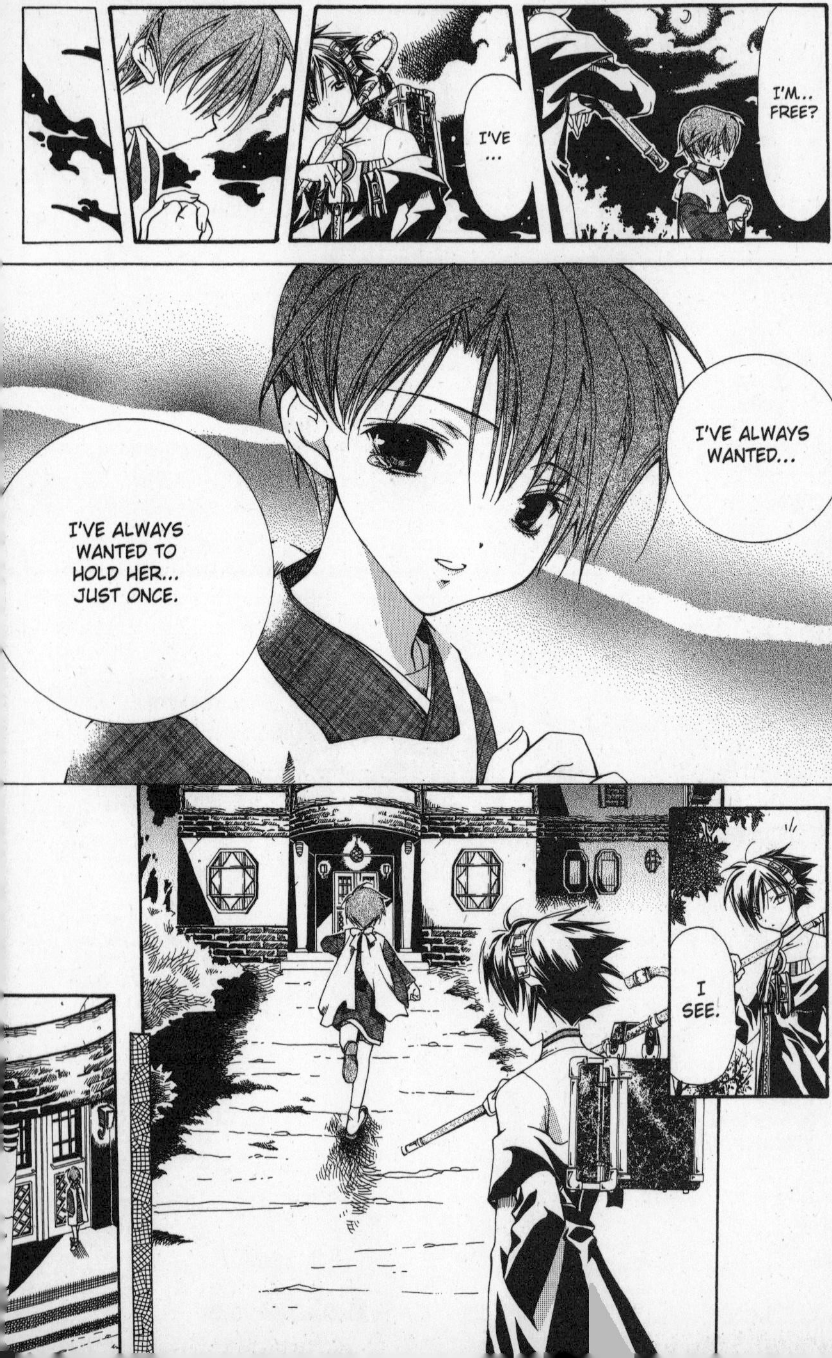
I'M.. FREE?
I'VE ...
I'VE ALWAYS WANTED...
I'VE ALWAYS WANTED TO HOLD HER... JUST ONCE.
I SEE.

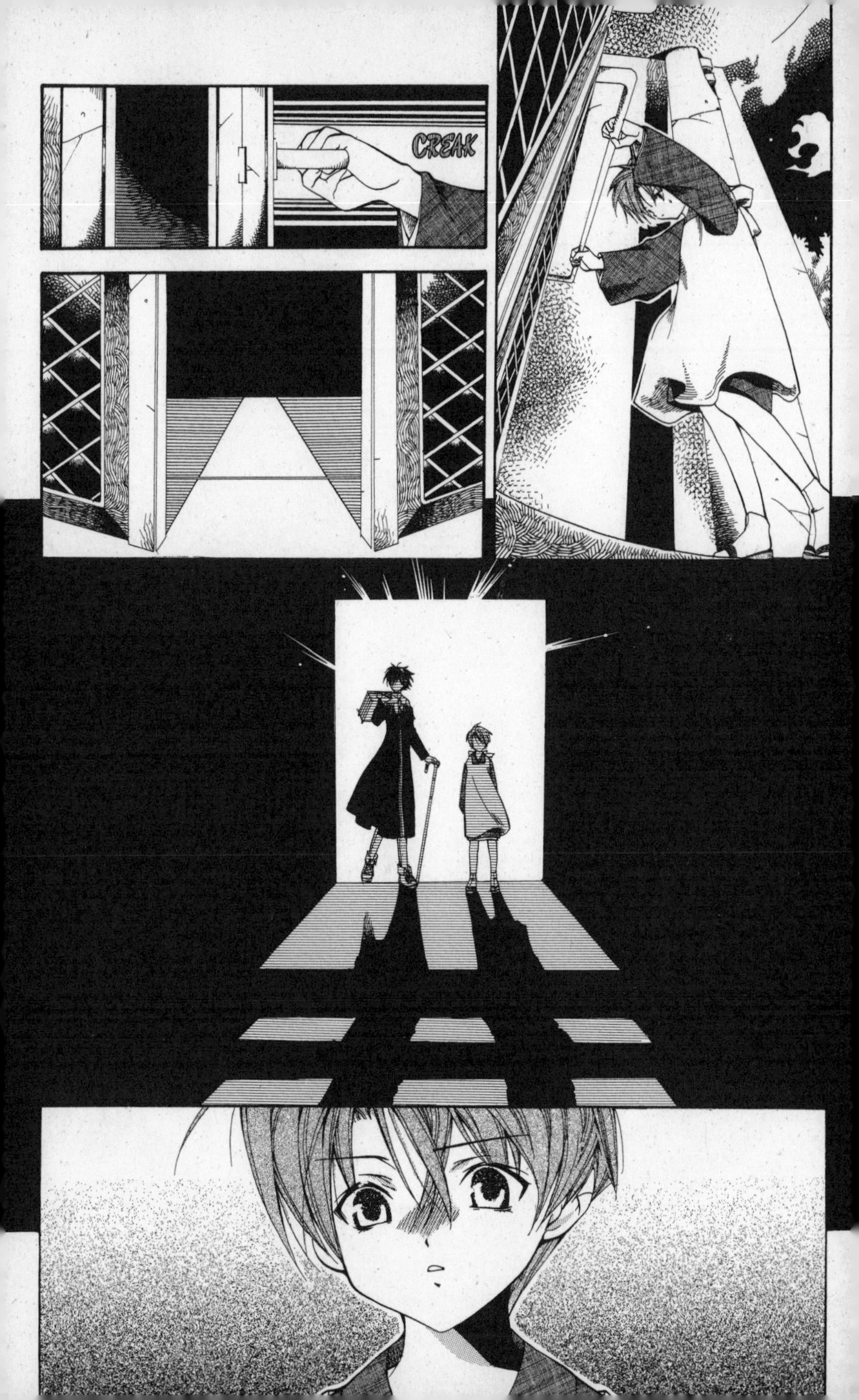
CREAK

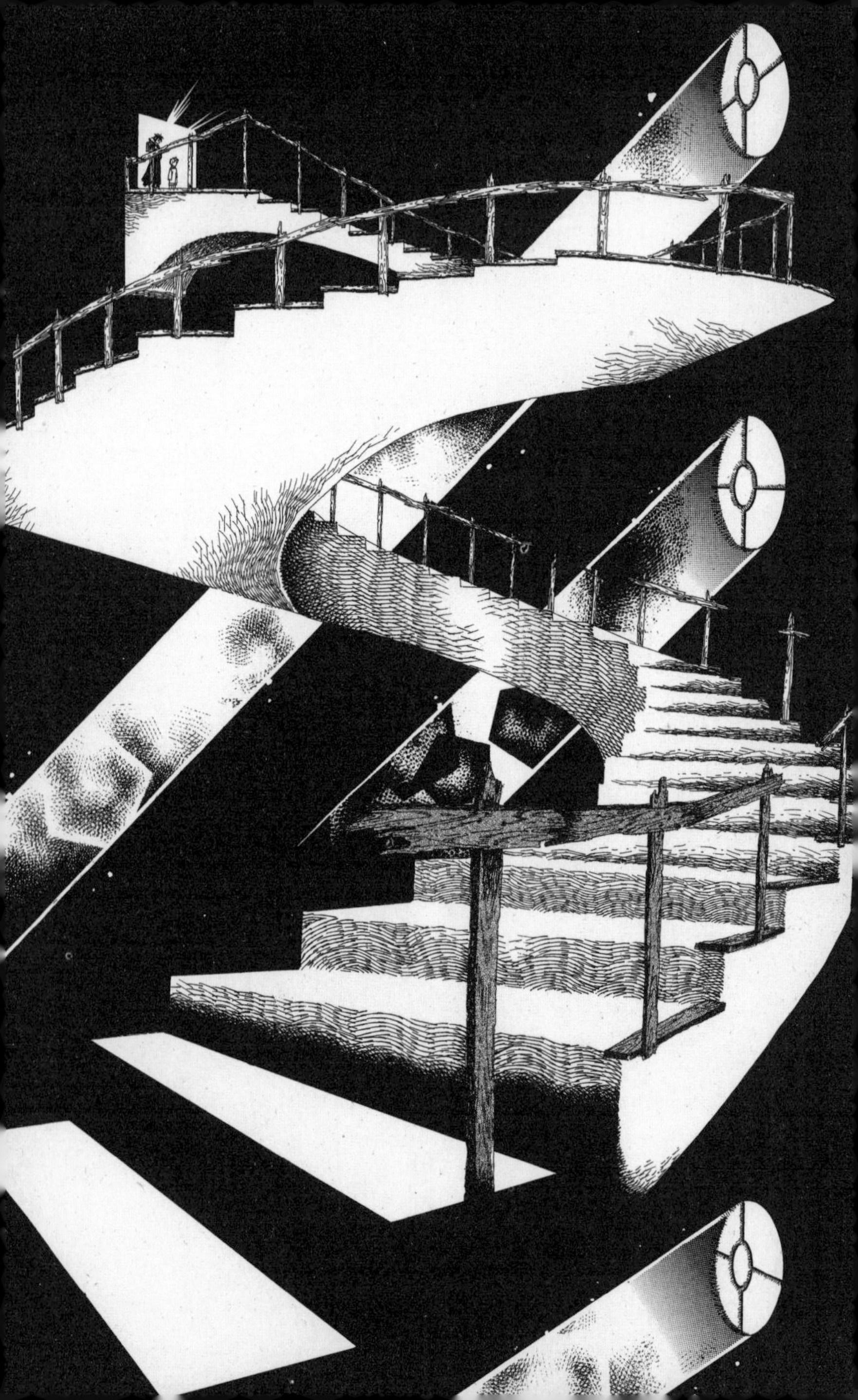

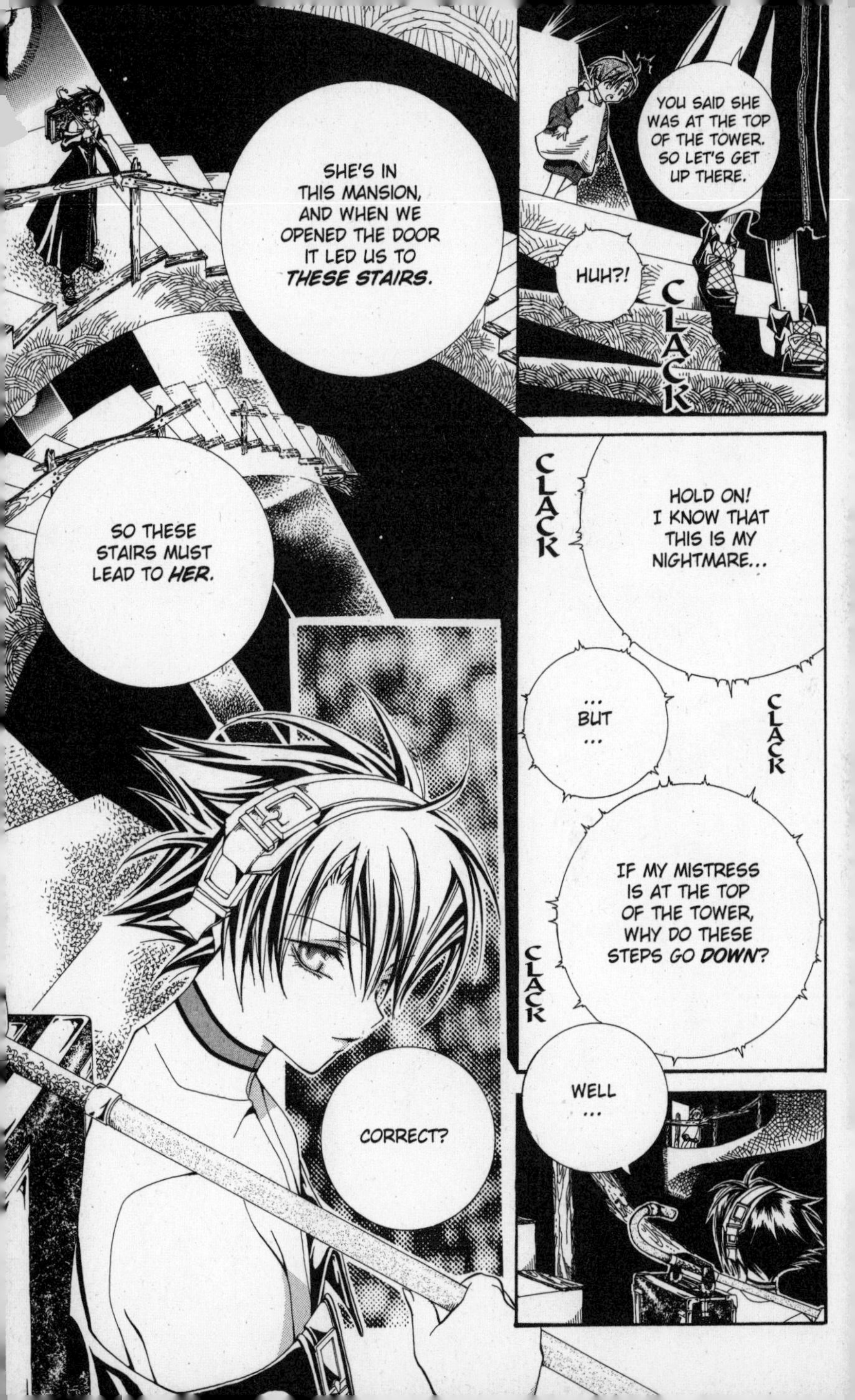
YOU SAID SHE WAS AT THE TOP OF THE TOWER. SO LET'S GET UP THERE.
HUH?!
CLACK
CLACK
HOLD ON! I KNOW THAT THIS IS MY NIGHTMARE...
... BUT ...
CLACK
IF MY MISTRESS IS AT THE TOP OF THE TOWER, WHY DO THESE STEPS GO DOWN?
CLACK
WELL ...
SHE'S IN THIS MANSION, AND WHEN WE OPENED THE DOOR IT LED US TO THESE STAIRS.
SO THESE STAIRS MUST LEAD TO HER.
CORRECT?

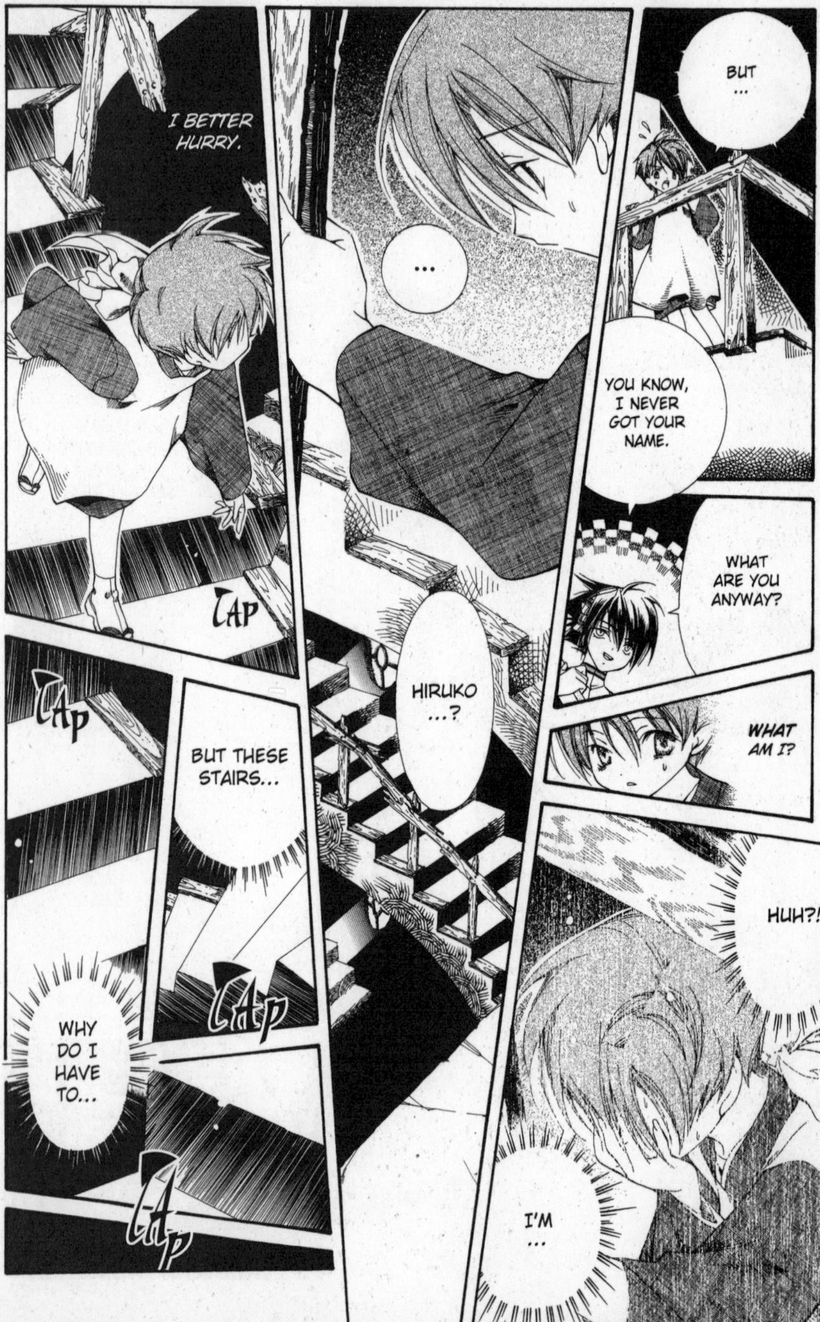
BUT ...
YOU KNOW, I NEVER GOT YOUR NAME.
WHAT ARE YOU ANYWAY?
WHAT AM I?
HUH?!
I'M ...
...
HIRUKO ...?
I BETTER HURRY.
TAP
TAP
BUT THESE STAIRS...
TAP
WHY DO I HAVE TO...
TAP

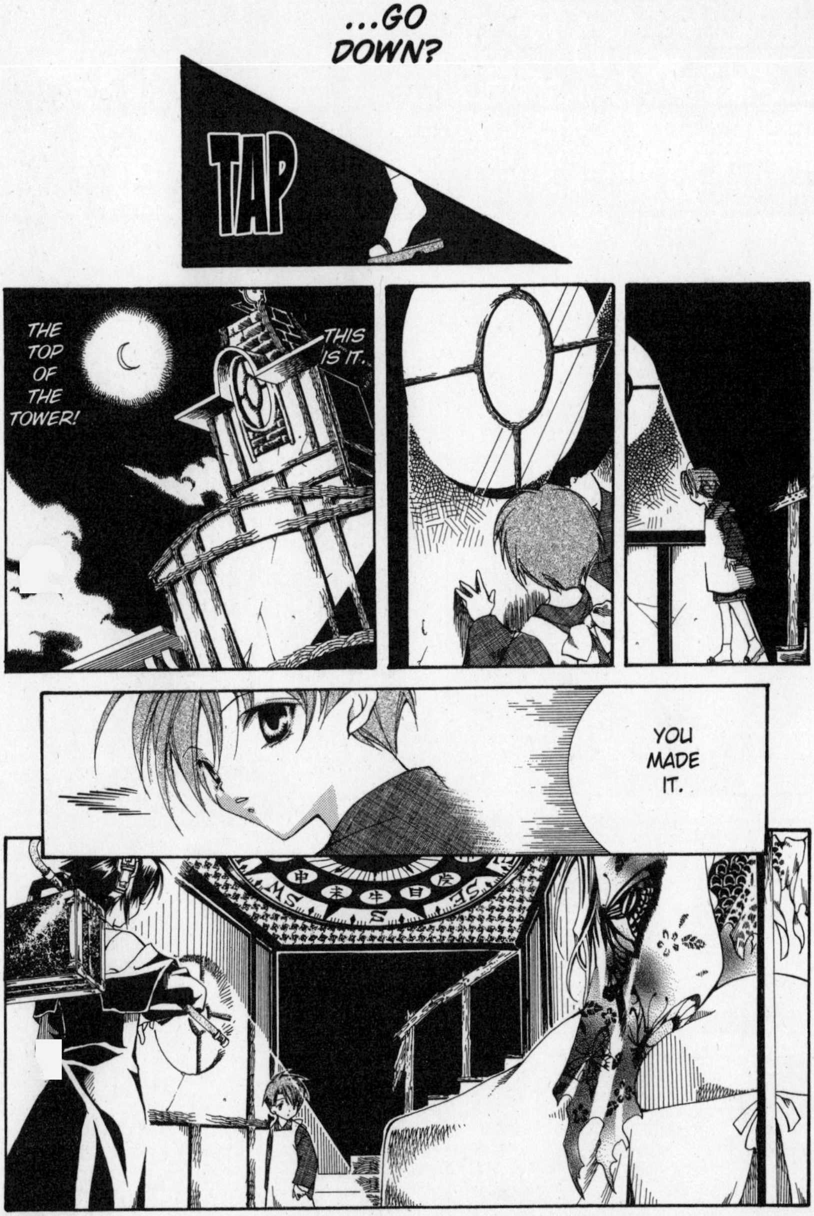
...GO DOWN?
TAP
THIS IS IT...
THE TOP OF THE TOWER!
YOU MADE IT.

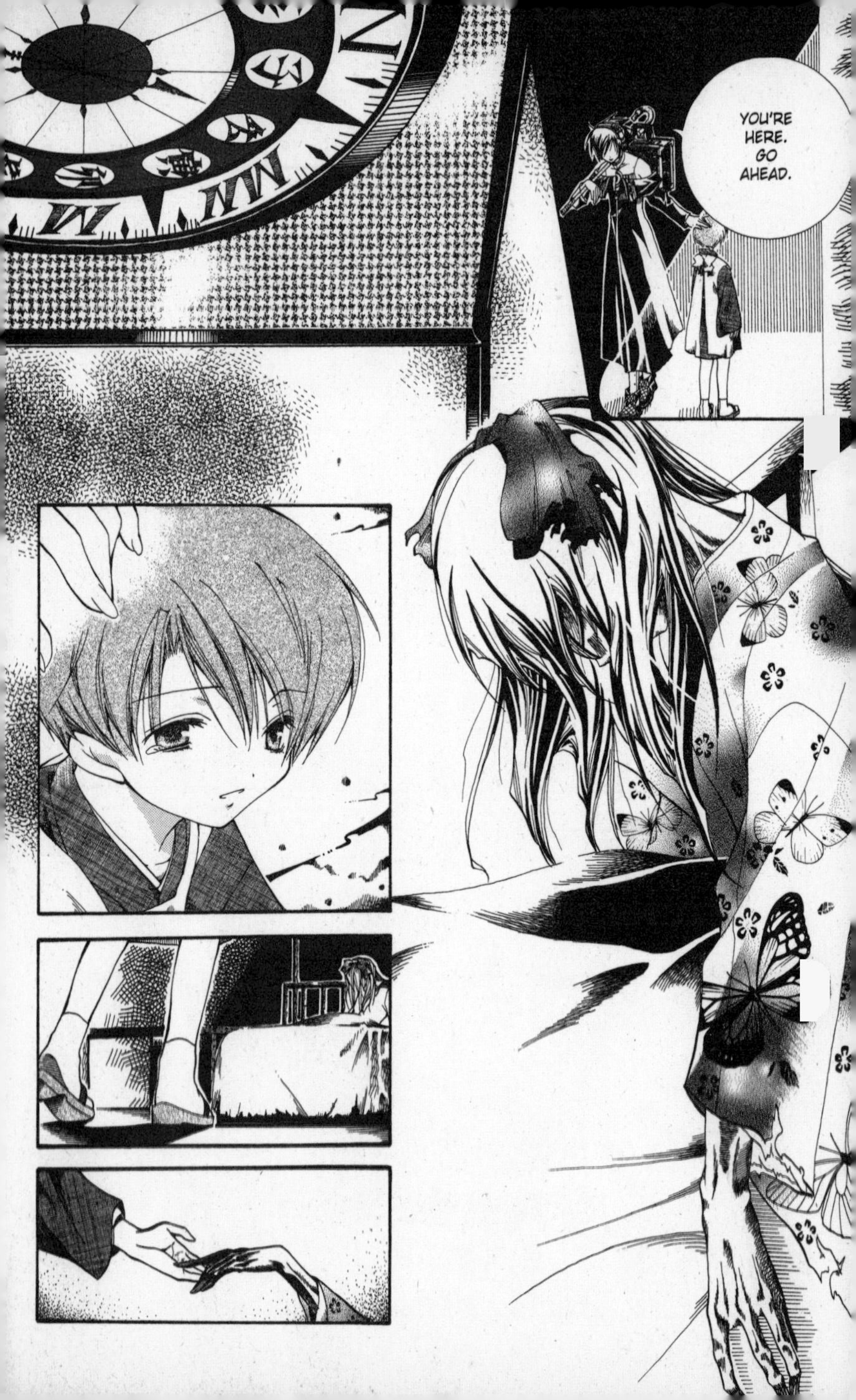
YOU'RE HERE. GO AHEAD.

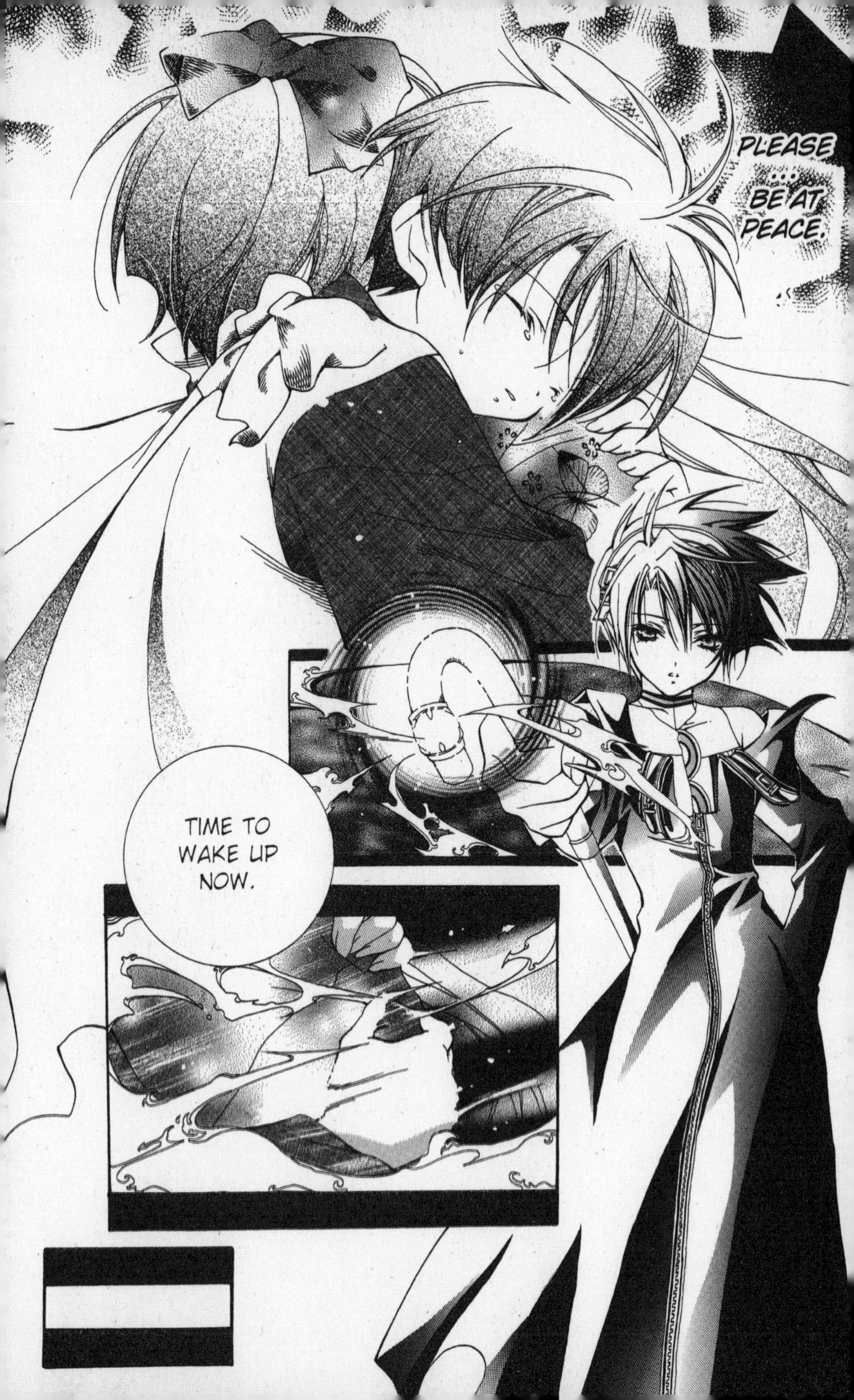
PLEASE ... BE AT PEACE.
TIME TO WAKE UP NOW.

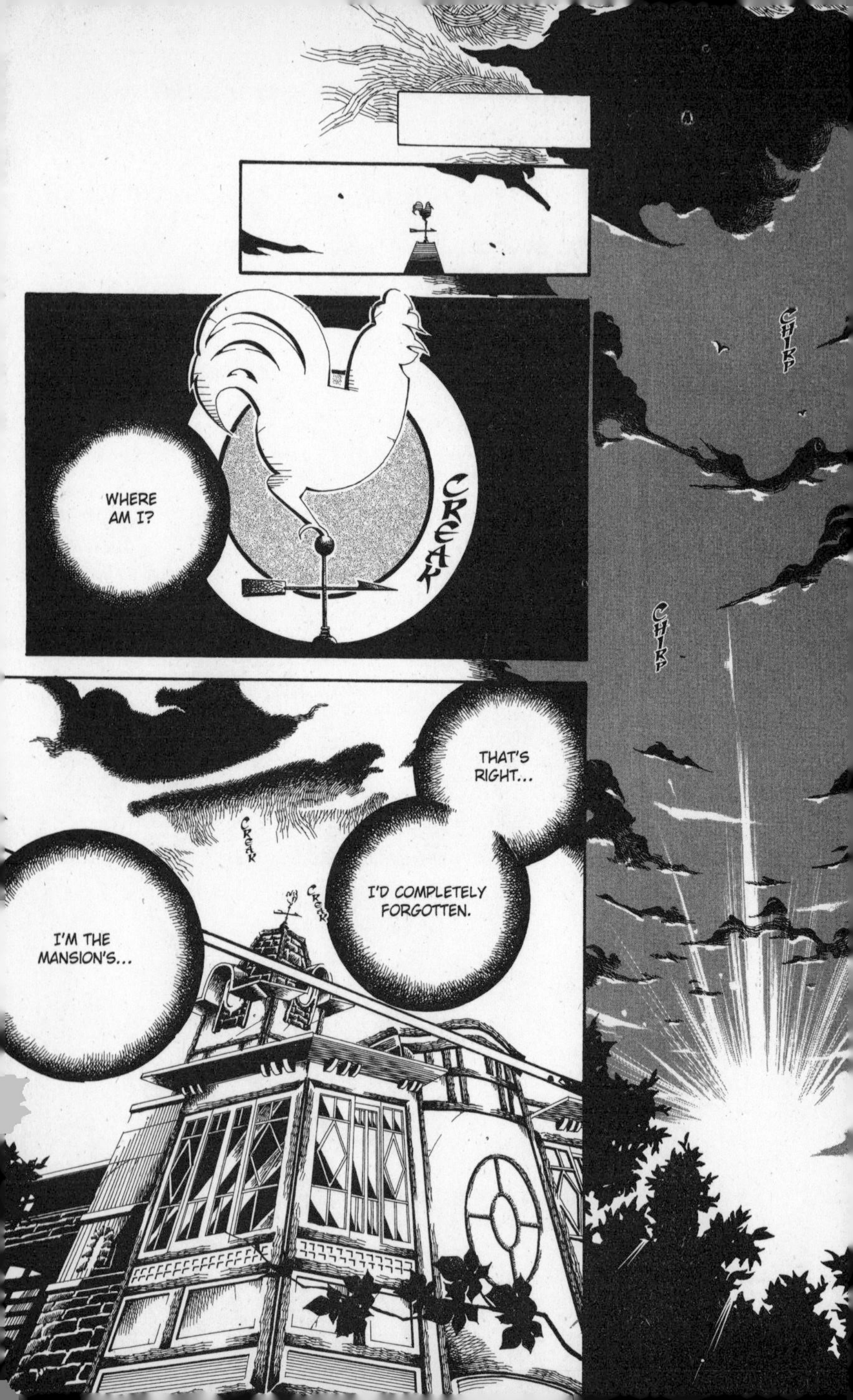
CHIRP
CHIRP
CREAK
WHERE AM I?
THAT'S RIGHT...
I'D COMPLETELY FORGOTTEN.
CREAK
CREAK
I'M THE MANSION'S...

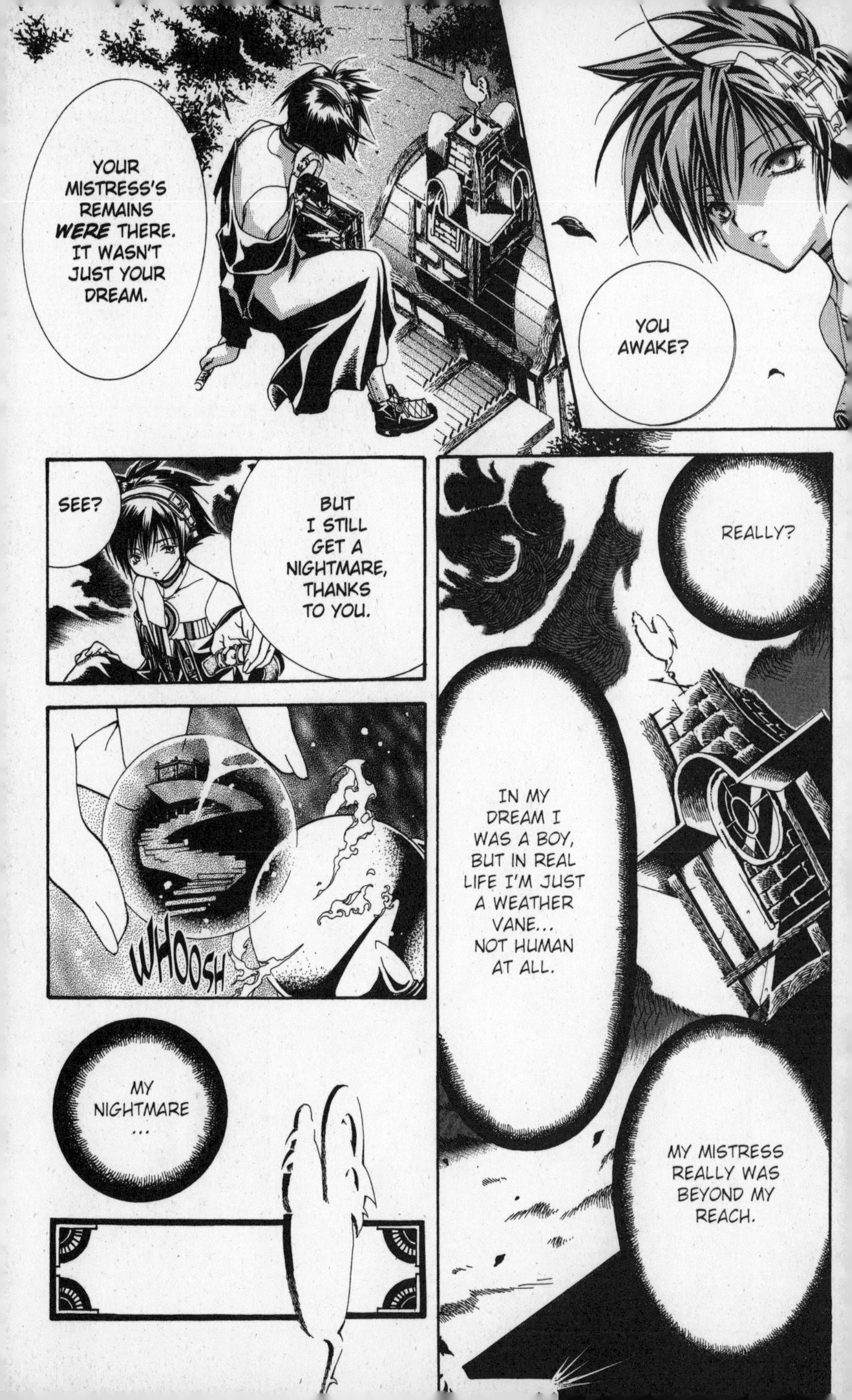
YOU AWAKE?
YOUR MISTRESS'S REMAINS *WERE* THERE. IT WASN'T JUST YOUR DREAM.
REALLY?
IN MY DREAM I WAS A BOY, BUT IN REAL LIFE I'M JUST A WEATHER VANE... NOT HUMAN AT ALL.
MY MISTRESS REALLY WAS BEYOND MY REACH.
BUT I STILL GET A NIGHTMARE, THANKS TO YOU.
SEE?
WHOOSH
MY NIGHTMARE ...

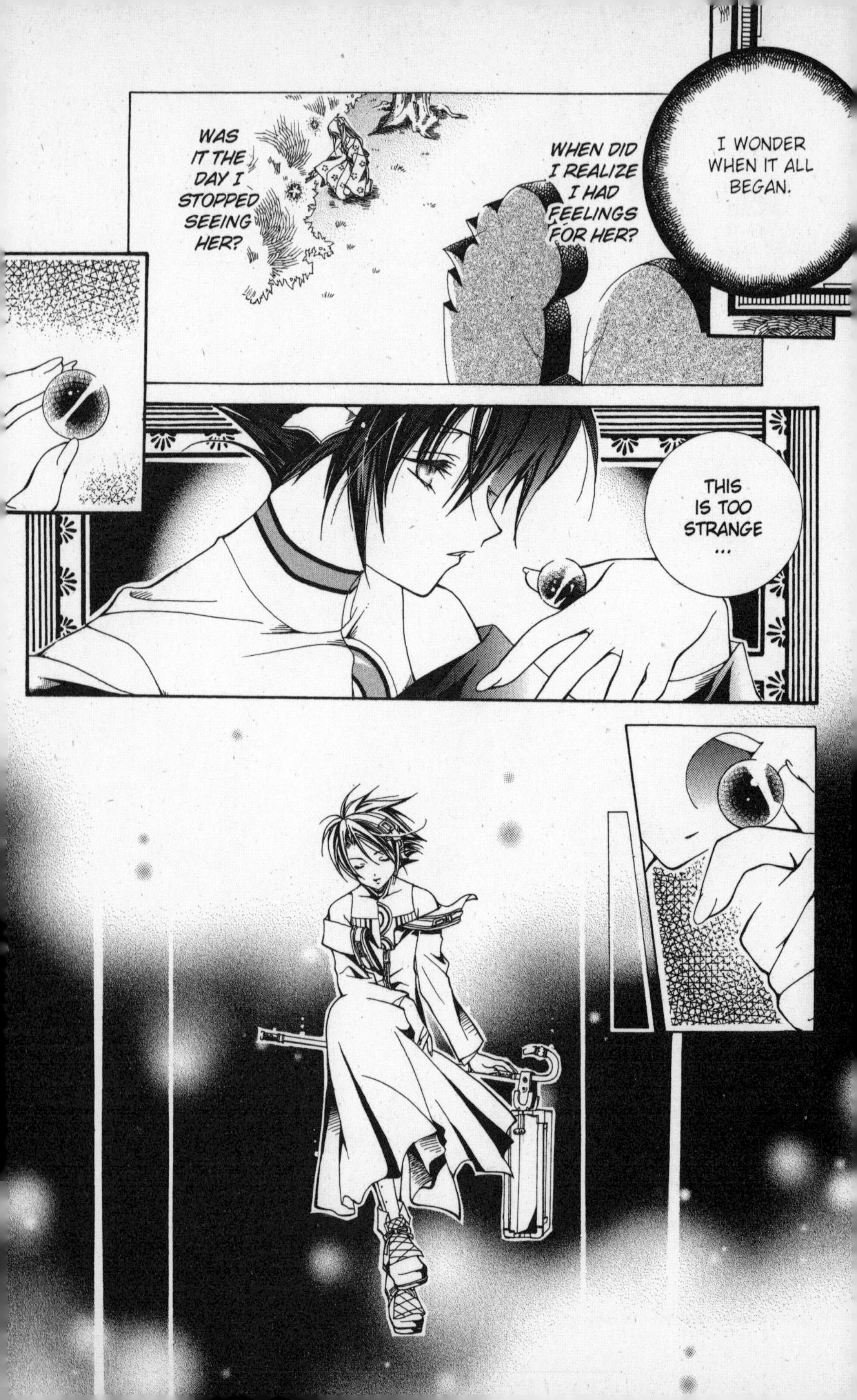
I WONDER WHEN IT ALL BEGAN.
WHEN DID I REALIZE I HAD FEELINGS FOR HER?
WAS IT THE DAY I STOPPED SEEING HER?
THIS IS TOO STRANGE ...

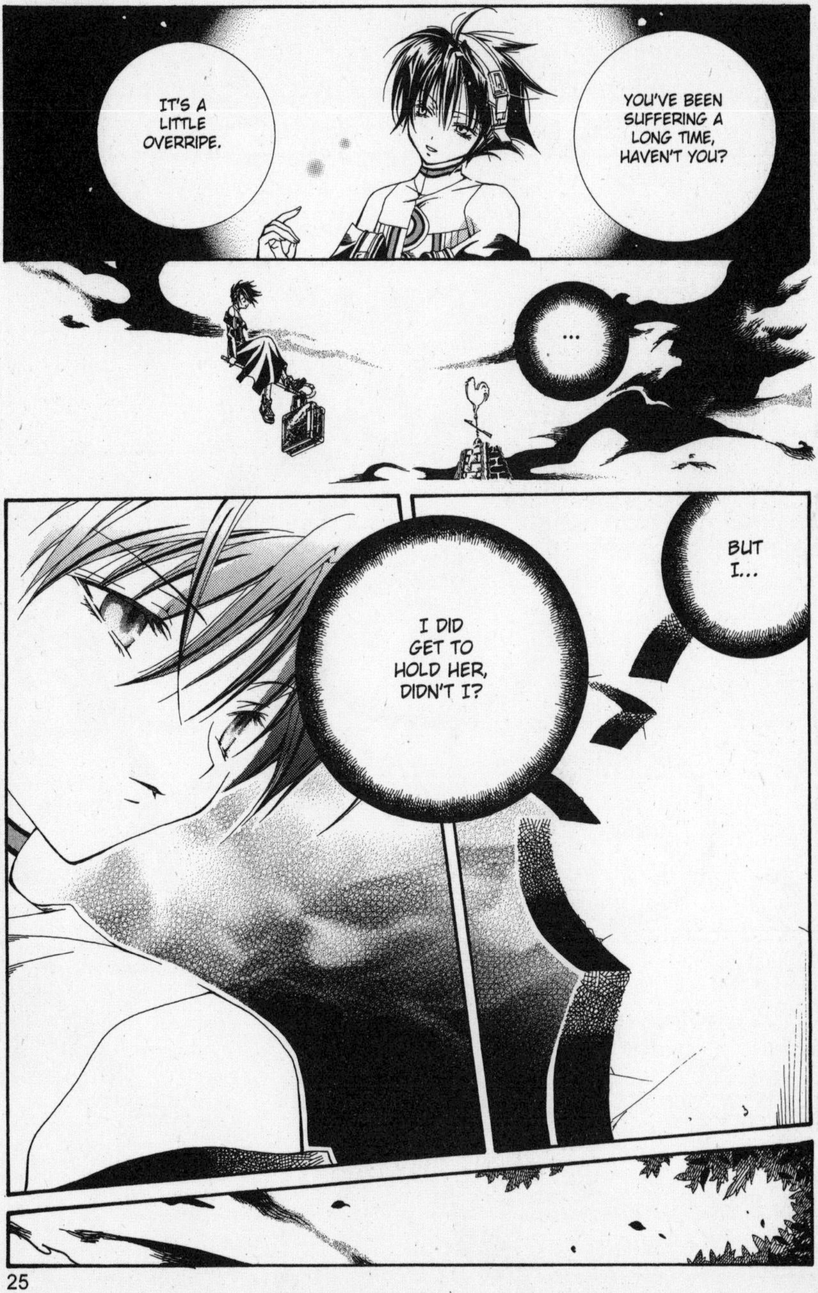
YOU'VE BEEN SUFFERING A LONG TIME, HAVEN'T YOU?
IT'S A LITTLE OVERRIPE.
...
BUT I...
I DID GET TO HOLD HER, DIDN'T I?

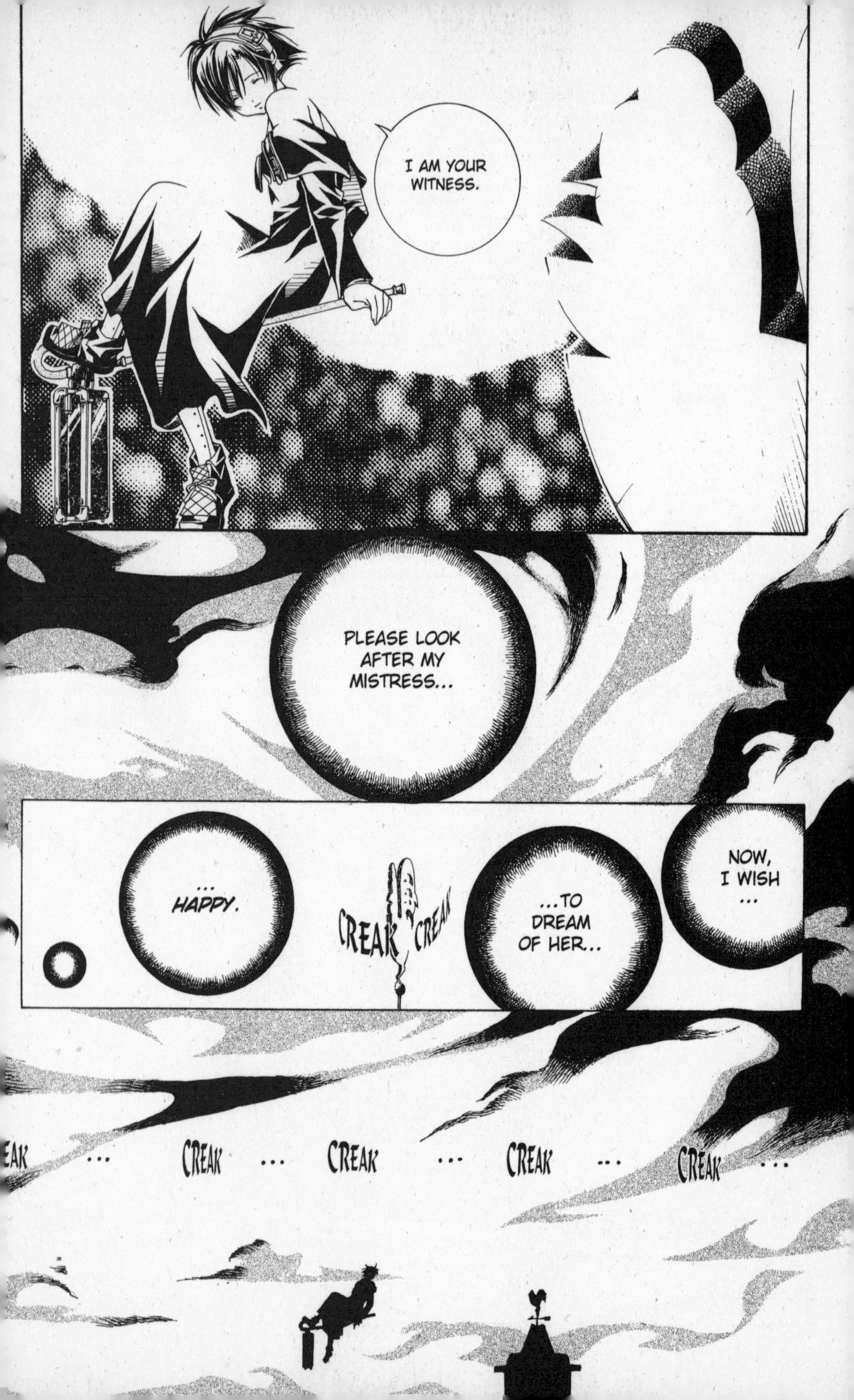
I AM YOUR WITNESS.
PLEASE LOOK AFTER MY MISTRESS...
NOW, I WISH ...
...TO DREAM OF HER..
CREAK CREAK
... HAPPY.
EAK ... CREAK ... CREAK ... CREAK ... CREAK ...

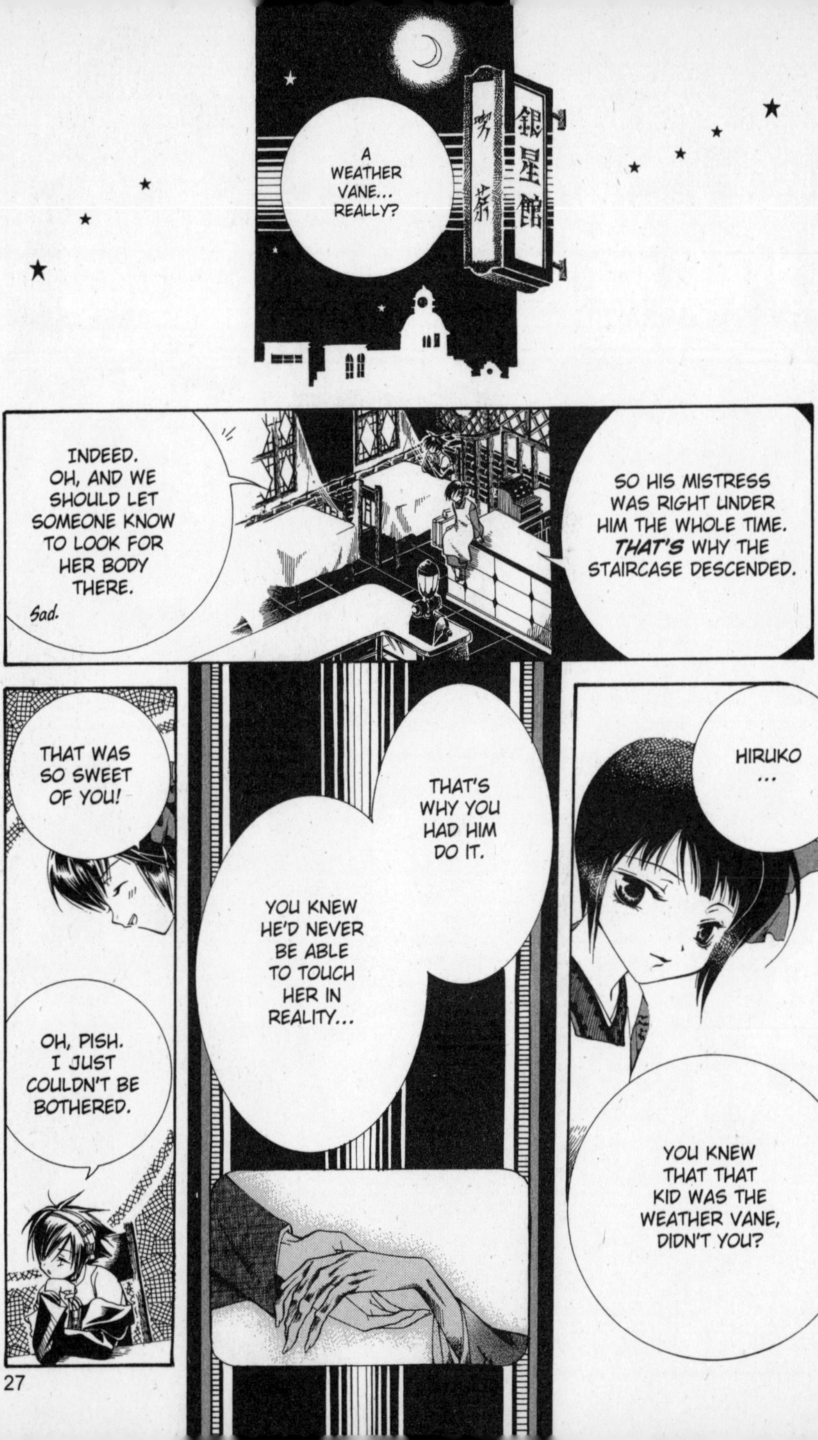
銀星館
喫茶
A WEATHER VANE... REALLY?
SO HIS MISTRESS WAS RIGHT UNDER HIM THE WHOLE TIME. ***THAT'S*** WHY THE STAIRCASE DESCENDED.
INDEED. OH, AND WE SHOULD LET SOMEONE KNOW TO LOOK FOR HER BODY THERE.
Sad.
HIRUKO ...
YOU KNEW THAT THAT KID WAS THE WEATHER VANE, DIDN'T YOU?
THAT'S WHY YOU HAD HIM DO IT.
YOU KNEW HE'D NEVER BE ABLE TO TOUCH HER IN REALITY...
THAT WAS SO SWEET OF YOU!
OH, PISH. I JUST COULDN'T BE BOTHERED.

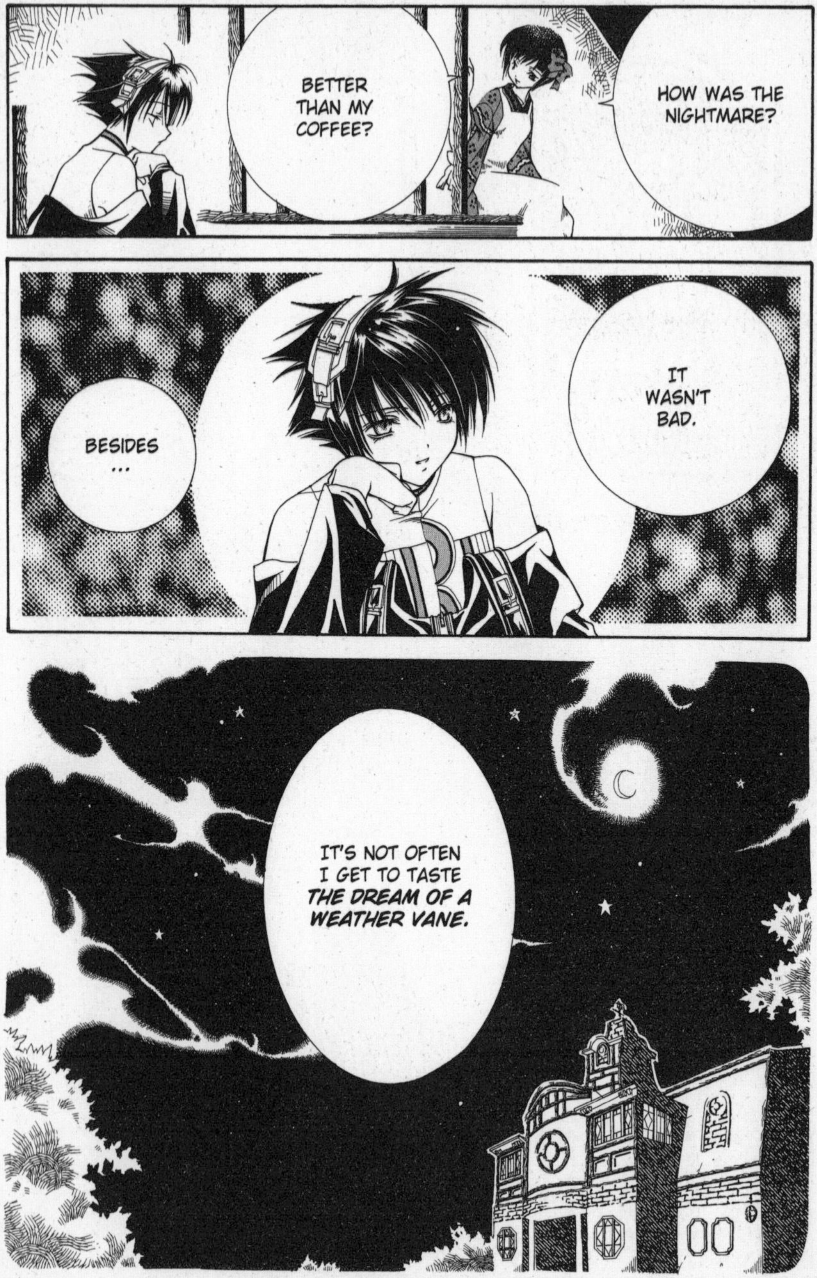
HOW WAS THE NIGHTMARE?
BETTER THAN MY COFFEE?
IT WASN'T BAD.
BESIDES ...
IT'S NOT OFTEN I GET TO TASTE *THE DREAM OF A WEATHER VANE.*

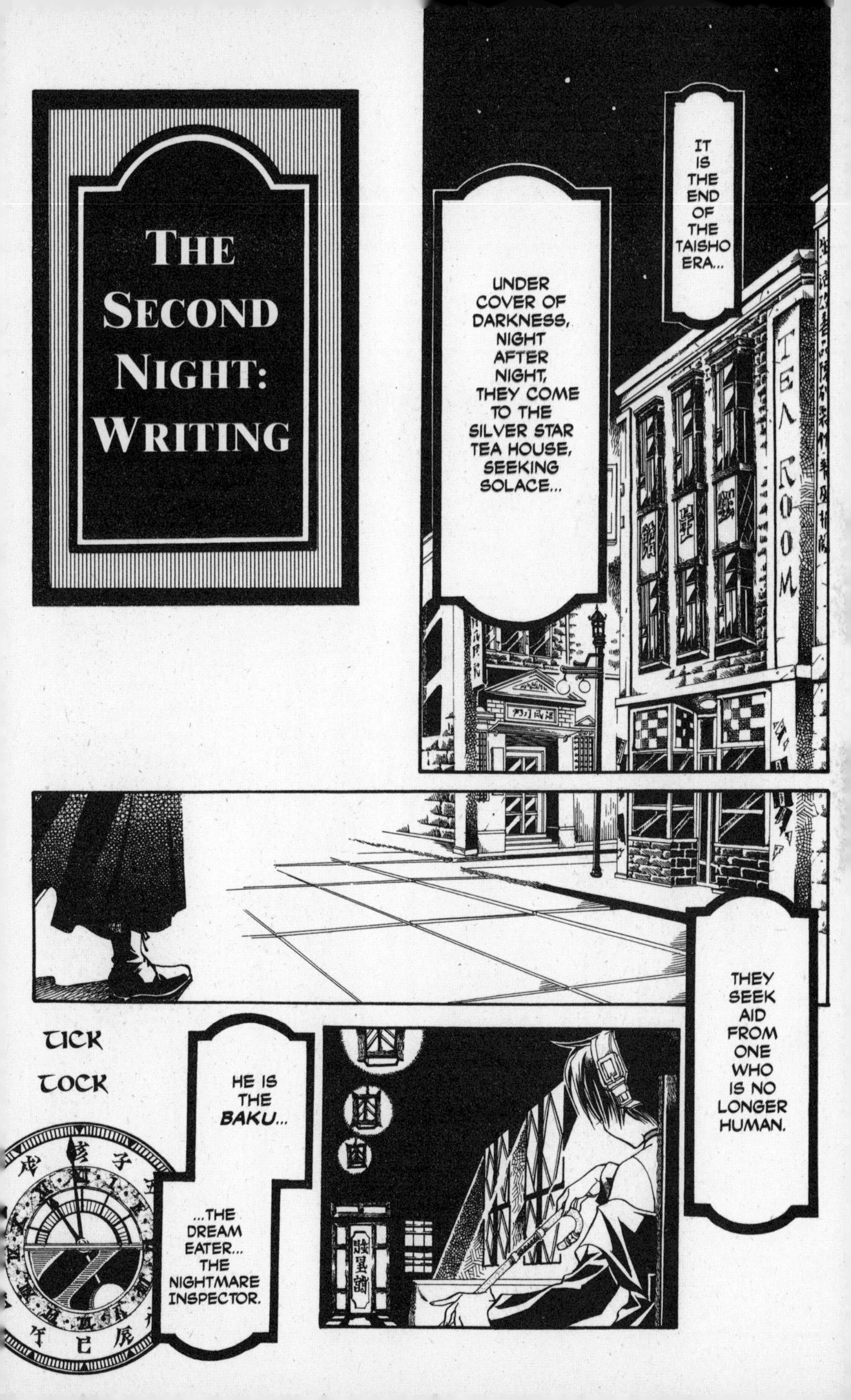
IT IS THE END OF THE TAISHO ERA...
UNDER COVER OF DARKNESS, NIGHT AFTER NIGHT, THEY COME TO THE SILVER STAR TEA HOUSE, SEEKING SOLACE...
TEA ROOM
THE SECOND NIGHT: WRITING
THEY SEEK AID FROM ONE WHO IS NO LONGER HUMAN.
HE IS THE *BAKU*...
...THE DREAM EATER... THE NIGHTMARE INSPECTOR.
TICK
TOCK

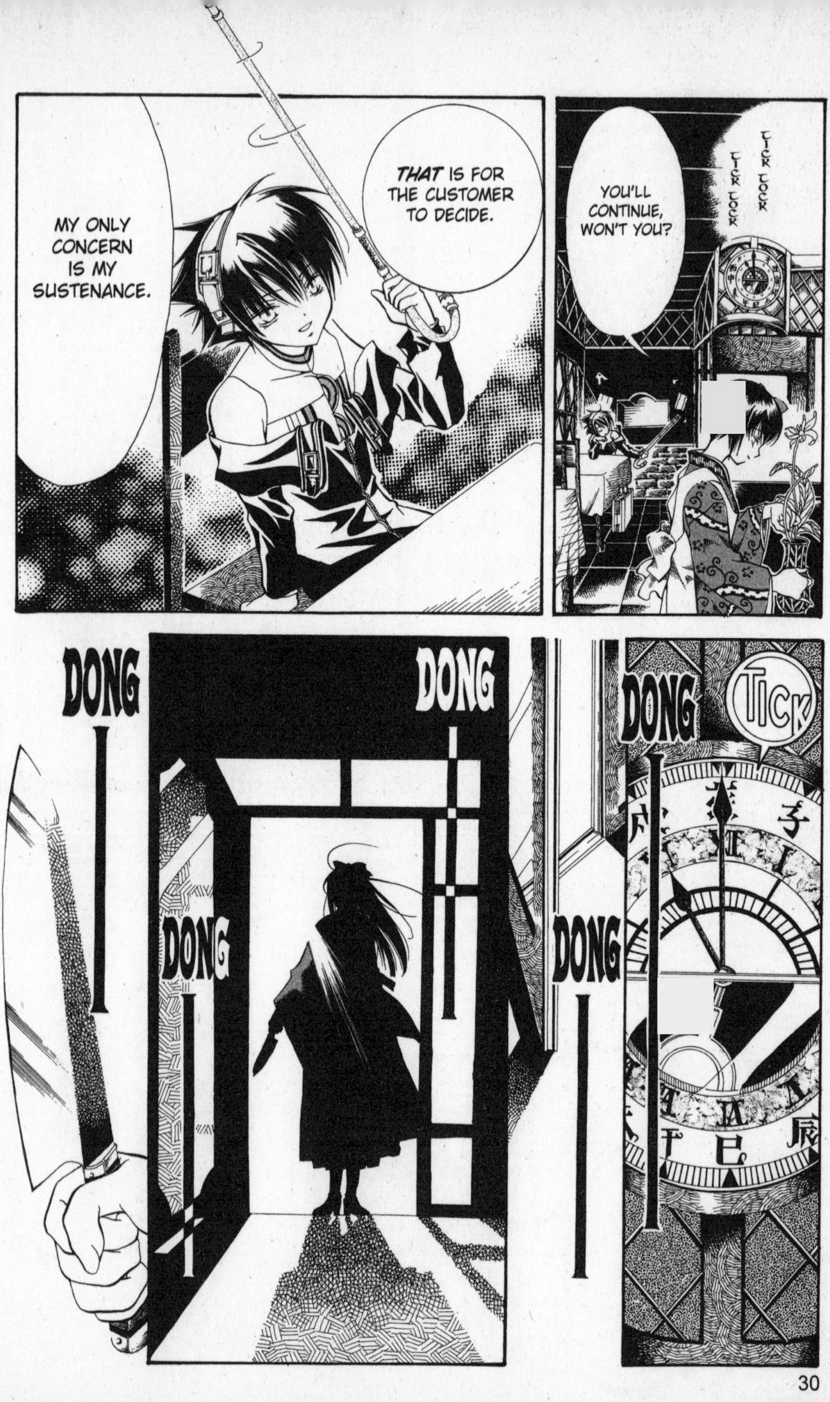
YOU'LL CONTINUE, WON'T YOU?
TICK TOCK
TICK TOCK
THAT IS FOR THE CUSTOMER TO DECIDE.
MY ONLY CONCERN IS MY SUSTENANCE.
TICK
DONG
DONG
DONG
DONG
DONG

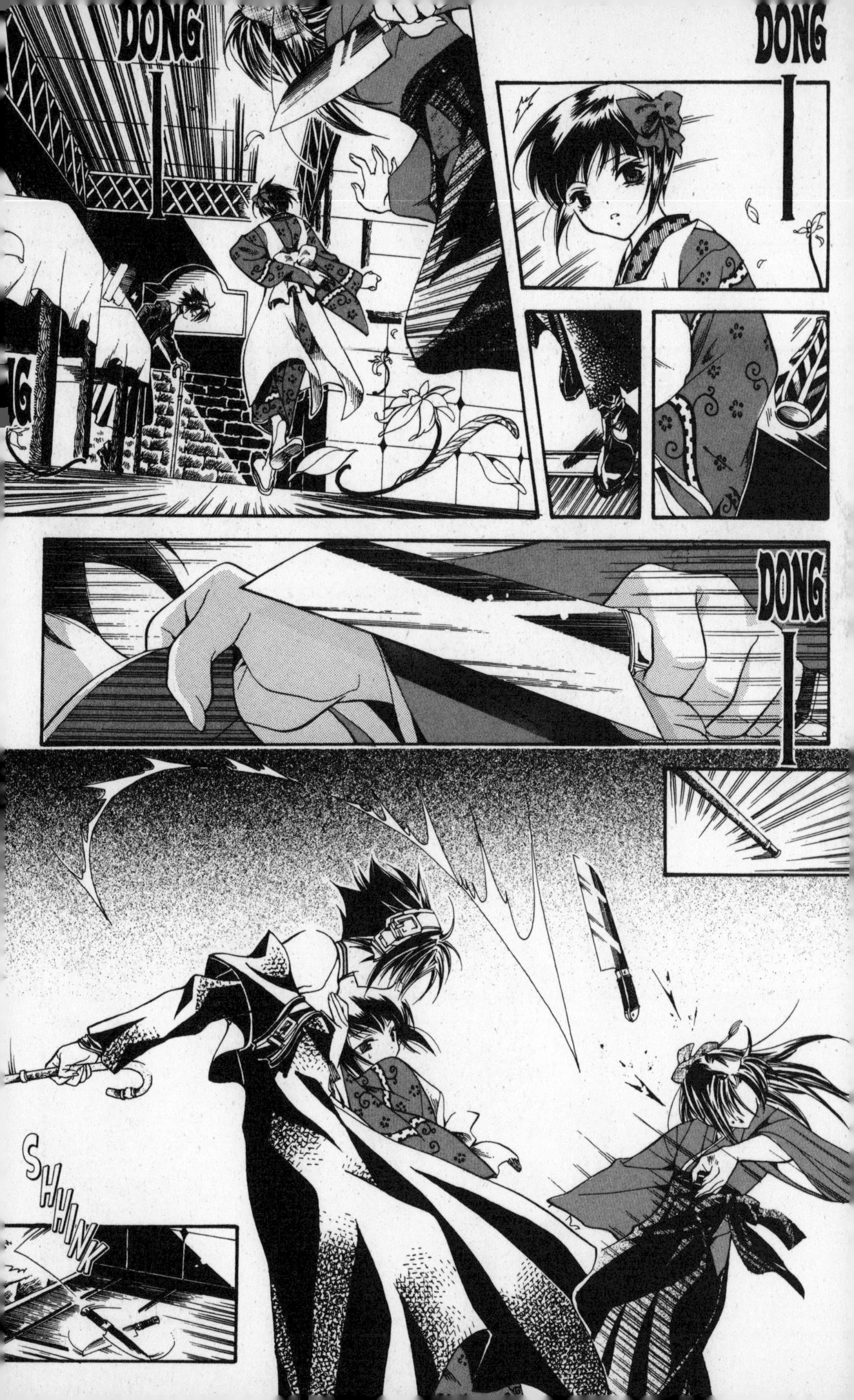
DONG
DONG
DONG
SHHHINK

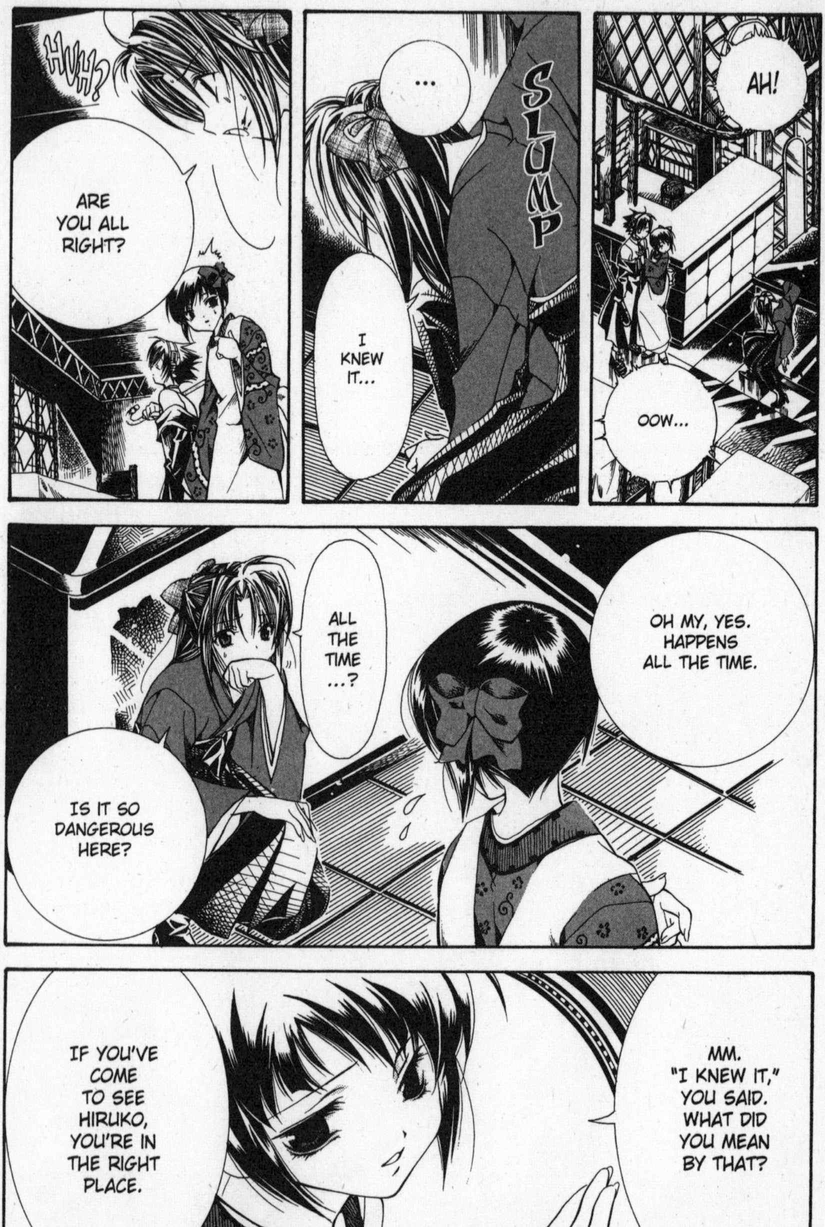
AH!
OOW...
...
SLUMP
I KNEW IT...
HUH?
ARE YOU ALL RIGHT?
OH MY, YES. HAPPENS ALL THE TIME.
ALL THE TIME ...?
IS IT SO DANGEROUS HERE?
MM. "I KNEW IT," YOU SAID. WHAT DID YOU MEAN BY THAT?
IF YOU'VE COME TO SEE HIRUKO, YOU'RE IN THE RIGHT PLACE.

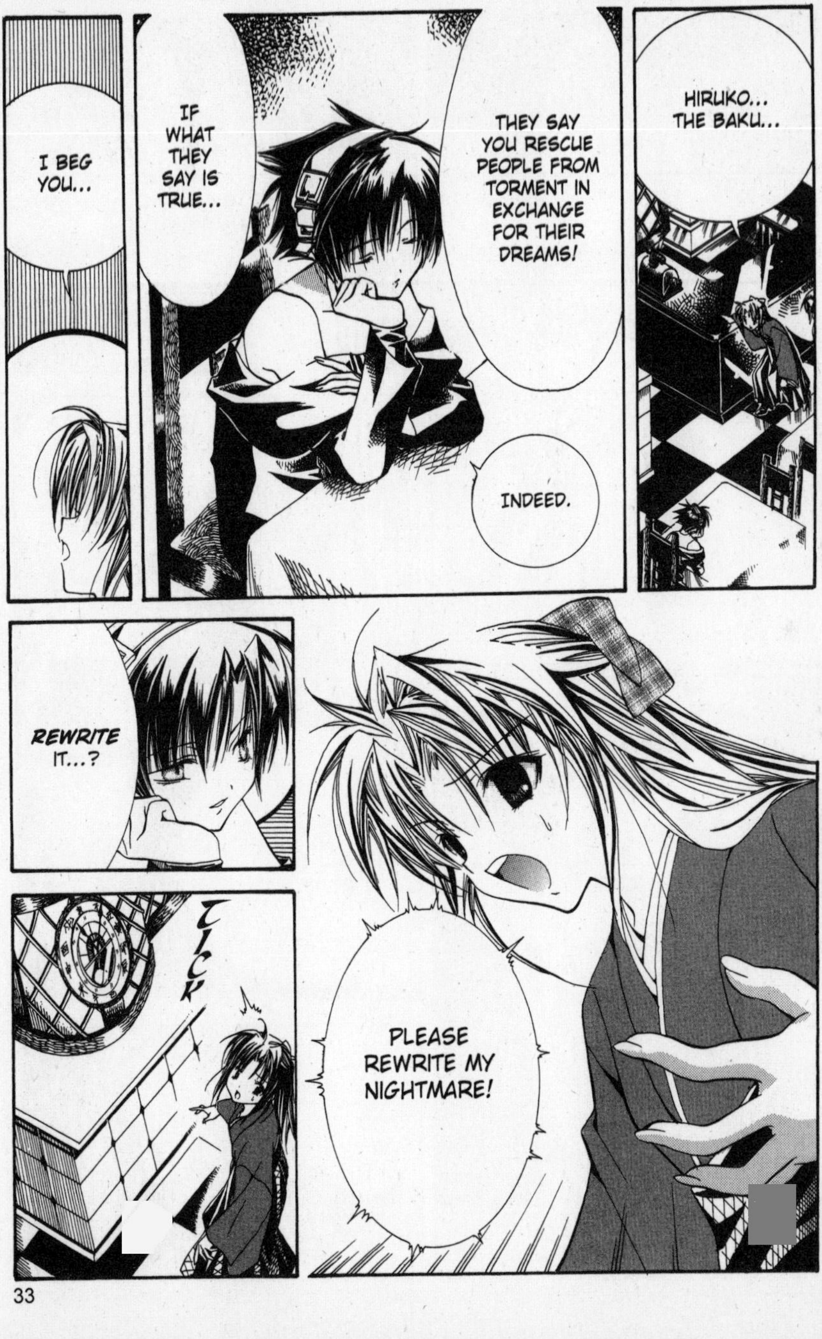
HIRUKO... THE BAKU...
THEY SAY YOU RESCUE PEOPLE FROM TORMENT IN EXCHANGE FOR THEIR DREAMS!
INDEED.
IF WHAT THEY SAY IS TRUE...
I BEG YOU...
PLEASE REWRITE MY NIGHTMARE!
REWRITE IT...?
TICK

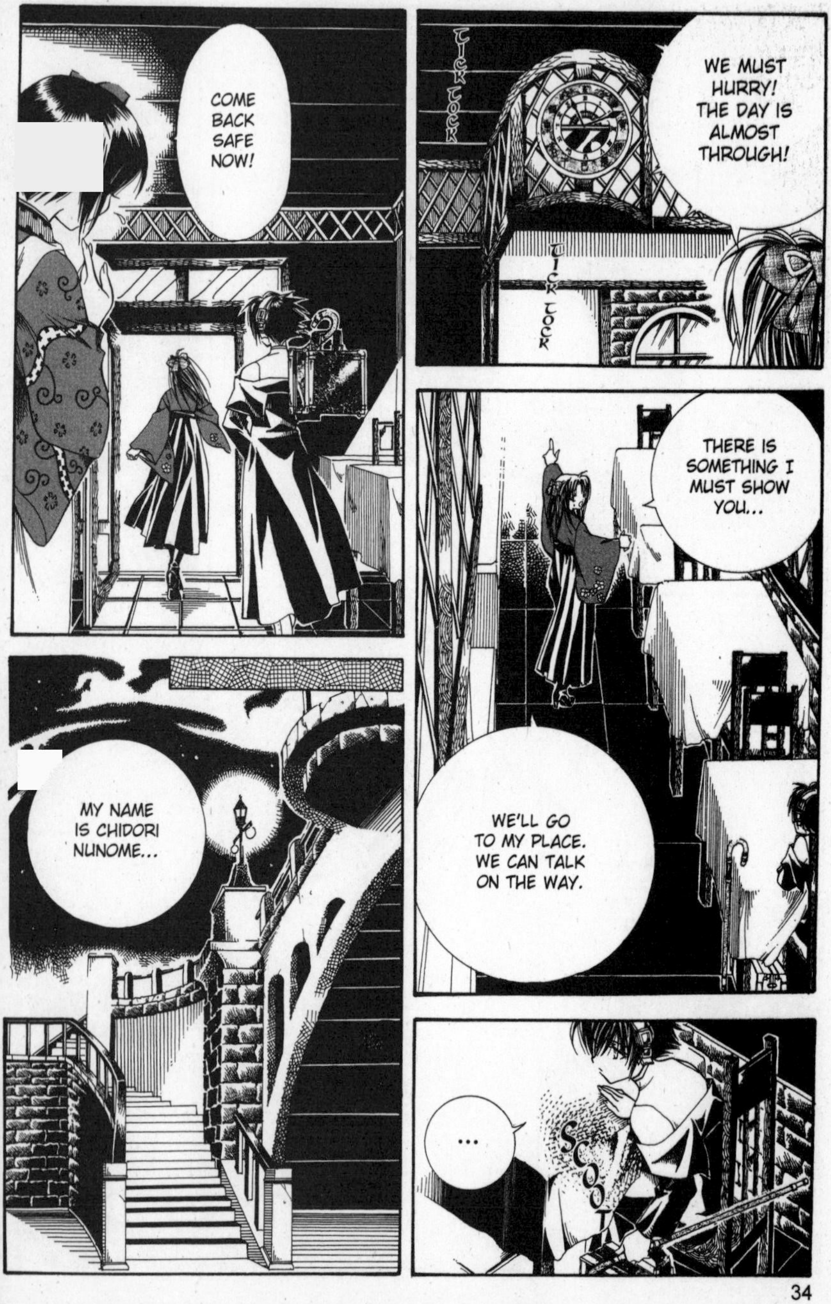
TICK TOCK
TICK TOCK
WE MUST HURRY! THE DAY IS ALMOST THROUGH!
COME BACK SAFE NOW!
THERE IS SOMETHING I MUST SHOW YOU...
WE'LL GO TO MY PLACE. WE CAN TALK ON THE WAY.
...
SCOOT
MY NAME IS CHIDORI NUNOME...

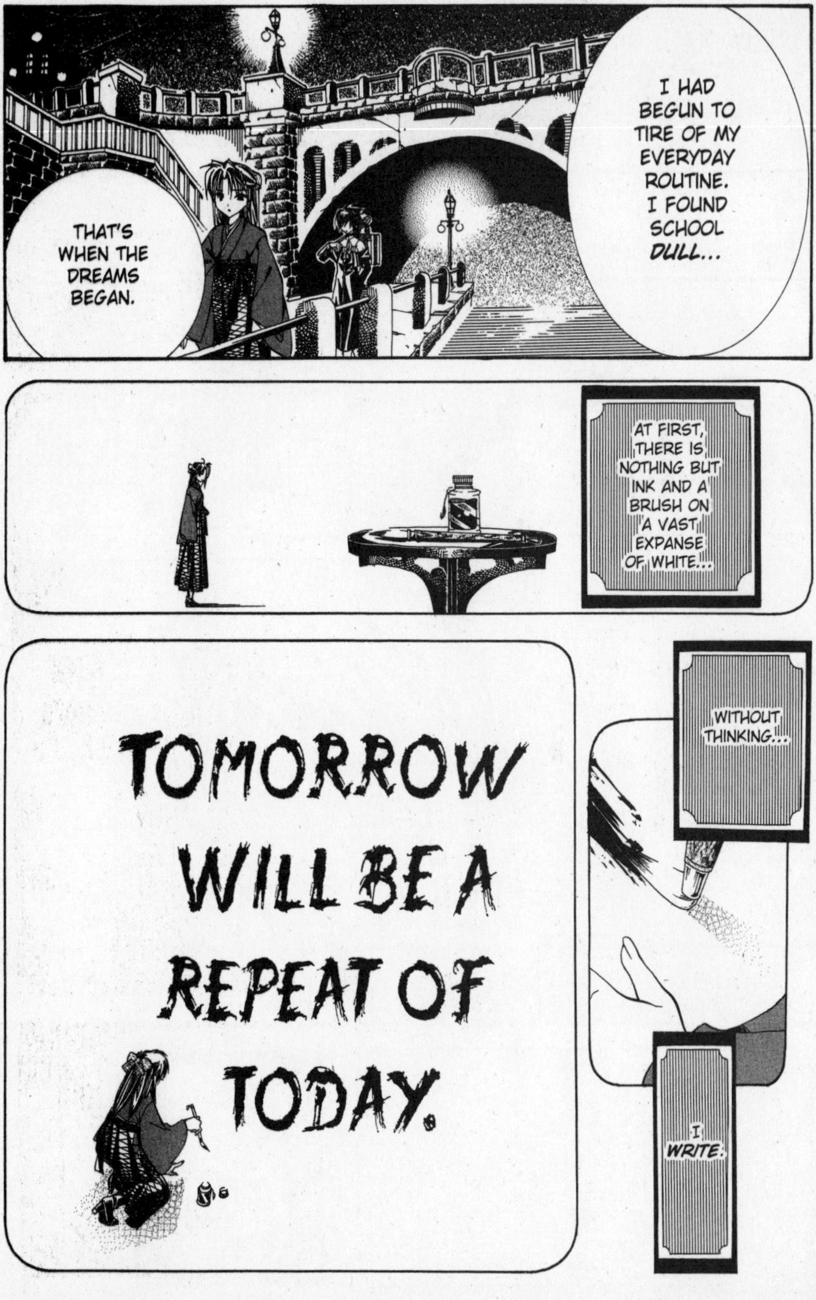
I HAD BEGUN TO TIRE OF MY EVERYDAY ROUTINE. I FOUND SCHOOL DULL...
THAT'S WHEN THE DREAMS BEGAN.
AT FIRST, THERE IS NOTHING BUT INK AND A BRUSH ON A VAST EXPANSE OF WHITE...
WITHOUT THINKING...
I WRITE.
TOMORROW WILL BE A REPEAT OF TODAY.

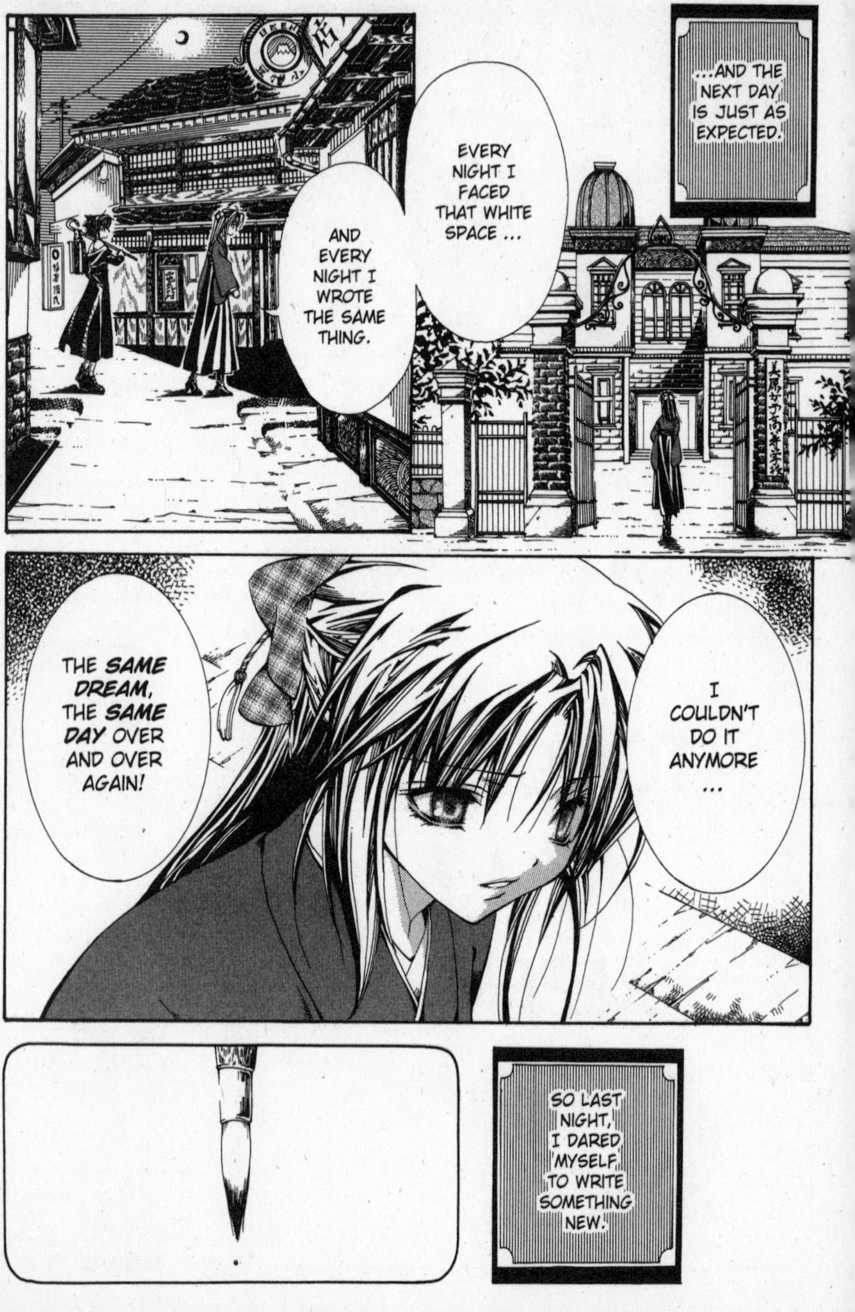
...AND THE NEXT DAY IS JUST AS EXPECTED.
EVERY NIGHT I FACED THAT WHITE SPACE ...
AND EVERY NIGHT I WROTE THE SAME THING.
I COULDN'T DO IT ANYMORE ...
THE ***SAME DREAM***, THE ***SAME DAY*** OVER AND OVER AGAIN!
SO LAST NIGHT, I DARED MYSELF TO WRITE SOMETHING NEW.

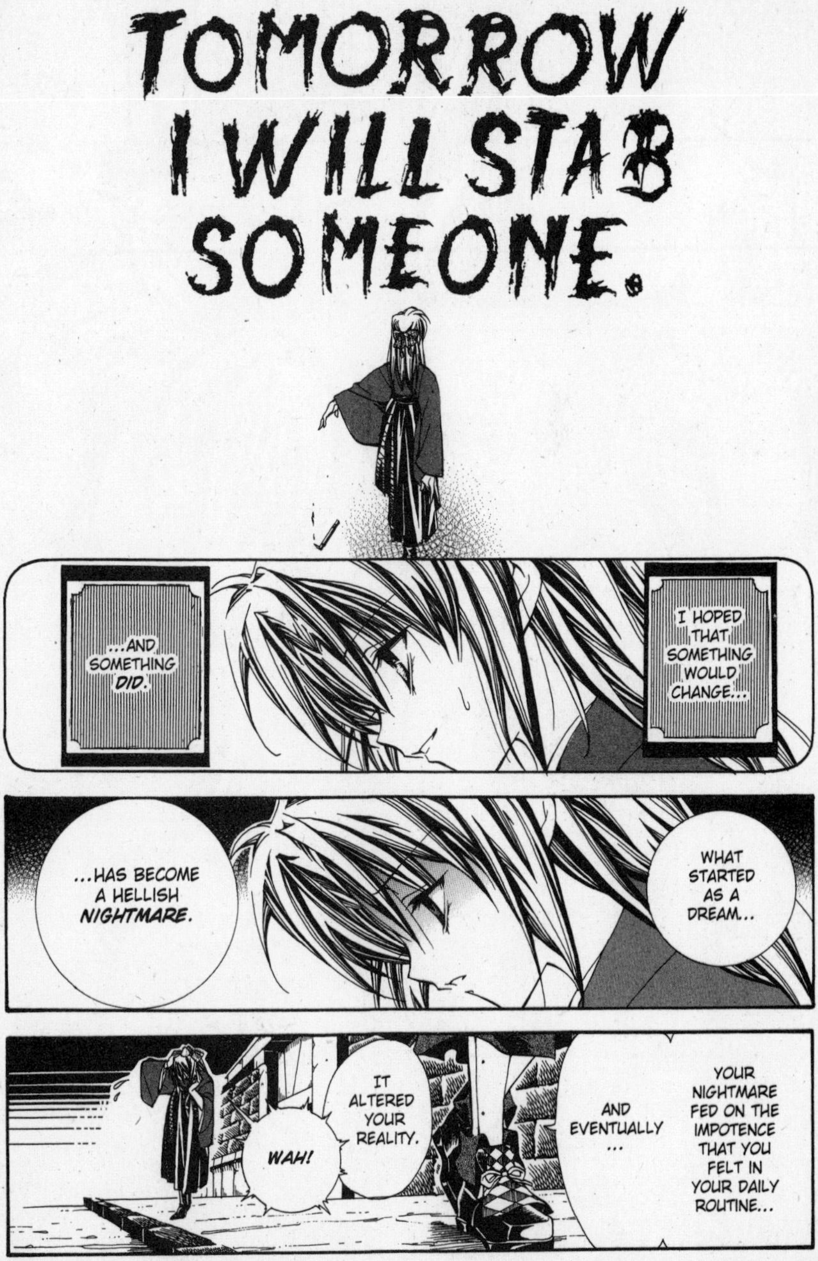
TOMORROW I WILL STAB SOMEONE.
I HOPED THAT SOMETHING WOULD CHANGE...
...AND SOMETHING DID.
WHAT STARTED AS A DREAM...
...HAS BECOME A HELLISH NIGHTMARE.
YOUR NIGHTMARE FED ON THE IMPOTENCE THAT YOU FELT IN YOUR DAILY ROUTINE...
AND EVENTUALLY ...
IT ALTERED YOUR REALITY.
WAH!

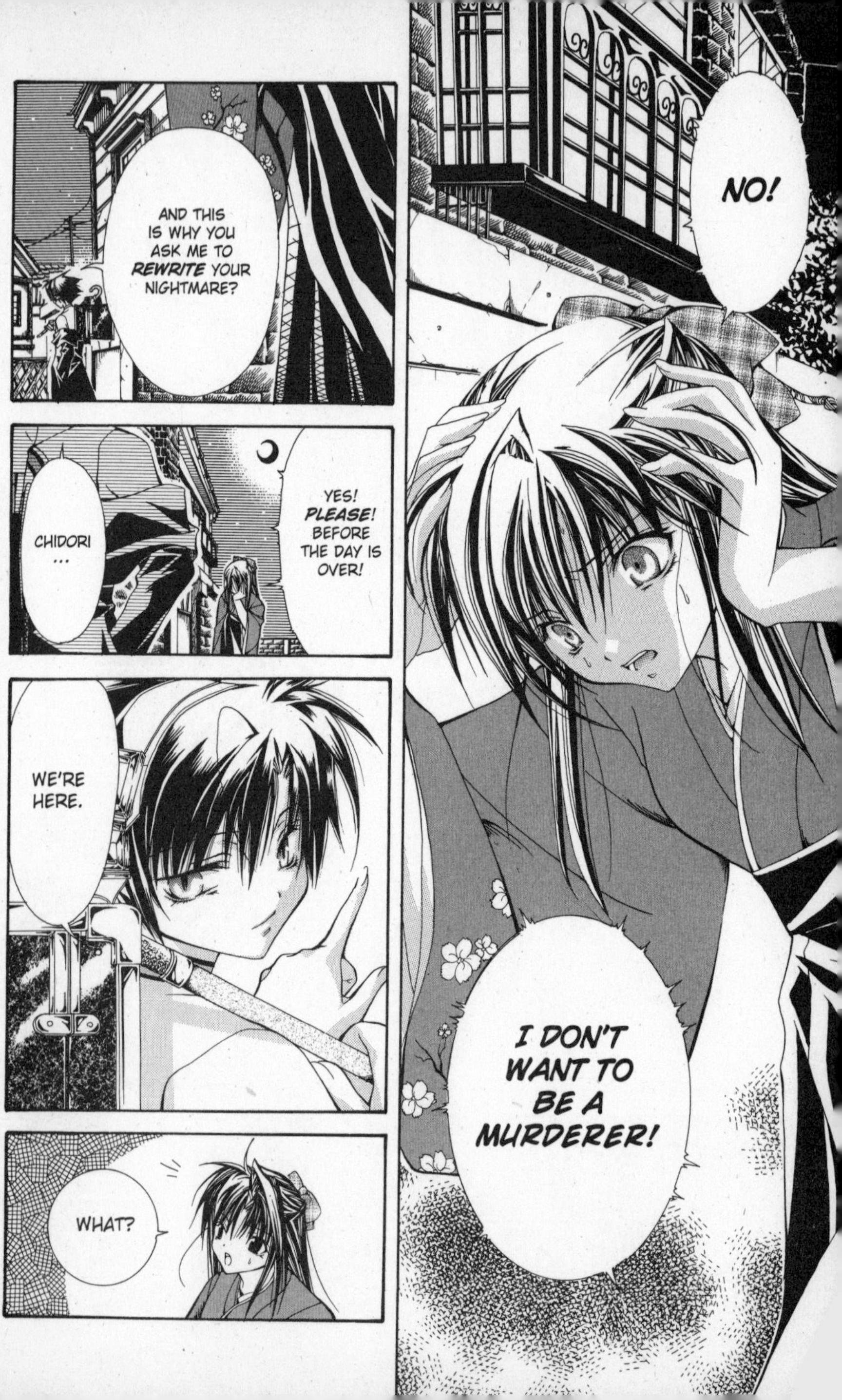
NO!
I DON'T WANT TO BE A MURDERER!
AND THIS IS WHY YOU ASK ME TO *REWRITE* YOUR NIGHTMARE?
YES! *PLEASE!* BEFORE THE DAY IS OVER!
CHIDORI...
WE'RE HERE.
WHAT?

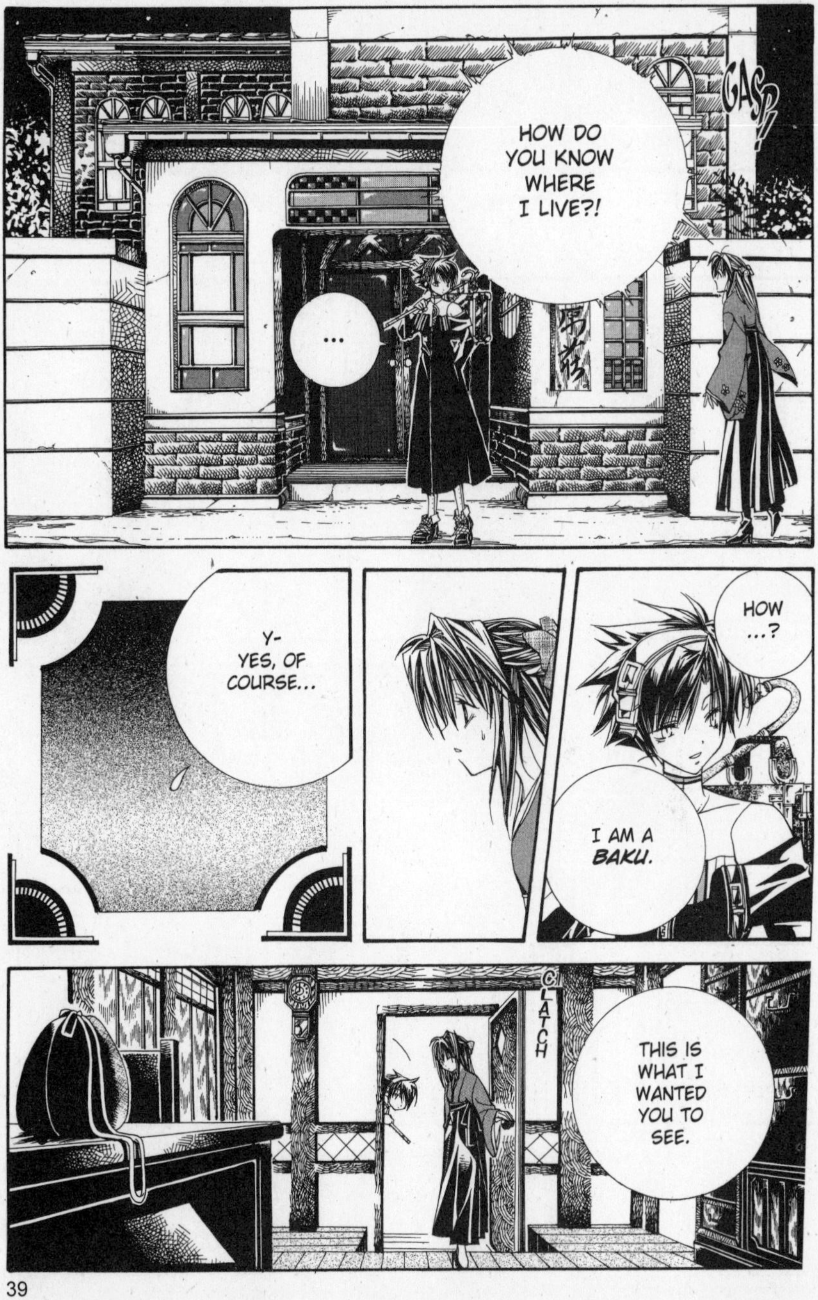
GASP!
HOW DO YOU KNOW WHERE I LIVE?!
...
HOW ...?
I AM A *BAKU*.
Y- YES, OF COURSE...
THIS IS WHAT I WANTED YOU TO SEE.
CLATCH

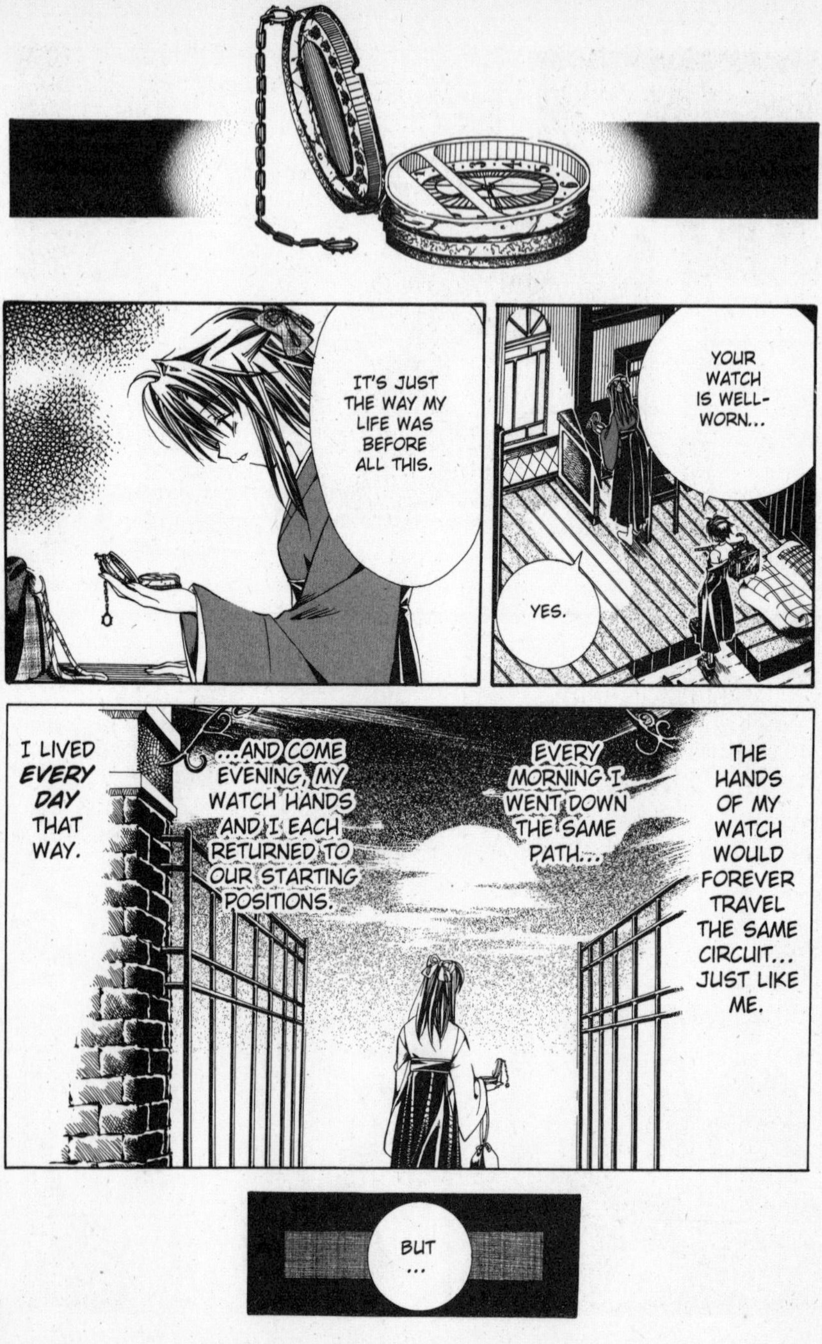
YOUR WATCH IS WELL-WORN...
YES.
IT'S JUST THE WAY MY LIFE WAS BEFORE ALL THIS.
THE HANDS OF MY WATCH WOULD FOREVER TRAVEL THE SAME CIRCUIT... JUST LIKE ME.
EVERY MORNING I WENT DOWN THE SAME PATH...
...AND COME EVENING, MY WATCH HANDS AND I EACH RETURNED TO OUR STARTING POSITIONS.
I LIVED *EVERY DAY* THAT WAY.
BUT...

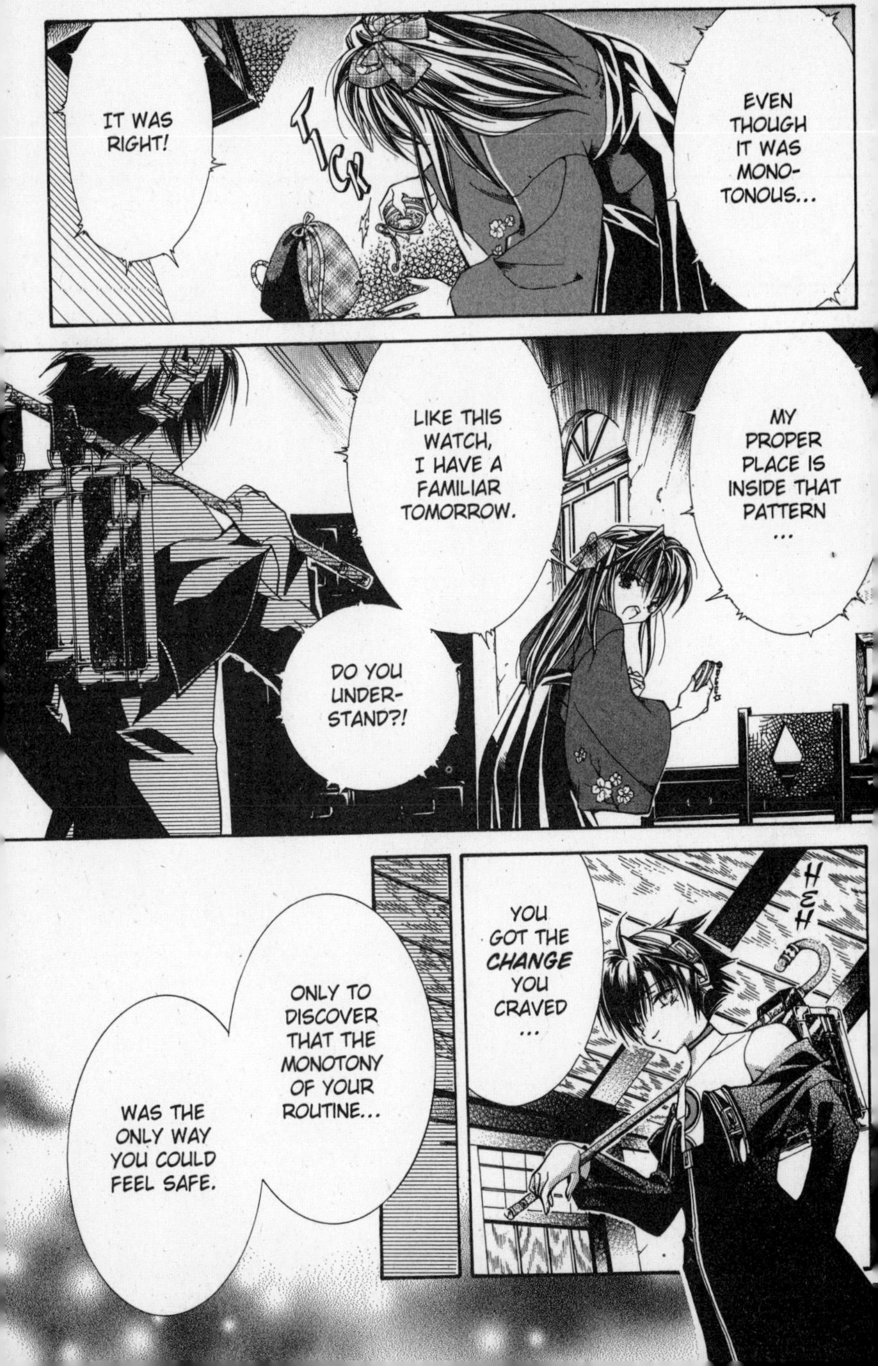
EVEN THOUGH IT WAS MONO- TONOUS...
TICK
IT WAS RIGHT!
MY PROPER PLACE IS INSIDE THAT PATTERN ...
LIKE THIS WATCH, I HAVE A FAMILIAR TOMORROW.
DO YOU UNDER- STAND?!
HEH
YOU GOT THE ***CHANGE*** YOU CRAVED ...
ONLY TO DISCOVER THAT THE MONOTONY OF YOUR ROUTINE...
WAS THE ONLY WAY YOU COULD FEEL SAFE.

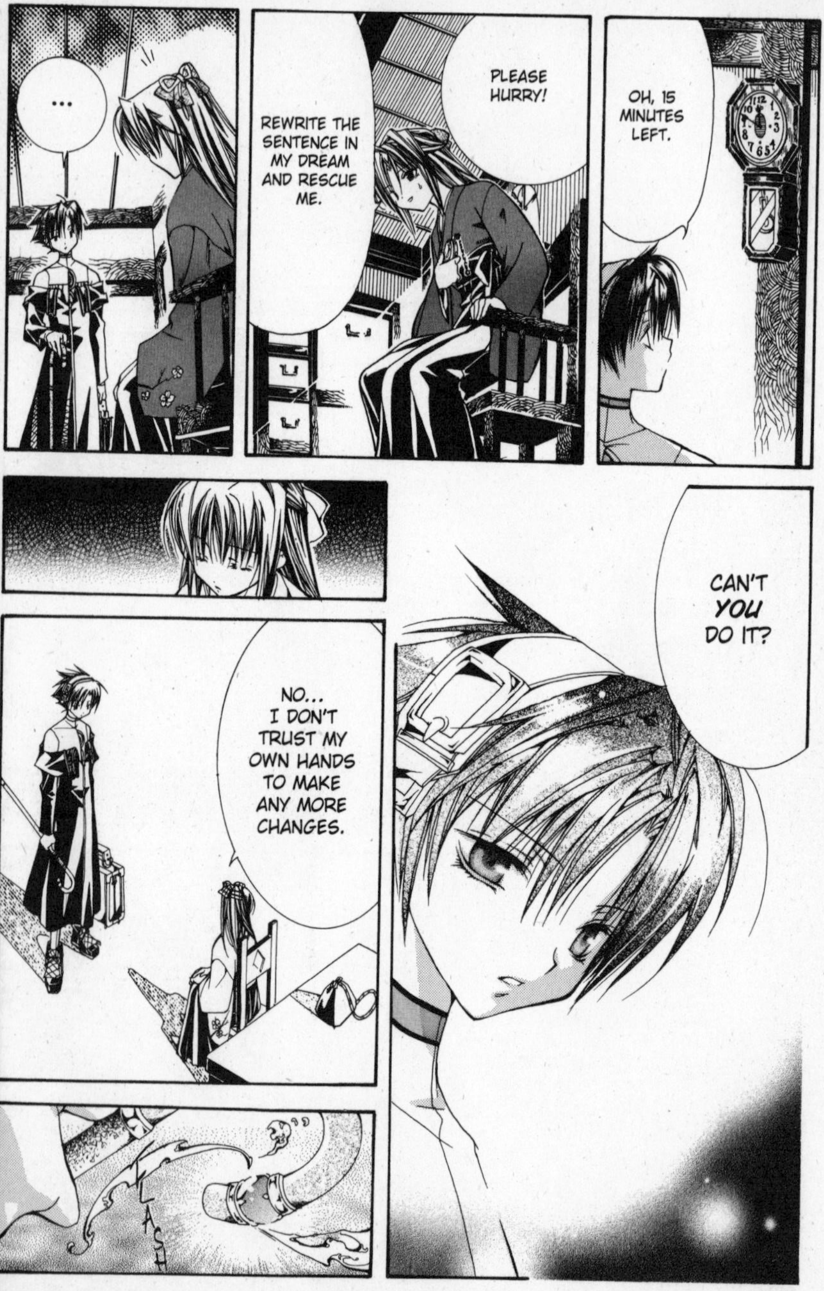
OH, 15 MINUTES LEFT.
PLEASE HURRY!
REWRITE THE SENTENCE IN MY DREAM AND RESCUE ME.
...
CAN'T *YOU* DO IT?
NO... I DON'T TRUST MY OWN HANDS TO MAKE ANY MORE CHANGES.
FLASH

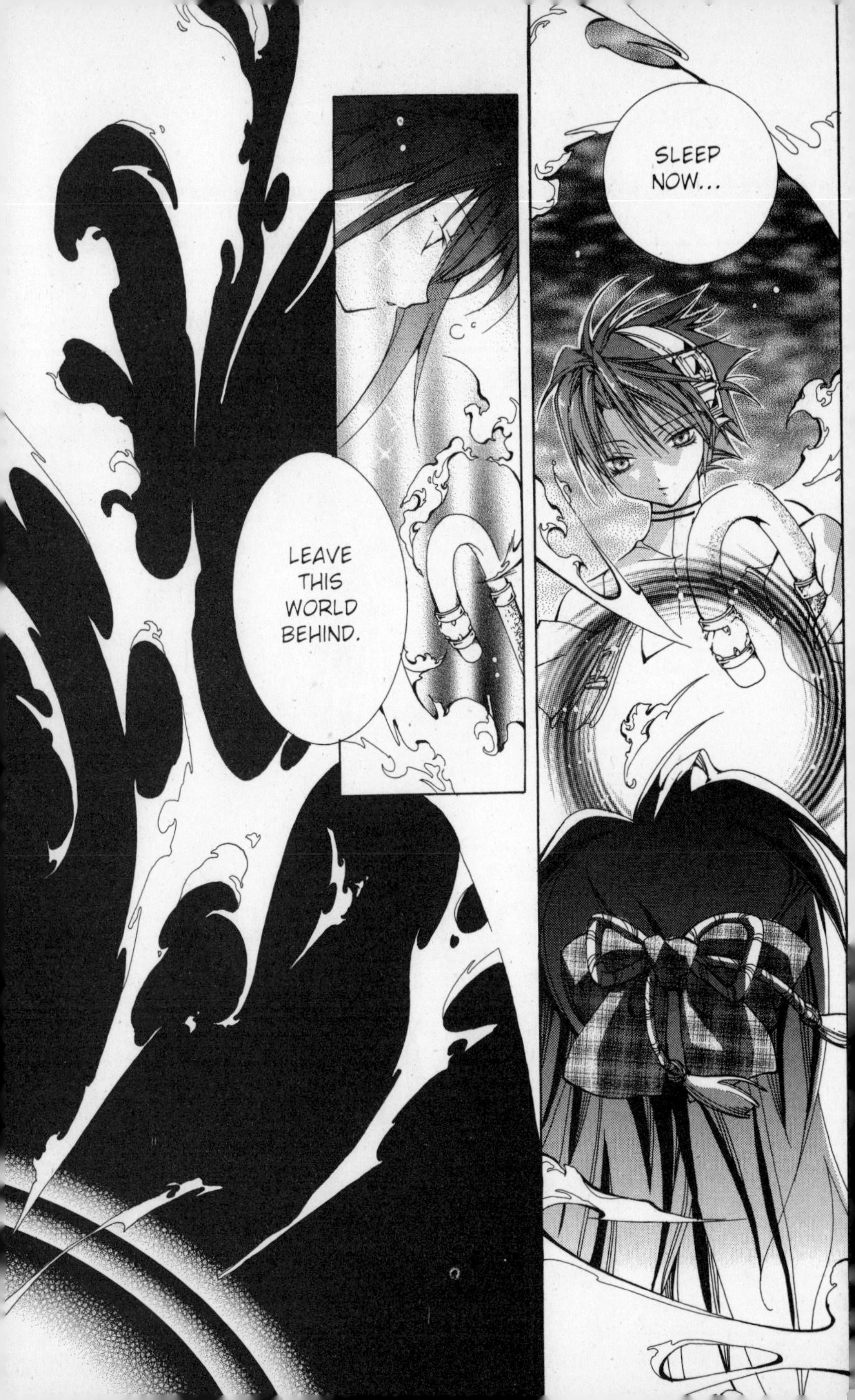
SLEEP NOW...
LEAVE THIS WORLD BEHIND.

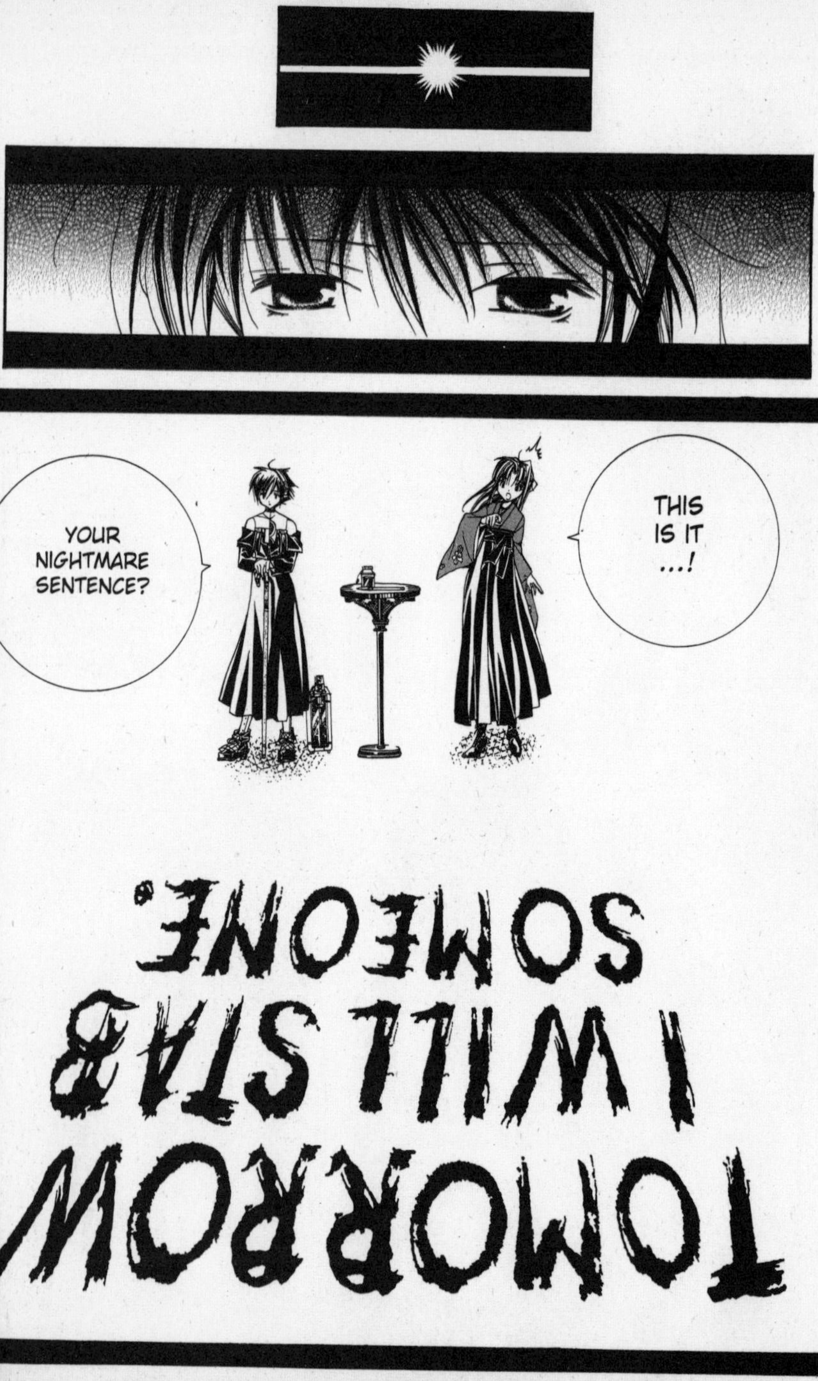
THIS IS IT ...!
YOUR NIGHTMARE SENTENCE?
TOMORROW I WILL STAB SOMEONE.

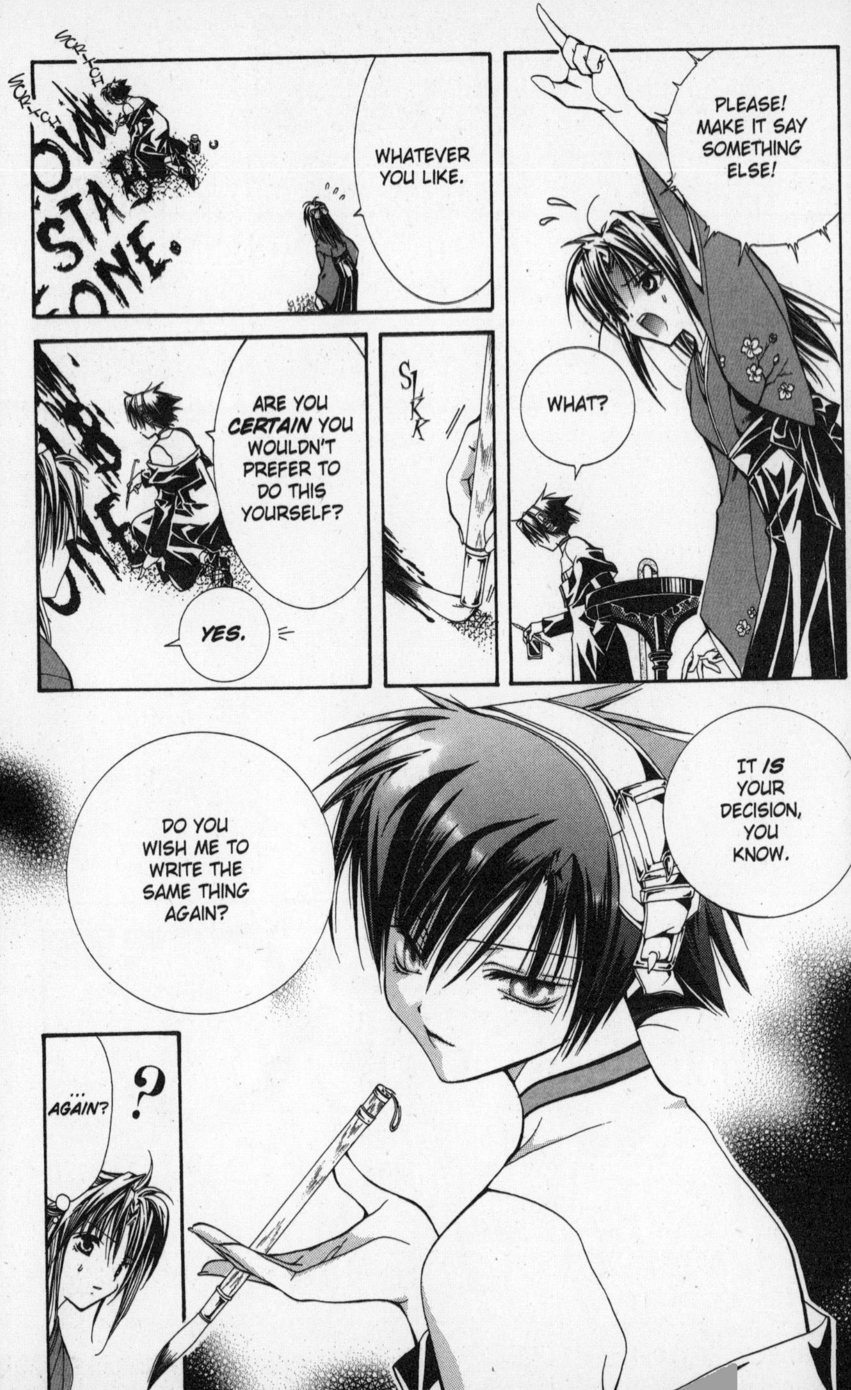
PLEASE! MAKE IT SAY SOMETHING ELSE!
WHAT?
SCRITCH
SCRITCH
WHATEVER YOU LIKE.
SLKK
ARE YOU *CERTAIN* YOU WOULDN'T PREFER TO DO THIS YOURSELF?
YES.
IT *IS* YOUR DECISION, YOU KNOW.
DO YOU WISH ME TO WRITE THE SAME THING AGAIN?
...AGAIN?
?

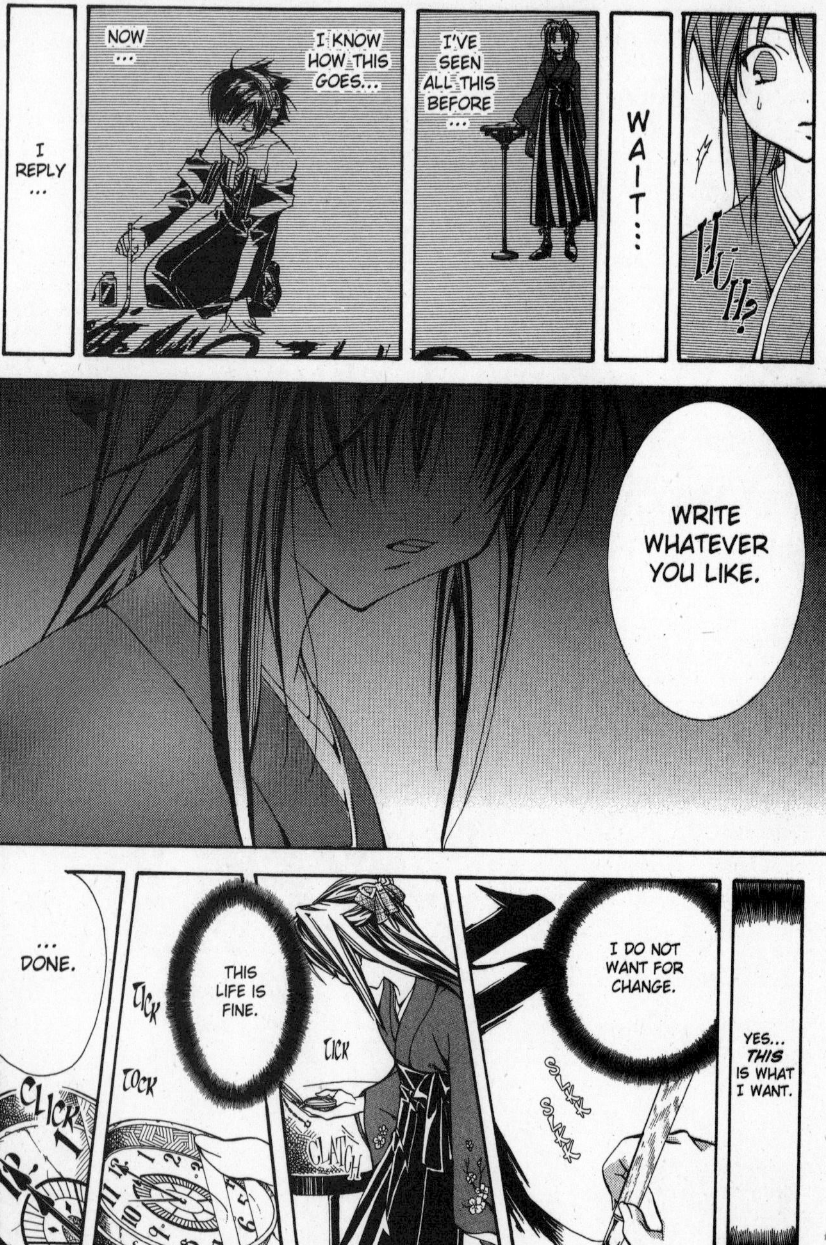

HUH!?
WAIT...
I'VE SEEN ALL THIS BEFORE...
I KNOW HOW THIS GOES...
NOW...
I REPLY...
WRITE WHATEVER YOU LIKE.
YES... THIS IS WHAT I WANT.
I DO NOT WANT FOR CHANGE.
TICK
CLATCH
THIS LIFE IS FINE.
TICK
TOCK
... DONE.
CLICK

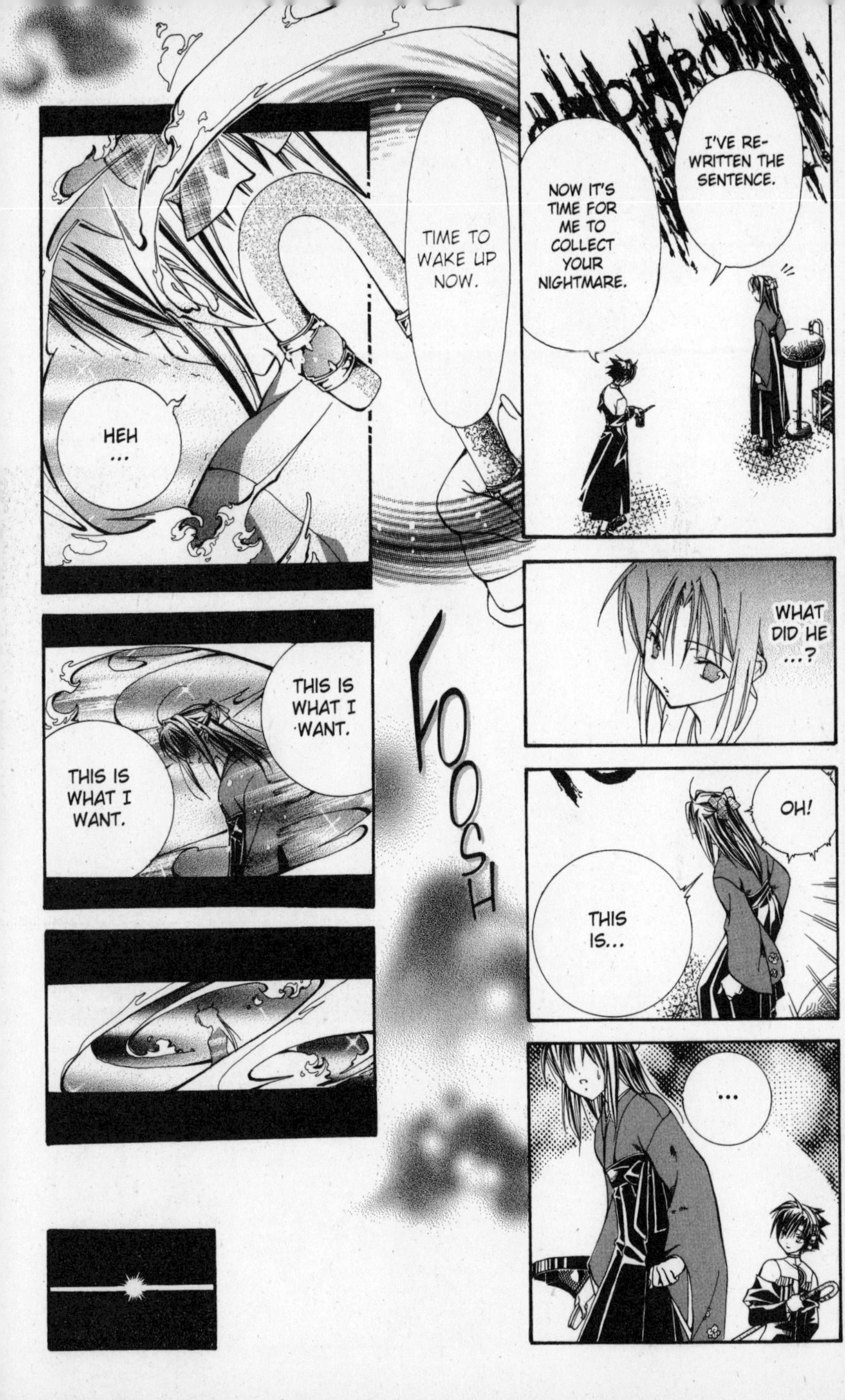
I'VE RE-WRITTEN THE SENTENCE.
NOW IT'S TIME FOR ME TO COLLECT YOUR NIGHTMARE.
TIME TO WAKE UP NOW.
HEH ...
WHAT DID HE ...?
OH!
THIS IS...
...
WOOSH
THIS IS WHAT I WANT.
THIS IS WHAT I WANT.

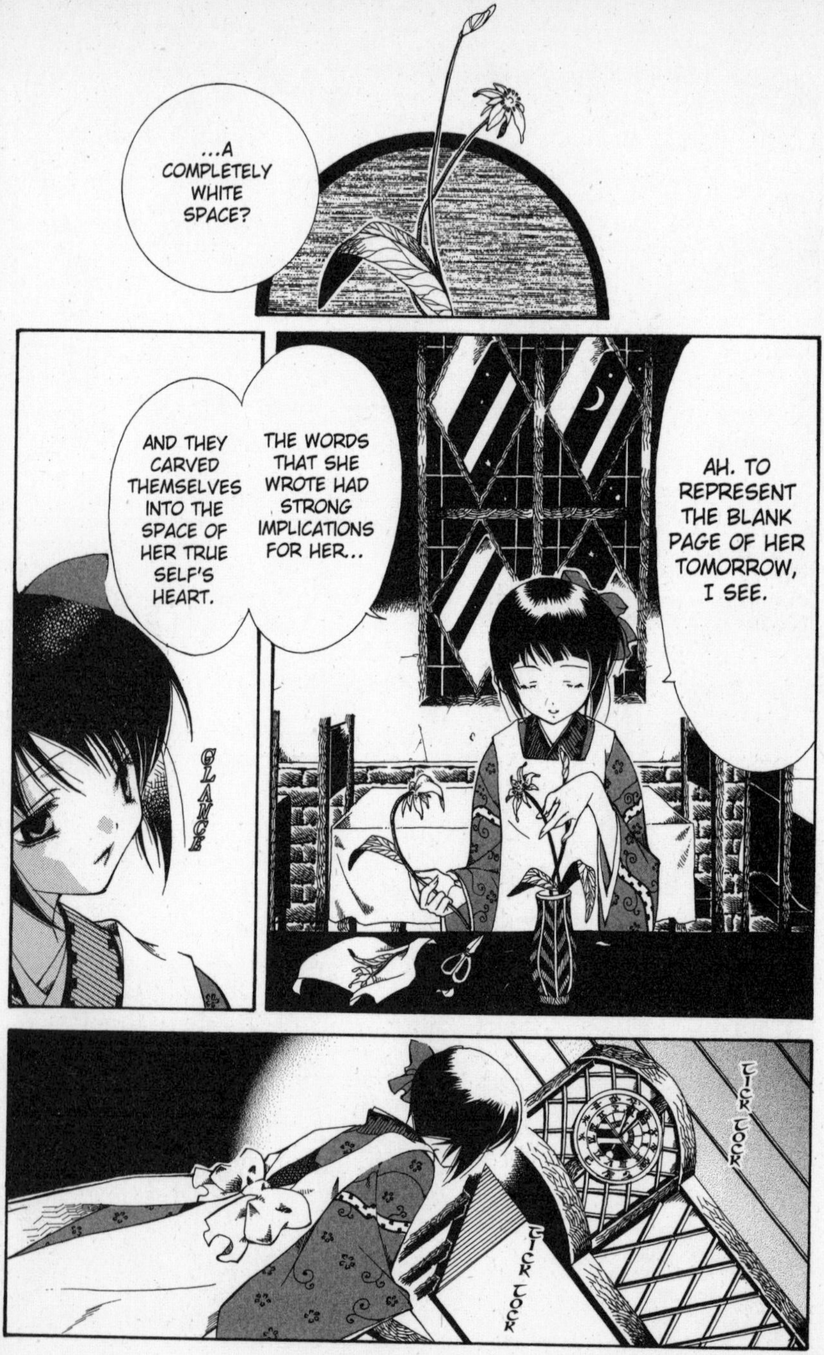
...A COMPLETELY WHITE SPACE?
AH. TO REPRESENT THE BLANK PAGE OF HER TOMORROW, I SEE.
THE WORDS THAT SHE WROTE HAD STRONG IMPLICATIONS FOR HER...
AND THEY CARVED THEMSELVES INTO THE SPACE OF HER TRUE SELF'S HEART.
GLANCE
TICK TOCK
TICK TOCK

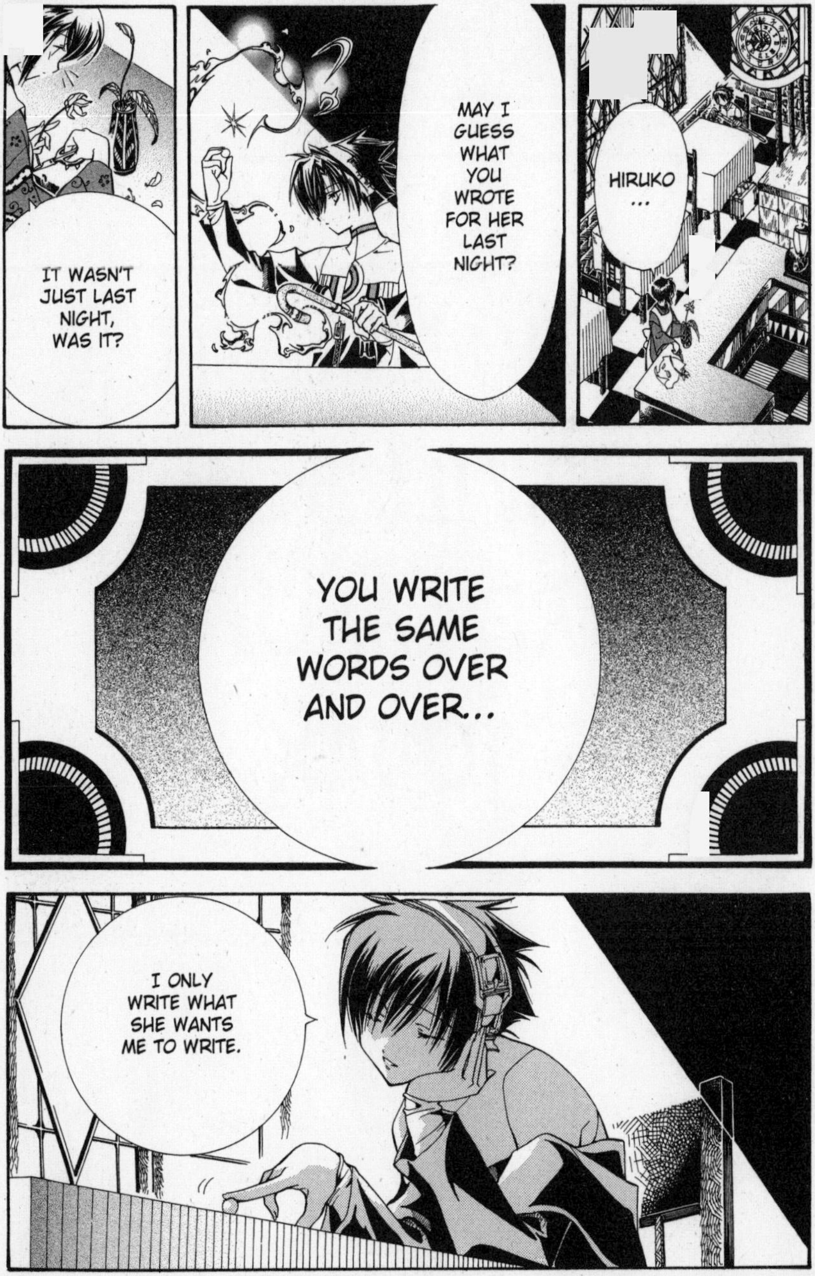
HIRUKO ...
MAY I GUESS WHAT YOU WROTE FOR HER LAST NIGHT?
IT WASN'T JUST LAST NIGHT, WAS IT?
YOU WRITE THE SAME WORDS OVER AND OVER...
I ONLY WRITE WHAT SHE WANTS ME TO WRITE.

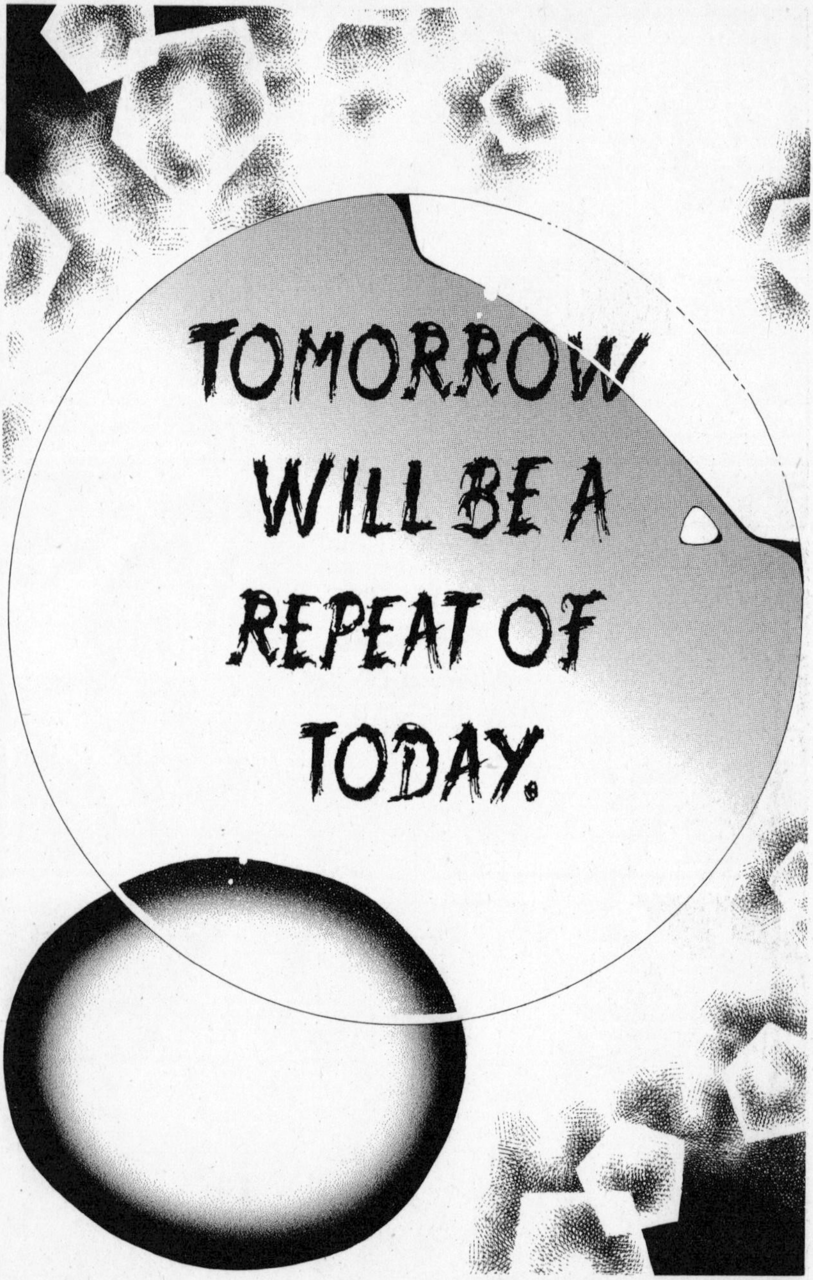
TOMORROW WILL BE A REPEAT OF TODAY.

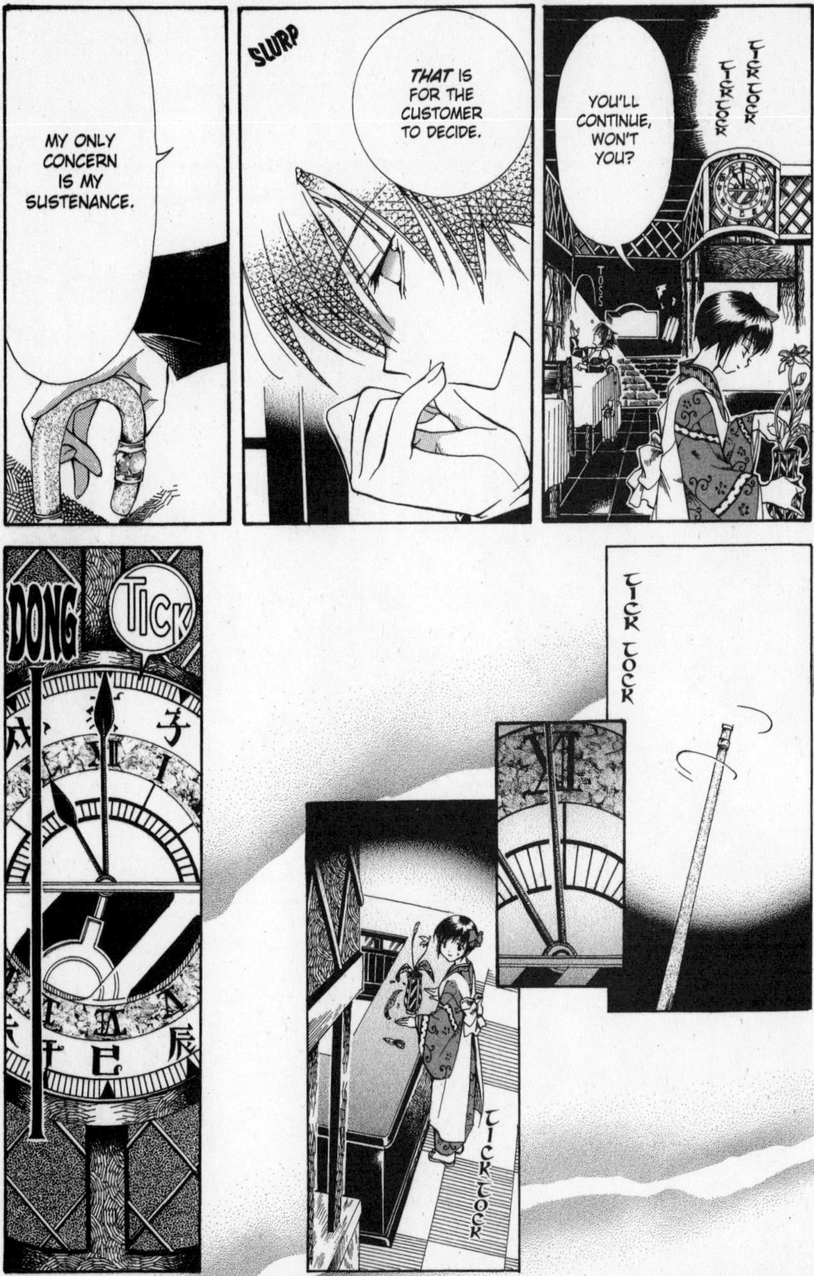
TICK TOCK
TICK TOCK
YOU'LL CONTINUE, WON'T YOU?
TOSS
SLURP
THAT IS FOR THE CUSTOMER TO DECIDE.
MY ONLY CONCERN IS MY SUSTENANCE.
TICK TOCK
TICK TOCK
TICK
DONG

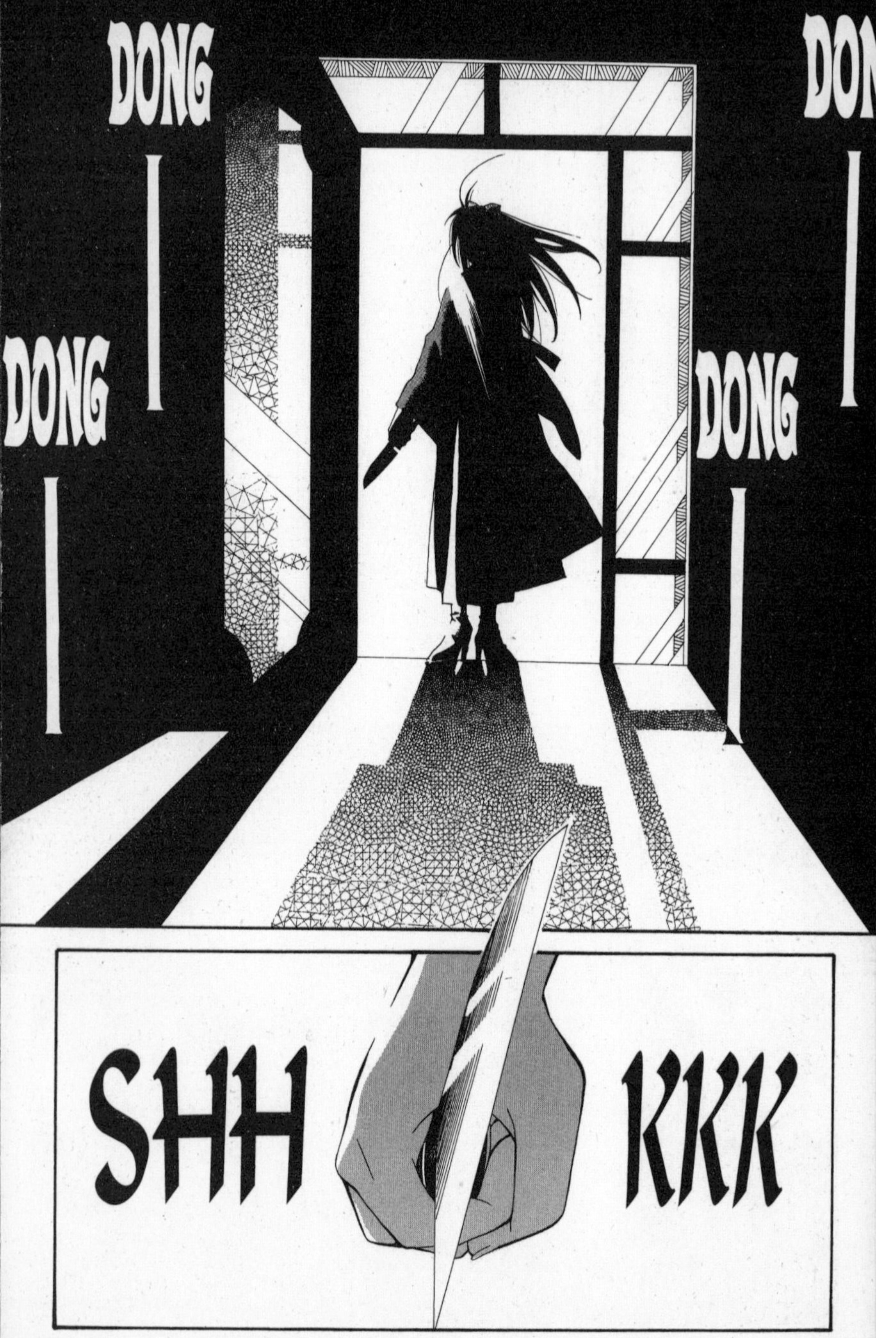
DON
DONG
DONG
DONG
SHH KKK

The Third Night: Lost Things

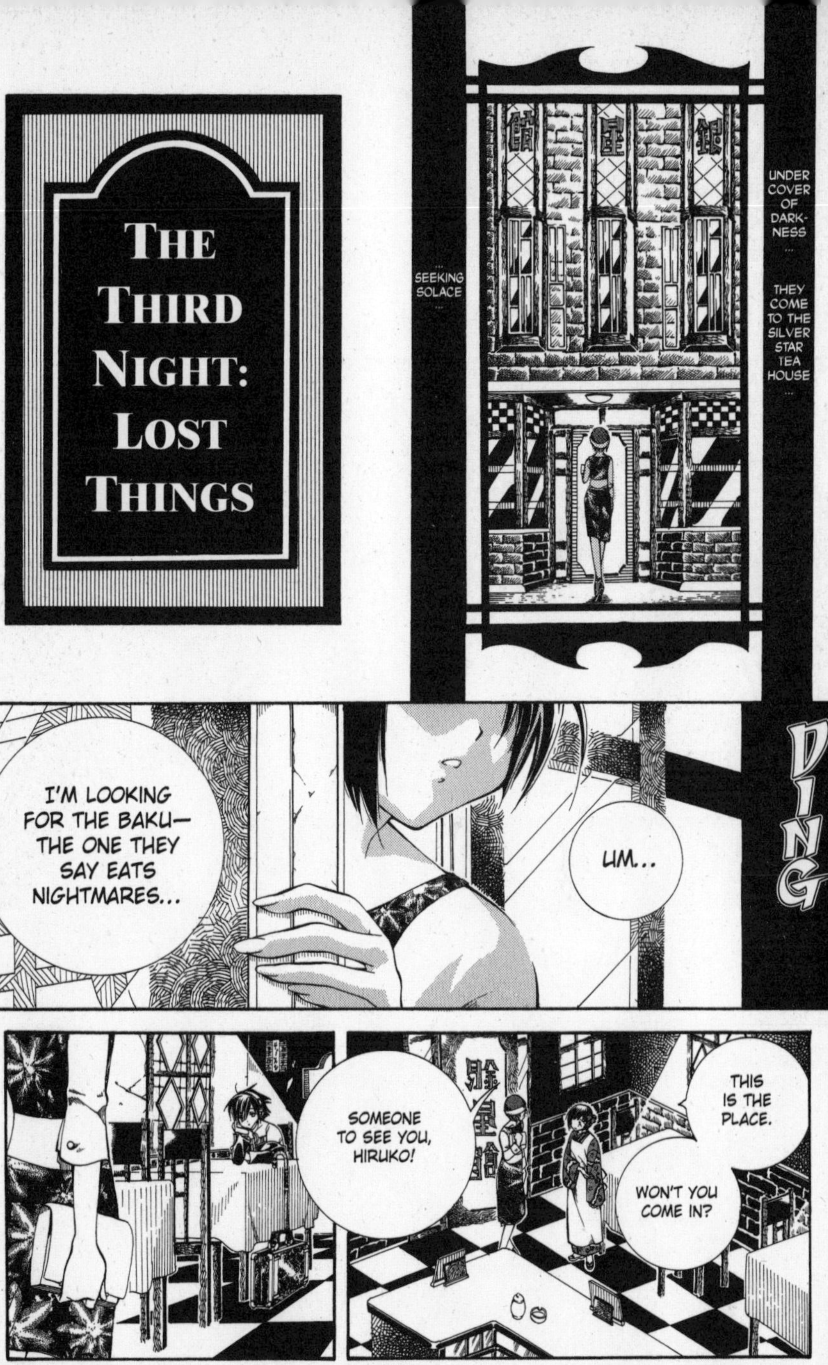
UNDER COVER OF DARKNESS...
THEY COME TO THE SILVER STAR TEA HOUSE...
...SEEKING SOLACE...
DING
UM...
I'M LOOKING FOR THE BAKU—THE ONE THEY SAY EATS NIGHTMARES...
THIS IS THE PLACE.
WON'T YOU COME IN?
SOMEONE TO SEE YOU, HIRUKO!

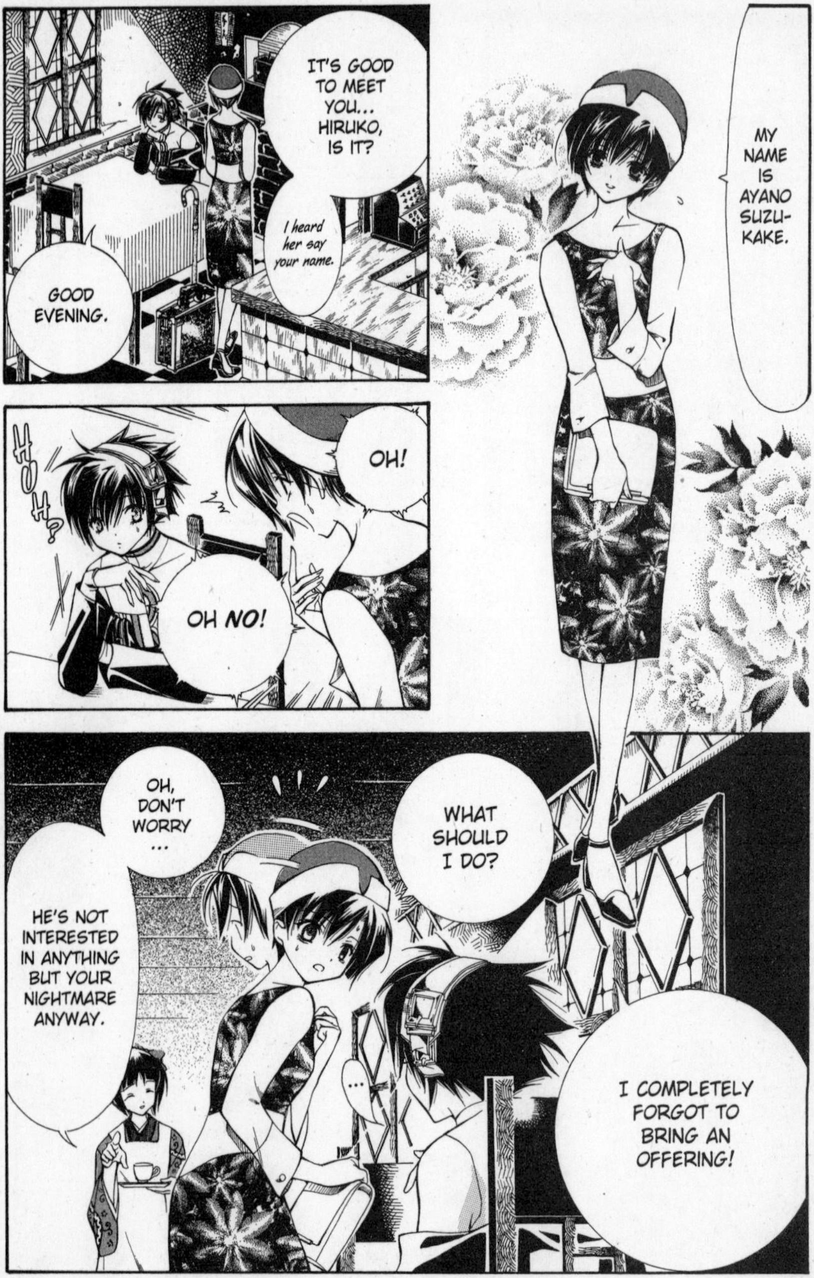
MY NAME IS AYANO SUZU-KAKE.
IT'S GOOD TO MEET YOU... HIRUKO, IS IT?
I heard her say your name.
GOOD EVENING.
OH!
HUH?
OH NO!
WHAT SHOULD I DO?
I COMPLETELY FORGOT TO BRING AN OFFERING!
...
OH, DON'T WORRY ...
HE'S NOT INTERESTED IN ANYTHING BUT YOUR NIGHTMARE ANYWAY.

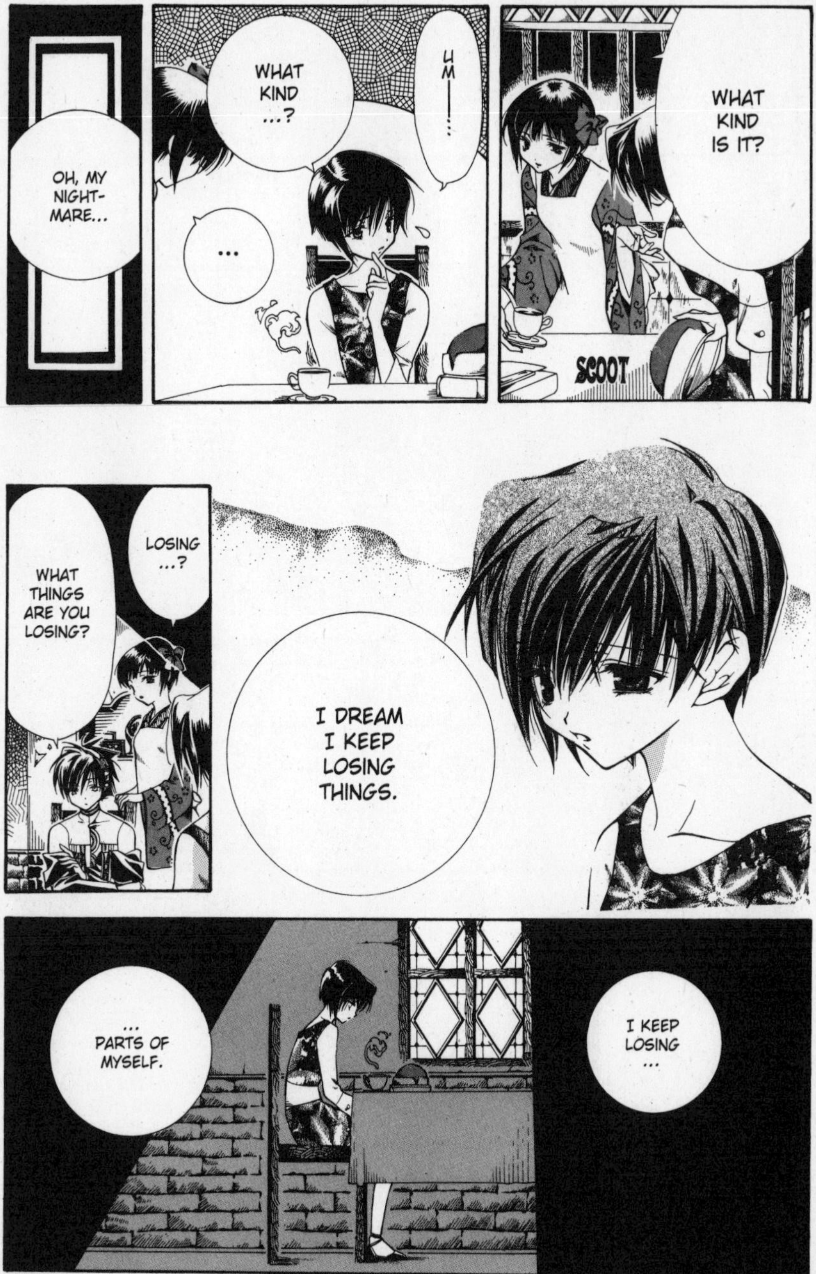
WHAT KIND IS IT?
SCOOT
UM—...
WHAT KIND ...?
...
OH, MY NIGHT-MARE...
I DREAM I KEEP LOSING THINGS.
LOSING ...?
WHAT THINGS ARE YOU LOSING?
I KEEP LOSING ...
... PARTS OF MYSELF.

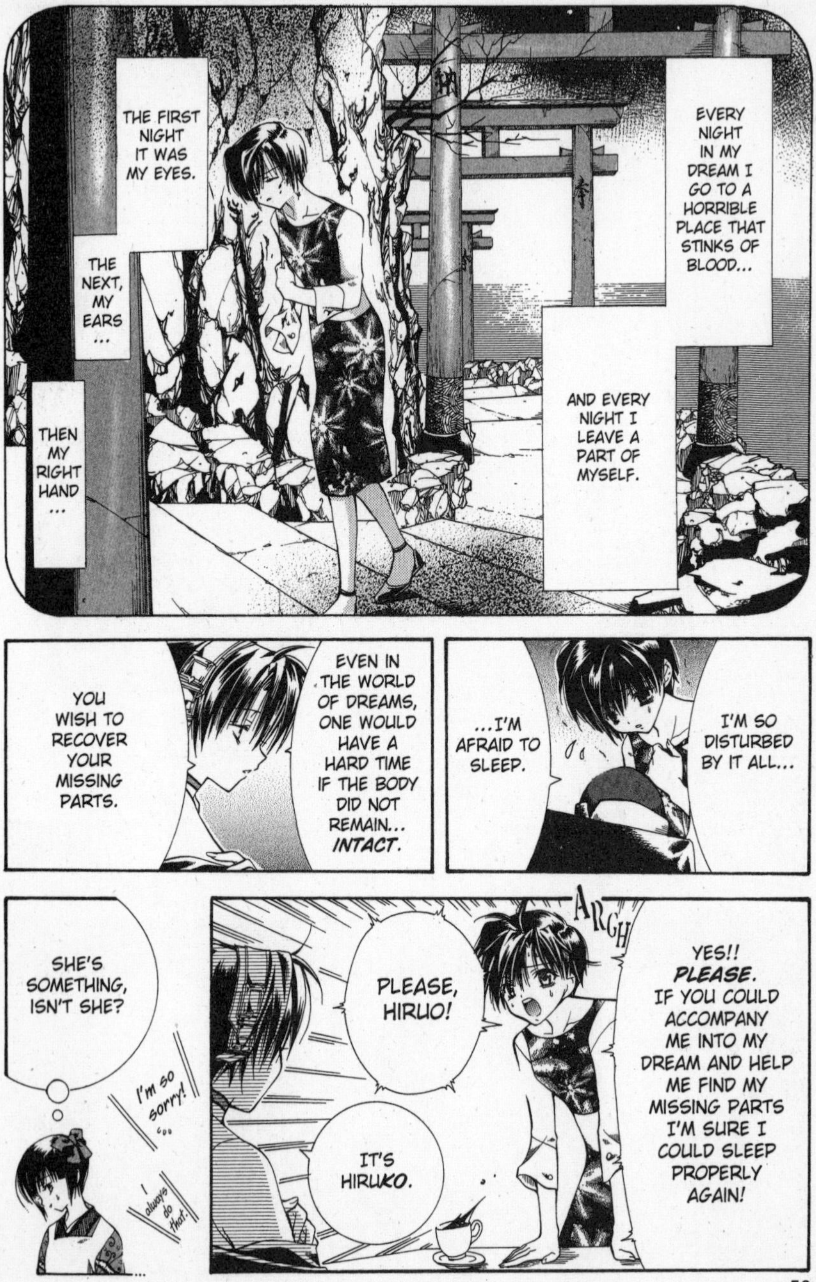
EVERY NIGHT IN MY DREAM I GO TO A HORRIBLE PLACE THAT STINKS OF BLOOD...
AND EVERY NIGHT I LEAVE A PART OF MYSELF.
THE FIRST NIGHT IT WAS MY EYES.
THE NEXT, MY EARS...
THEN MY RIGHT HAND...
I'M SO DISTURBED BY IT ALL...
...I'M AFRAID TO SLEEP.
EVEN IN THE WORLD OF DREAMS, ONE WOULD HAVE A HARD TIME IF THE BODY DID NOT REMAIN... ***INTACT***.
YOU WISH TO RECOVER YOUR MISSING PARTS.
ARGH
YES!! ***PLEASE.*** IF YOU COULD ACCOMPANY ME INTO MY DREAM AND HELP ME FIND MY MISSING PARTS I'M SURE I COULD SLEEP PROPERLY AGAIN!
PLEASE, HIRUO!
IT'S HIRU**KO**.
SHE'S SOMETHING, ISN'T SHE?
I'm so sorry!...
I always do that.
...

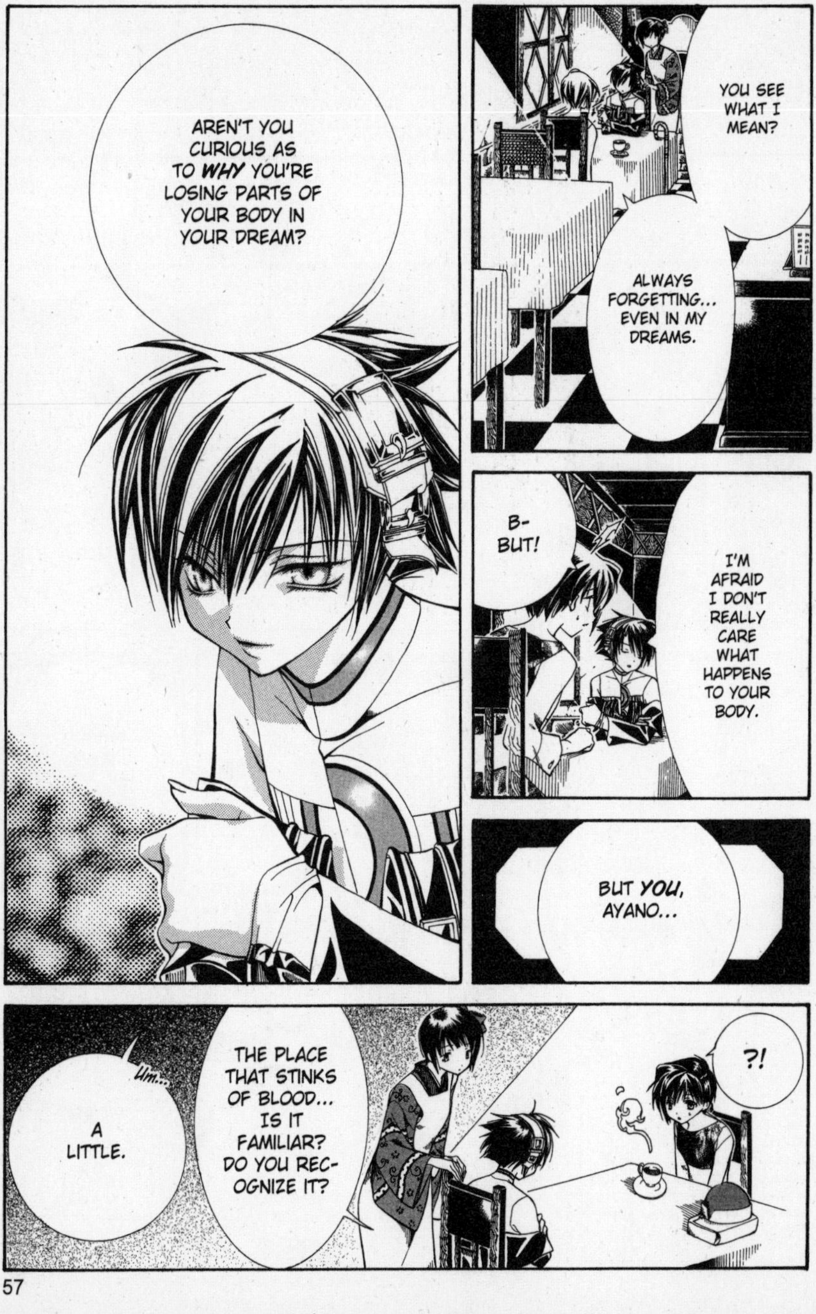

YOU SEE WHAT I MEAN?
ALWAYS FORGETTING... EVEN IN MY DREAMS.
I'M AFRAID I DON'T REALLY CARE WHAT HAPPENS TO YOUR BODY.
B-BUT!
BUT *YOU*, AYANO...
AREN'T YOU CURIOUS AS TO ***WHY*** YOU'RE LOSING PARTS OF YOUR BODY IN YOUR DREAM?
?!
THE PLACE THAT STINKS OF BLOOD... IS IT FAMILIAR? DO YOU RECOGNIZE IT?
Um...
A LITTLE.

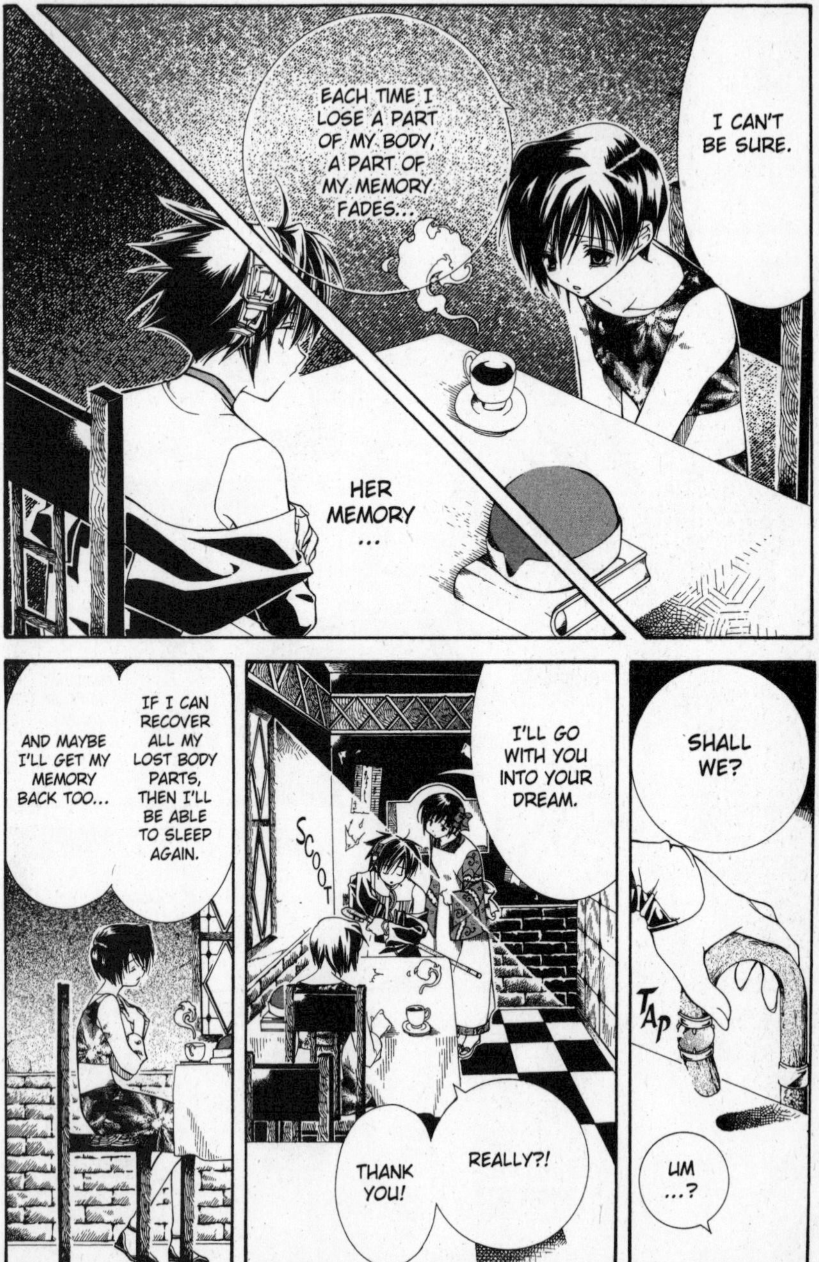
I CAN'T BE SURE.
EACH TIME I LOSE A PART OF MY BODY, A PART OF MY MEMORY FADES...
HER MEMORY ...
SHALL WE?
TAP
UM ...?
I'LL GO WITH YOU INTO YOUR DREAM.
SCOOT
REALLY?!
THANK YOU!
IF I CAN RECOVER ALL MY LOST BODY PARTS, THEN I'LL BE ABLE TO SLEEP AGAIN.
AND MAYBE I'LL GET MY MEMORY BACK TOO...

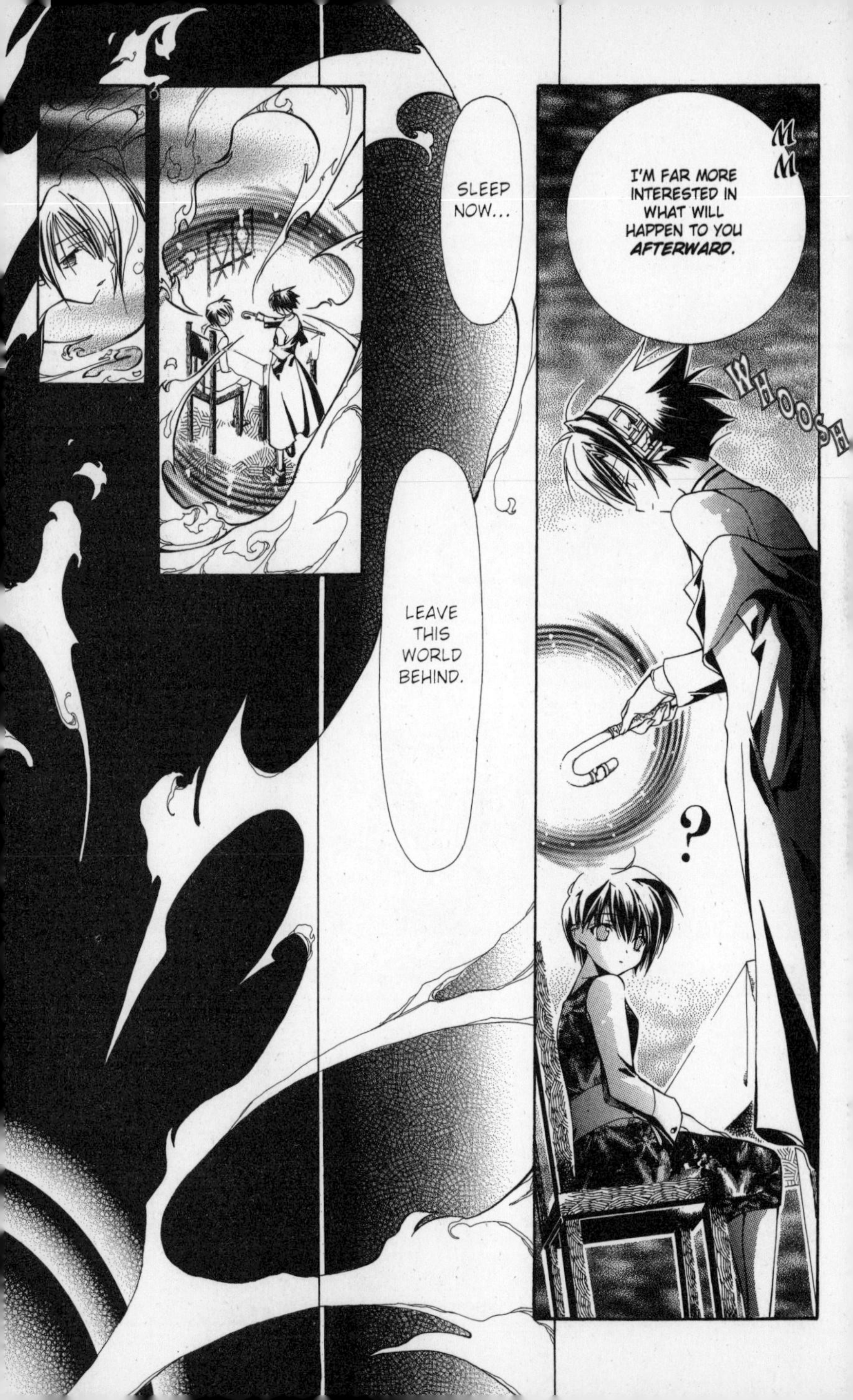
MM
I'M FAR MORE INTERESTED IN WHAT WILL HAPPEN TO YOU AFTERWARD.
WHOOSH
?
SLEEP NOW...
LEAVE THIS WORLD BEHIND.

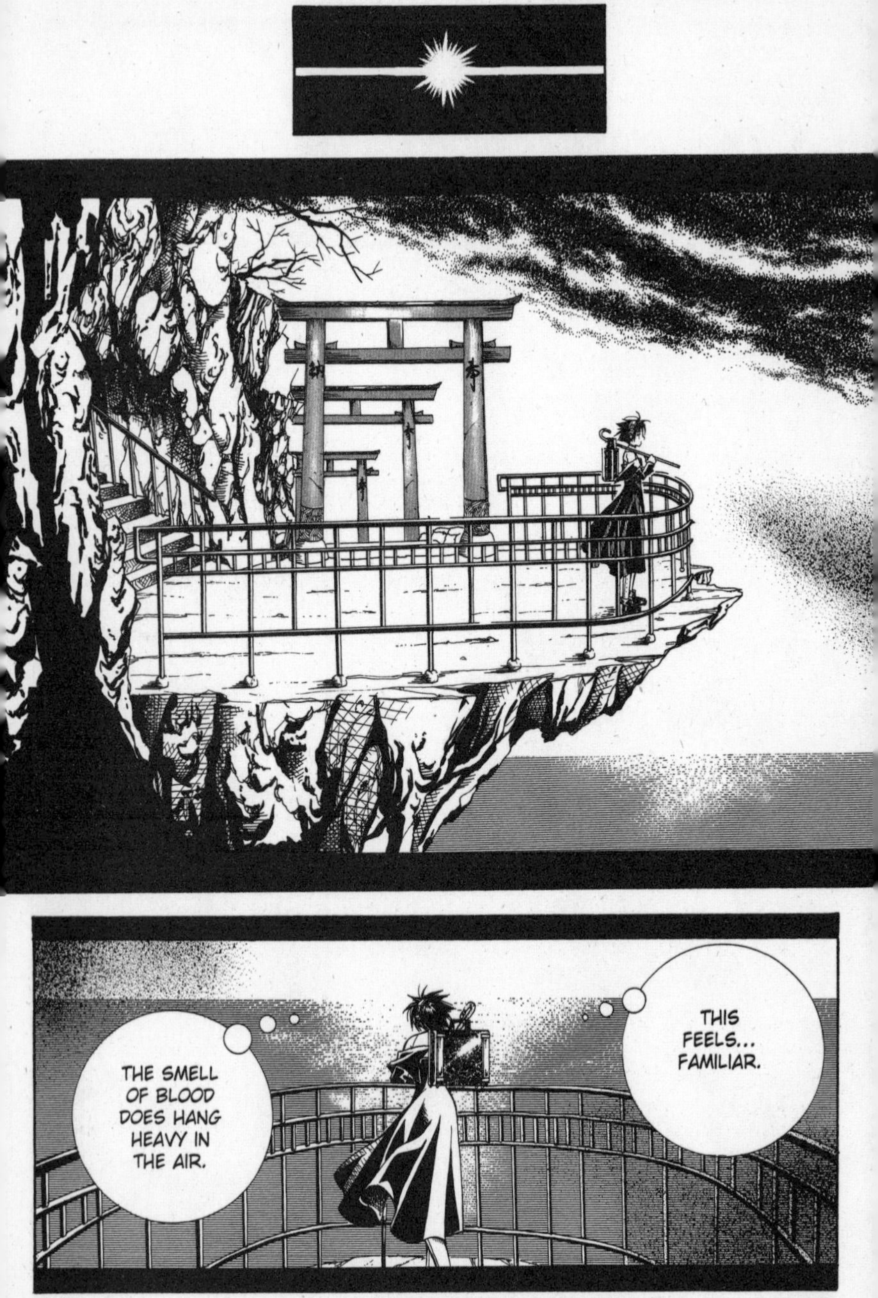
THIS FEELS... FAMILIAR.
THE SMELL OF BLOOD DOES HANG HEAVY IN THE AIR.

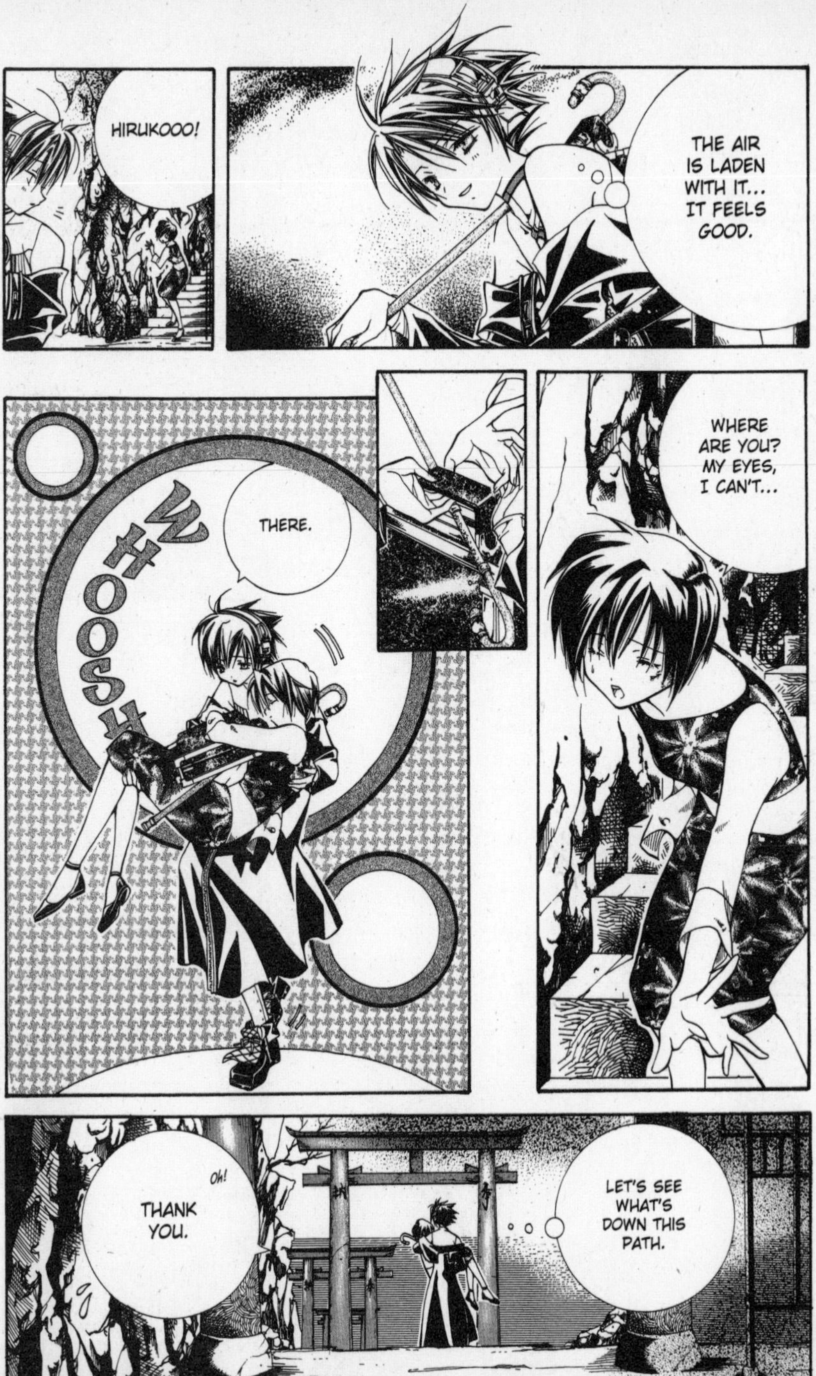
THE AIR IS LADEN WITH IT... IT FEELS GOOD.
HIRUKOOO!
WHERE ARE YOU? MY EYES, I CAN'T...
THERE.
WHOOSH
LET'S SEE WHAT'S DOWN THIS PATH.
Oh!
THANK YOU.

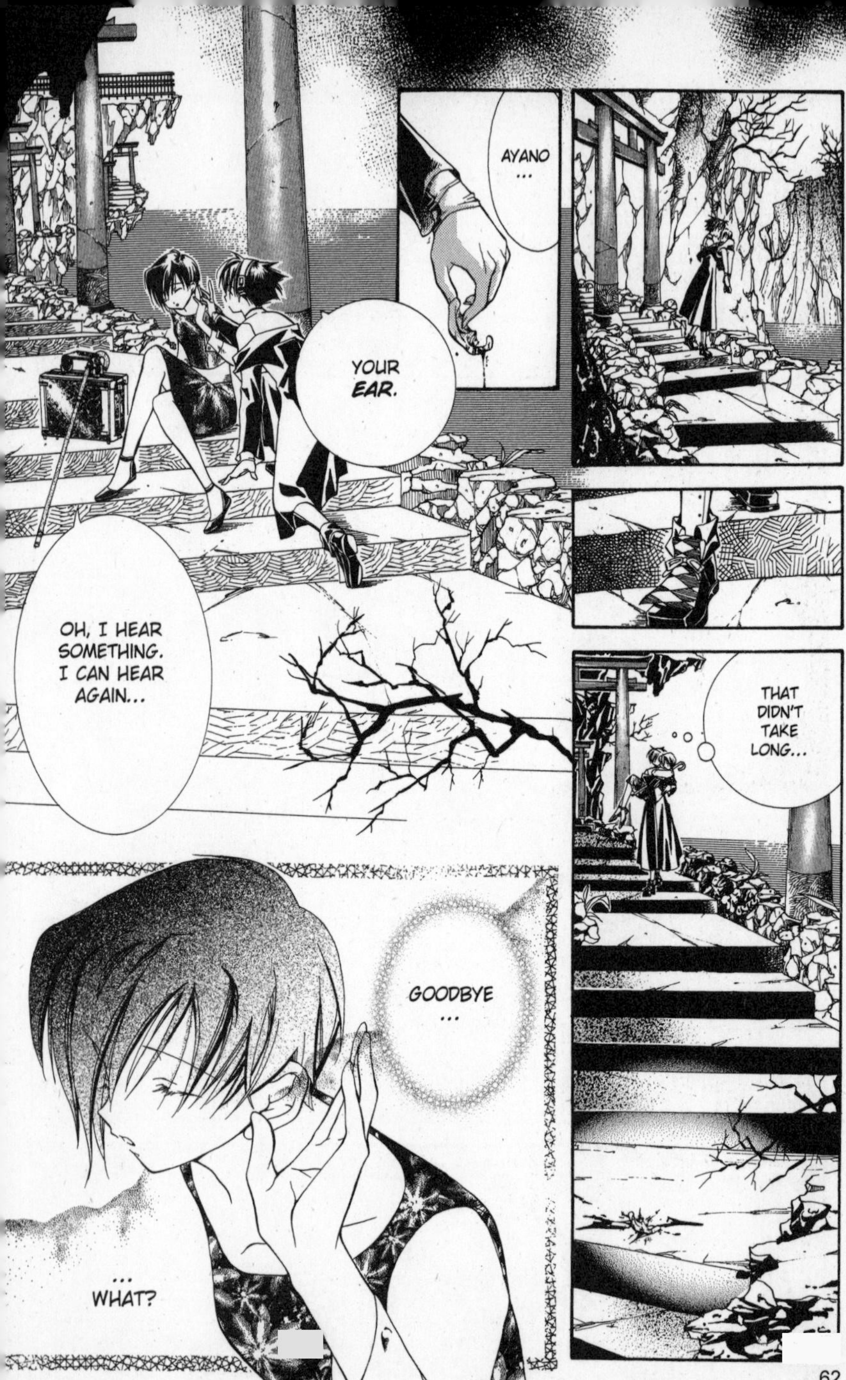
AYANO ...
YOUR EAR.
OH, I HEAR SOMETHING. I CAN HEAR AGAIN...
THAT DIDN'T TAKE LONG...
GOODBYE ...
... WHAT?

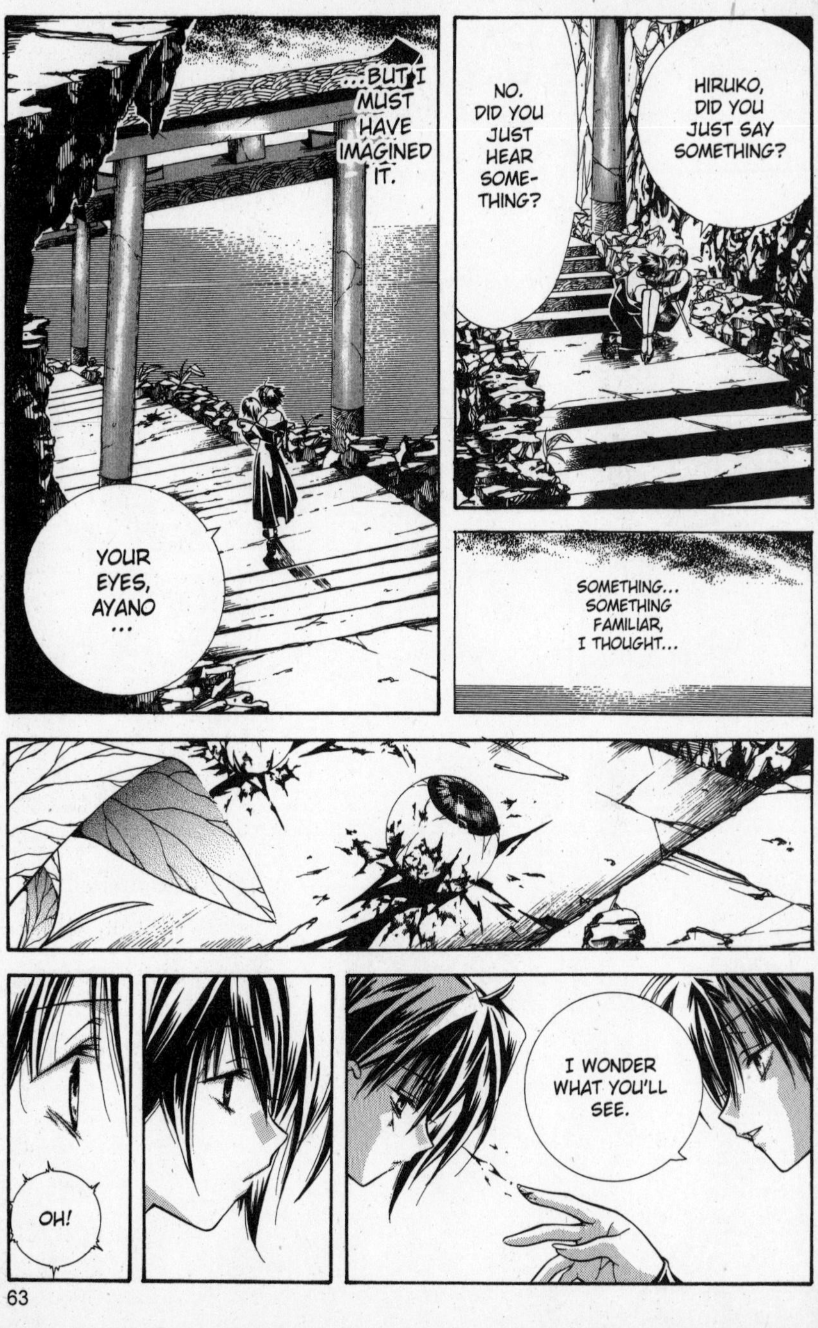
HIRUKO, DID YOU JUST SAY SOMETHING?
NO. DID YOU JUST HEAR SOME-THING?
SOMETHING... SOMETHING FAMILIAR, I THOUGHT...
...BUT I MUST HAVE IMAGINED IT.
YOUR EYES, AYANO...
I WONDER WHAT YOU'LL SEE.
OH!

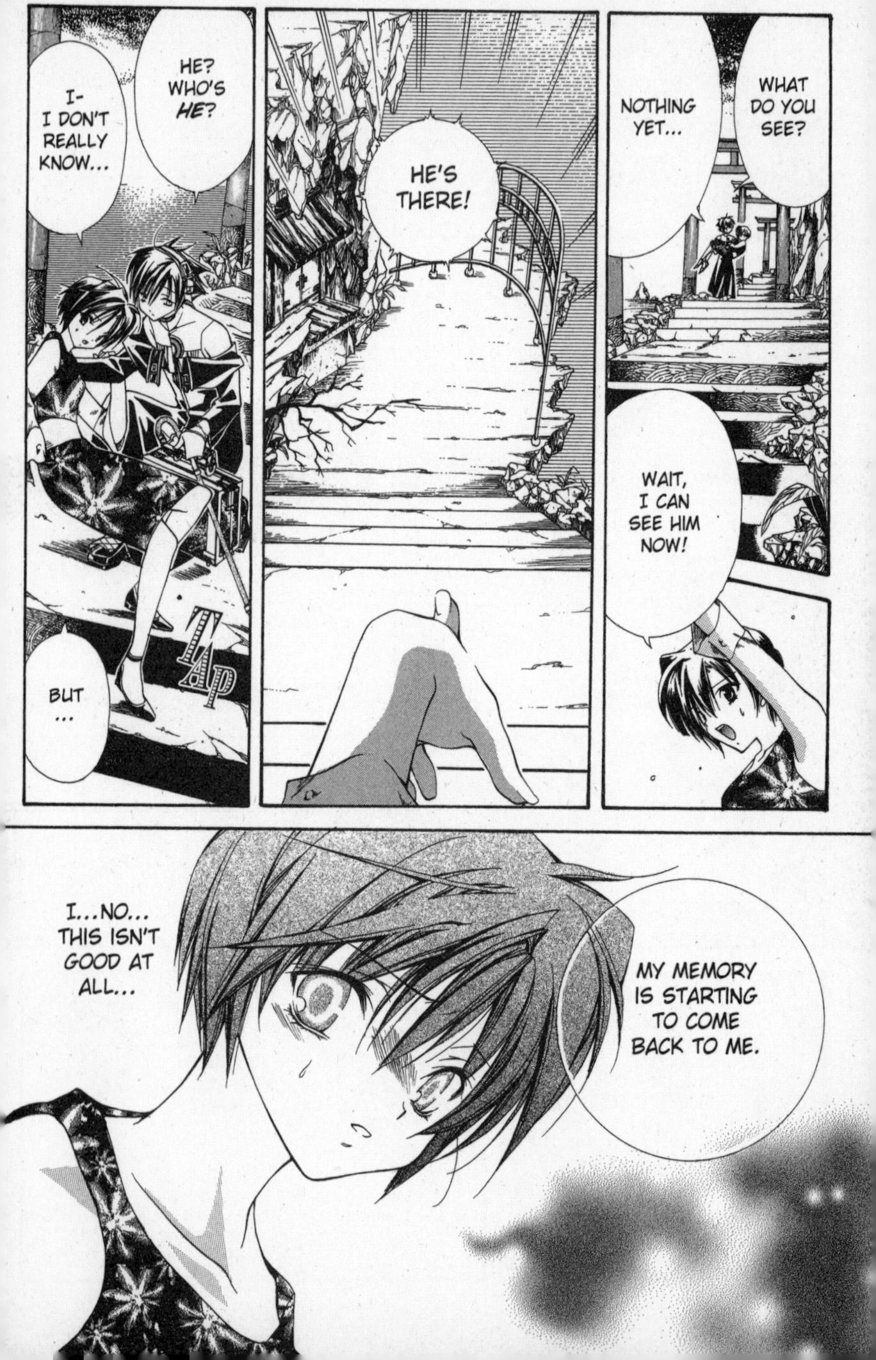
WHAT DO YOU SEE?
NOTHING YET...
WAIT, I CAN SEE HIM NOW!
HE'S THERE!
HE? WHO'S HE?
I- I DON'T REALLY KNOW...
TAP
BUT ...
MY MEMORY IS STARTING TO COME BACK TO ME.
I...NO... THIS ISN'T GOOD AT ALL...

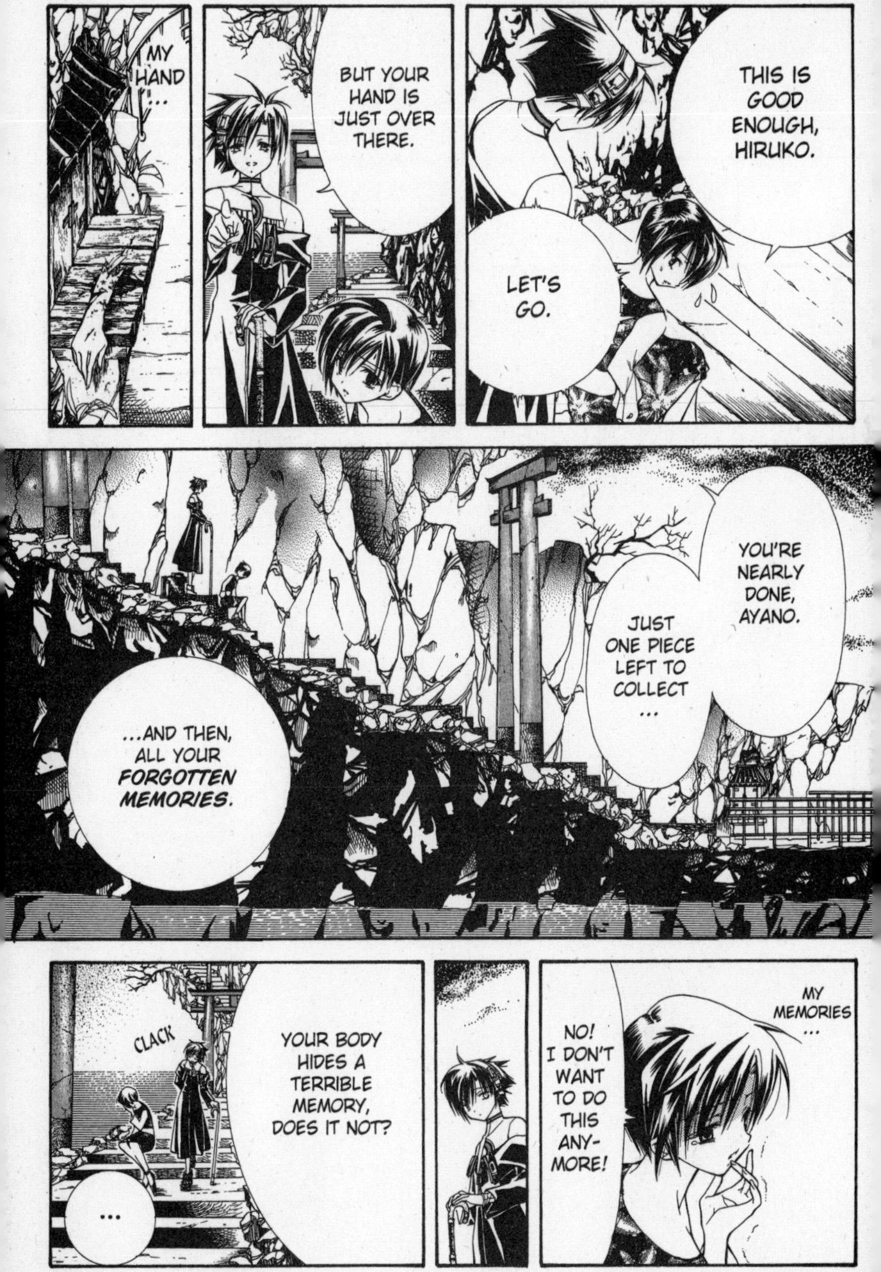
THIS IS GOOD ENOUGH, HIRUKO.
LET'S GO.
BUT YOUR HAND IS JUST OVER THERE.
MY HAND ...
YOU'RE NEARLY DONE, AYANO.
JUST ONE PIECE LEFT TO COLLECT ...
...AND THEN, ALL YOUR *FORGOTTEN MEMORIES.*
MY MEMORIES ...
NO! I DON'T WANT TO DO THIS ANY-MORE!
YOUR BODY HIDES A TERRIBLE MEMORY, DOES IT NOT?
CLACK
...

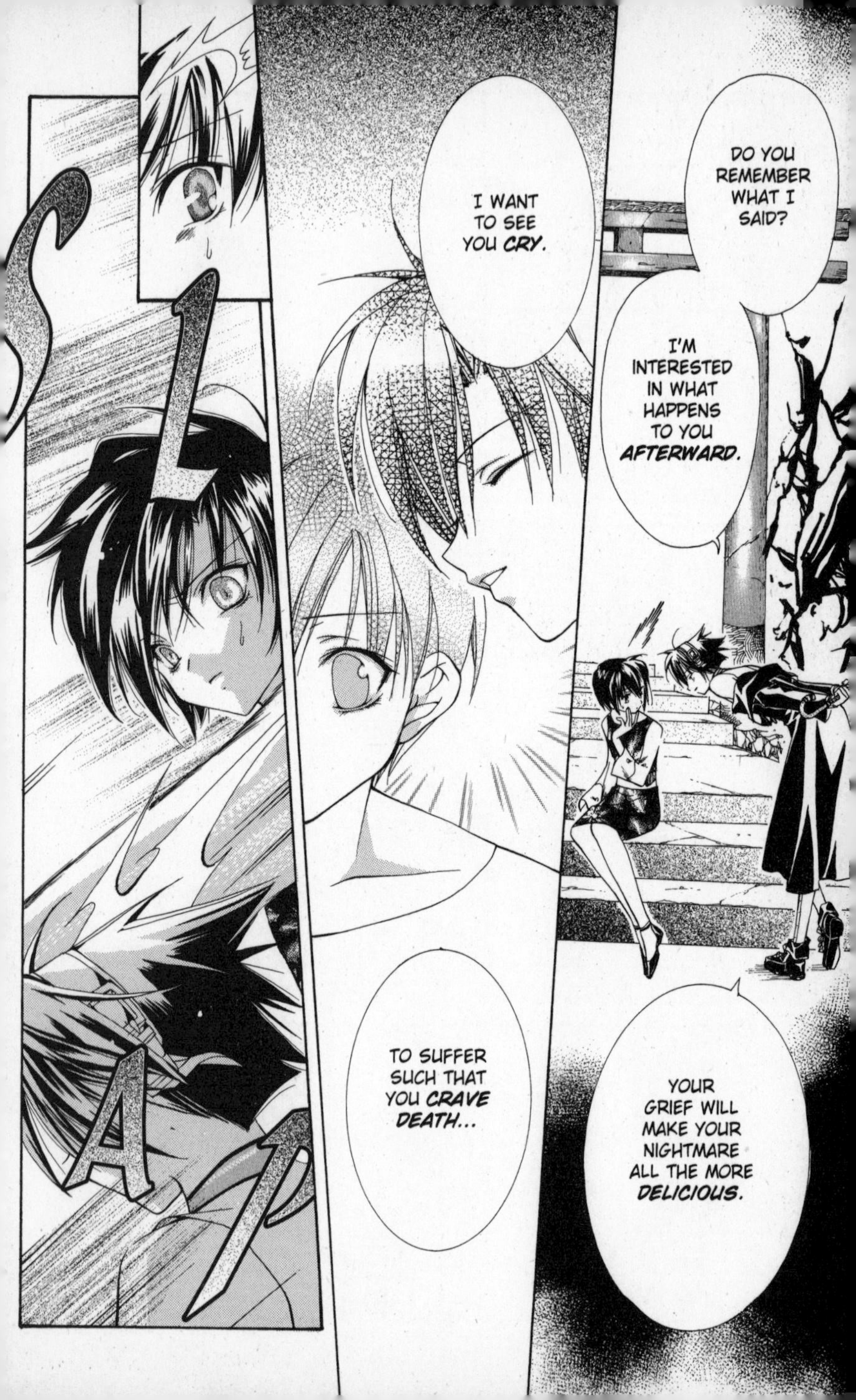
DO YOU REMEMBER WHAT I SAID?
I'M INTERESTED IN WHAT HAPPENS TO YOU AFTERWARD.
YOUR GRIEF WILL MAKE YOUR NIGHTMARE ALL THE MORE DELICIOUS.
I WANT TO SEE YOU CRY.
TO SUFFER SUCH THAT YOU CRAVE DEATH...
SLA

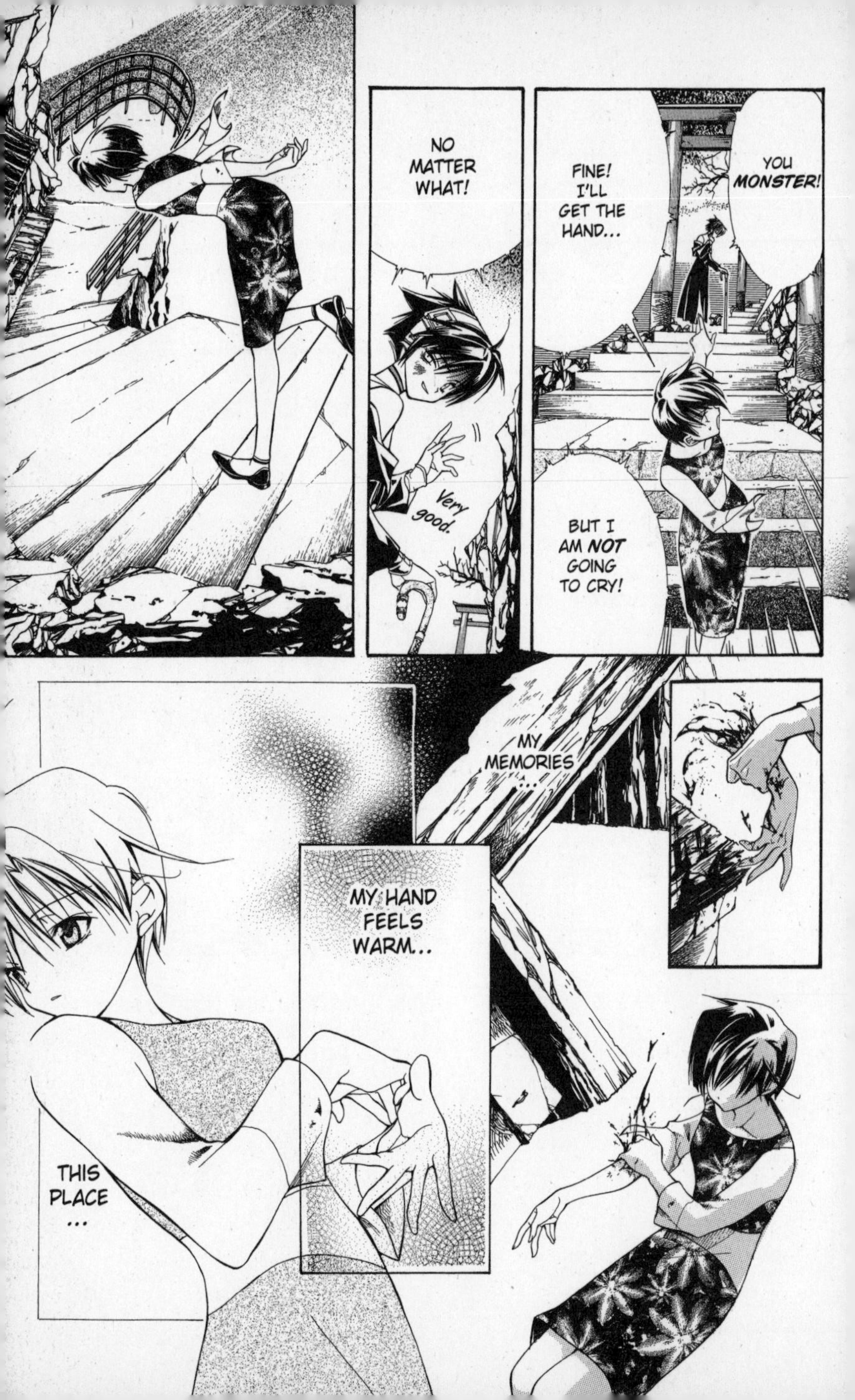
YOU MONSTER!
FINE! I'LL GET THE HAND...
BUT I AM NOT GOING TO CRY!
NO MATTER WHAT!
Very good.
MY MEMORIES...
MY HAND FEELS WARM...
THIS PLACE...

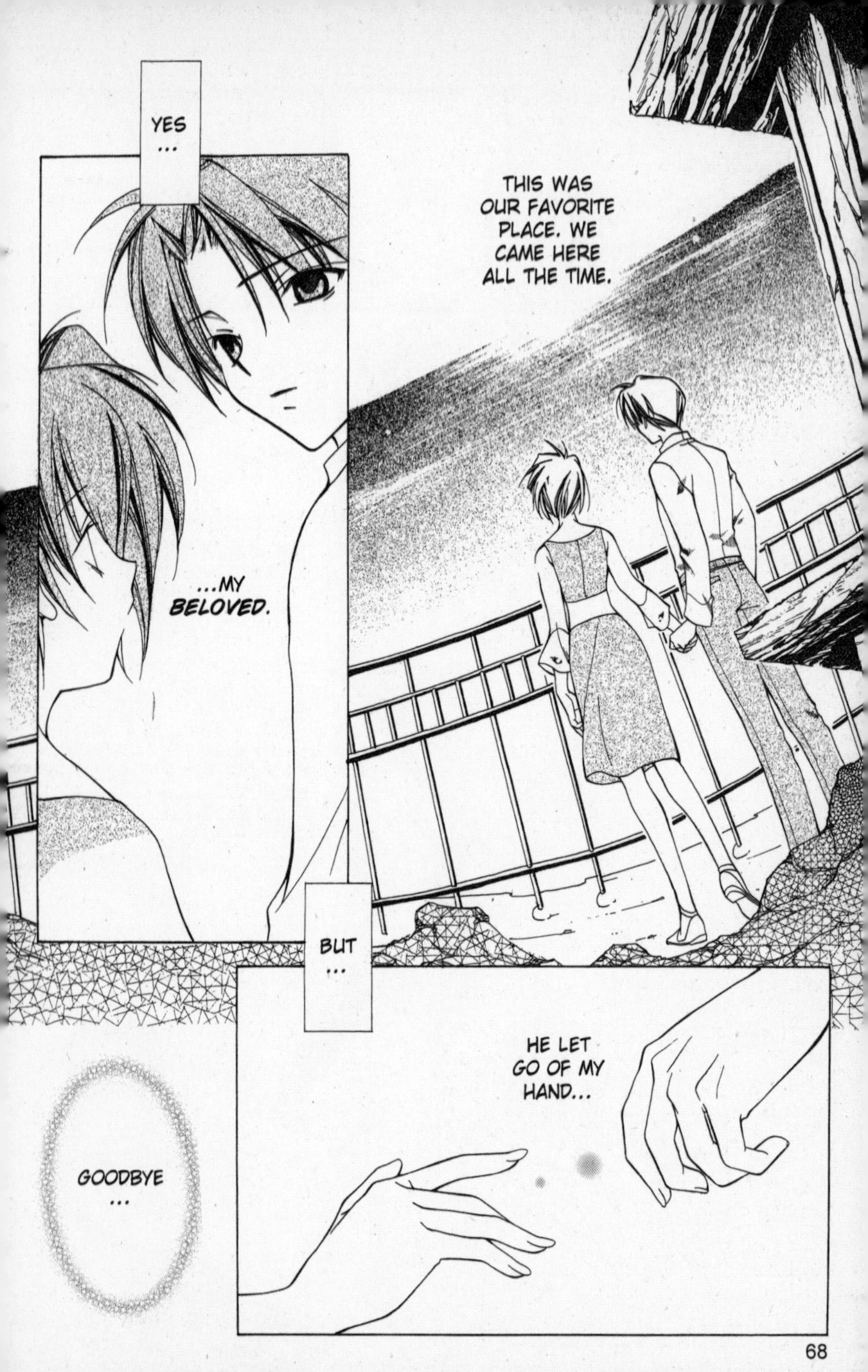
THIS WAS OUR FAVORITE PLACE. WE CAME HERE ALL THE TIME.
YES...
...MY BELOVED.
BUT...
HE LET GO OF MY HAND...
GOODBYE...

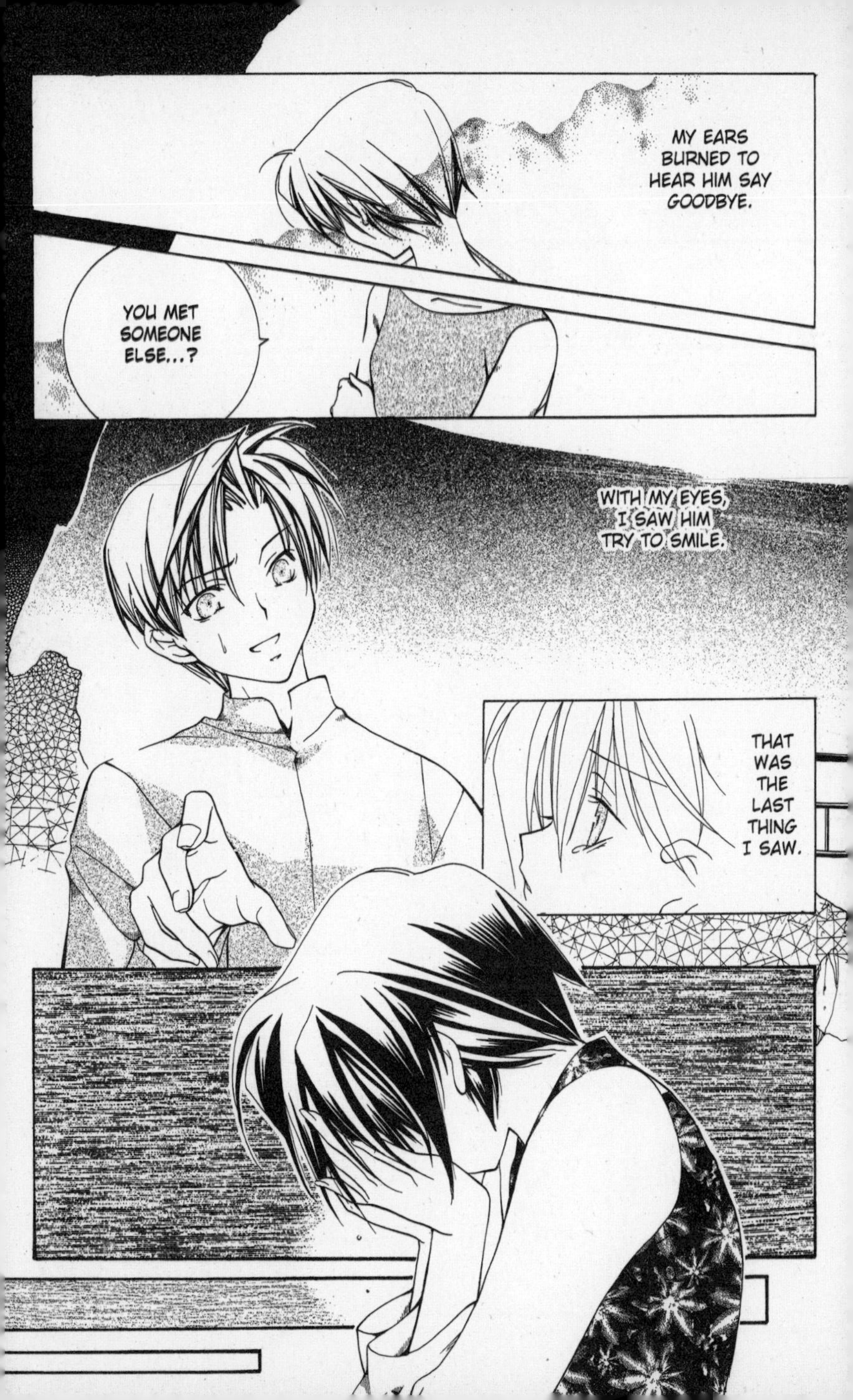
MY EARS BURNED TO HEAR HIM SAY GOODBYE.
YOU MET SOMEONE ELSE...?
WITH MY EYES, I SAW HIM TRY TO SMILE.
THAT WAS THE LAST THING I SAW.

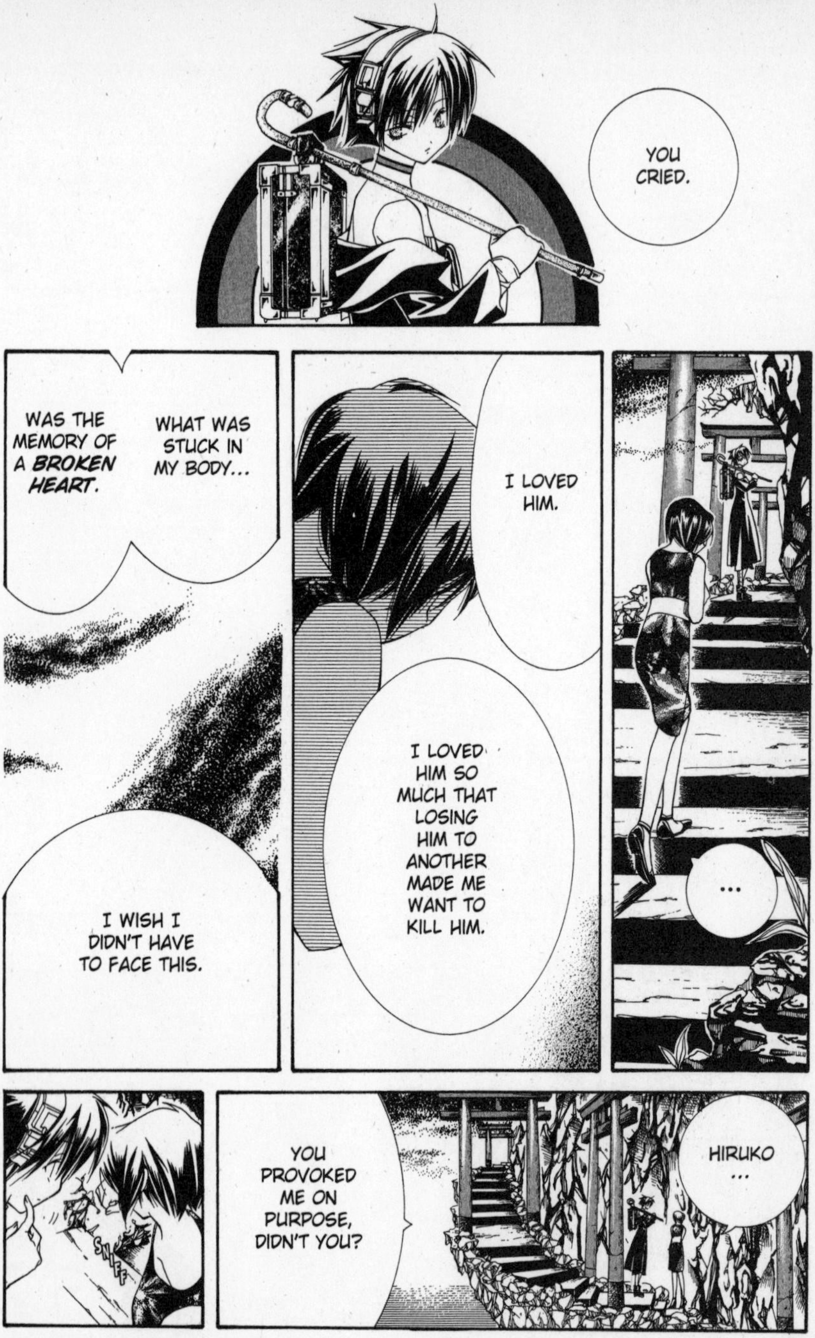
YOU CRIED.
...
I LOVED HIM.
I LOVED HIM SO MUCH THAT LOSING HIM TO ANOTHER MADE ME WANT TO KILL HIM.
WHAT WAS STUCK IN MY BODY...
WAS THE MEMORY OF A **BROKEN HEART**.
I WISH I DIDN'T HAVE TO FACE THIS.
HIRUKO ...
YOU PROVOKED ME ON PURPOSE, DIDN'T YOU?
SNIFF

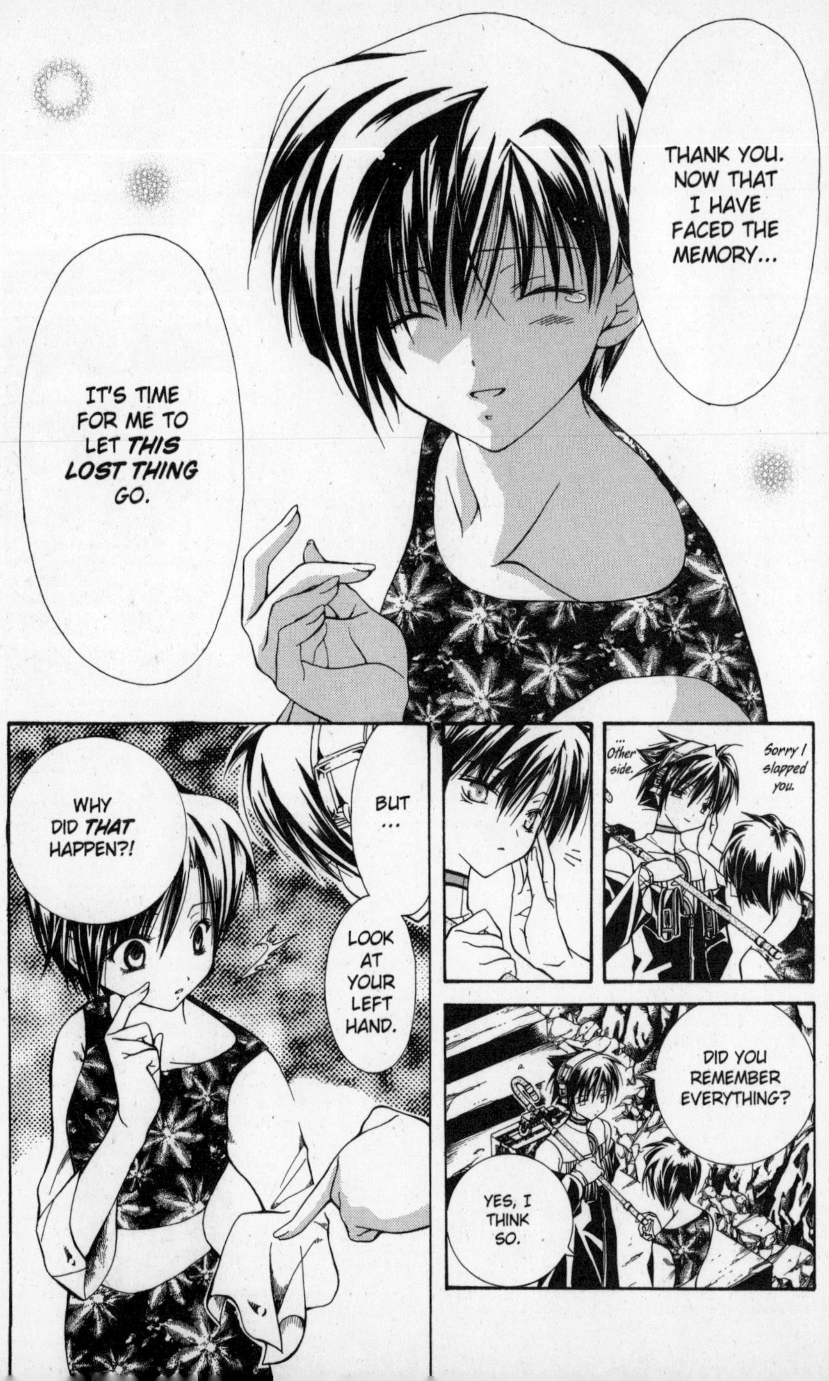
THANK YOU. NOW THAT I HAVE FACED THE MEMORY...
IT'S TIME FOR ME TO LET *THIS LOST THING* GO.
Sorry I slapped you.
...Other side.
DID YOU REMEMBER EVERYTHING?
YES, I THINK SO.
BUT ...
LOOK AT YOUR LEFT HAND.
WHY DID *THAT* HAPPEN?!

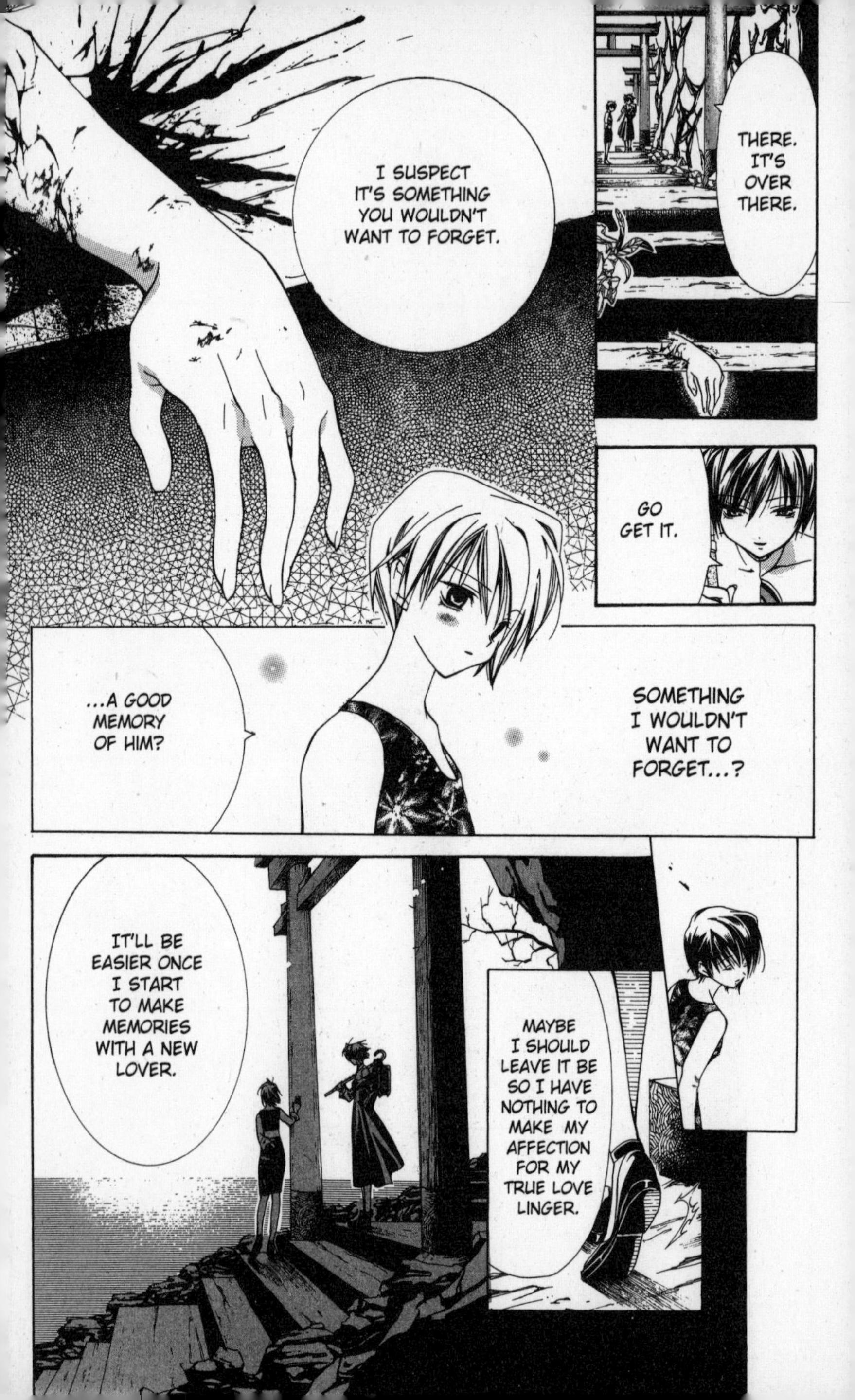
THERE. IT'S OVER THERE.
GO GET IT.
I SUSPECT IT'S SOMETHING YOU WOULDN'T WANT TO FORGET.
SOMETHING I WOULDN'T WANT TO FORGET...?
...A GOOD MEMORY OF HIM?
MAYBE I SHOULD LEAVE IT BE SO I HAVE NOTHING TO MAKE MY AFFECTION FOR MY TRUE LOVE LINGER.
IT'LL BE EASIER ONCE I START TO MAKE MEMORIES WITH A NEW LOVER.

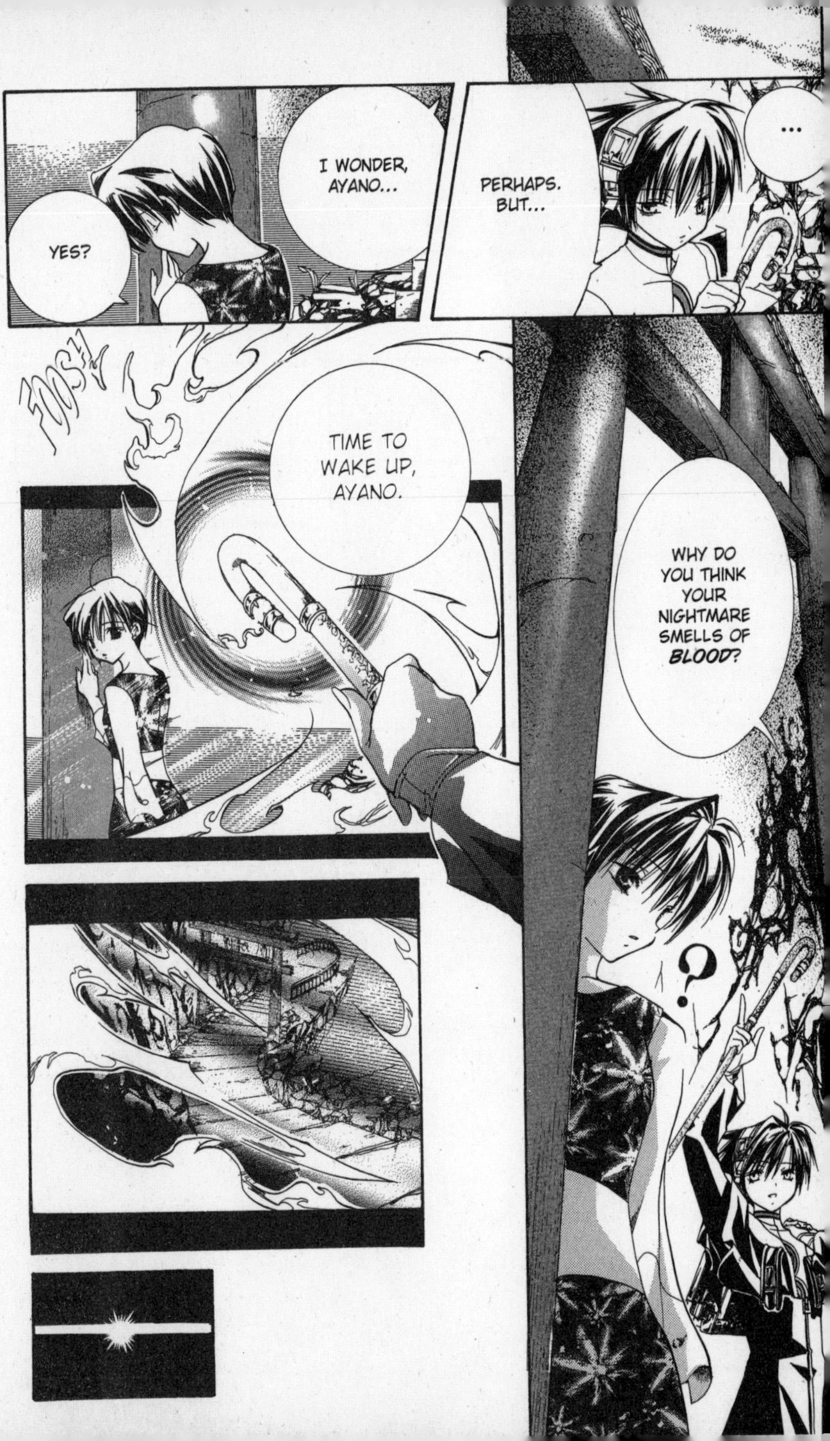
...
PERHAPS. BUT...
I WONDER, AYANO...
YES?
WHY DO YOU THINK YOUR NIGHTMARE SMELLS OF BLOOD?
TIME TO WAKE UP, AYANO.
FOOSH

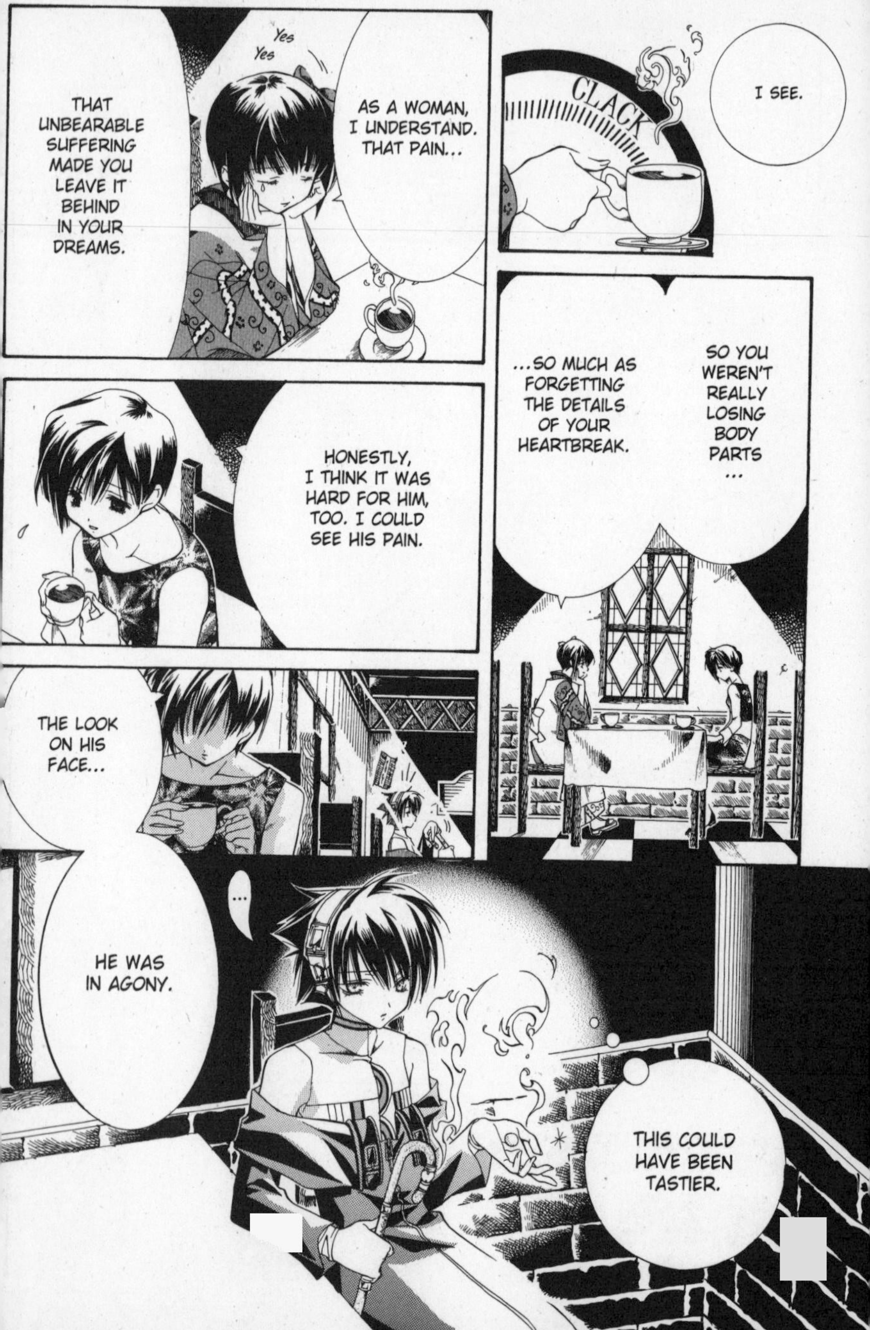

CLACK
I SEE.
Yes
Yes
AS A WOMAN, I UNDERSTAND. THAT PAIN...
THAT UNBEARABLE SUFFERING MADE YOU LEAVE IT BEHIND IN YOUR DREAMS.
SO YOU WEREN'T REALLY LOSING BODY PARTS ...
...SO MUCH AS FORGETTING THE DETAILS OF YOUR HEARTBREAK.
HONESTLY, I THINK IT WAS HARD FOR HIM, TOO. I COULD SEE HIS PAIN.
THE LOOK ON HIS FACE...
HE WAS IN AGONY.
...
THIS COULD HAVE BEEN TASTIER.

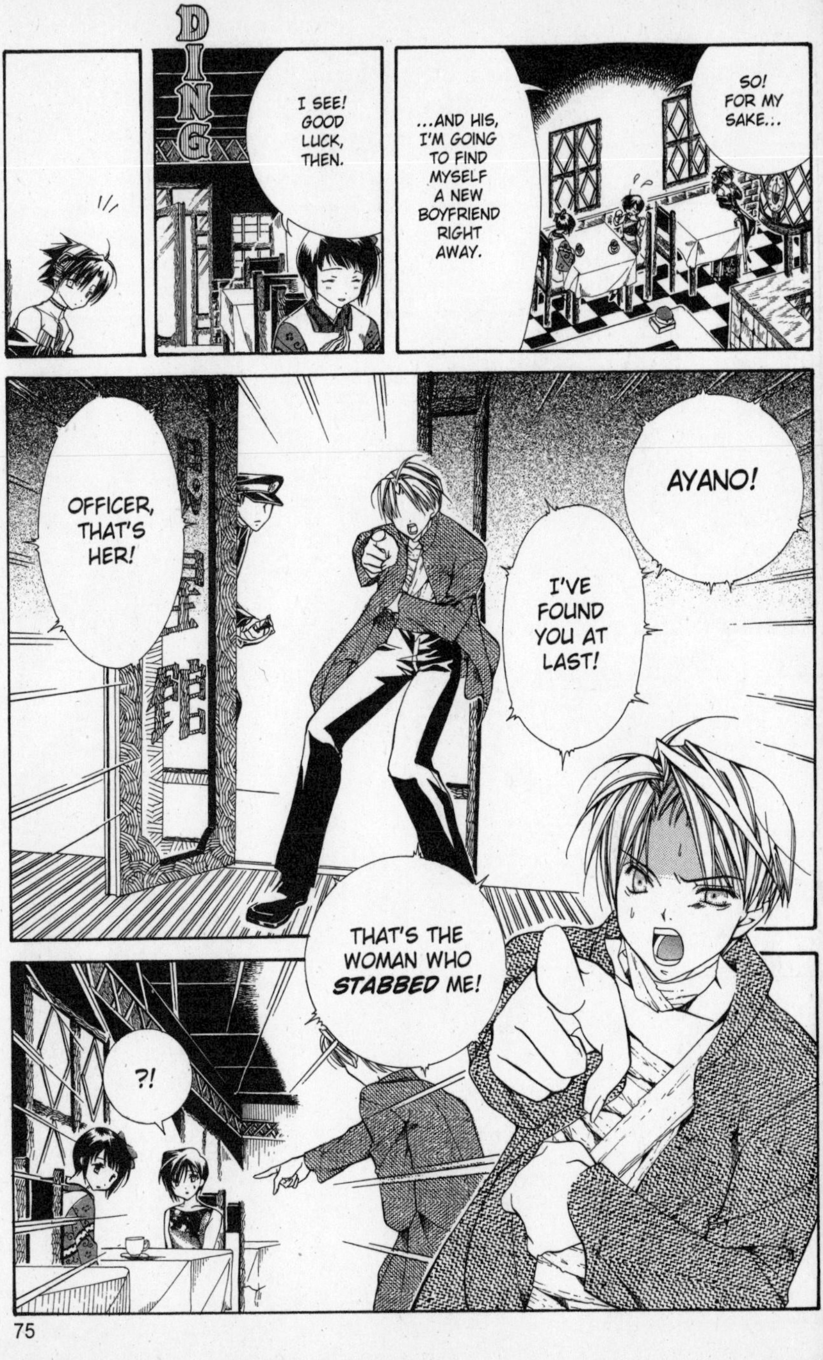
SO! FOR MY SAKE...
...AND HIS, I'M GOING TO FIND MYSELF A NEW BOYFRIEND RIGHT AWAY.
DING
I SEE! GOOD LUCK, THEN.
AYANO!
I'VE FOUND YOU AT LAST!
OFFICER, THAT'S HER!
THAT'S THE WOMAN WHO *STABBED* ME!
?!

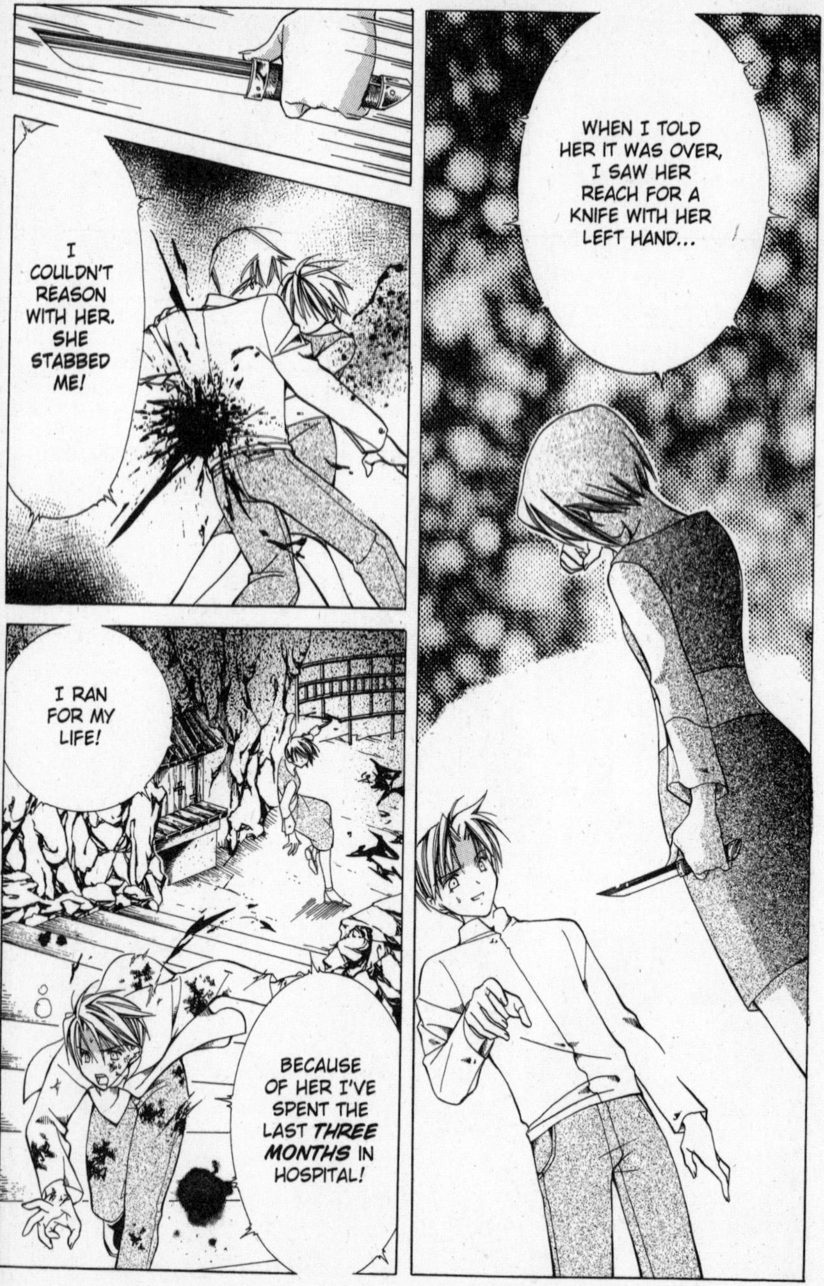
WHEN I TOLD HER IT WAS OVER, I SAW HER REACH FOR A KNIFE WITH HER LEFT HAND...
I COULDN'T REASON WITH HER. SHE STABBED ME!
I RAN FOR MY LIFE!
BECAUSE OF HER I'VE SPENT THE LAST ***THREE MONTHS*** IN HOSPITAL!

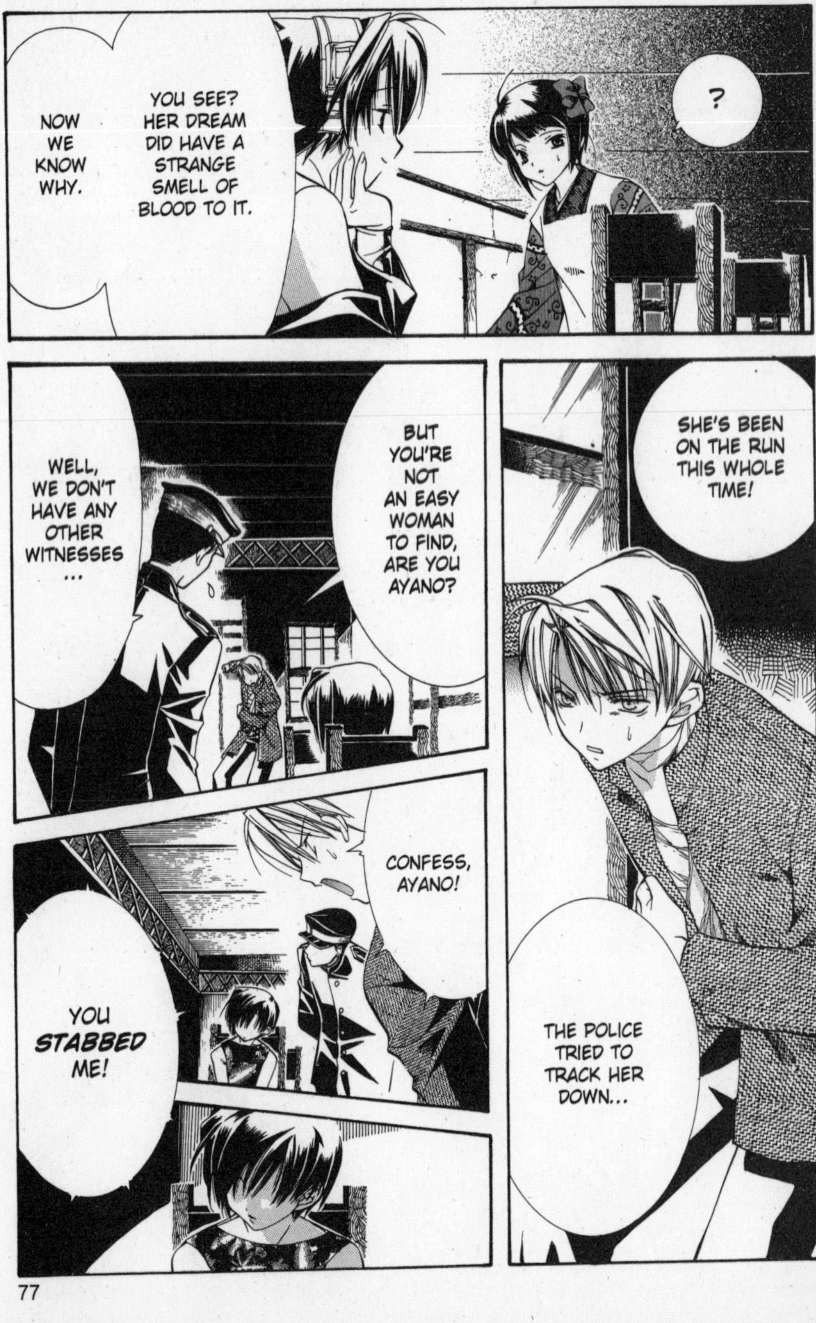
?
YOU SEE? HER DREAM DID HAVE A STRANGE SMELL OF BLOOD TO IT.
NOW WE KNOW WHY.
SHE'S BEEN ON THE RUN THIS WHOLE TIME!
THE POLICE TRIED TO TRACK HER DOWN...
BUT YOU'RE NOT AN EASY WOMAN TO FIND, ARE YOU AYANO?
WELL, WE DON'T HAVE ANY OTHER WITNESSES...
CONFESS, AYANO!
YOU STABBED ME!

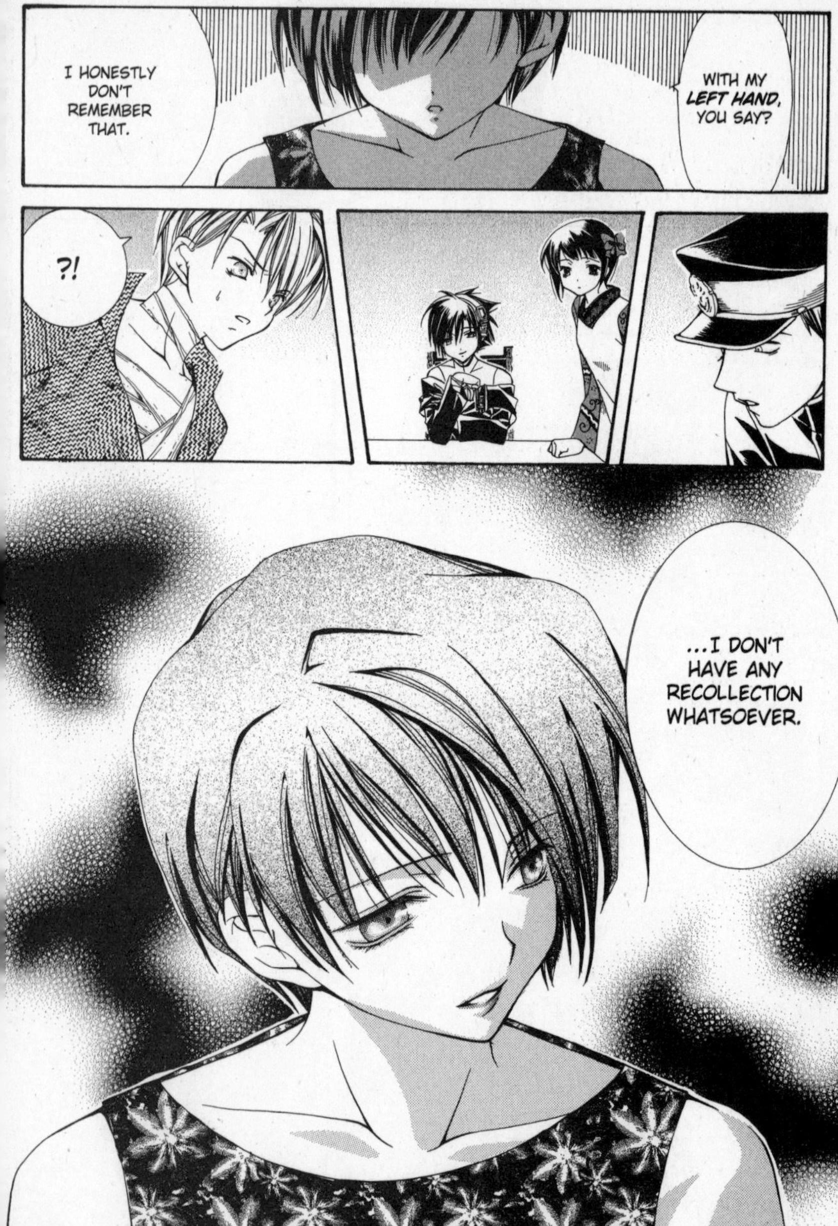
WITH MY *LEFT HAND*, YOU SAY?
I HONESTLY DON'T REMEMBER THAT.
?!
...I DON'T HAVE ANY RECOLLECTION WHATSOEVER.

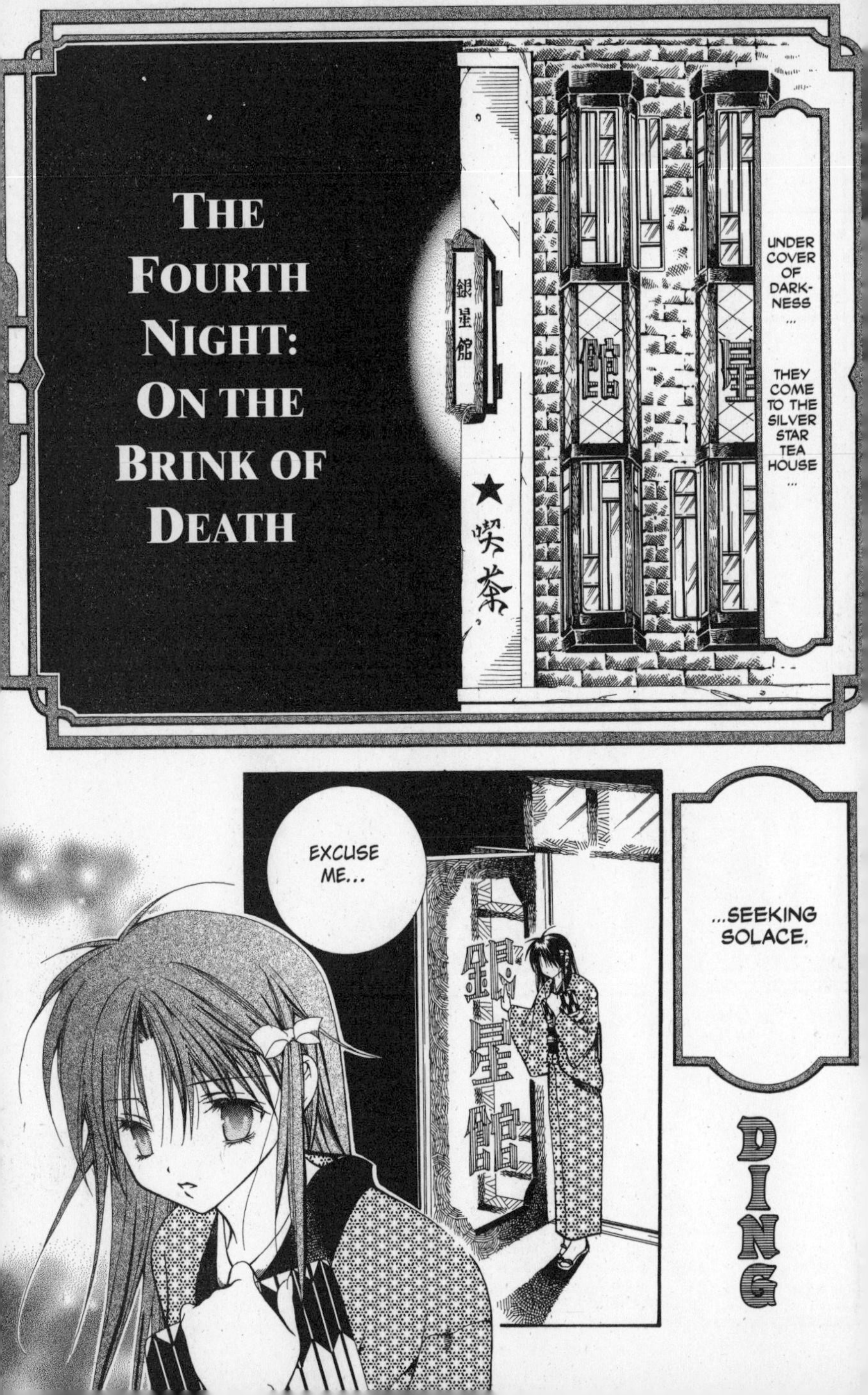
UNDER COVER OF DARKNESS...
THEY COME TO THE SILVER STAR TEA HOUSE...
喫茶
銀星館
THE FOURTH NIGHT: ON THE BRINK OF DEATH
...SEEKING SOLACE.
DING
銀星館
EXCUSE ME...

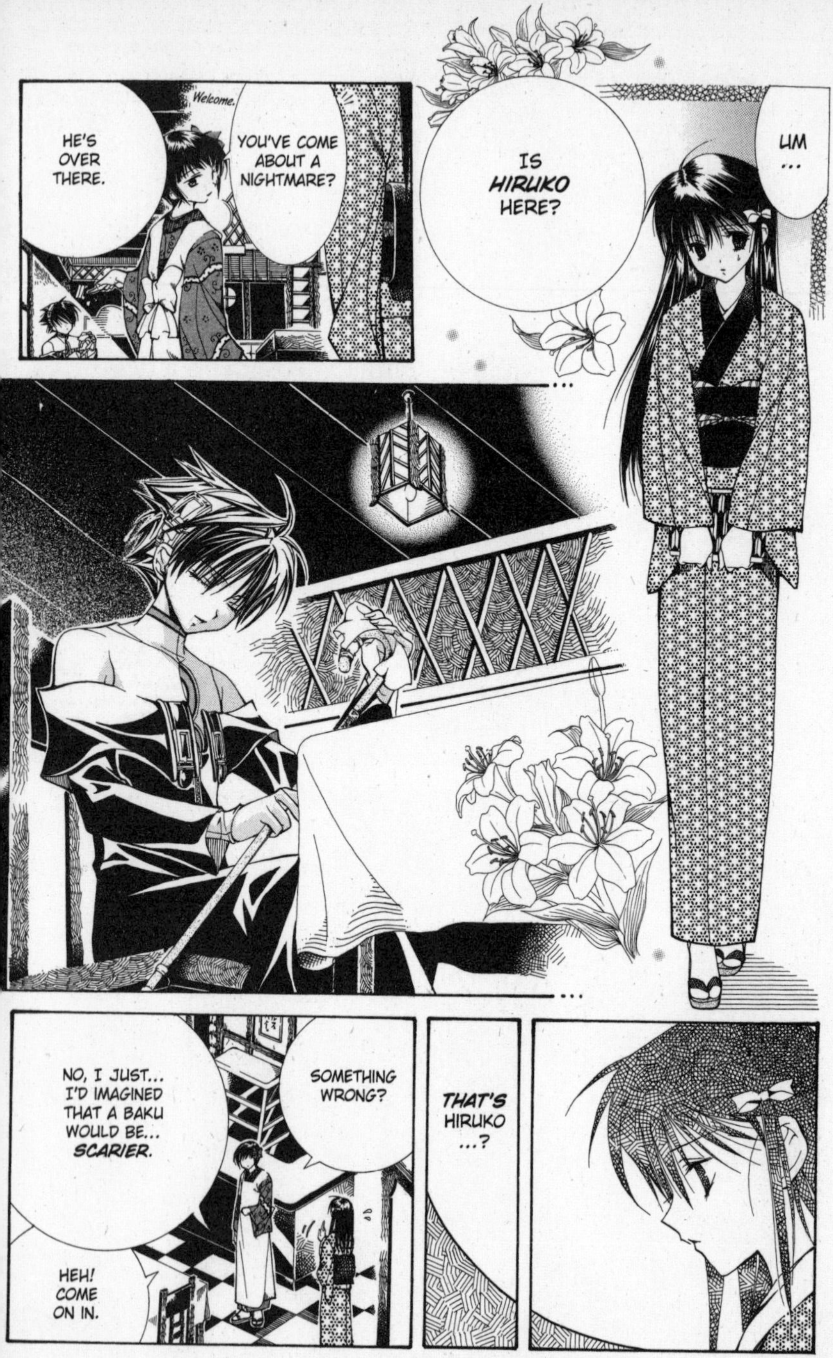
UM ...
IS HIRUKO HERE?
Welcome.
YOU'VE COME ABOUT A NIGHTMARE?
HE'S OVER THERE.
...
...
THAT'S HIRUKO ...?
SOMETHING WRONG?
NO, I JUST... I'D IMAGINED THAT A BAKU WOULD BE... SCARIER.
HEH! COME ON IN.

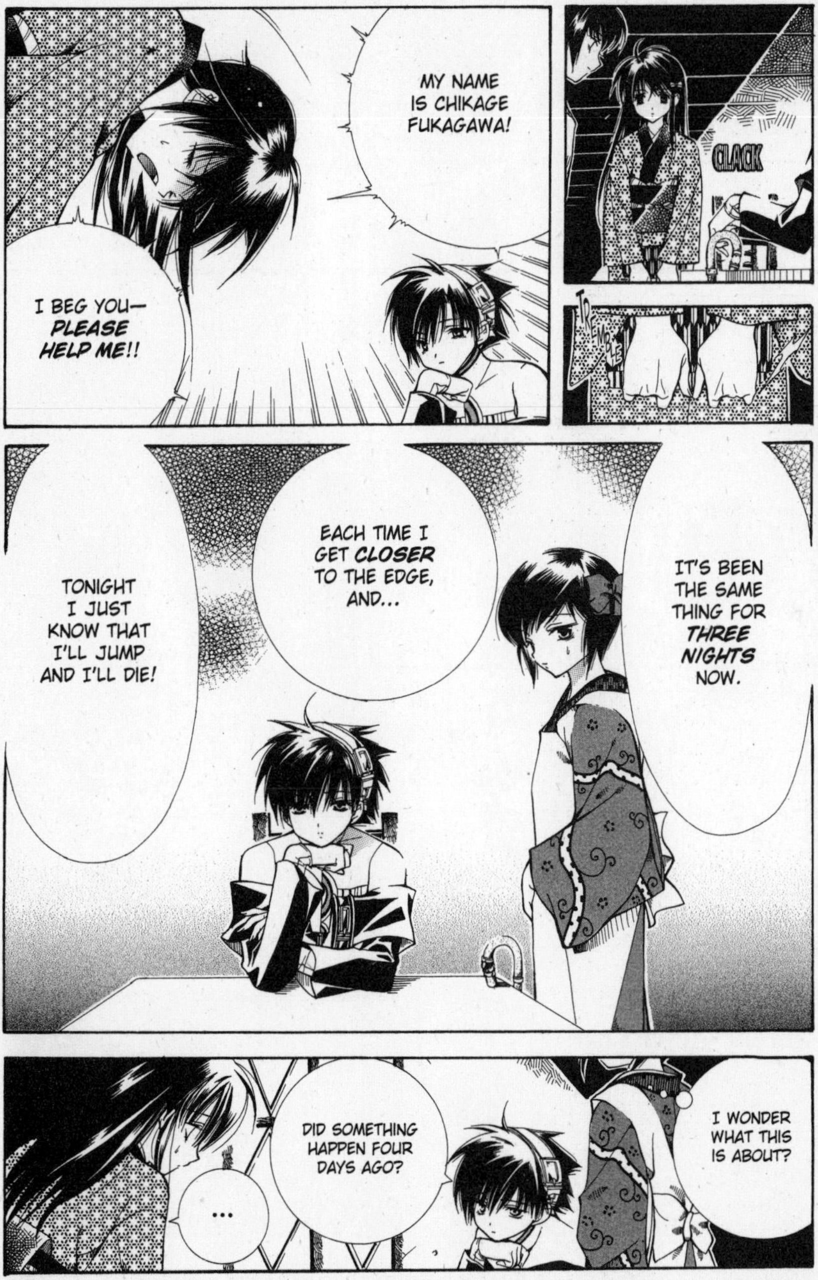
CLACK
TREMBLE
MY NAME IS CHIKAGE FUKAGAWA!
I BEG YOU— *PLEASE HELP ME!!*
IT'S BEEN THE SAME THING FOR *THREE NIGHTS* NOW.
EACH TIME I GET *CLOSER* TO THE EDGE, AND...
TONIGHT I JUST KNOW THAT I'LL JUMP AND I'LL DIE!
I WONDER WHAT THIS IS ABOUT?
DID SOMETHING HAPPEN FOUR DAYS AGO?
...

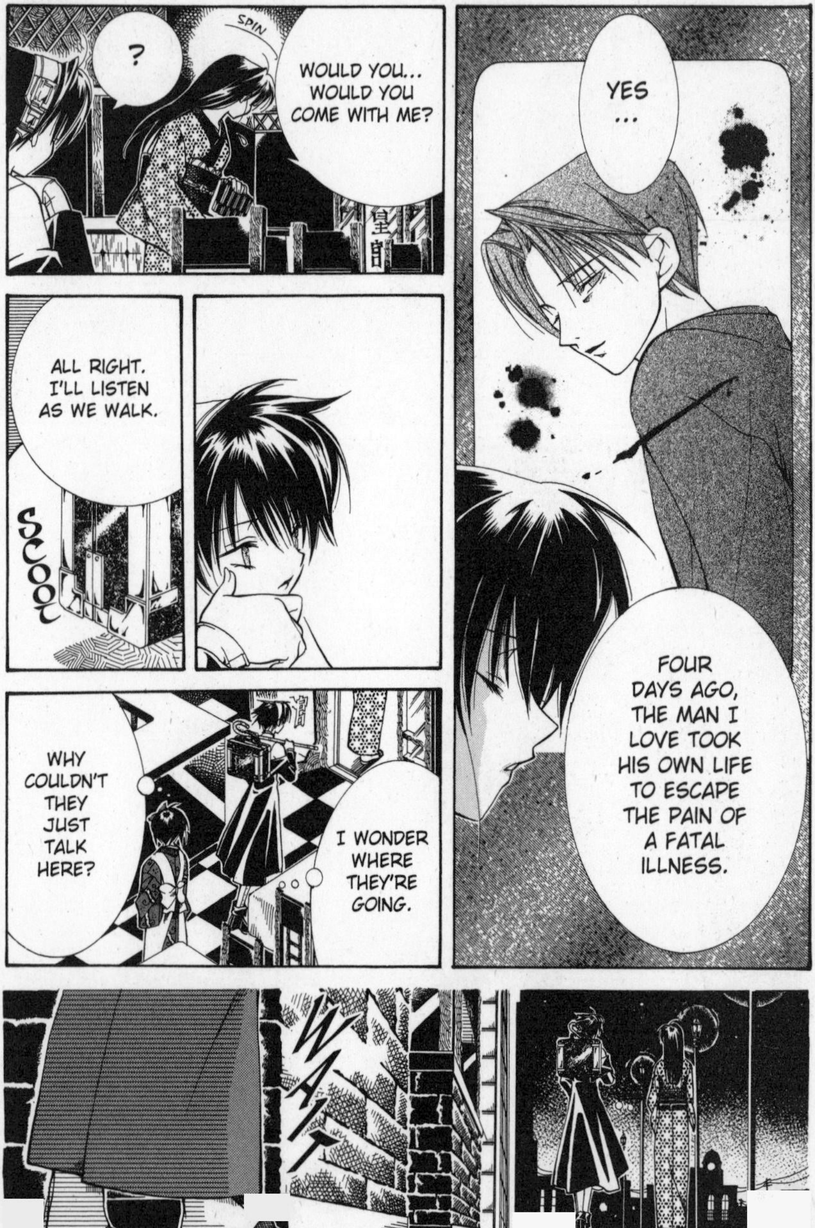
YES ...
FOUR DAYS AGO, THE MAN I LOVE TOOK HIS OWN LIFE TO ESCAPE THE PAIN OF A FATAL ILLNESS.
SPIN
WOULD YOU... WOULD YOU COME WITH ME?
?
ALL RIGHT. I'LL LISTEN AS WE WALK.
SCOOT
I WONDER WHERE THEY'RE GOING.
WHY COULDN'T THEY JUST TALK HERE?
WAIT

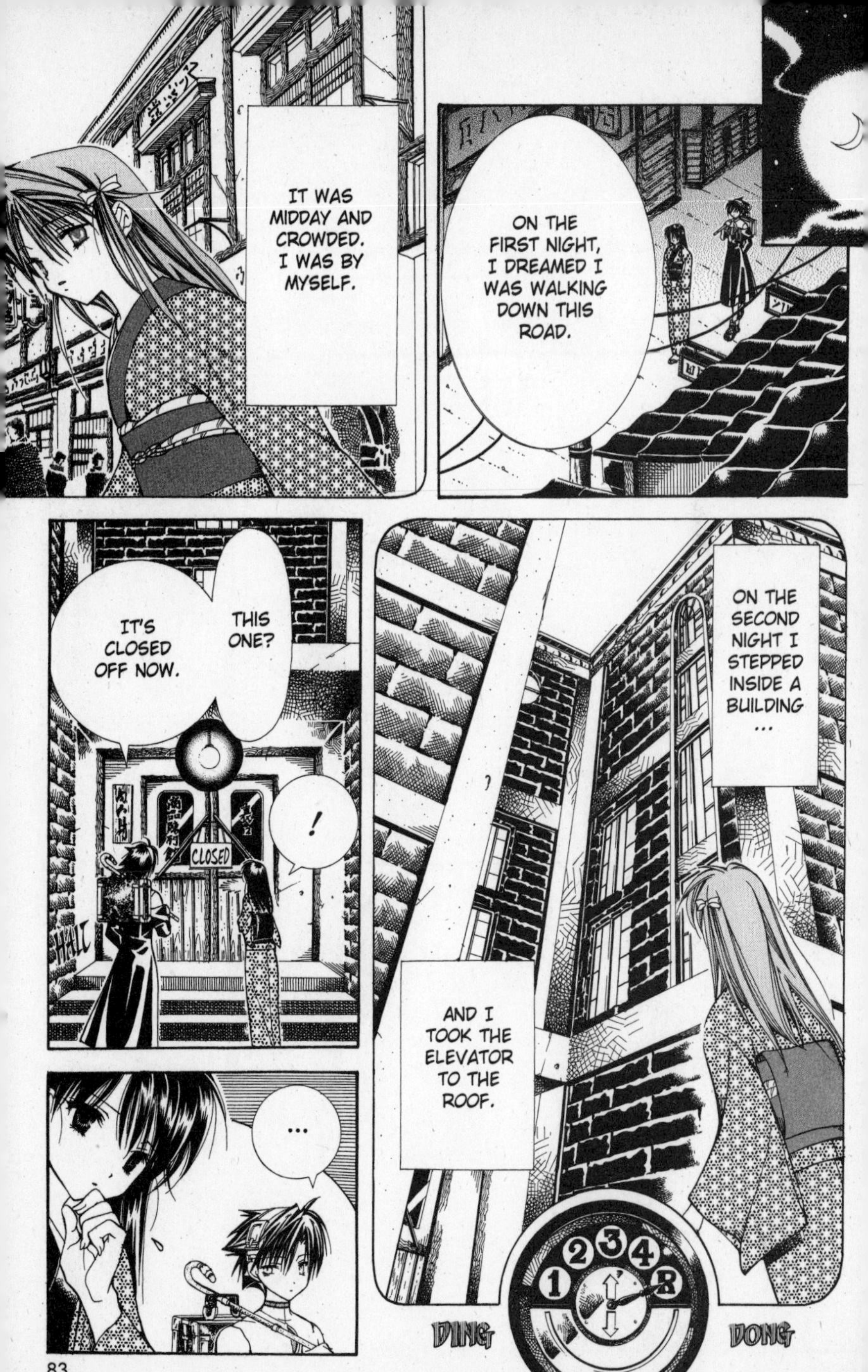
ON THE FIRST NIGHT, I DREAMED I WAS WALKING DOWN THIS ROAD.
IT WAS MIDDAY AND CROWDED. I WAS BY MYSELF.
ON THE SECOND NIGHT I STEPPED INSIDE A BUILDING...
AND I TOOK THE ELEVATOR TO THE ROOF.
DING
DONG
THIS ONE?
IT'S CLOSED OFF NOW.
CLOSED
HALL
!
...

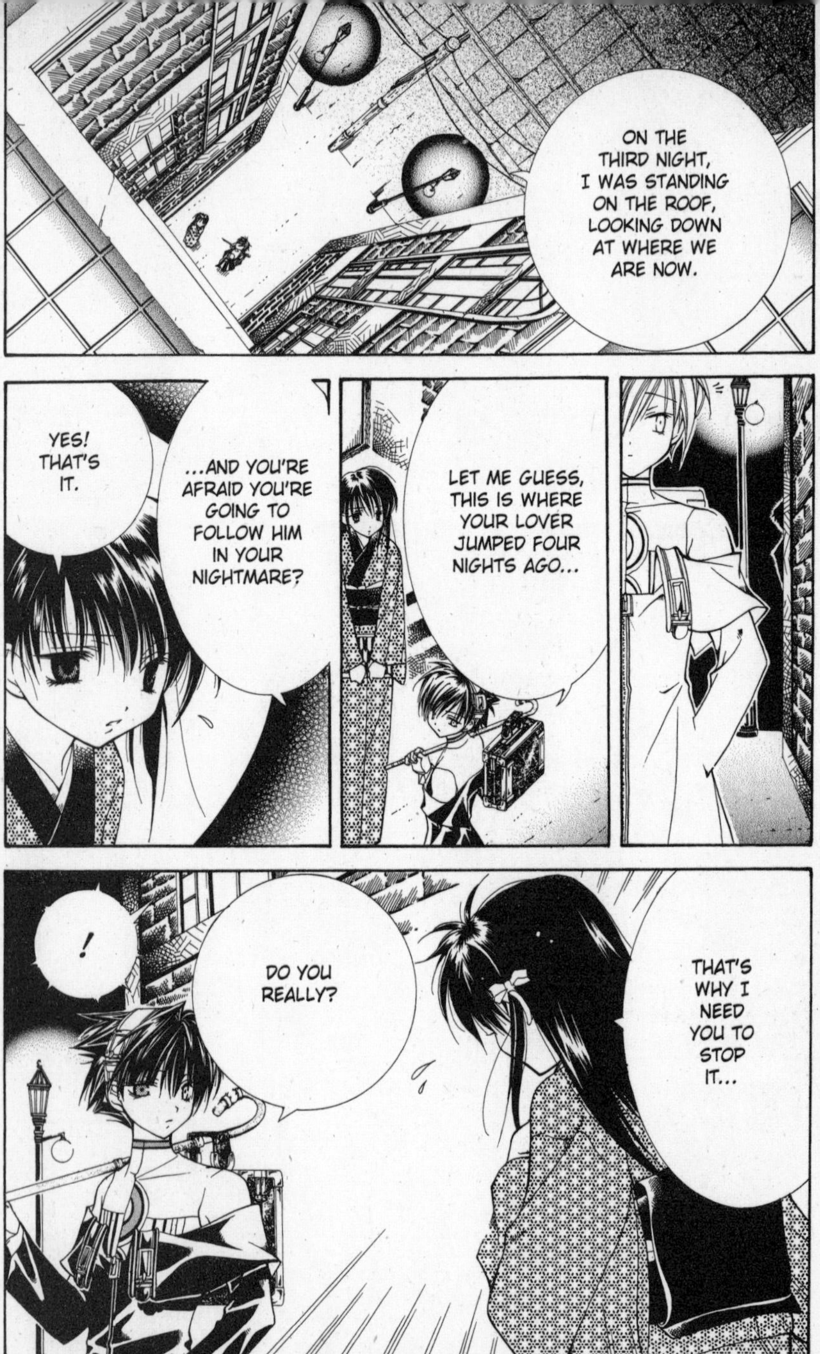

ON THE THIRD NIGHT, I WAS STANDING ON THE ROOF, LOOKING DOWN AT WHERE WE ARE NOW.
LET ME GUESS, THIS IS WHERE YOUR LOVER JUMPED FOUR NIGHTS AGO...
...AND YOU'RE AFRAID YOU'RE GOING TO FOLLOW HIM IN YOUR NIGHTMARE?
YES! THAT'S IT.
THAT'S WHY I NEED YOU TO STOP IT...
DO YOU REALLY?
!

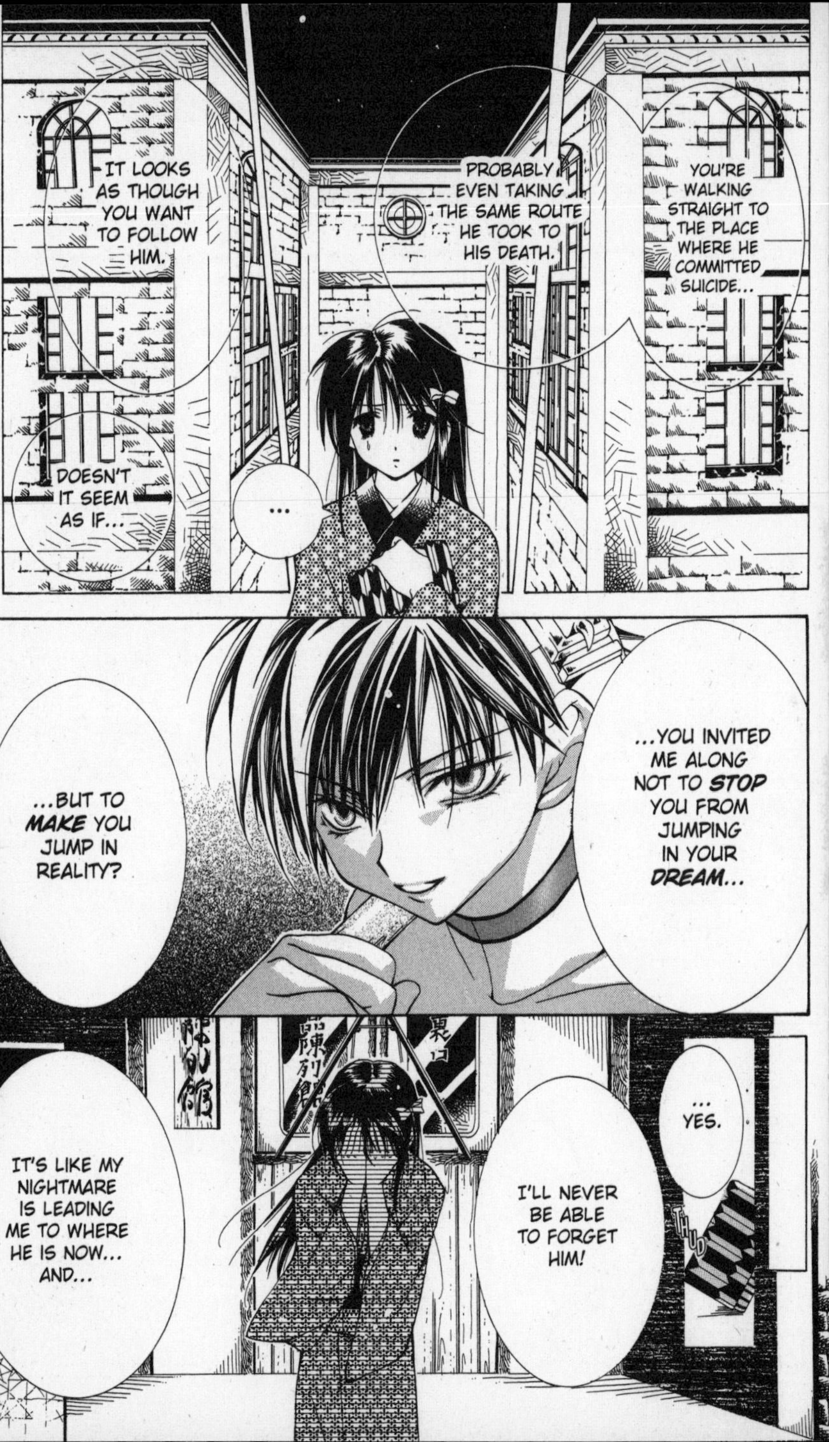
YOU'RE WALKING STRAIGHT TO THE PLACE WHERE HE COMMITTED SUICIDE...
PROBABLY EVEN TAKING THE SAME ROUTE HE TOOK TO HIS DEATH.
IT LOOKS AS THOUGH YOU WANT TO FOLLOW HIM.
...
DOESN'T IT SEEM AS IF...
...YOU INVITED ME ALONG NOT TO STOP YOU FROM JUMPING IN YOUR DREAM...
...BUT TO MAKE YOU JUMP IN REALITY?
... YES.
THUD
I'LL NEVER BE ABLE TO FORGET HIM!
IT'S LIKE MY NIGHTMARE IS LEADING ME TO WHERE HE IS NOW... AND...

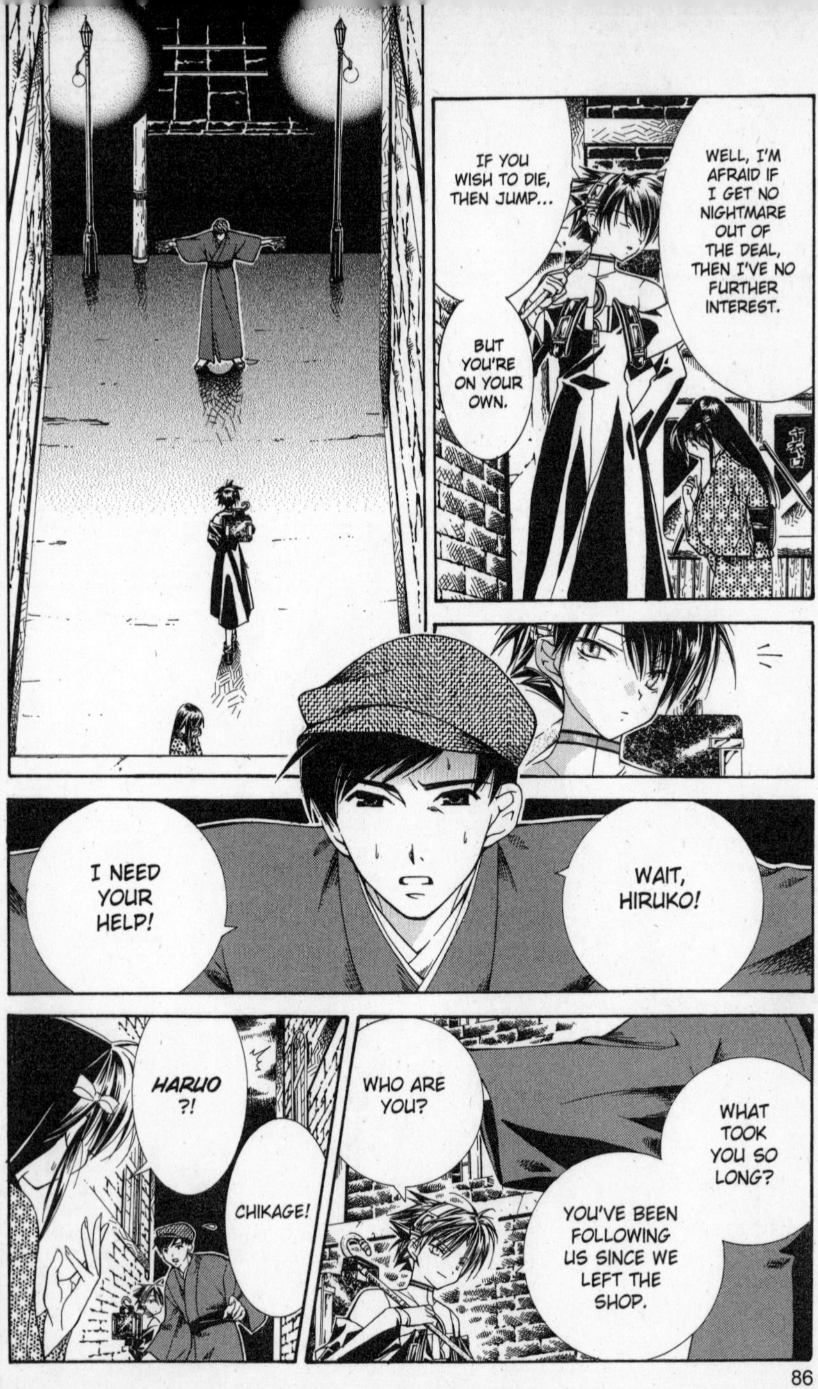
WELL, I'M AFRAID IF I GET NO NIGHTMARE OUT OF THE DEAL, THEN I'VE NO FURTHER INTEREST.
IF YOU WISH TO DIE, THEN JUMP...
BUT YOU'RE ON YOUR OWN.
WAIT, HIRUKO!
I NEED YOUR HELP!
WHAT TOOK YOU SO LONG?
YOU'VE BEEN FOLLOWING US SINCE WE LEFT THE SHOP.
WHO ARE YOU?
CHIKAGE!
HARUO ?!

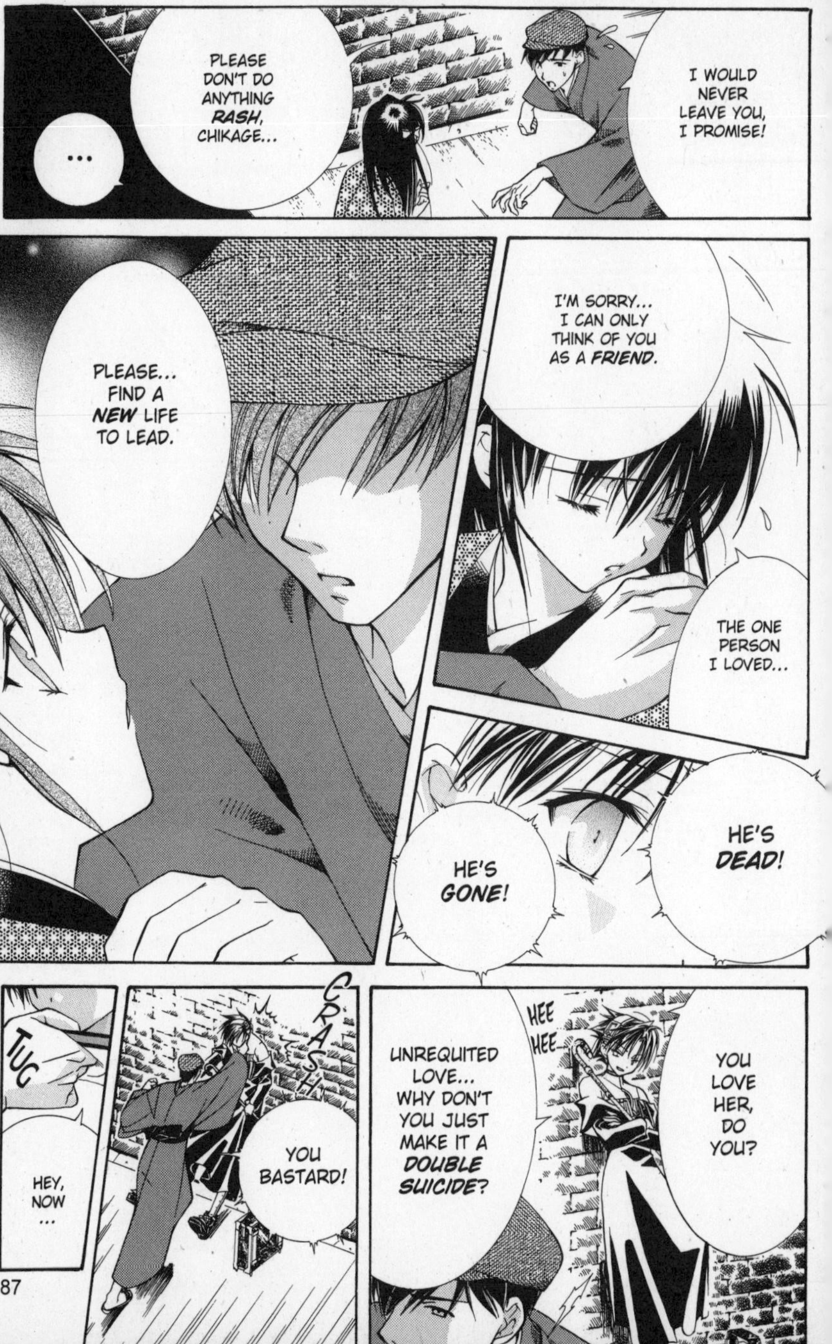
I WOULD NEVER LEAVE YOU, I PROMISE!
PLEASE DON'T DO ANYTHING *RASH*, CHIKAGE...
...
I'M SORRY... I CAN ONLY THINK OF YOU AS A *FRIEND*.
THE ONE PERSON I LOVED...
HE'S *DEAD*!
HE'S *GONE*!
PLEASE... FIND A *NEW* LIFE TO LEAD.
YOU LOVE HER, DO YOU?
HEE HEE
UNREQUITED LOVE... WHY DON'T YOU JUST MAKE IT A *DOUBLE SUICIDE*?
CRASH
YOU BASTARD!
TUG
HEY, NOW ...

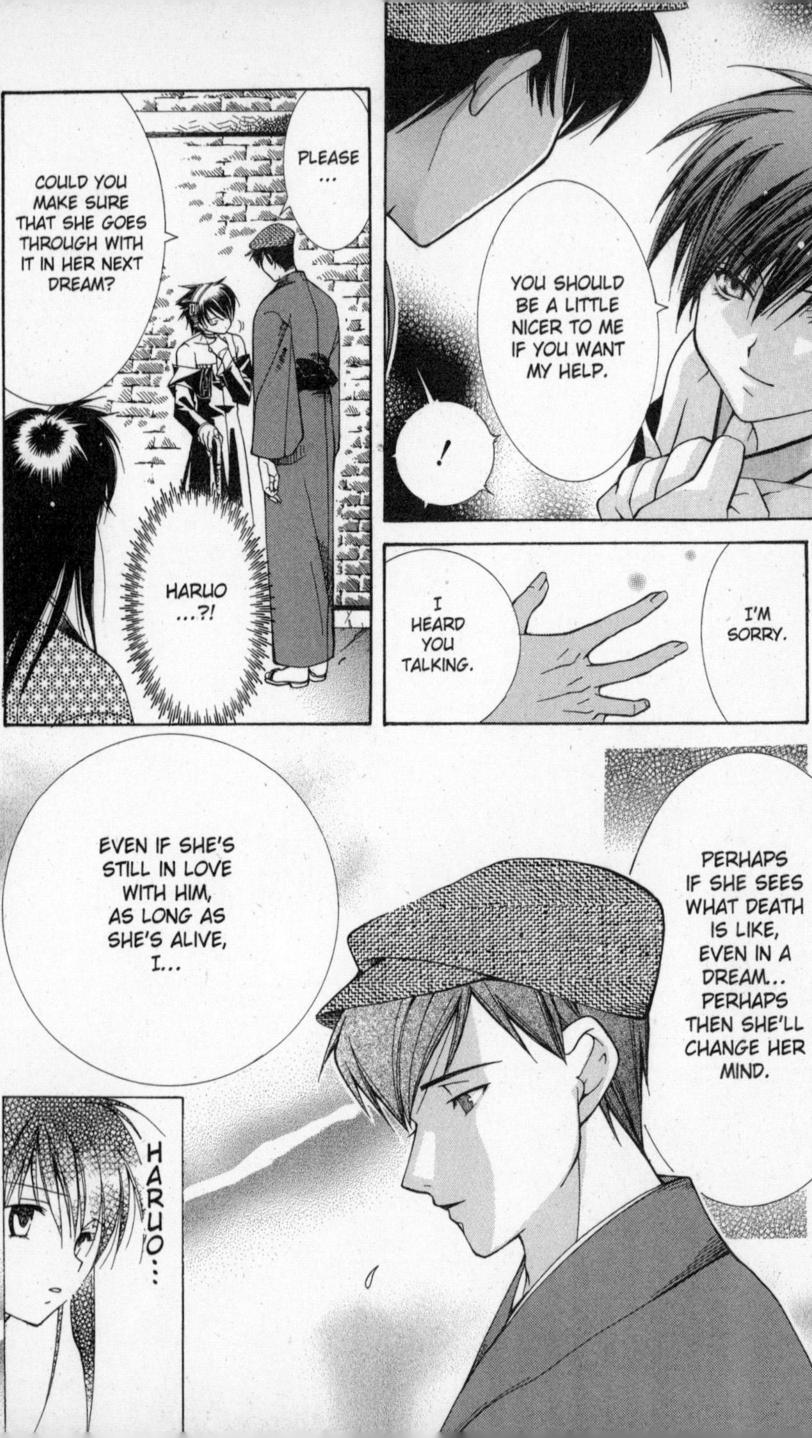
YOU SHOULD BE A LITTLE NICER TO ME IF YOU WANT MY HELP.
!
I'M SORRY.
I HEARD YOU TALKING.
PLEASE ...
COULD YOU MAKE SURE THAT SHE GOES THROUGH WITH IT IN HER NEXT DREAM?
HARUO ...?!
PERHAPS IF SHE SEES WHAT DEATH IS LIKE, EVEN IN A DREAM... PERHAPS THEN SHE'LL CHANGE HER MIND.
EVEN IF SHE'S STILL IN LOVE WITH HIM, AS LONG AS SHE'S ALIVE, I...
HARUO...

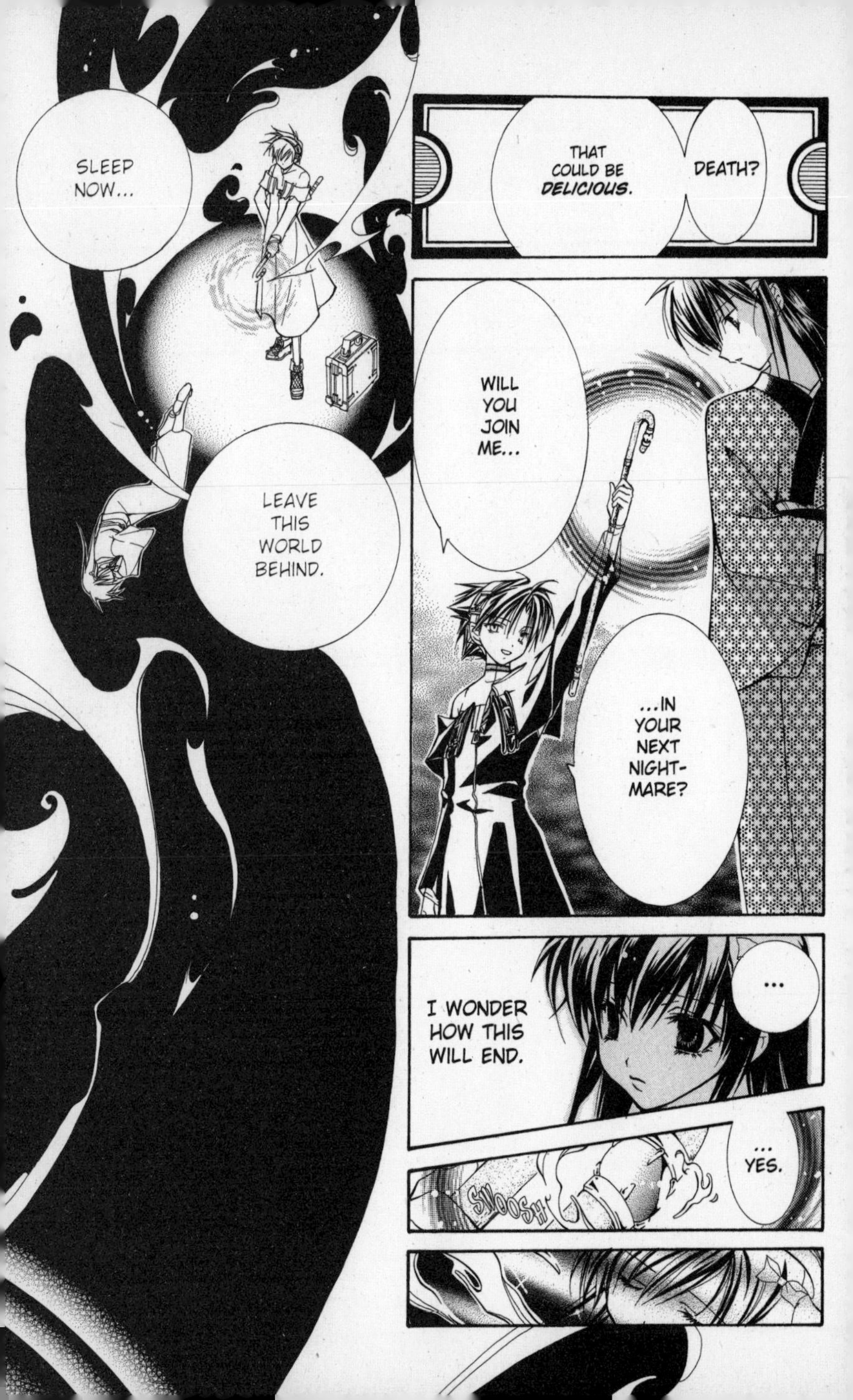
DEATH?
THAT COULD BE DELICIOUS.
WILL YOU JOIN ME...
...IN YOUR NEXT NIGHTMARE?
...
I WONDER HOW THIS WILL END.
...YES.
SNOOSH
SLEEP NOW...
LEAVE THIS WORLD BEHIND.

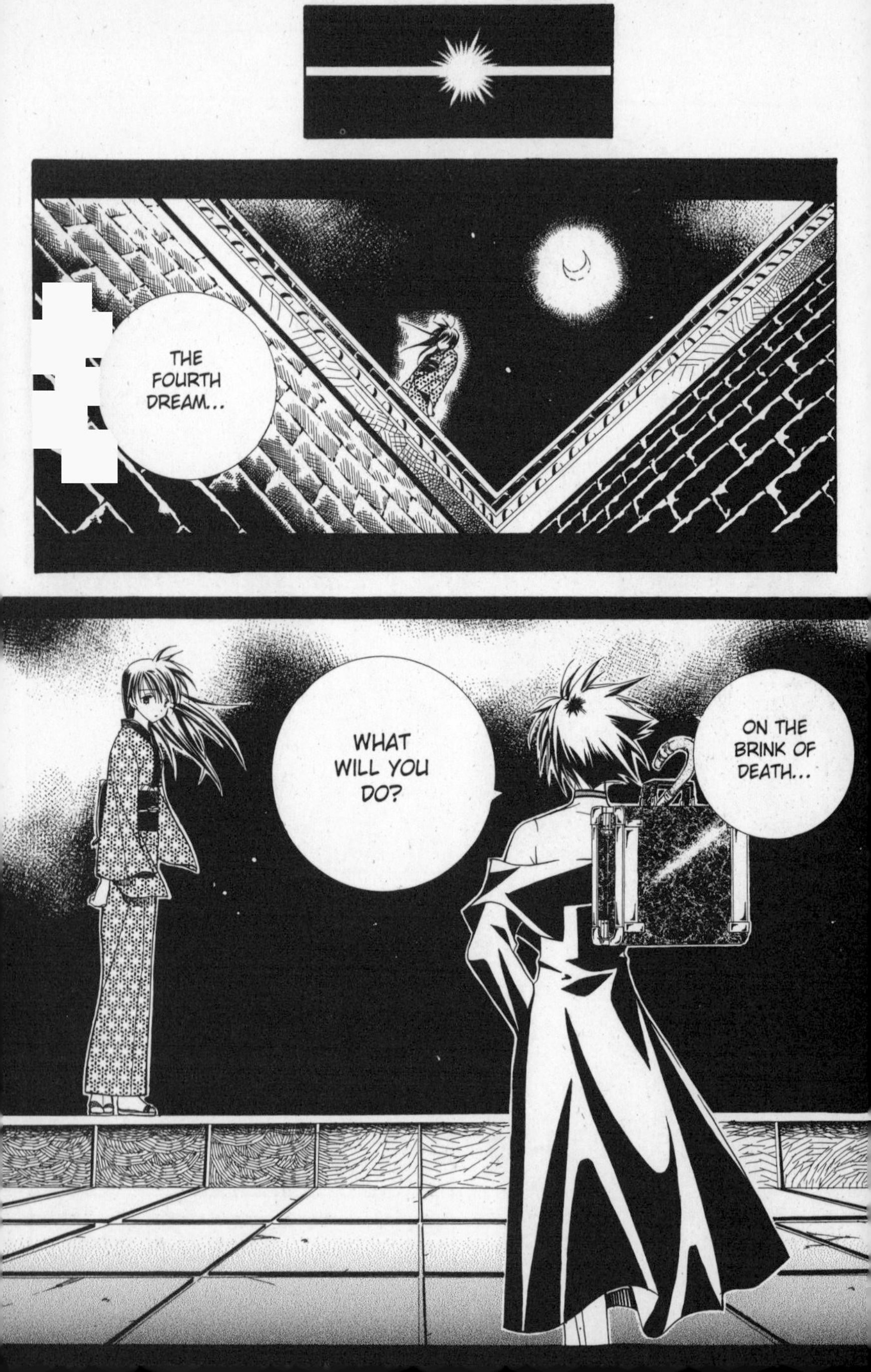
THE FOURTH DREAM...
ON THE BRINK OF DEATH...
WHAT WILL YOU DO?

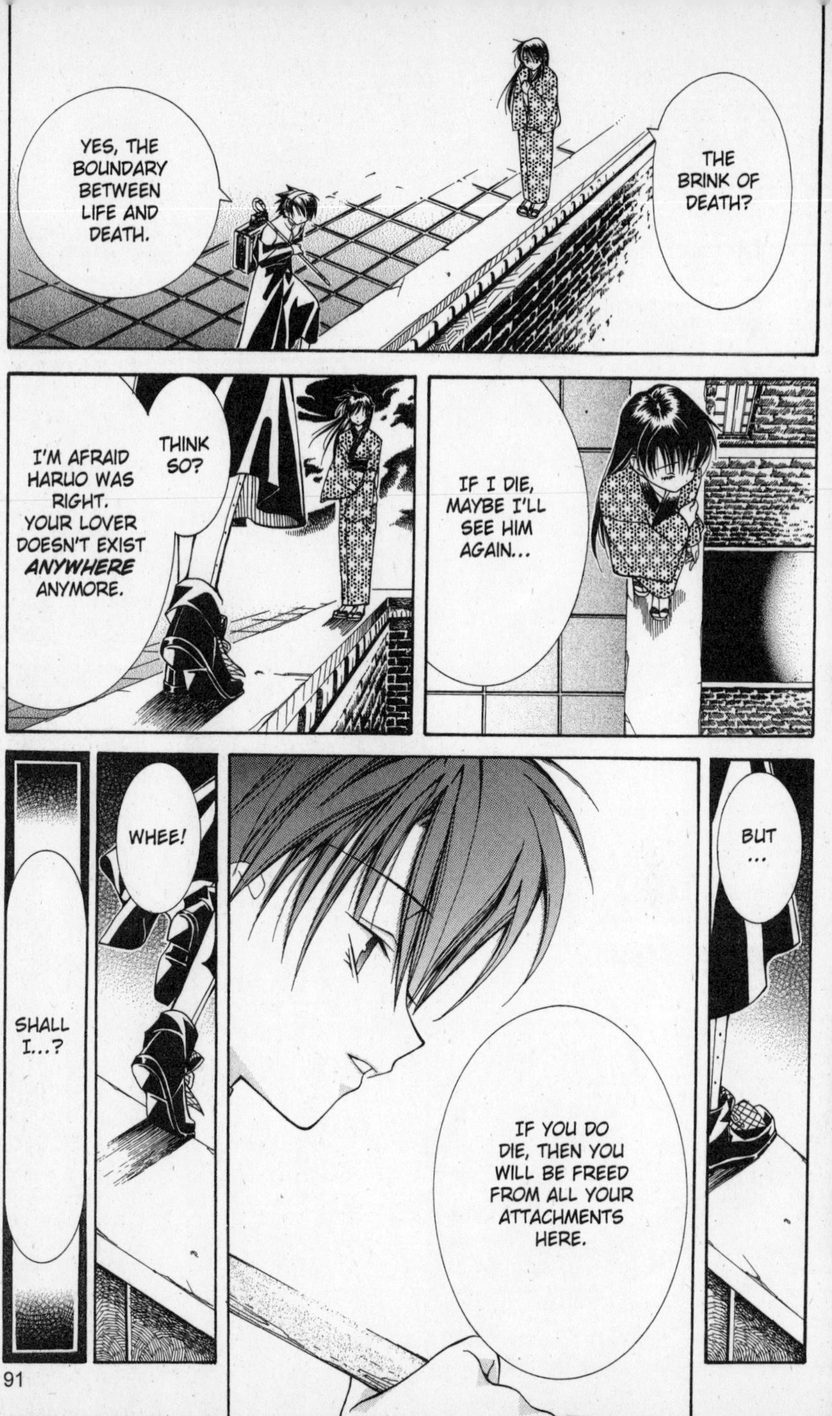
THE BRINK OF DEATH?
YES, THE BOUNDARY BETWEEN LIFE AND DEATH.
IF I DIE, MAYBE I'LL SEE HIM AGAIN...
THINK SO?
I'M AFRAID HARUO WAS RIGHT. YOUR LOVER DOESN'T EXIST *ANYWHERE* ANYMORE.
BUT ...
IF YOU DO DIE, THEN YOU WILL BE FREED FROM ALL YOUR ATTACHMENTS HERE.
WHEE!
SHALL I...?

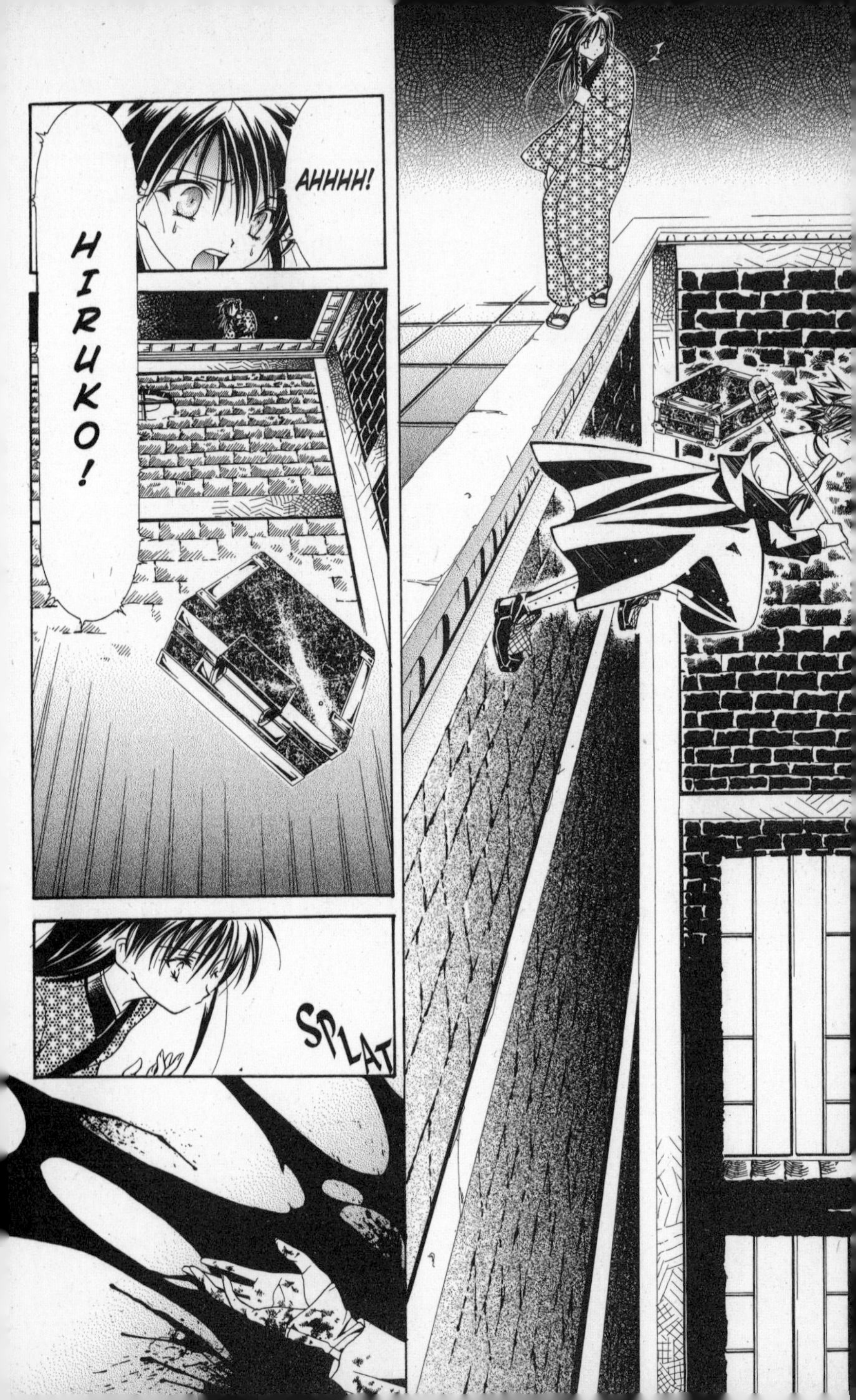
AHHHH!
HIRUKO!
SPLAT

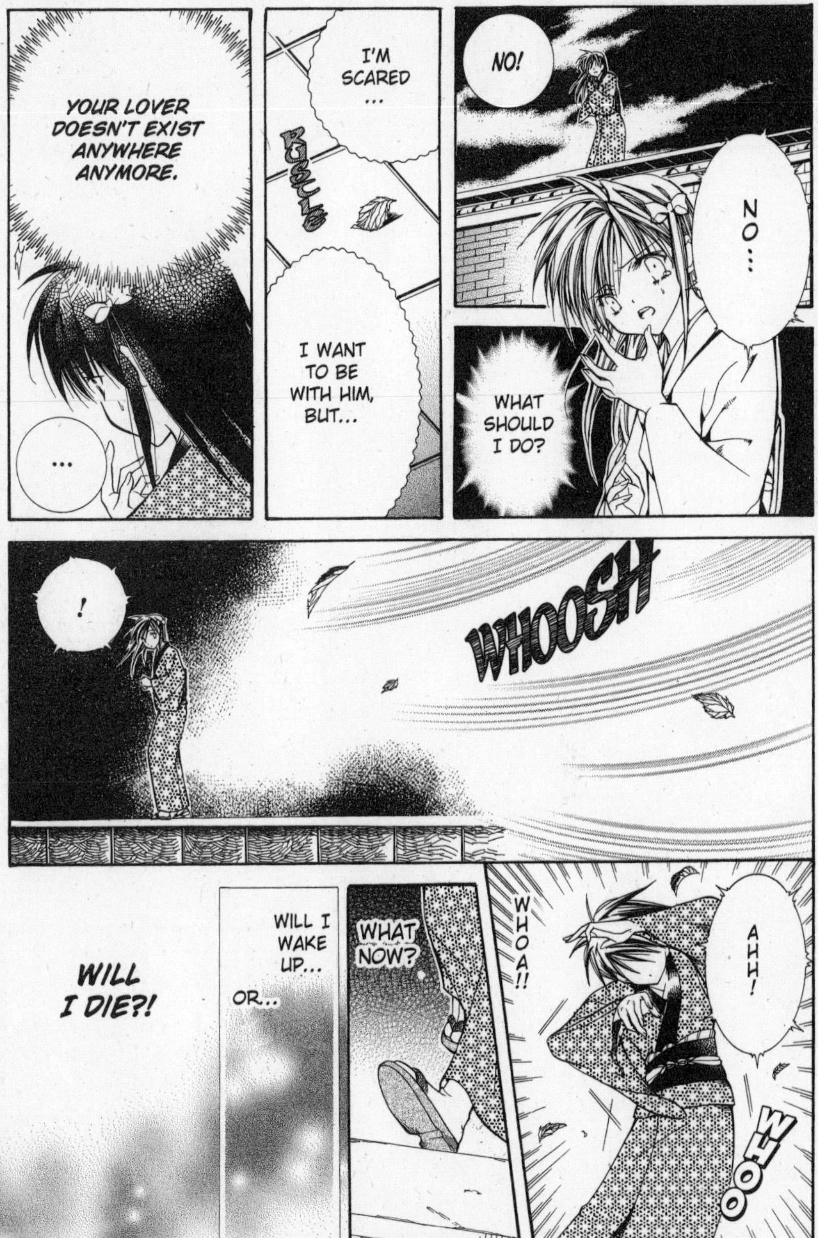
NO!
NO...
WHAT SHOULD I DO?
I'M SCARED...
I WANT TO BE WITH HIM, BUT...
YOUR LOVER DOESN'T EXIST ANYWHERE ANYMORE.
...
WHOOSH
!
AHH!
WHOA!!
WHOOO
WHAT NOW?
WILL I WAKE UP...
OR...
WILL I DIE?!

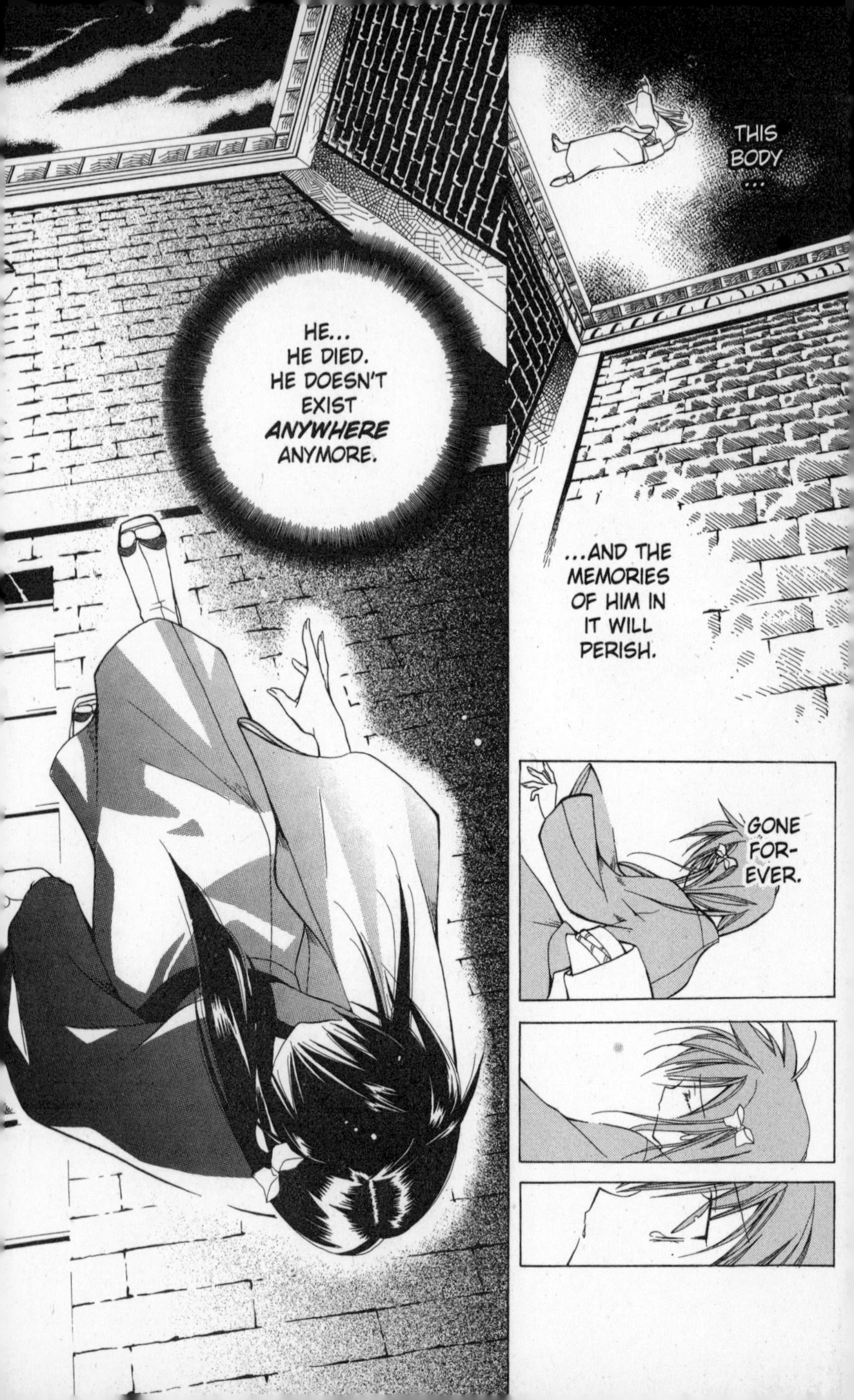
THIS BODY...
...AND THE MEMORIES OF HIM IN IT WILL PERISH.
GONE FOR-EVER.
HE... HE DIED. HE DOESN'T EXIST *ANYWHERE* ANYMORE.

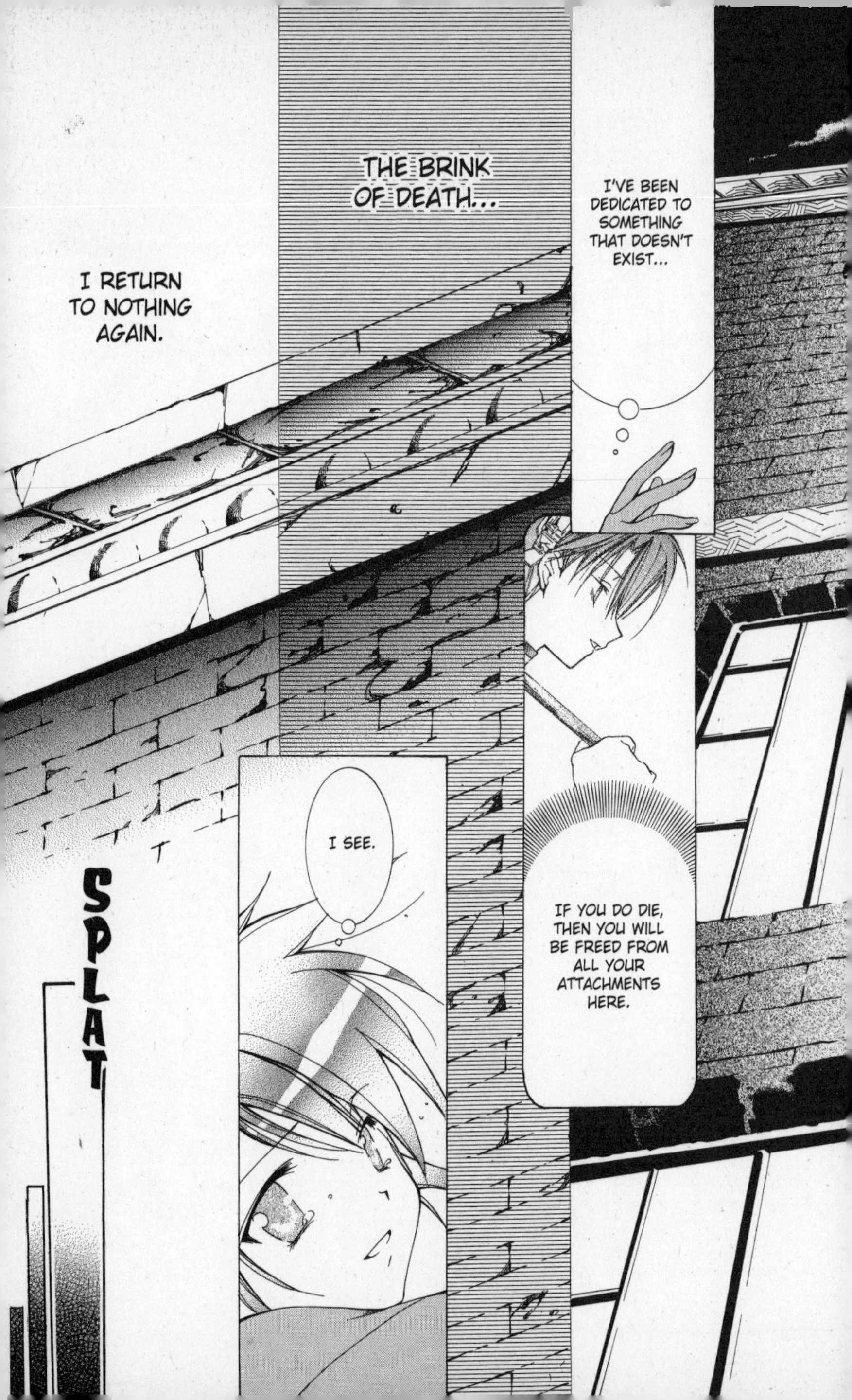

I'VE BEEN DEDICATED TO SOMETHING THAT DOESN'T EXIST...
THE BRINK OF DEATH...
I RETURN TO NOTHING AGAIN.
IF YOU DO DIE, THEN YOU WILL BE FREED FROM ALL YOUR ATTACHMENTS HERE.
I SEE.
SPLAT

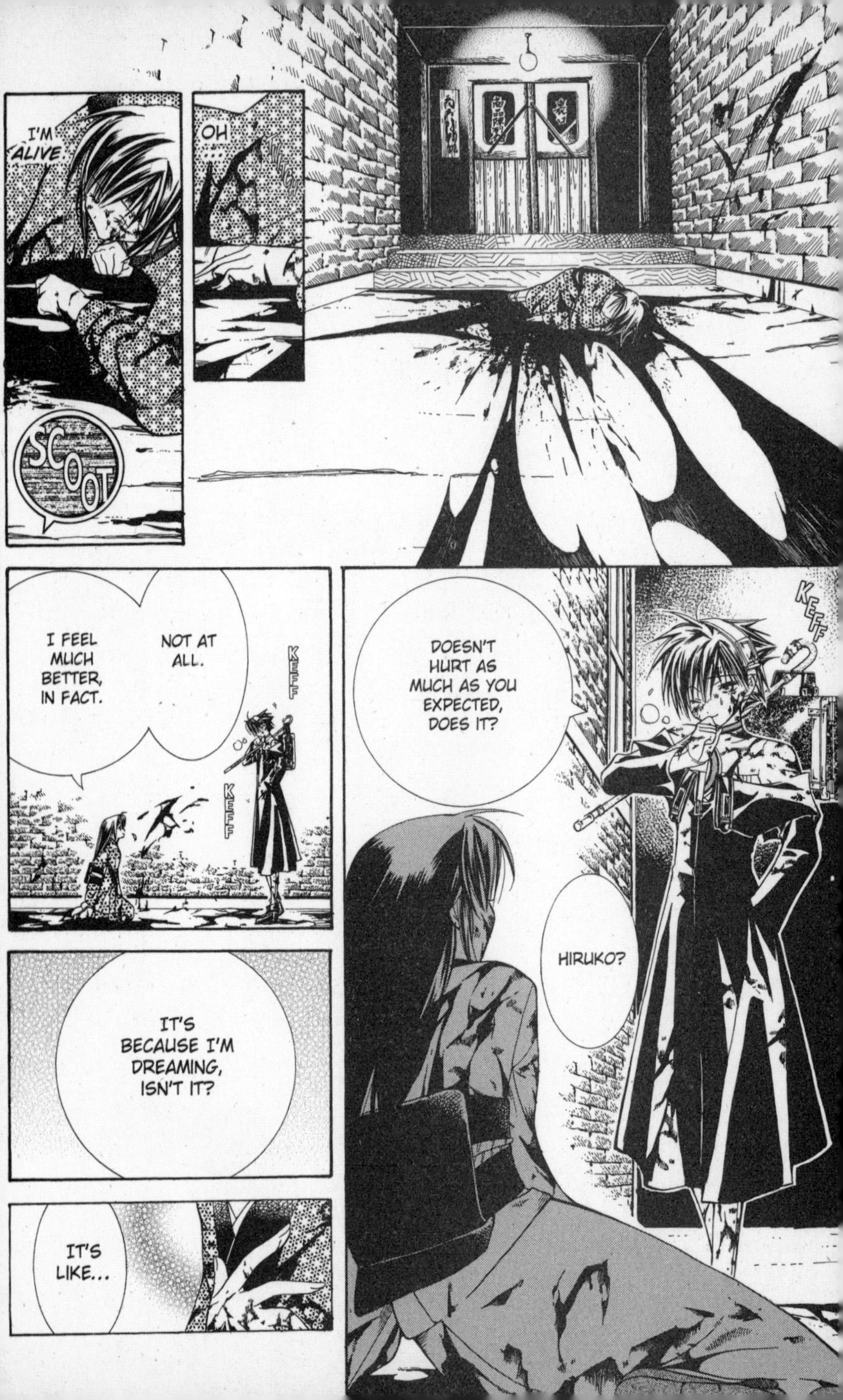
OH...
TWITCH
I'M ALIVE.
SCOOT
DOESN'T HURT AS MUCH AS YOU EXPECTED, DOES IT?
KEFF
HIRUKO?
NOT AT ALL.
I FEEL MUCH BETTER, IN FACT.
KEFF
KEFF
IT'S BECAUSE I'M DREAMING, ISN'T IT?
IT'S LIKE...

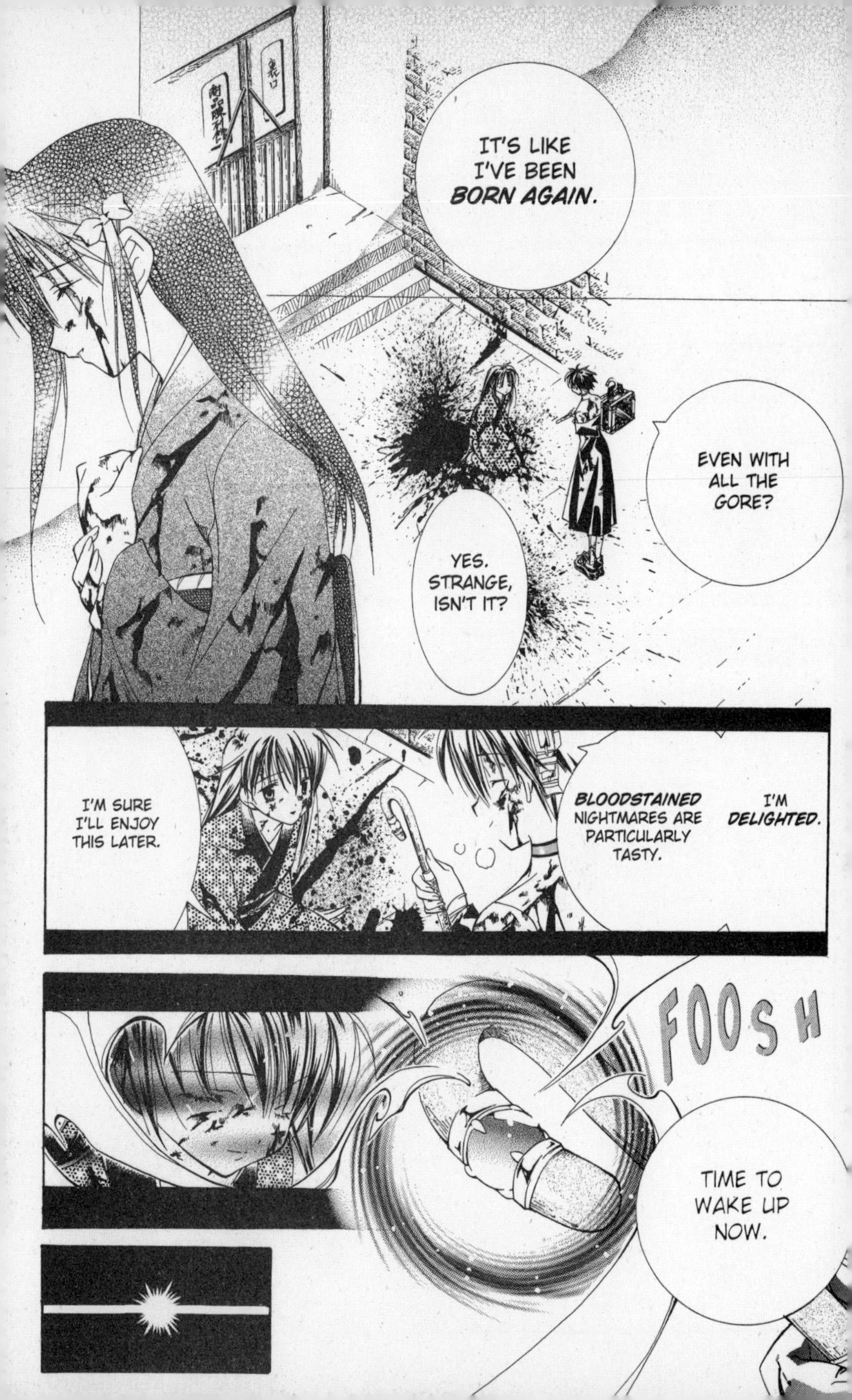
IT'S LIKE I'VE BEEN **BORN AGAIN**.
EVEN WITH ALL THE GORE?
YES. STRANGE, ISN'T IT?
I'M **DELIGHTED**.
BLOODSTAINED NIGHTMARES ARE PARTICULARLY TASTY.
I'M SURE I'LL ENJOY THIS LATER.
FOOSH
TIME TO WAKE UP NOW.

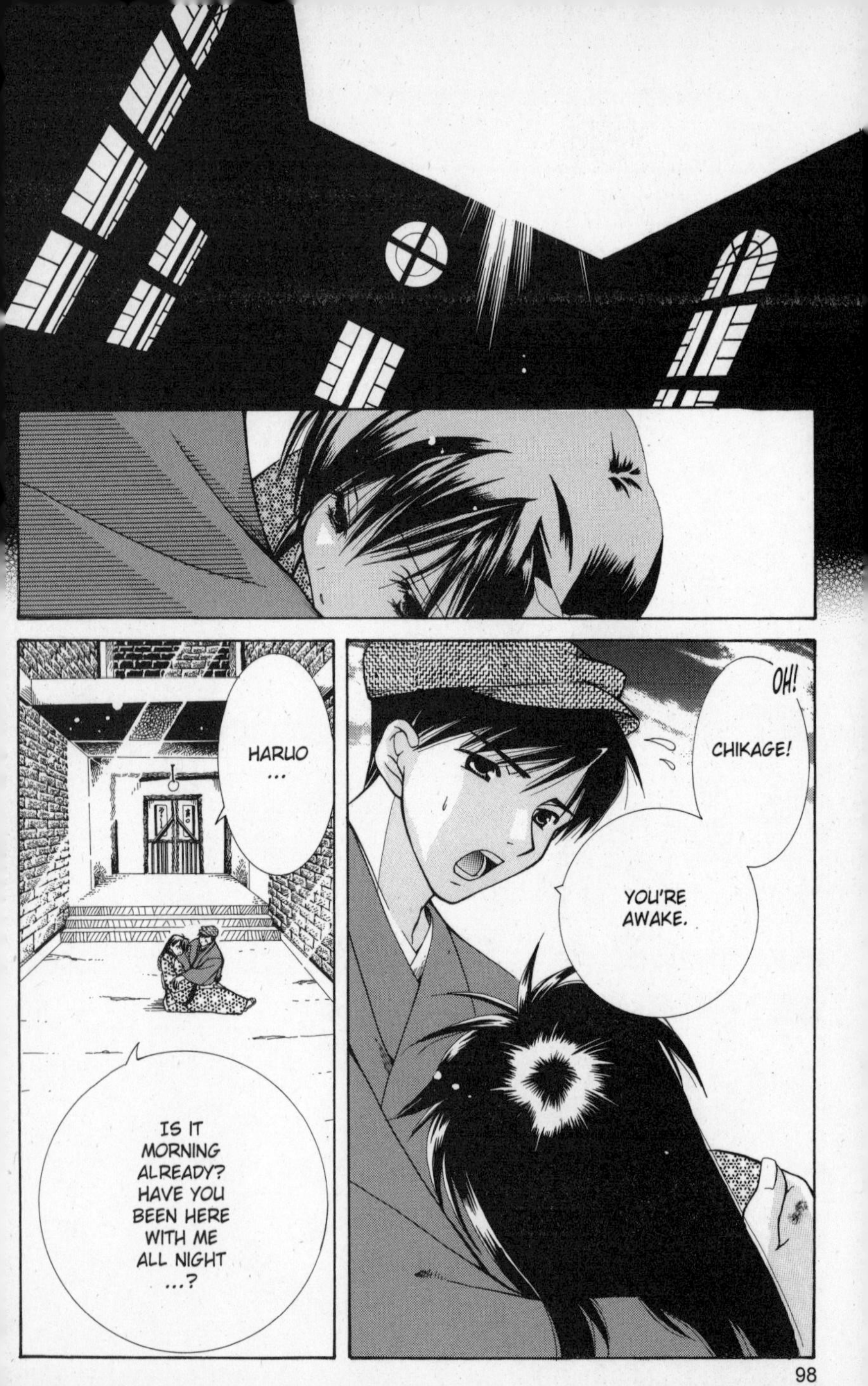
OH!
CHIKAGE!
YOU'RE AWAKE.
HARUO ...
IS IT MORNING ALREADY? HAVE YOU BEEN HERE WITH ME ALL NIGHT ...?

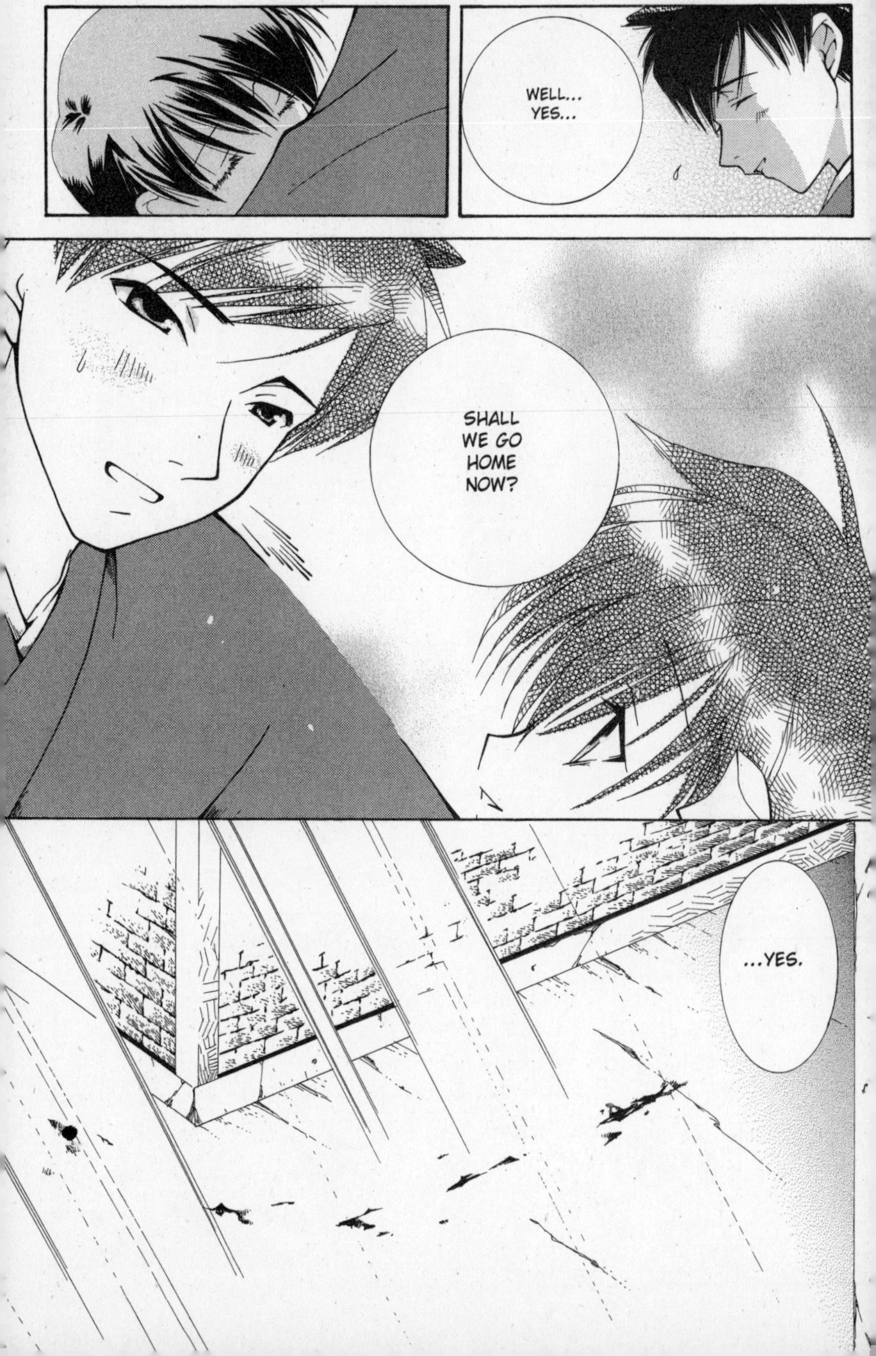
WELL... YES...
SHALL WE GO HOME NOW?
...YES.

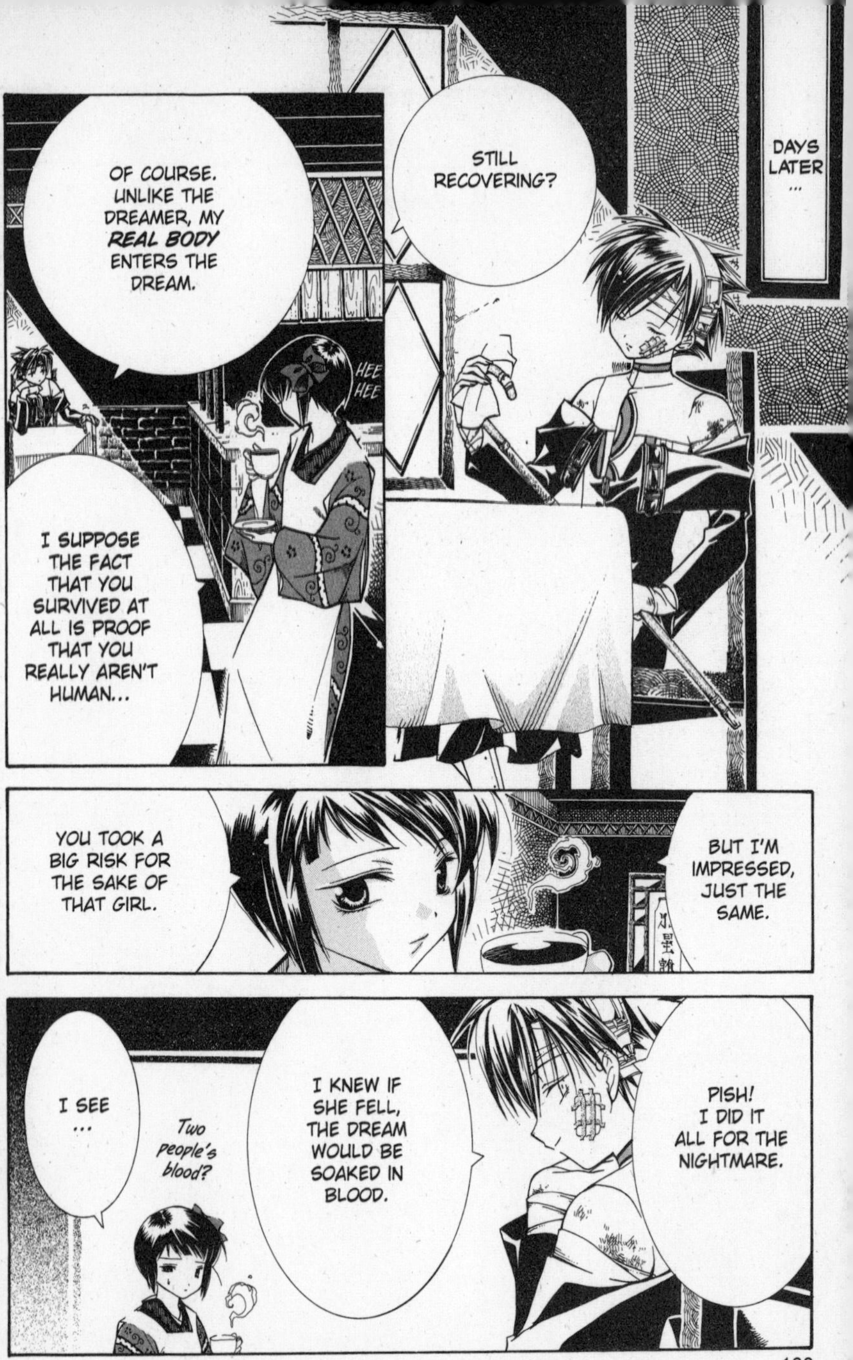
DAYS LATER ...
STILL RECOVERING?
OF COURSE. UNLIKE THE DREAMER, MY ***REAL BODY*** ENTERS THE DREAM.
HEE HEE
I SUPPOSE THE FACT THAT YOU SURVIVED AT ALL IS PROOF THAT YOU REALLY AREN'T HUMAN...
BUT I'M IMPRESSED, JUST THE SAME.
YOU TOOK A BIG RISK FOR THE SAKE OF THAT GIRL.
PISH! I DID IT ALL FOR THE NIGHTMARE.
I KNEW IF SHE FELL, THE DREAM WOULD BE SOAKED IN BLOOD.
Two people's blood?
I SEE ...

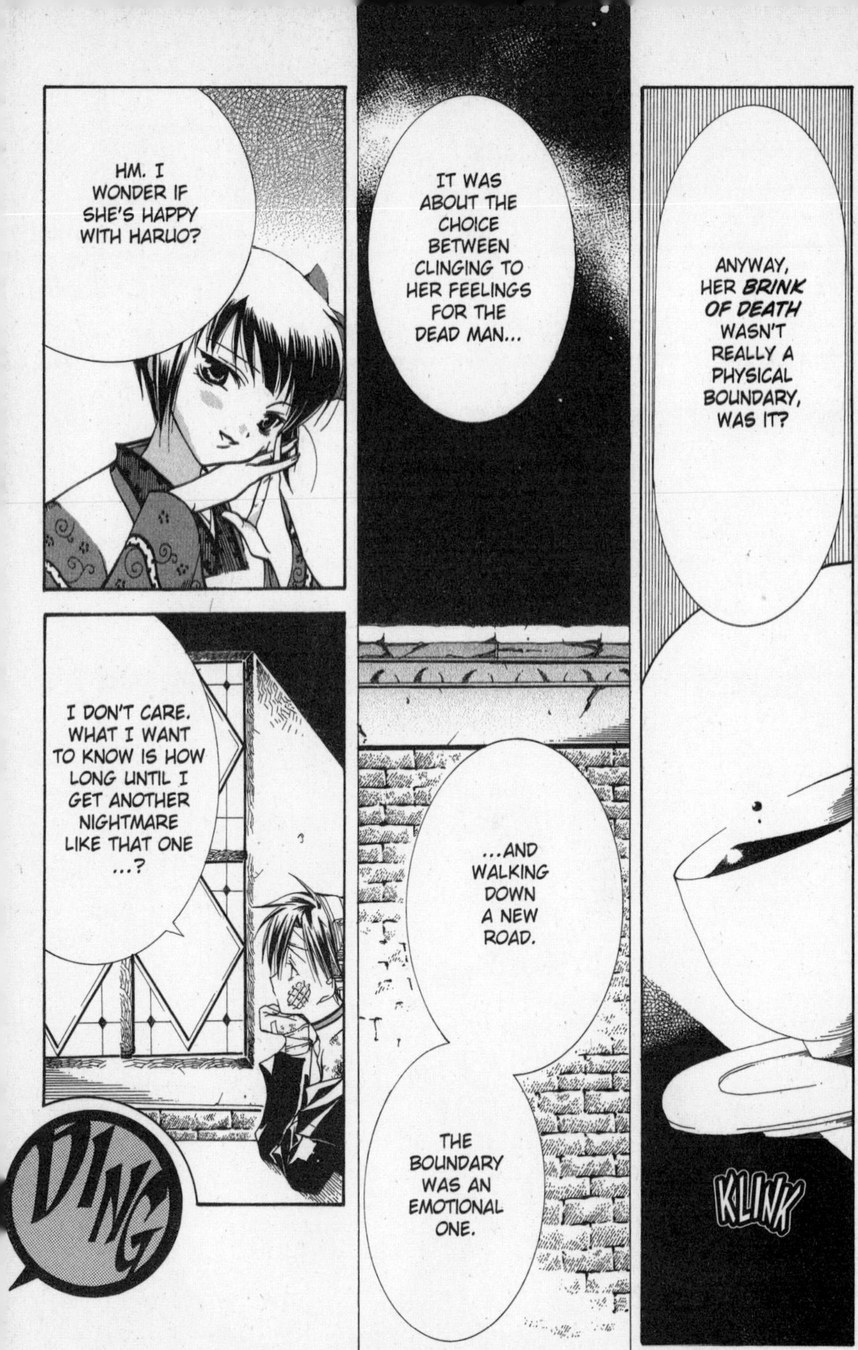
ANYWAY, HER ***BRINK OF DEATH*** WASN'T REALLY A PHYSICAL BOUNDARY, WAS IT?
KLINK
IT WAS ABOUT THE CHOICE BETWEEN CLINGING TO HER FEELINGS FOR THE DEAD MAN...
...AND WALKING DOWN A NEW ROAD.
THE BOUNDARY WAS AN EMOTIONAL ONE.
HM. I WONDER IF SHE'S HAPPY WITH HARUO?
I DON'T CARE. WHAT I WANT TO KNOW IS HOW LONG UNTIL I GET ANOTHER NIGHTMARE LIKE THAT ONE ...?
DING

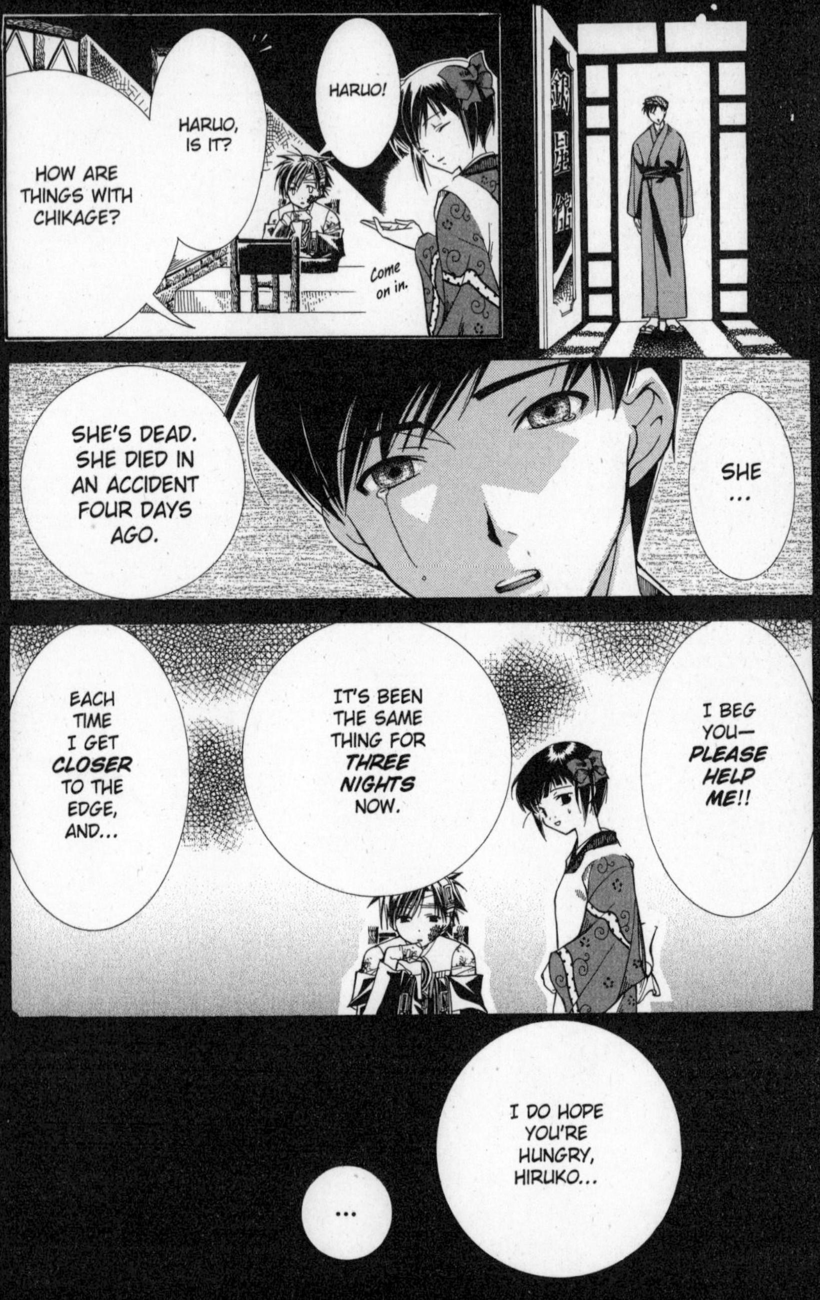
HARUO!
Come on in.
HARUO, IS IT?
HOW ARE THINGS WITH CHIKAGE?
SHE...
SHE'S DEAD. SHE DIED IN AN ACCIDENT FOUR DAYS AGO.
I BEG YOU—PLEASE HELP ME!!
IT'S BEEN THE SAME THING FOR THREE NIGHTS NOW.
EACH TIME I GET CLOSER TO THE EDGE, AND...
I DO HOPE YOU'RE HUNGRY, HIRUKO...
...

THE FIFTH NIGHT: CHARACTERS

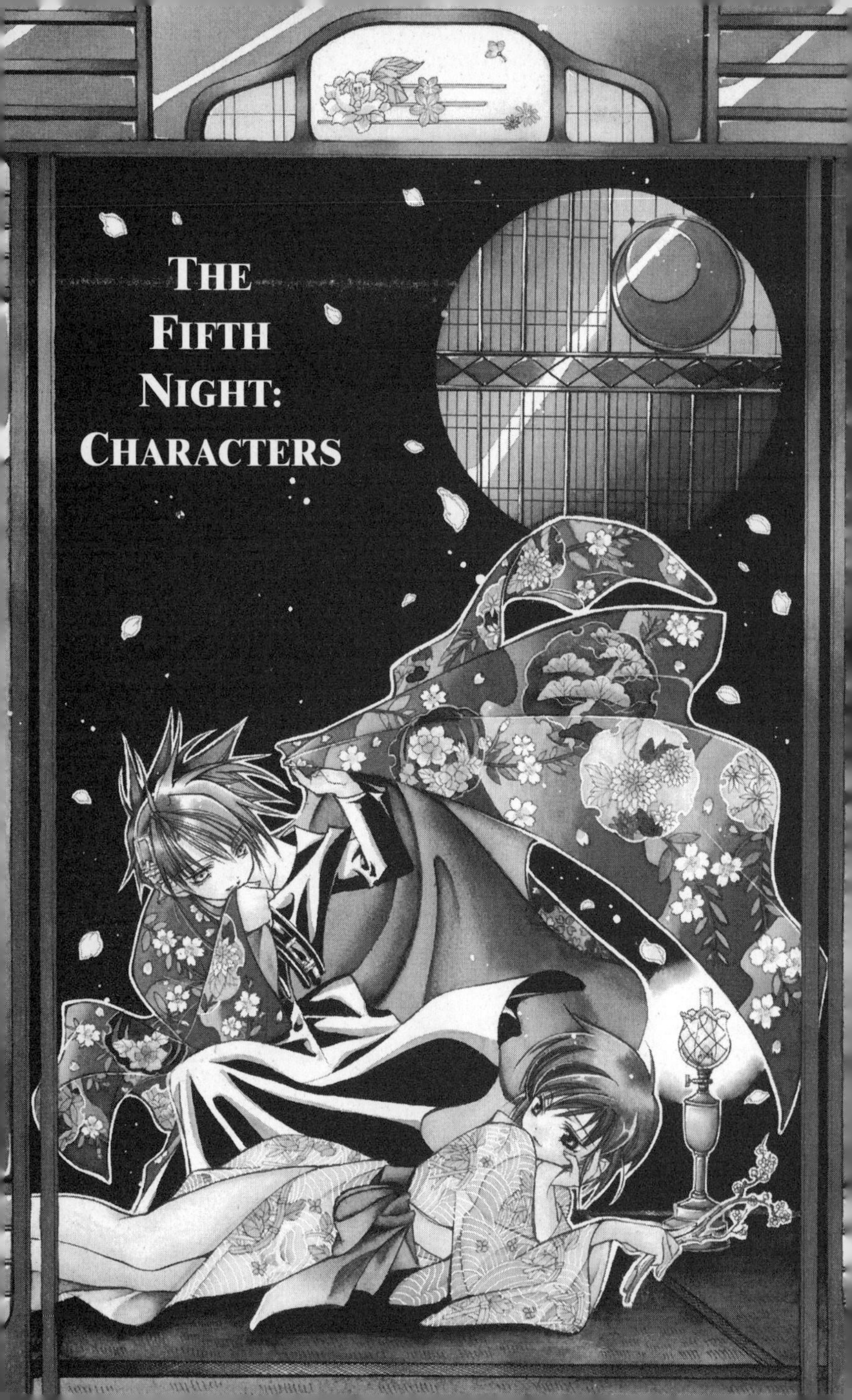

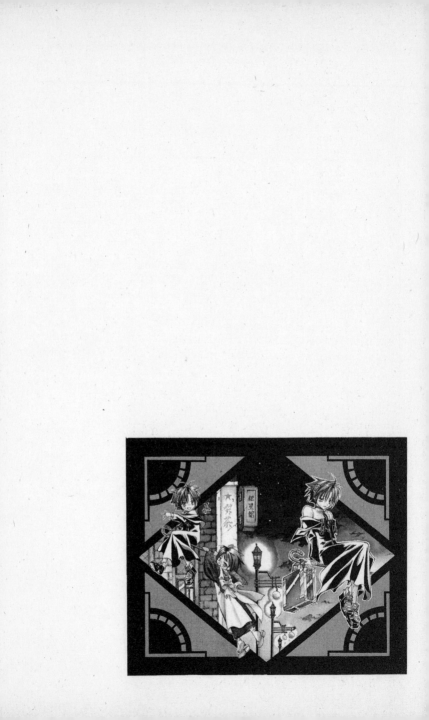

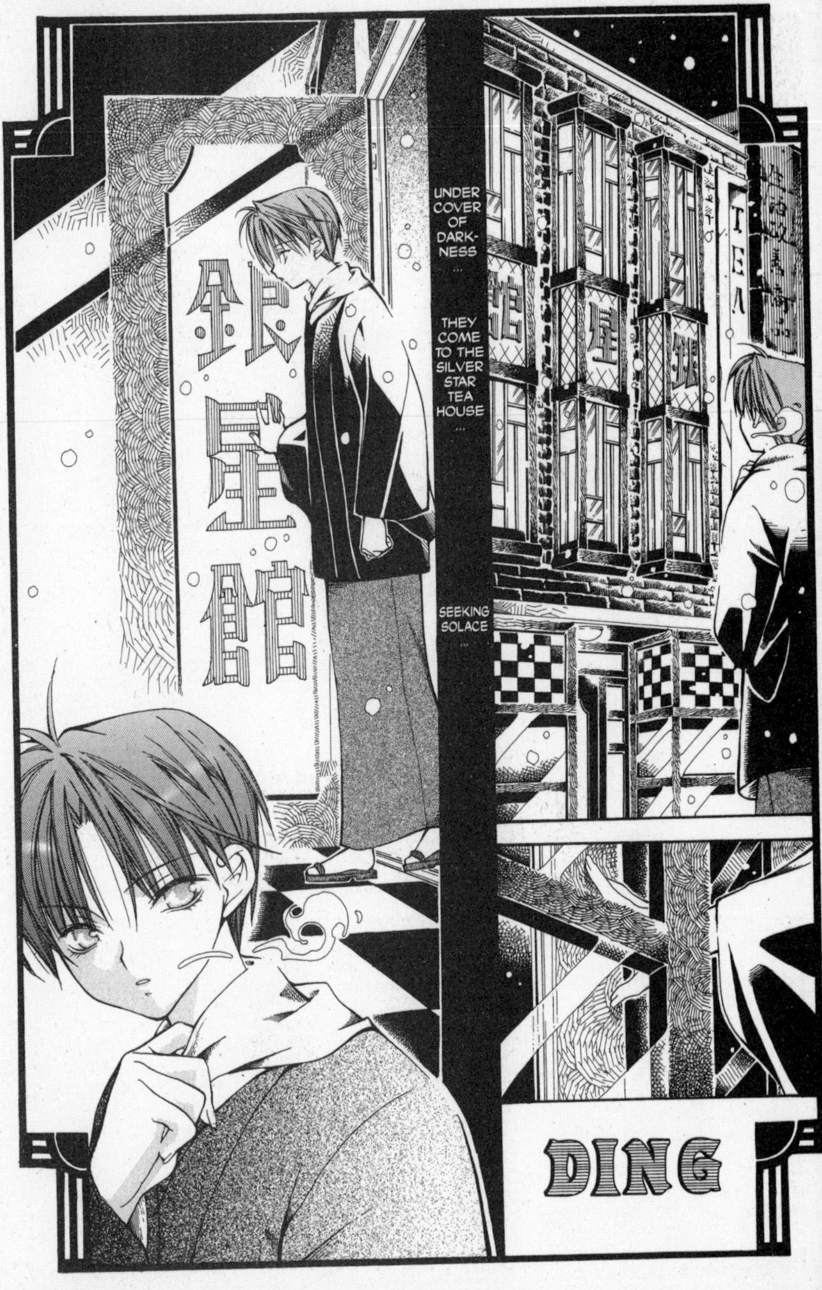
TEA
UNDER COVER OF DARKNESS...
THEY COME TO THE SILVER STAR TEA HOUSE...
SEEKING SOLACE...
DING
銀星館

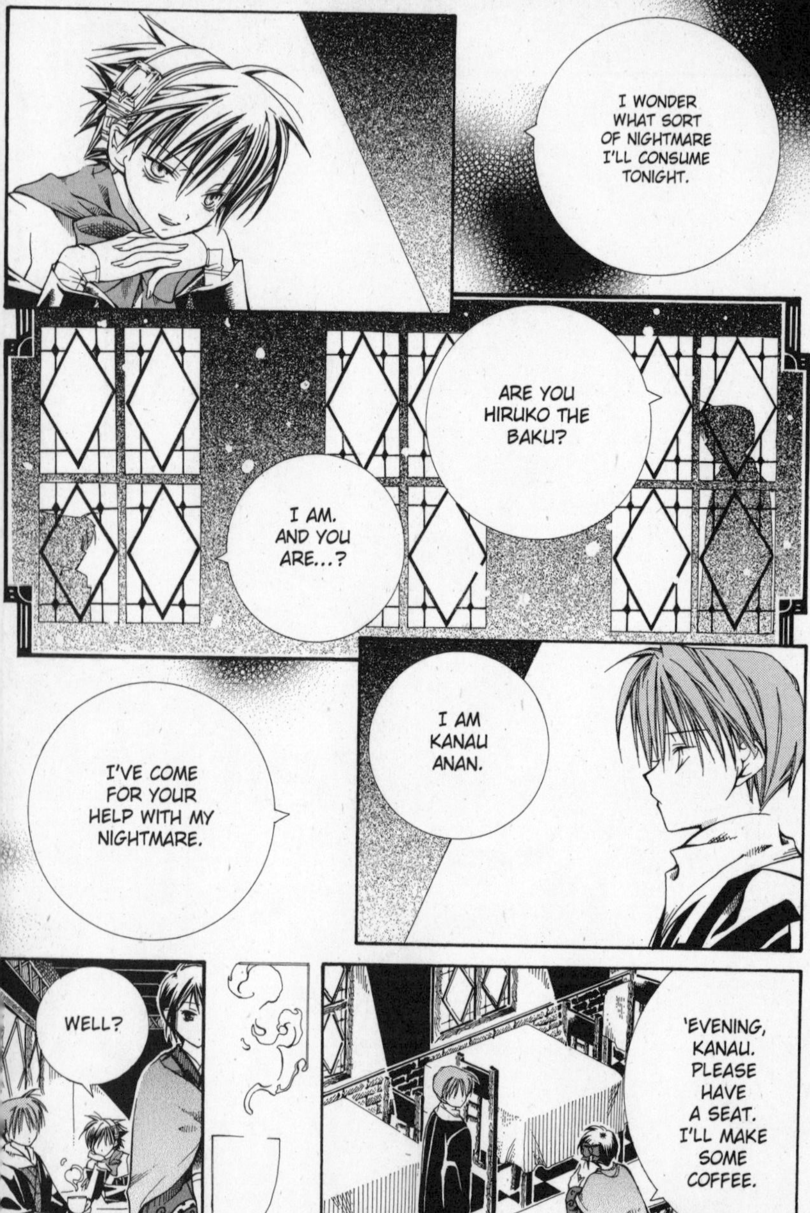

I WONDER WHAT SORT OF NIGHTMARE I'LL CONSUME TONIGHT.
ARE YOU HIRUKO THE BAKU?
I AM. AND YOU ARE...?
I AM KANAU ANAN.
I'VE COME FOR YOUR HELP WITH MY NIGHTMARE.
'EVENING, KANAU. PLEASE HAVE A SEAT. I'LL MAKE SOME COFFEE.
WELL?

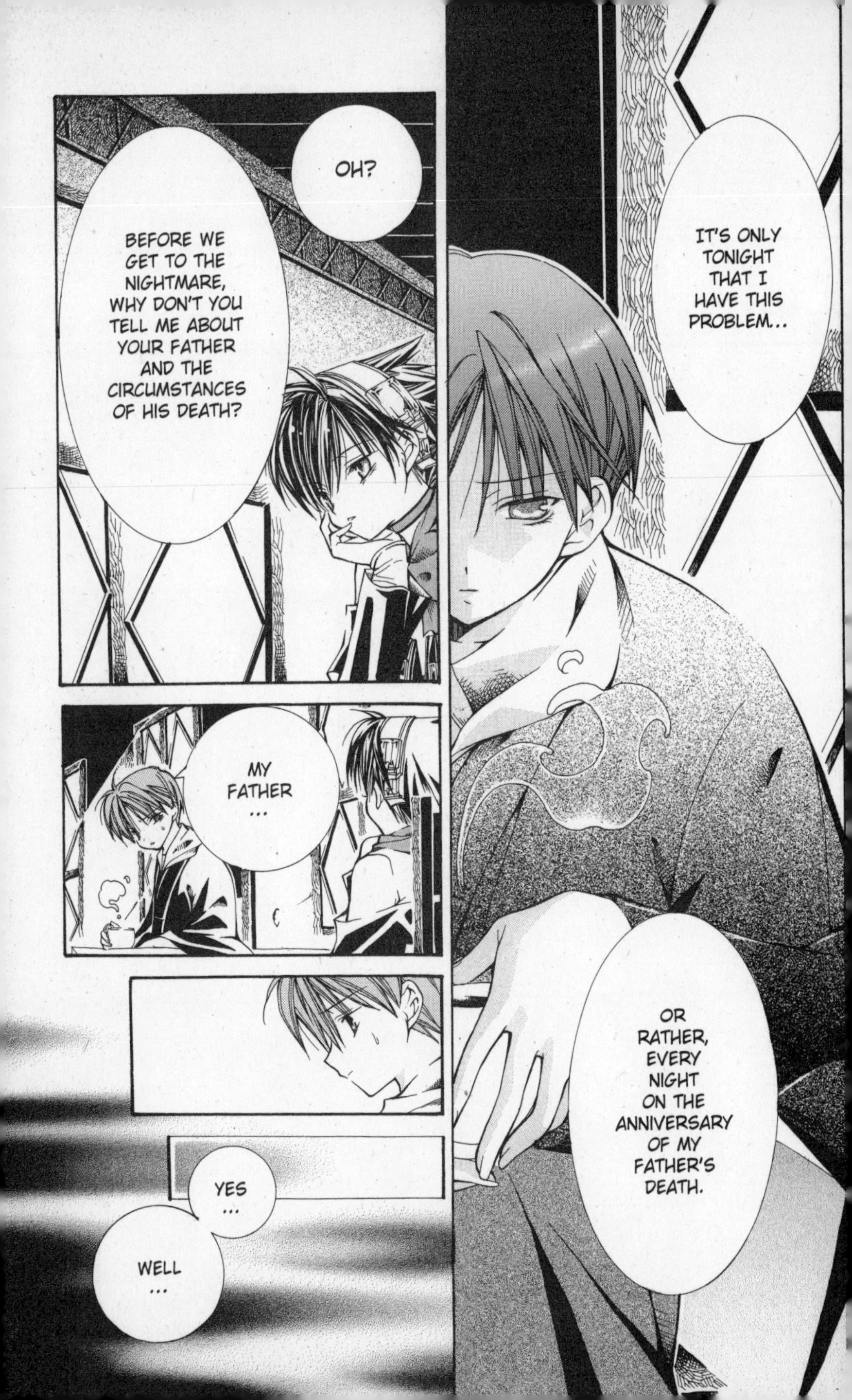
IT'S ONLY TONIGHT THAT I HAVE THIS PROBLEM...
OR RATHER, EVERY NIGHT ON THE ANNIVERSARY OF MY FATHER'S DEATH.
OH?
BEFORE WE GET TO THE NIGHTMARE, WHY DON'T YOU TELL ME ABOUT YOUR FATHER AND THE CIRCUMSTANCES OF HIS DEATH?
MY FATHER ...
YES ...
WELL ...

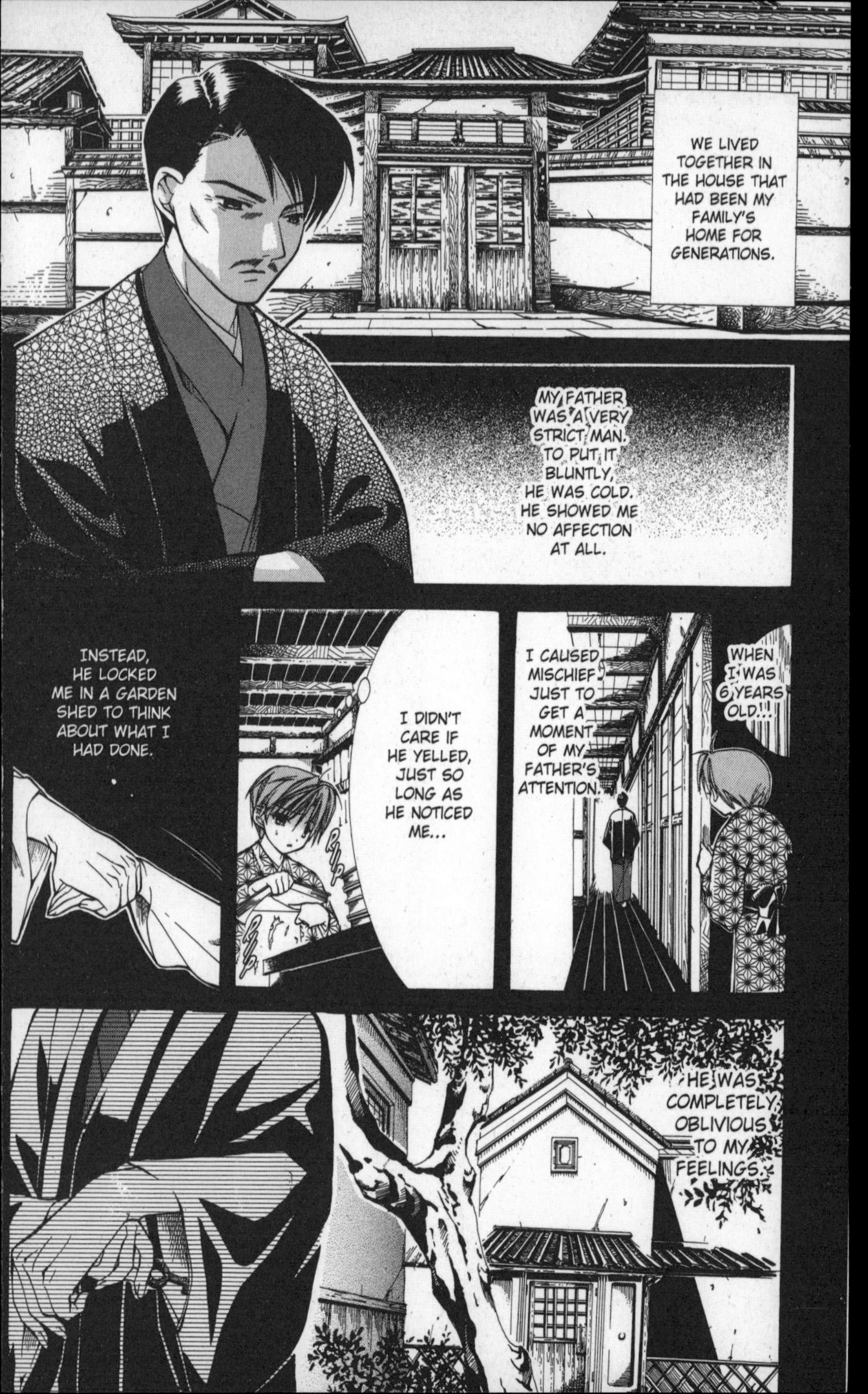
WE LIVED TOGETHER IN THE HOUSE THAT HAD BEEN MY FAMILY'S HOME FOR GENERATIONS.
MY FATHER WAS A VERY STRICT MAN. TO PUT IT BLUNTLY, HE WAS COLD. HE SHOWED ME NO AFFECTION AT ALL.
WHEN I WAS 6 YEARS OLD!!
I CAUSED MISCHIEF JUST TO GET A MOMENT OF MY FATHER'S ATTENTION.
I DIDN'T CARE IF HE YELLED, JUST SO LONG AS HE NOTICED ME...
INSTEAD, HE LOCKED ME IN A GARDEN SHED TO THINK ABOUT WHAT I HAD DONE.
HE WAS COMPLETELY OBLIVIOUS TO MY FEELINGS.

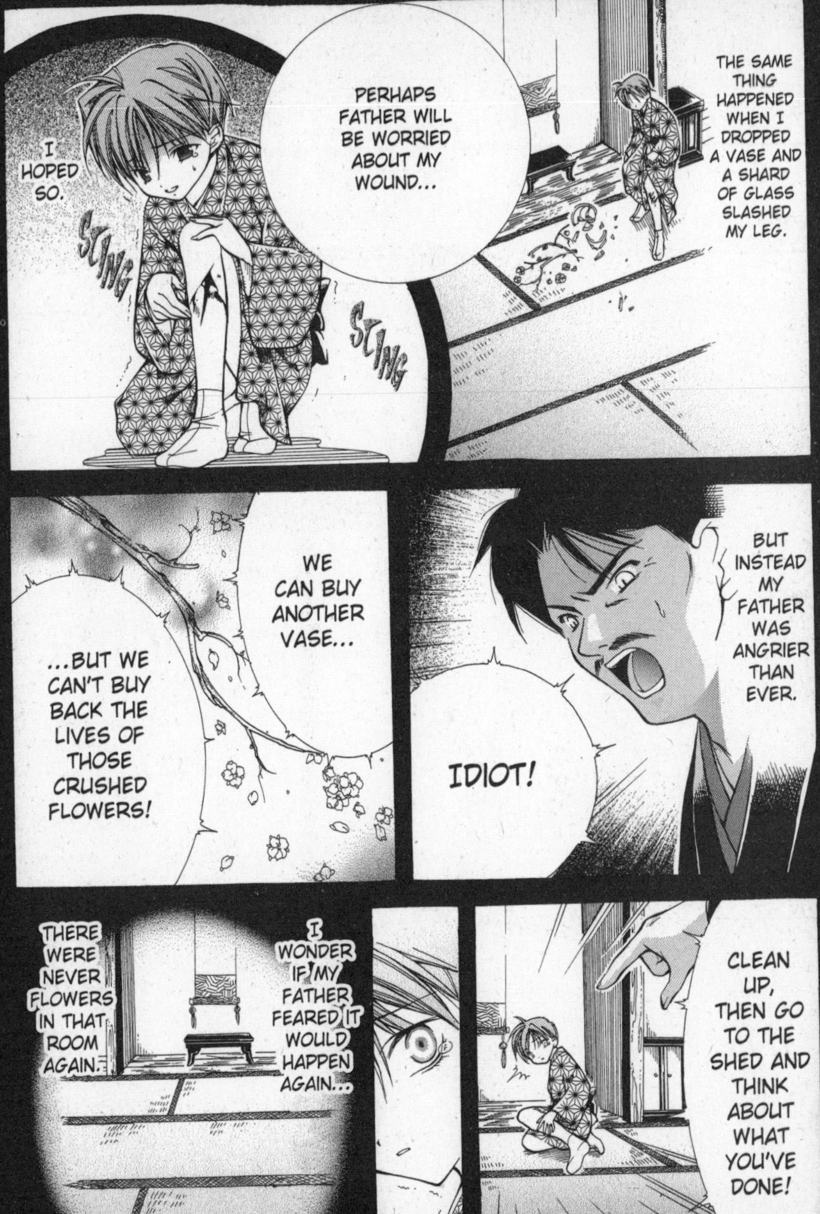
THE SAME THING HAPPENED WHEN I DROPPED A VASE AND A SHARD OF GLASS SLASHED MY LEG.
PERHAPS FATHER WILL BE WORRIED ABOUT MY WOUND...
STING
STING
I HOPED SO.
BUT INSTEAD MY FATHER WAS ANGRIER THAN EVER.
IDIOT!
WE CAN BUY ANOTHER VASE...
...BUT WE CAN'T BUY BACK THE LIVES OF THOSE CRUSHED FLOWERS!
CLEAN UP, THEN GO TO THE SHED AND THINK ABOUT WHAT YOU'VE DONE!
I WONDER IF MY FATHER FEARED IT WOULD HAPPEN AGAIN...
THERE WERE NEVER FLOWERS IN THAT ROOM AGAIN.

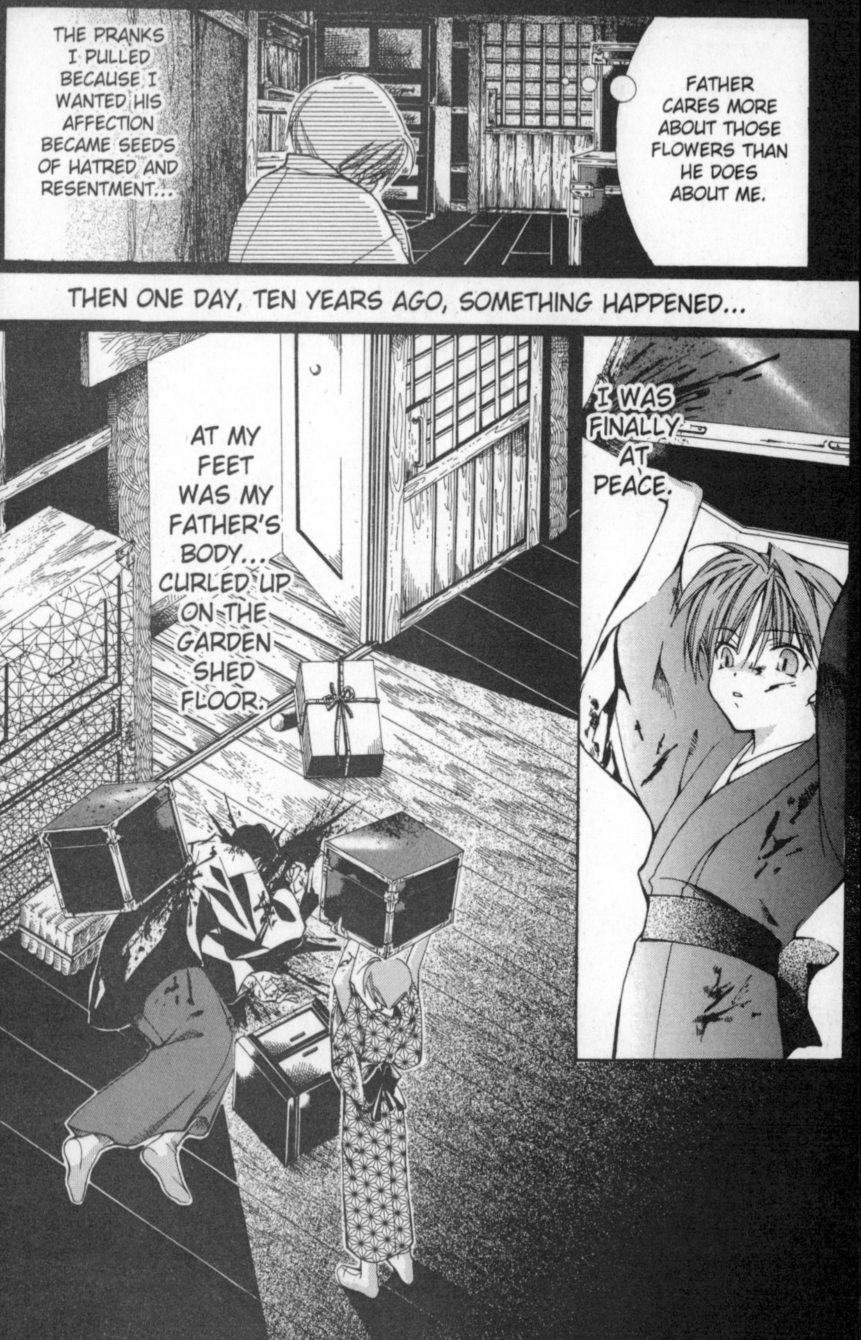
FATHER CARES MORE ABOUT THOSE FLOWERS THAN HE DOES ABOUT ME.
THE PRANKS I PULLED BECAUSE I WANTED HIS AFFECTION BECAME SEEDS OF HATRED AND RESENTMENT...
THEN ONE DAY, TEN YEARS AGO, SOMETHING HAPPENED...
I WAS FINALLY AT PEACE.
AT MY FEET WAS MY FATHER'S BODY... CURLED UP ON THE GARDEN SHED FLOOR.

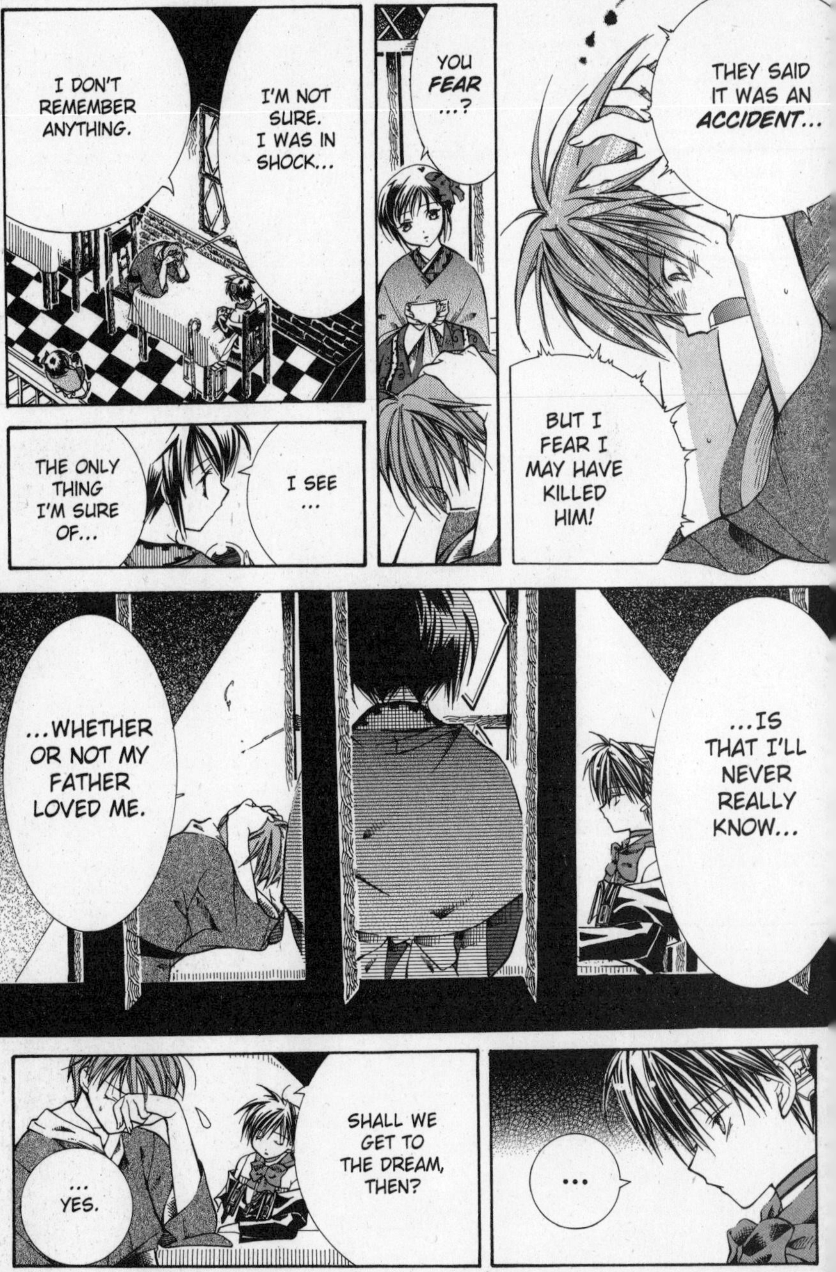
THEY SAID IT WAS AN *ACCIDENT*...
BUT I FEAR I MAY HAVE KILLED HIM!
YOU *FEAR*...?
I'M NOT SURE. I WAS IN SHOCK...
I DON'T REMEMBER ANYTHING.
I SEE...
THE ONLY THING I'M SURE OF...
...IS THAT I'LL NEVER REALLY KNOW...
...WHETHER OR NOT MY FATHER LOVED ME.
...
SHALL WE GET TO THE DREAM, THEN?
... YES.

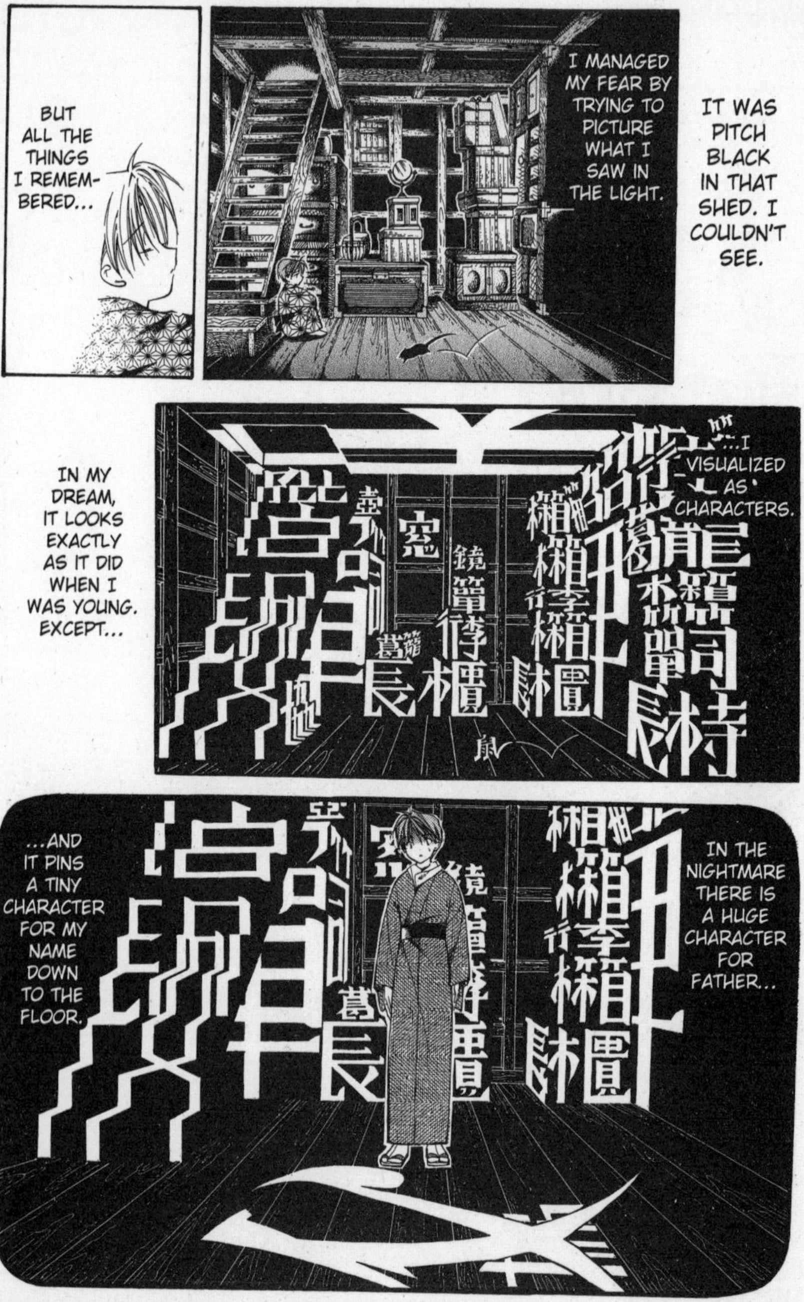
IT WAS PITCH BLACK IN THAT SHED. I COULDN'T SEE.
I MANAGED MY FEAR BY TRYING TO PICTURE WHAT I SAW IN THE LIGHT.
BUT ALL THE THINGS I REMEMBERED...
...I VISUALIZED AS CHARACTERS.
IN MY DREAM, IT LOOKS EXACTLY AS IT DID WHEN I WAS YOUNG. EXCEPT...
IN THE NIGHTMARE THERE IS A HUGE CHARACTER FOR FATHER...
...AND IT PINS A TINY CHARACTER FOR MY NAME DOWN TO THE FLOOR.

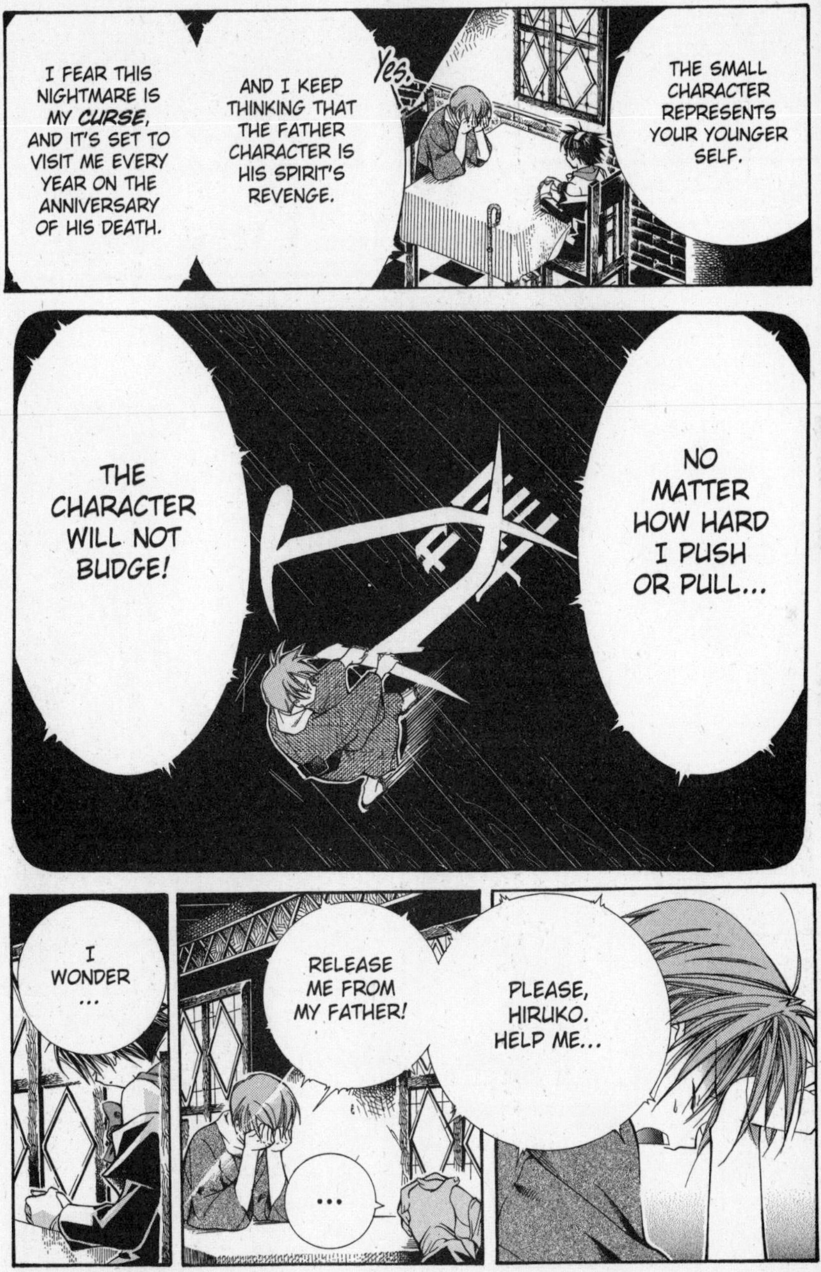
THE SMALL CHARACTER REPRESENTS YOUR YOUNGER SELF.
Yes.
AND I KEEP THINKING THAT THE FATHER CHARACTER IS HIS SPIRIT'S REVENGE.
I FEAR THIS NIGHTMARE IS MY *CURSE*, AND IT'S SET TO VISIT ME EVERY YEAR ON THE ANNIVERSARY OF HIS DEATH.
NO MATTER HOW HARD I PUSH OR PULL...
THE CHARACTER WILL NOT BUDGE!
PLEASE, HIRUKO. HELP ME...
RELEASE ME FROM MY FATHER!
...
I WONDER ...

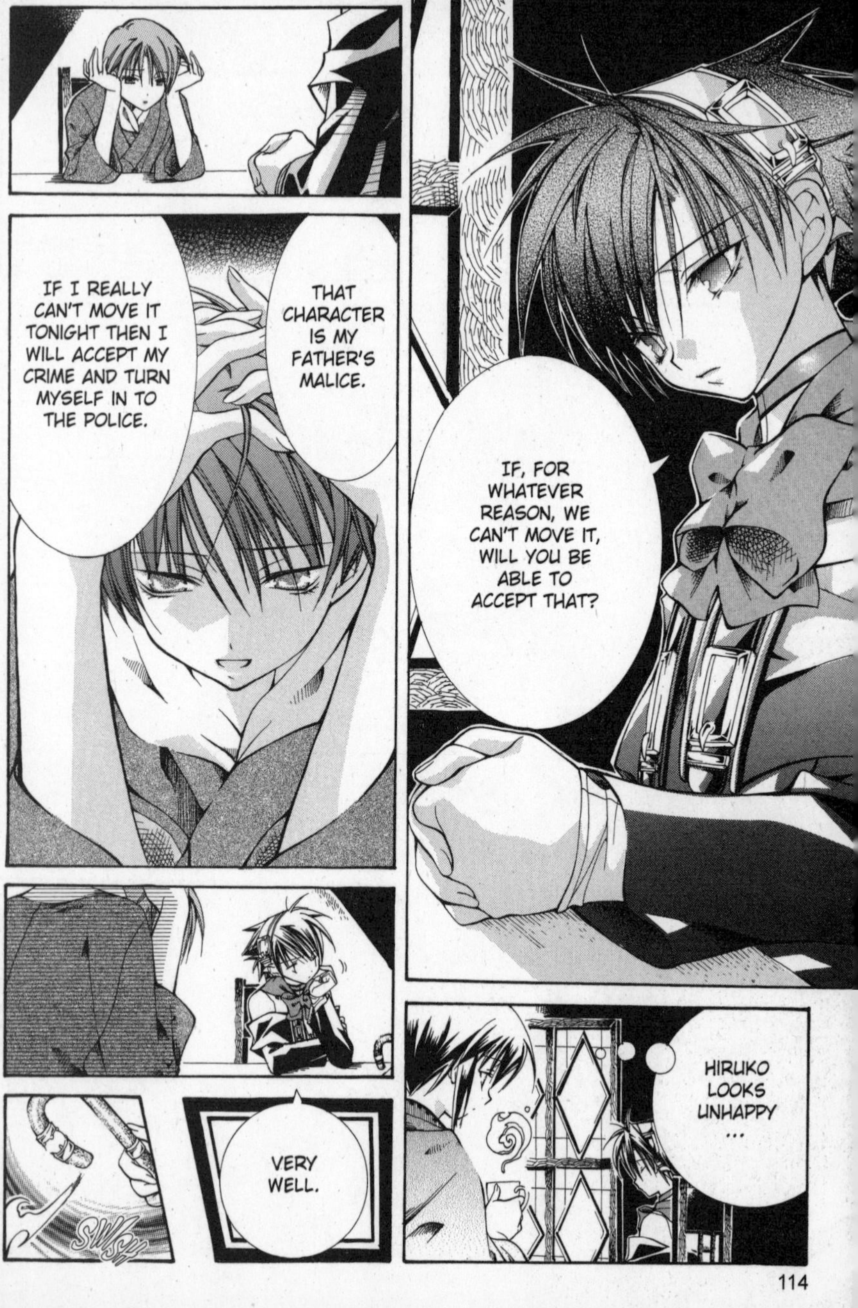
IF, FOR WHATEVER REASON, WE CAN'T MOVE IT, WILL YOU BE ABLE TO ACCEPT THAT?
THAT CHARACTER IS MY FATHER'S MALICE.
IF I REALLY CAN'T MOVE IT TONIGHT THEN I WILL ACCEPT MY CRIME AND TURN MYSELF IN TO THE POLICE.
HIRUKO LOOKS UNHAPPY ...
VERY WELL.
SWISH

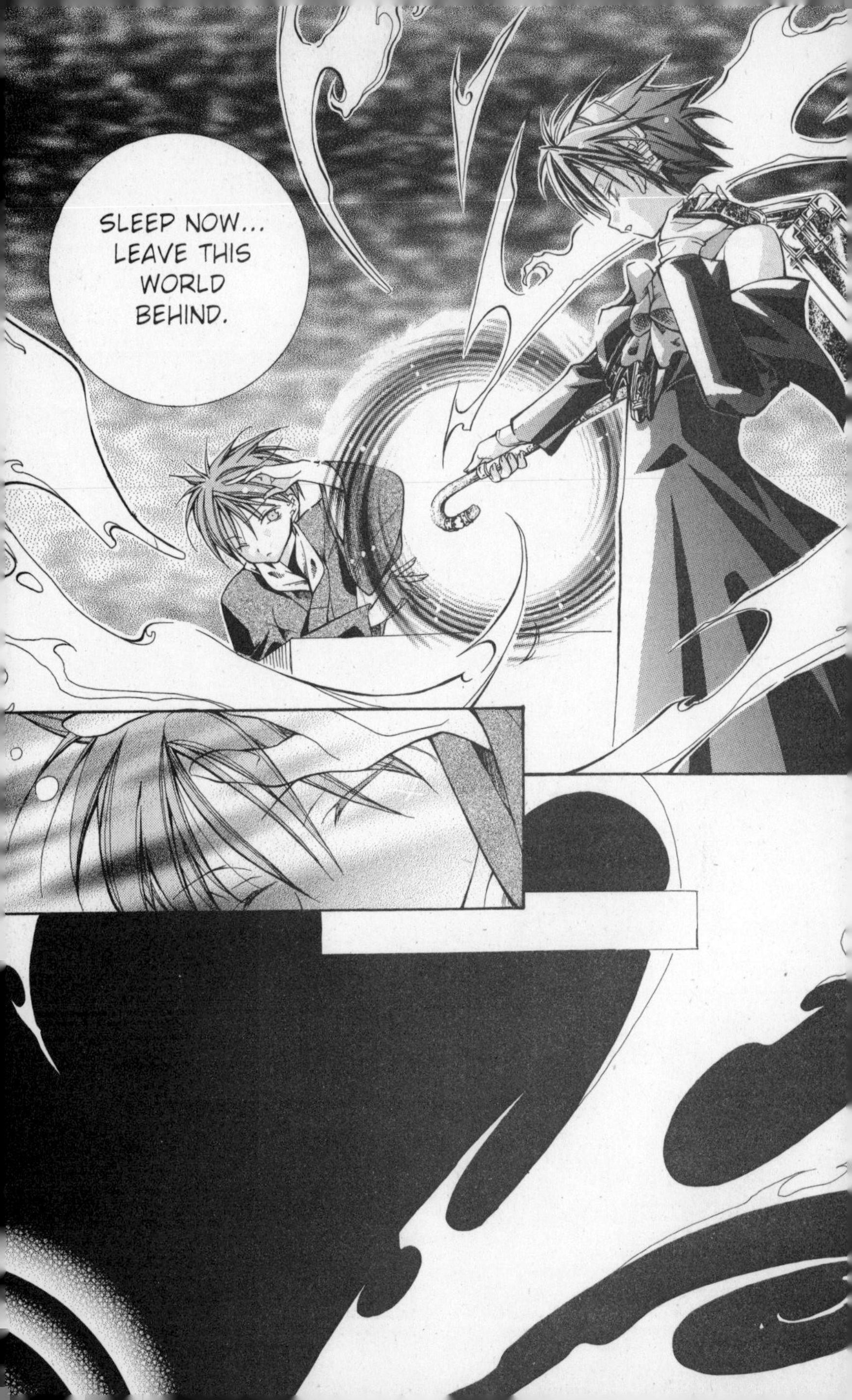
SLEEP NOW... LEAVE THIS WORLD BEHIND.

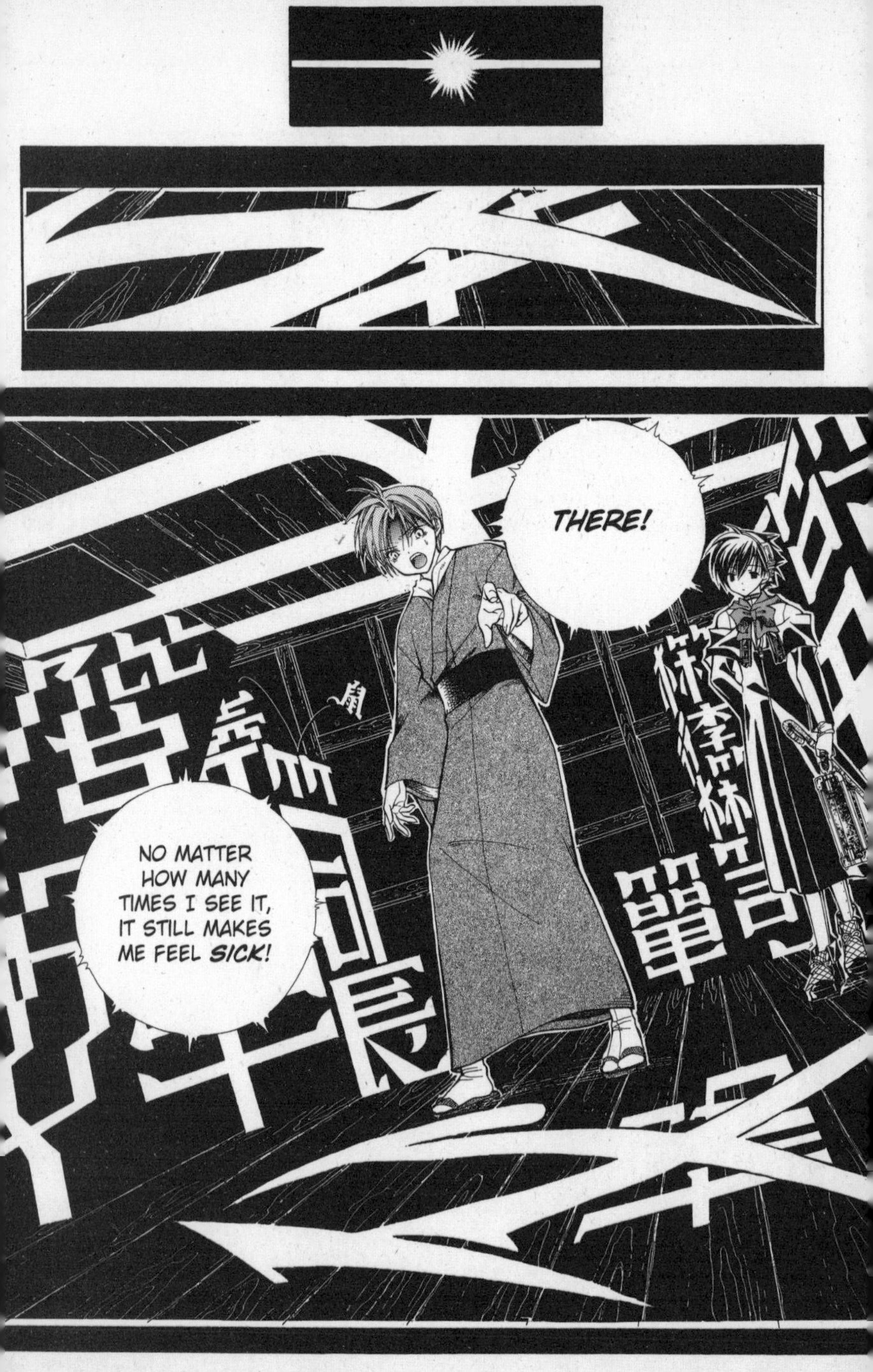
THERE!
NO MATTER HOW MANY TIMES I SEE IT, IT STILL MAKES ME FEEL SICK!

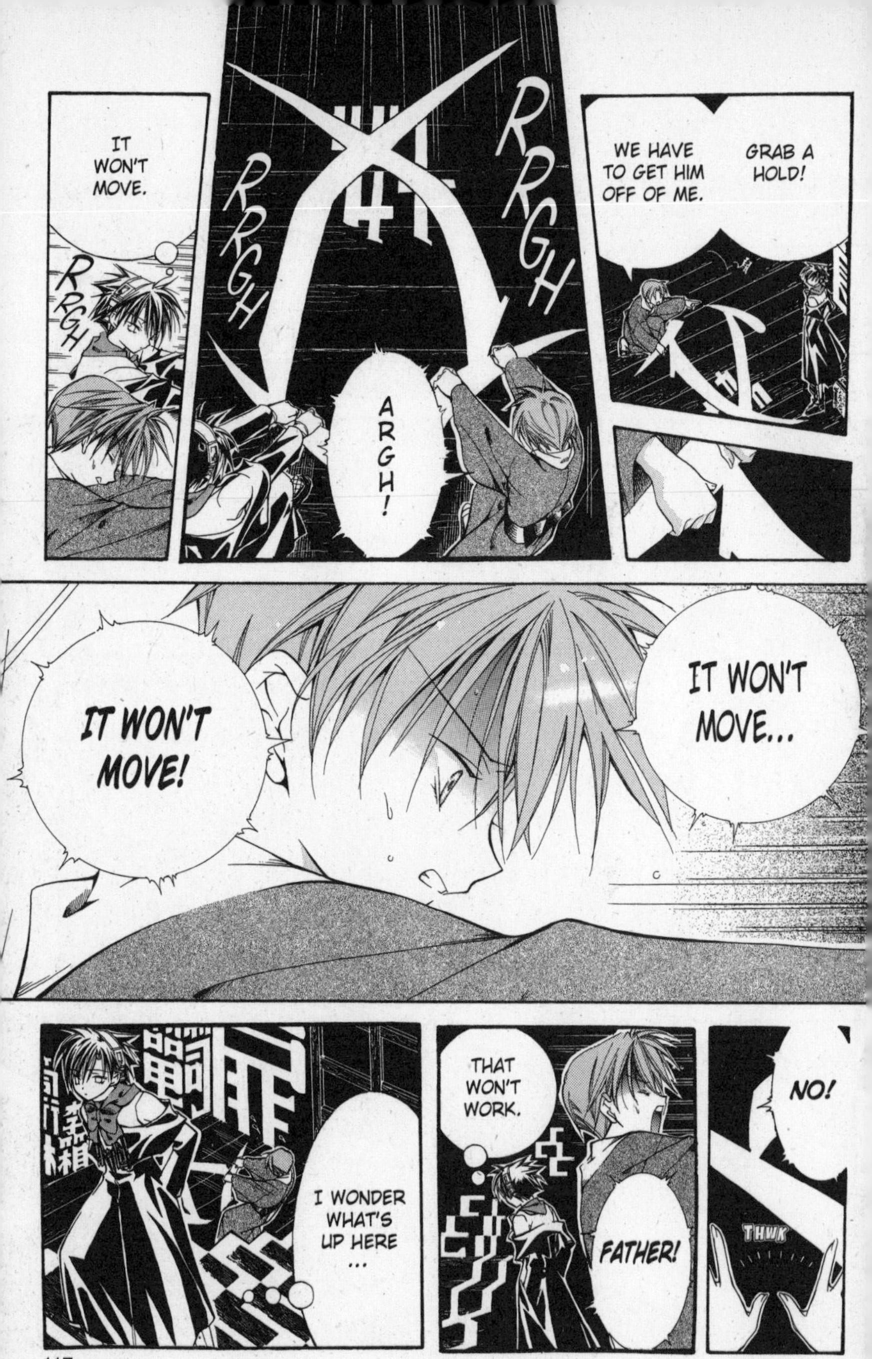
GRAB A HOLD!
WE HAVE TO GET HIM OFF OF ME.
RRGH
RRGH
ARGH!
IT WON'T MOVE.
RRGH
IT WON'T MOVE...
IT WON'T MOVE!
NO!
THWK
THAT WON'T WORK.
FATHER!
I WONDER WHAT'S UP HERE ...

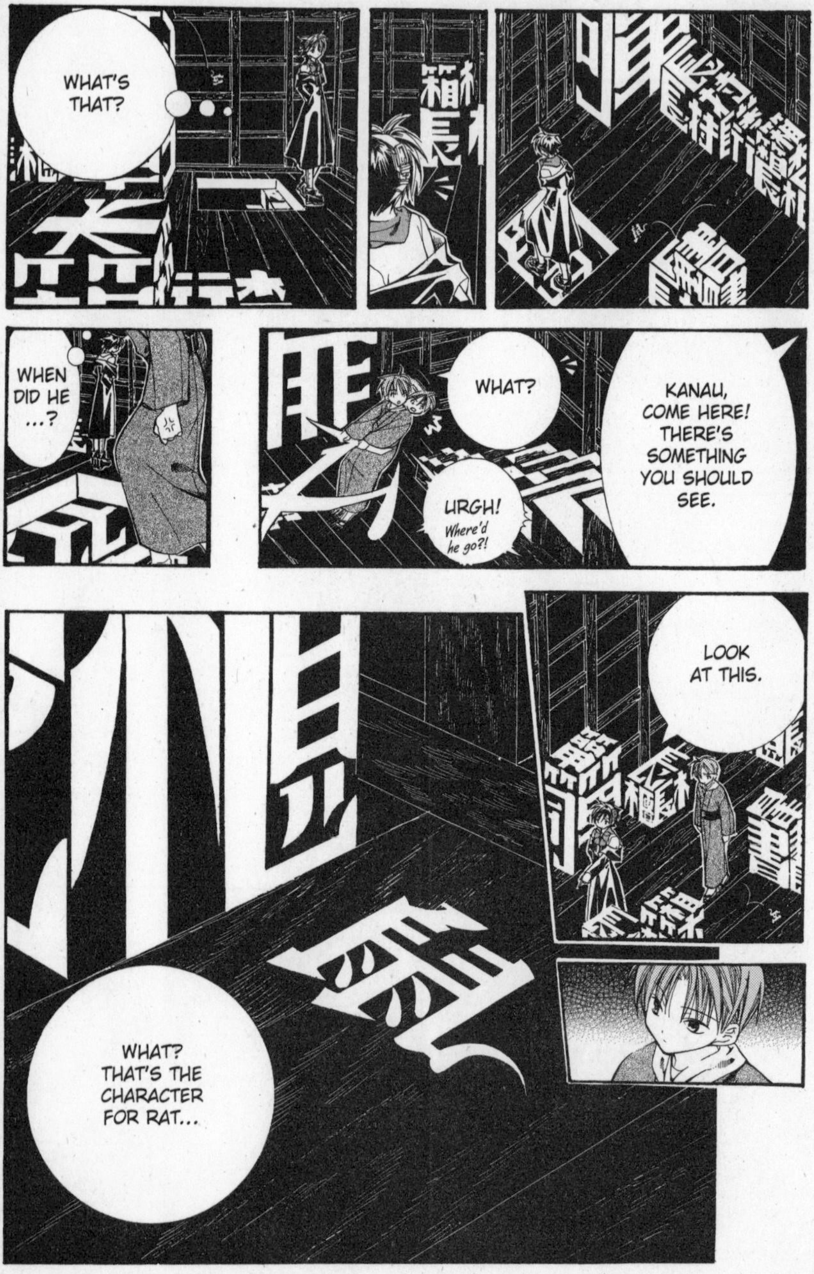
WHAT'S THAT?
KANAU, COME HERE! THERE'S SOMETHING YOU SHOULD SEE.
WHAT?
URGH! Where'd he go?!
WHEN DID HE ...?
LOOK AT THIS.
WHAT? THAT'S THE CHARACTER FOR RAT...

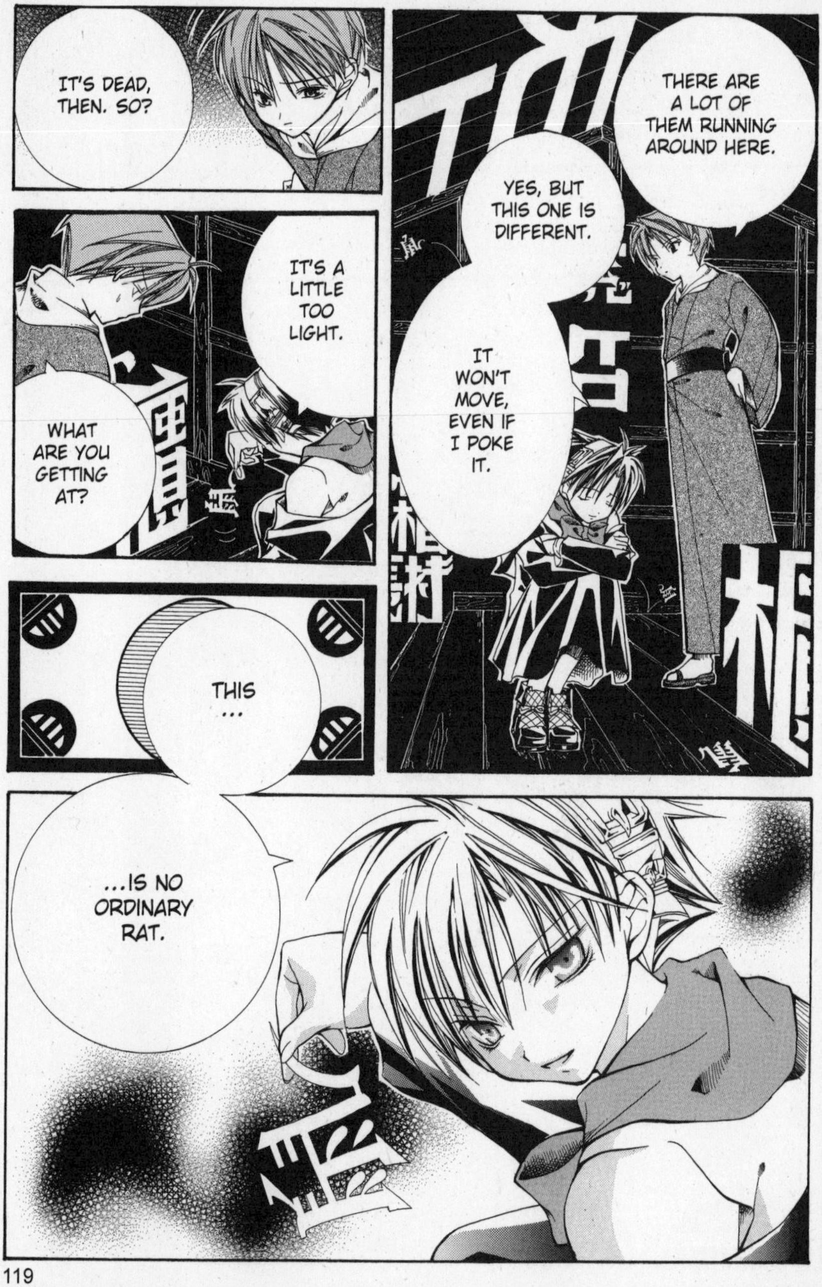
THERE ARE A LOT OF THEM RUNNING AROUND HERE.
YES, BUT THIS ONE IS DIFFERENT.
IT WON'T MOVE, EVEN IF I POKE IT.
IT'S DEAD, THEN. SO?
IT'S A LITTLE TOO LIGHT.
WHAT ARE YOU GETTING AT?
THIS...
...IS NO ORDINARY RAT.

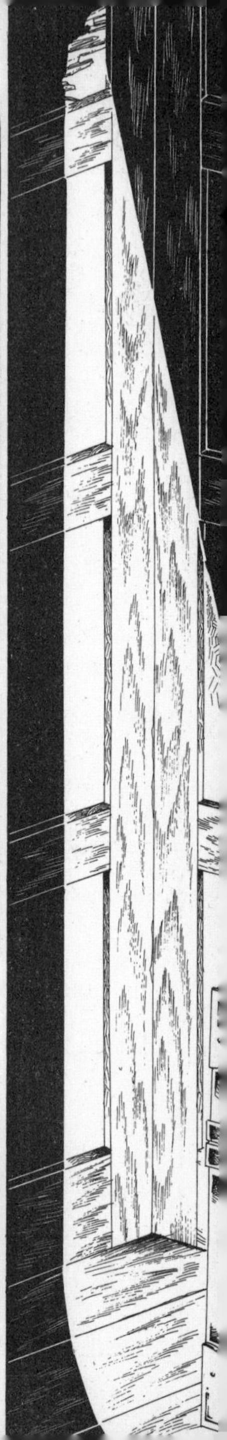

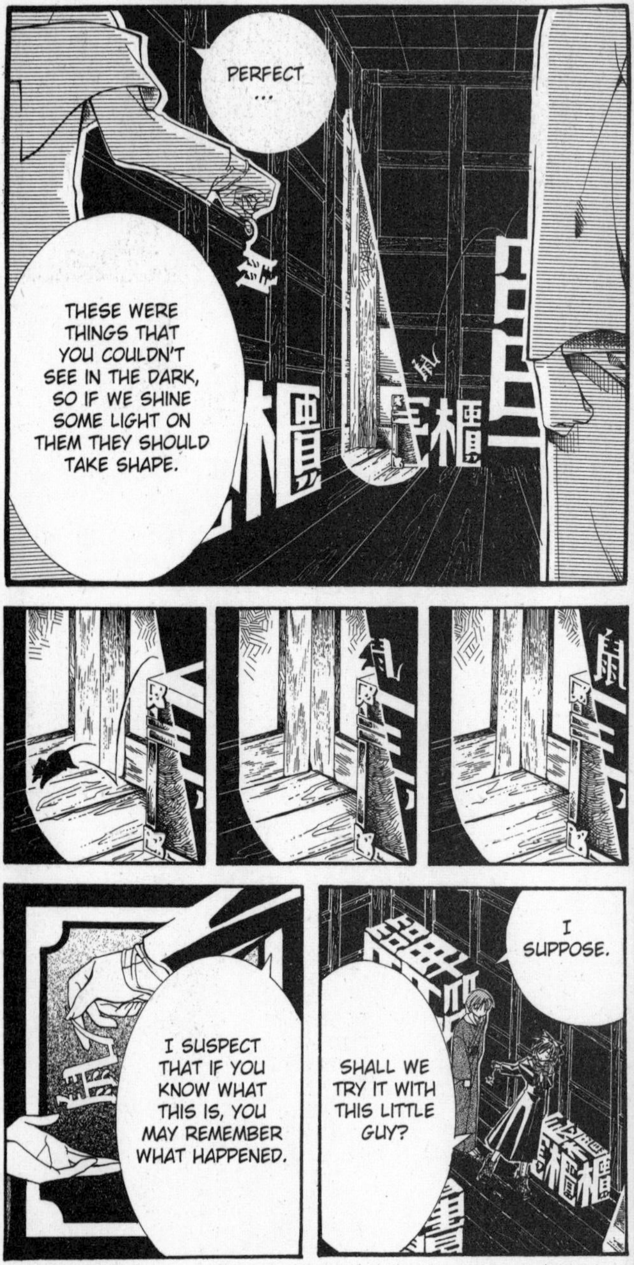
PERFECT ...
THESE WERE THINGS THAT YOU COULDN'T SEE IN THE DARK, SO IF WE SHINE SOME LIGHT ON THEM THEY SHOULD TAKE SHAPE.
I SUPPOSE.
SHALL WE TRY IT WITH THIS LITTLE GUY?
I SUSPECT THAT IF YOU KNOW WHAT THIS IS, YOU MAY REMEMBER WHAT HAPPENED.

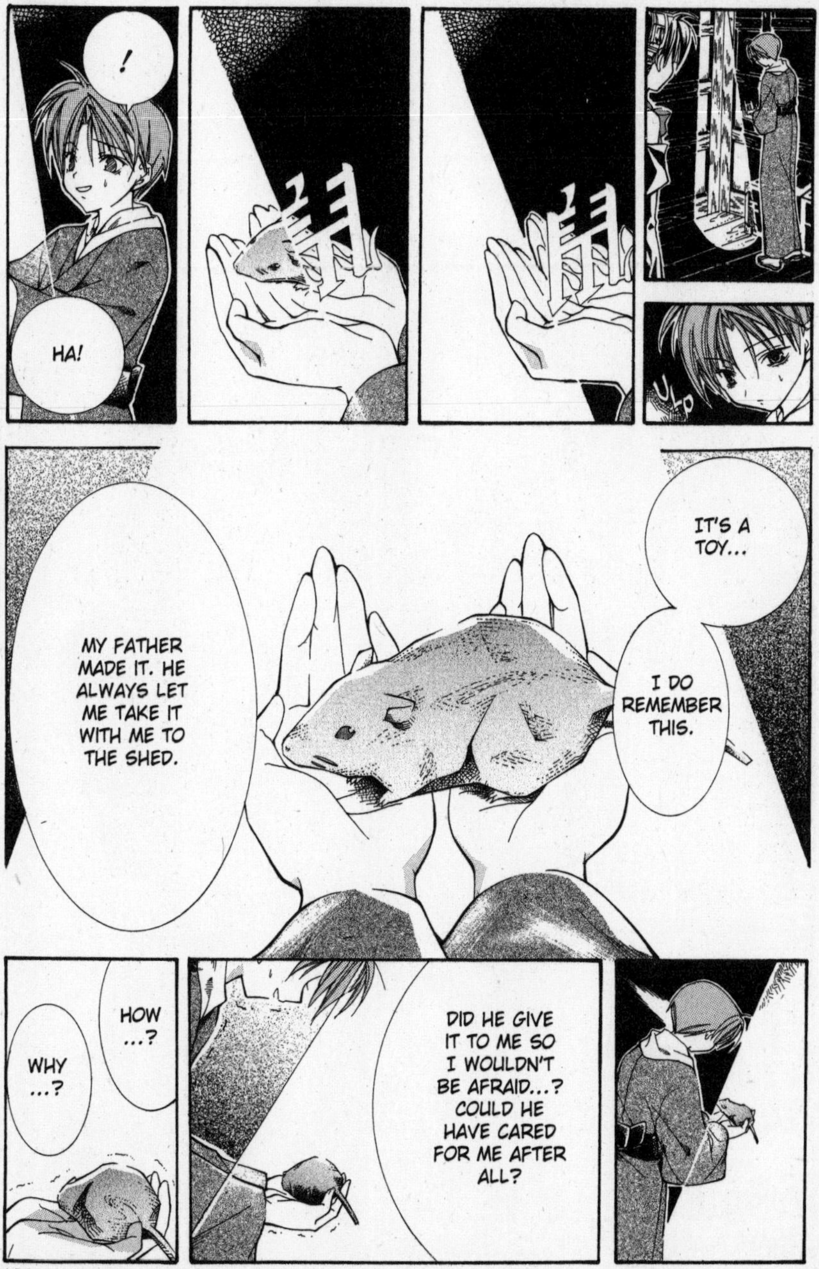
ULP
!
HA!
IT'S A TOY...
I DO REMEMBER THIS.
MY FATHER MADE IT. HE ALWAYS LET ME TAKE IT WITH ME TO THE SHED.
DID HE GIVE IT TO ME SO I WOULDN'T BE AFRAID...? COULD HE HAVE CARED FOR ME AFTER ALL?
HOW ...?
WHY ...?

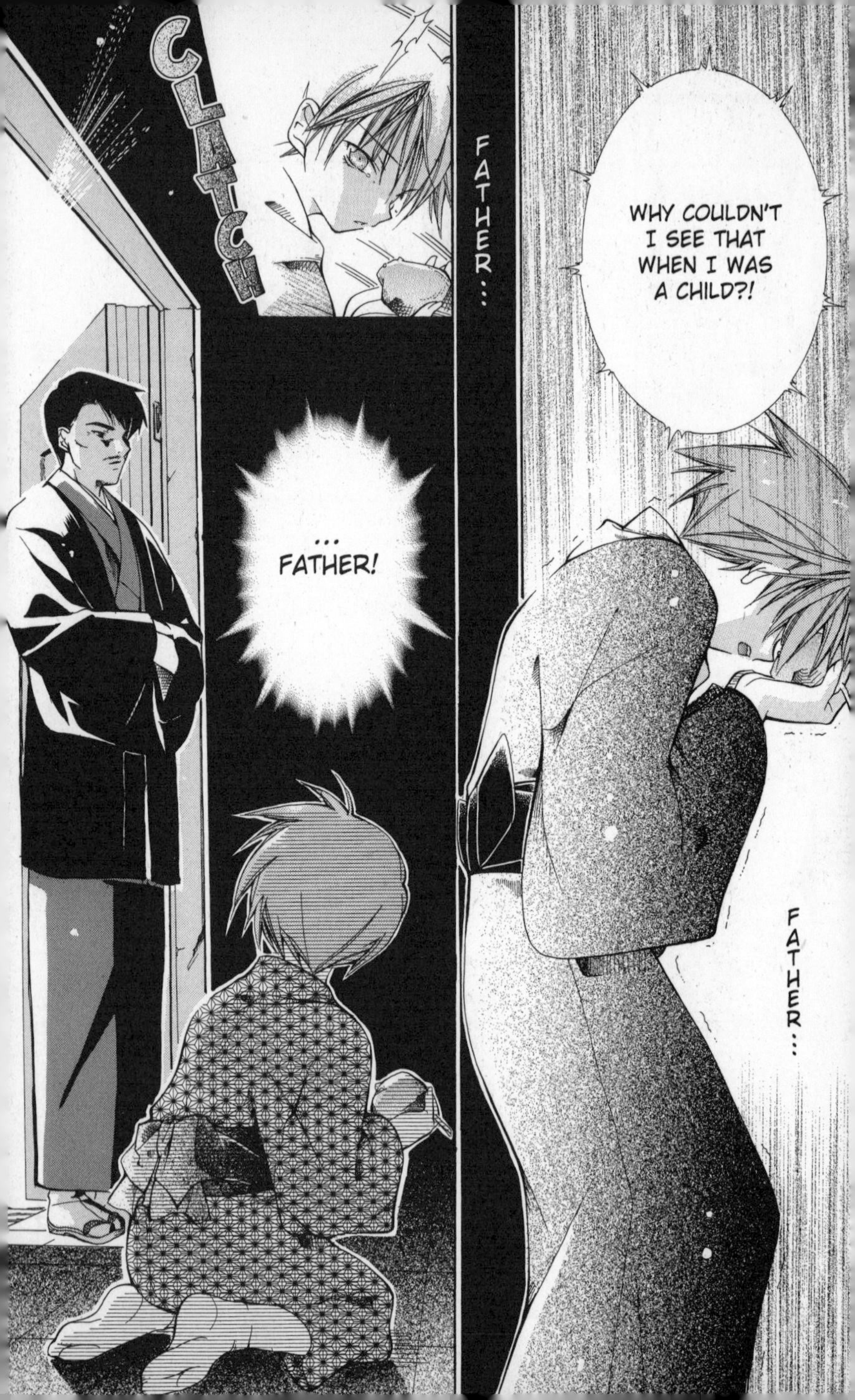
WHY COULDN'T I SEE THAT WHEN I WAS A CHILD?!
FATHER...
FATHER...
CLATCH
...FATHER!

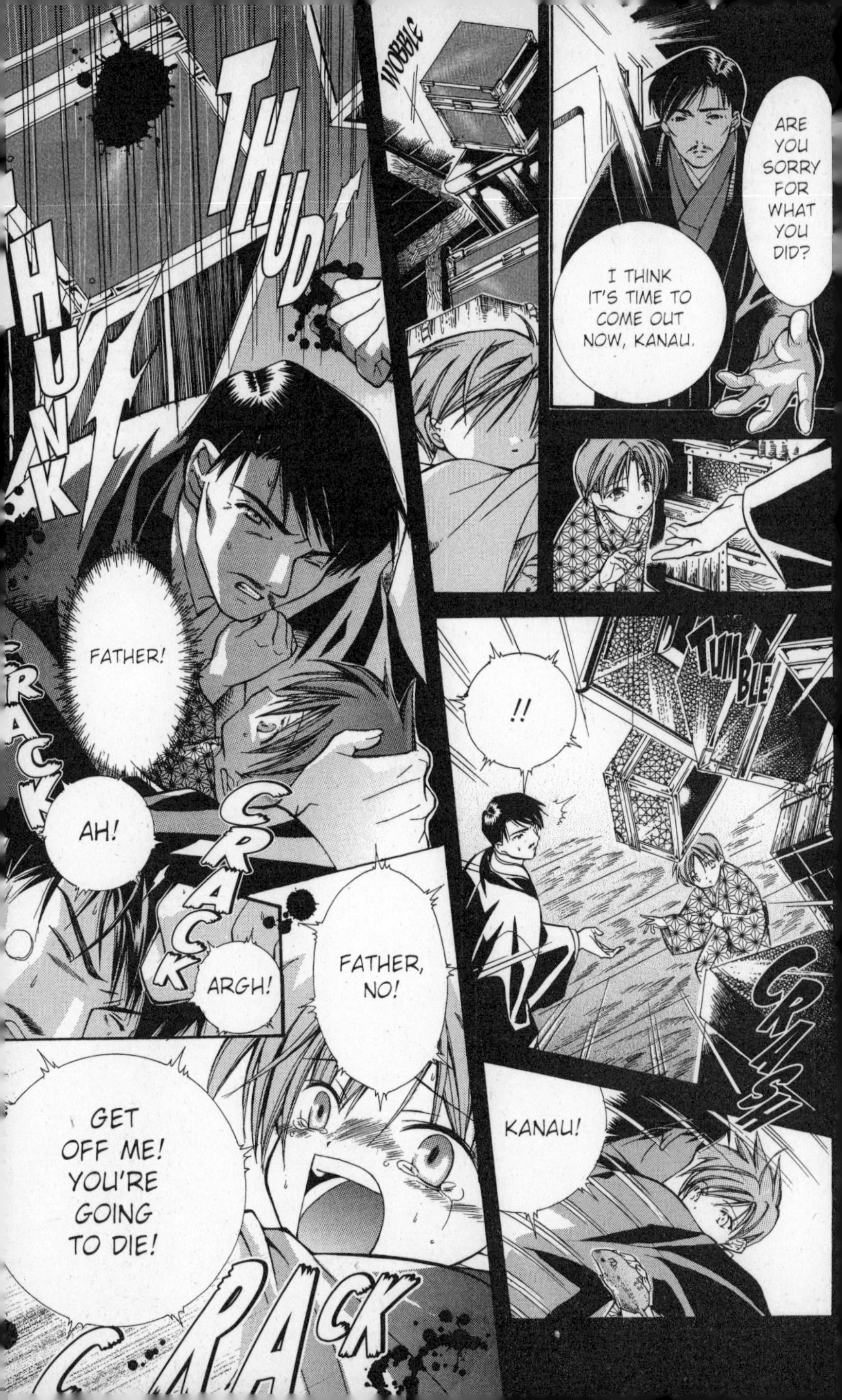

ARE YOU SORRY FOR WHAT YOU DID?
I THINK IT'S TIME TO COME OUT NOW, KANAU.
WOBBLE
!!
TUMBLE
CRASH
KANAU!
THUD
THUNK
FATHER!
CRACK
AH!
CRACK
ARGH!
FATHER, NO!
GET OFF ME! YOU'RE GOING TO DIE!
CRACK

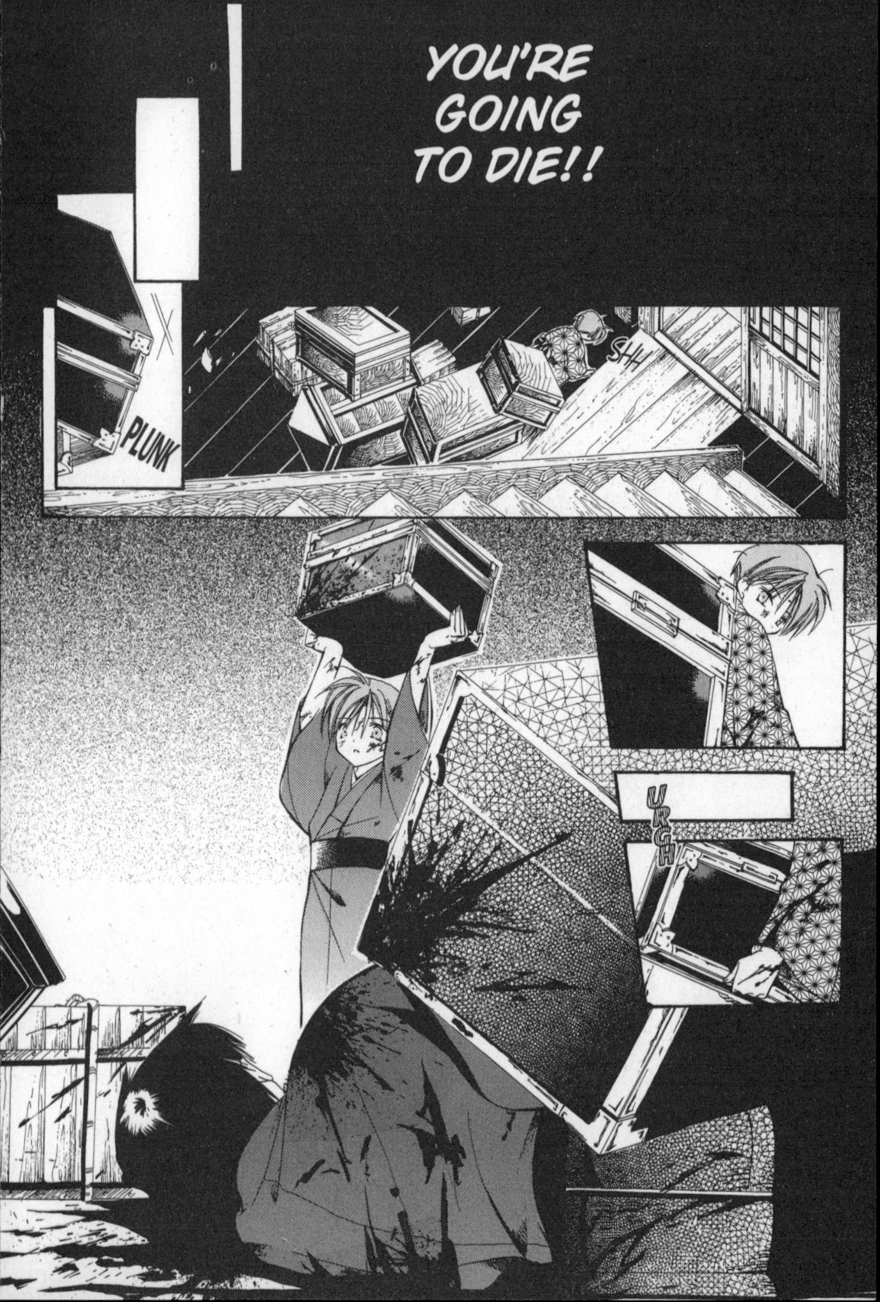
YOU'RE GOING TO DIE!!
SHH
PLUNK
URGH

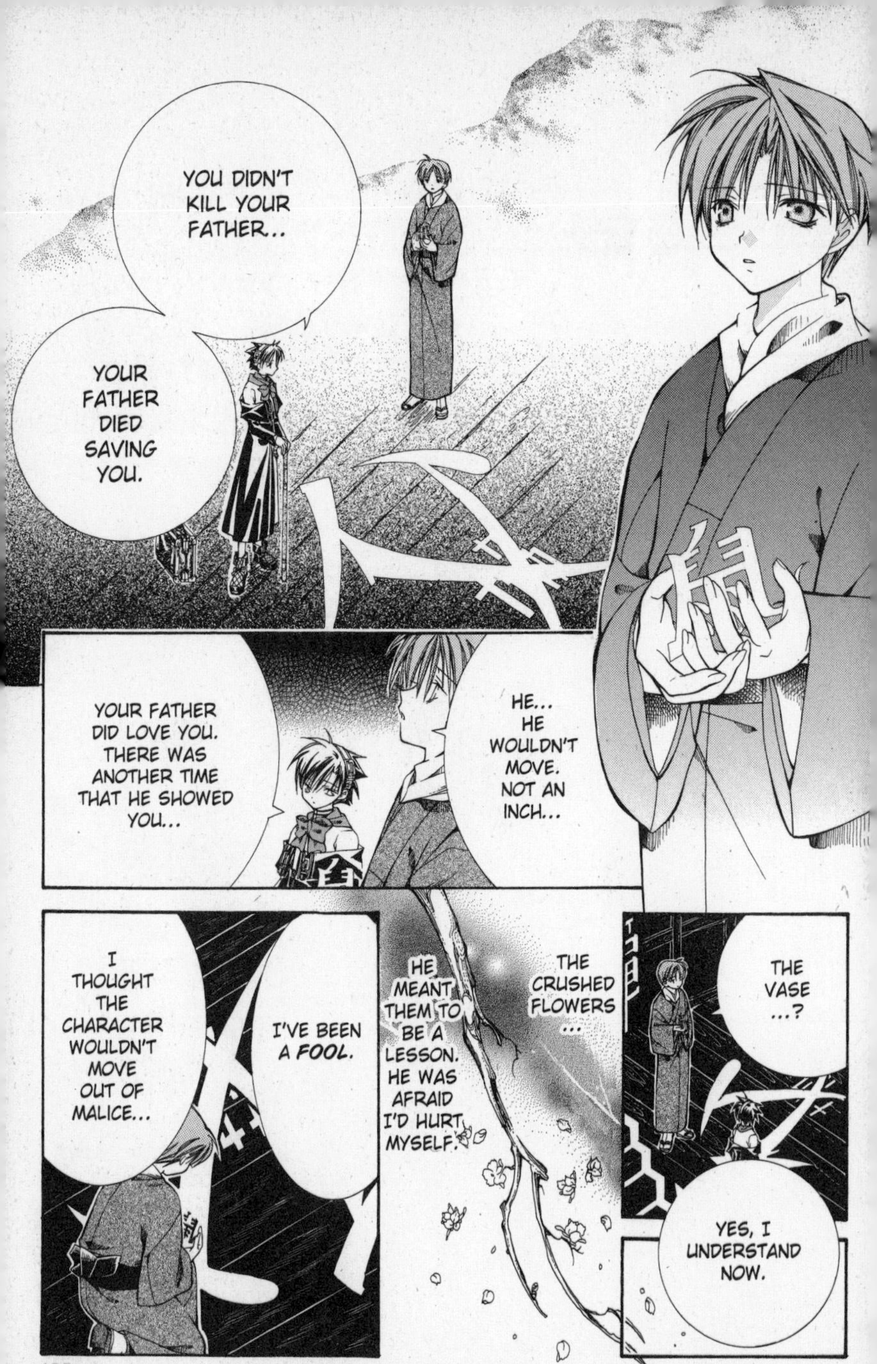
YOU DIDN'T KILL YOUR FATHER...
YOUR FATHER DIED SAVING YOU.
HE... HE WOULDN'T MOVE. NOT AN INCH...
YOUR FATHER DID LOVE YOU. THERE WAS ANOTHER TIME THAT HE SHOWED YOU...
THE VASE ...?
YES, I UNDERSTAND NOW.
THE CRUSHED FLOWERS ...
HE MEANT THEM TO BE A LESSON. HE WAS AFRAID I'D HURT MYSELF.
I'VE BEEN A *FOOL*.
I THOUGHT THE CHARACTER WOULDN'T MOVE OUT OF MALICE...

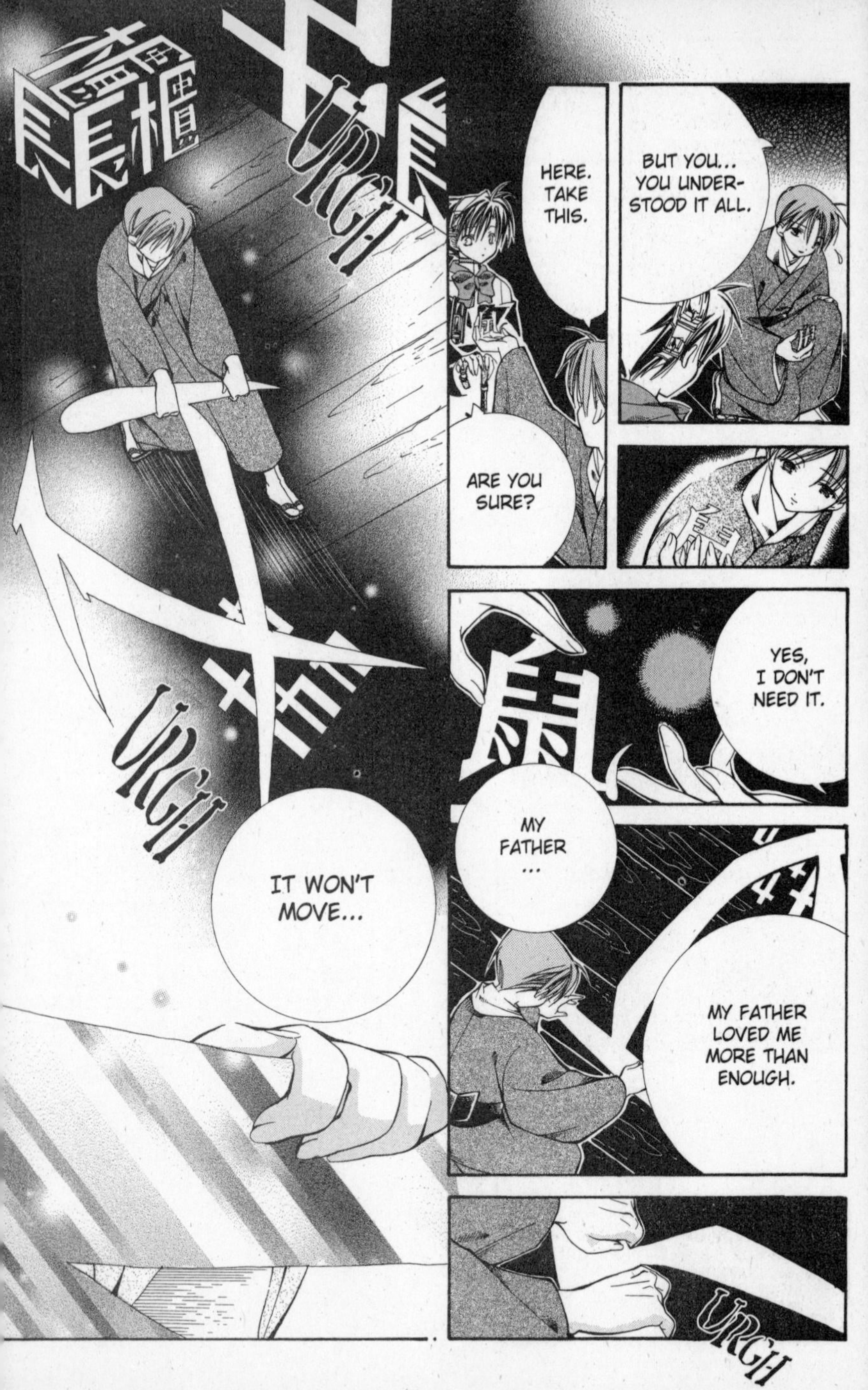
BUT YOU... YOU UNDER-STOOD IT ALL.
HERE. TAKE THIS.
ARE YOU SURE?
鼠
YES, I DON'T NEED IT.
MY FATHER...
MY FATHER LOVED ME MORE THAN ENOUGH.
URGH
URGH
URGH
IT WON'T MOVE...

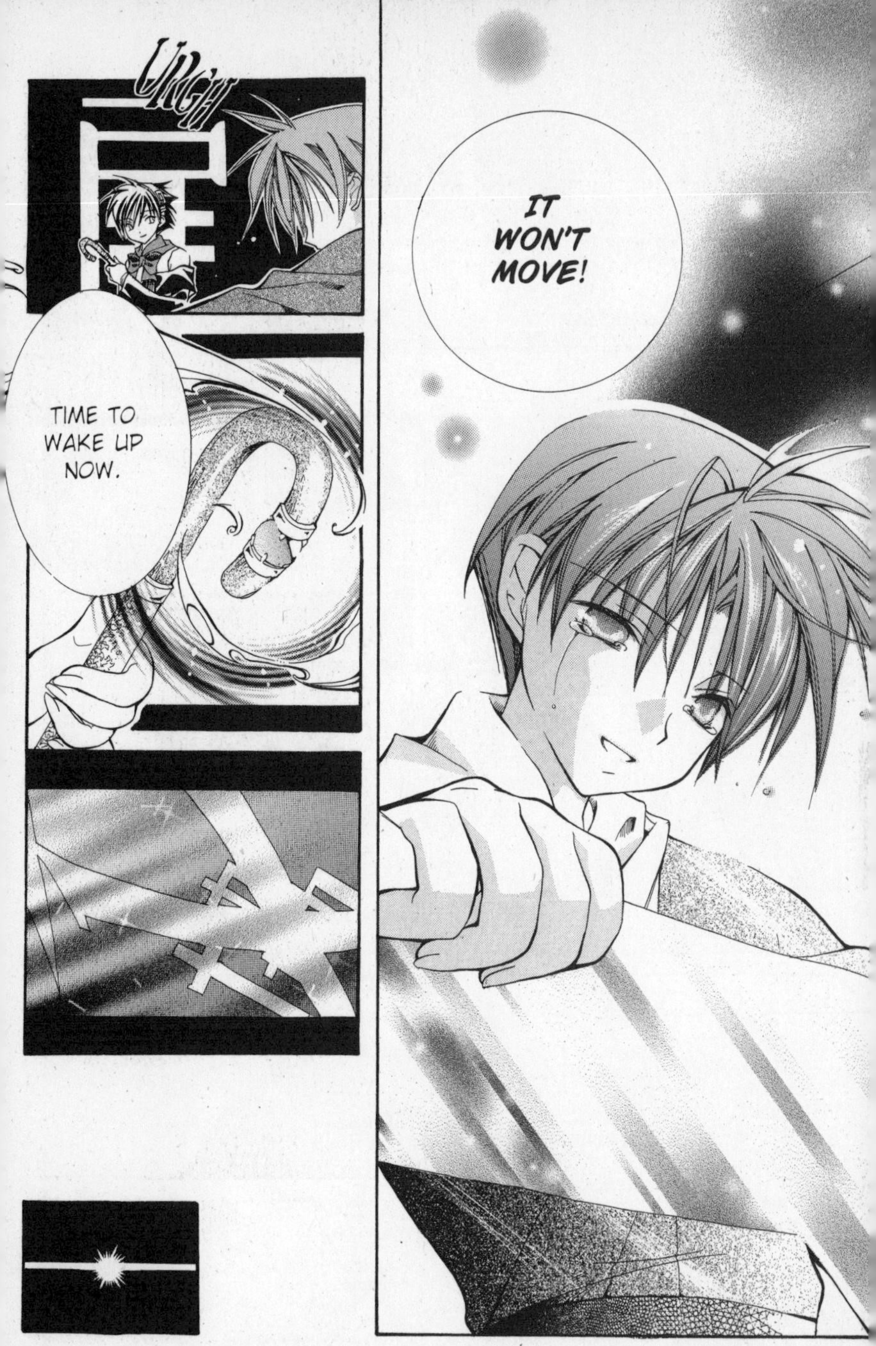
IT WON'T MOVE!
URGH
TIME TO WAKE UP NOW.

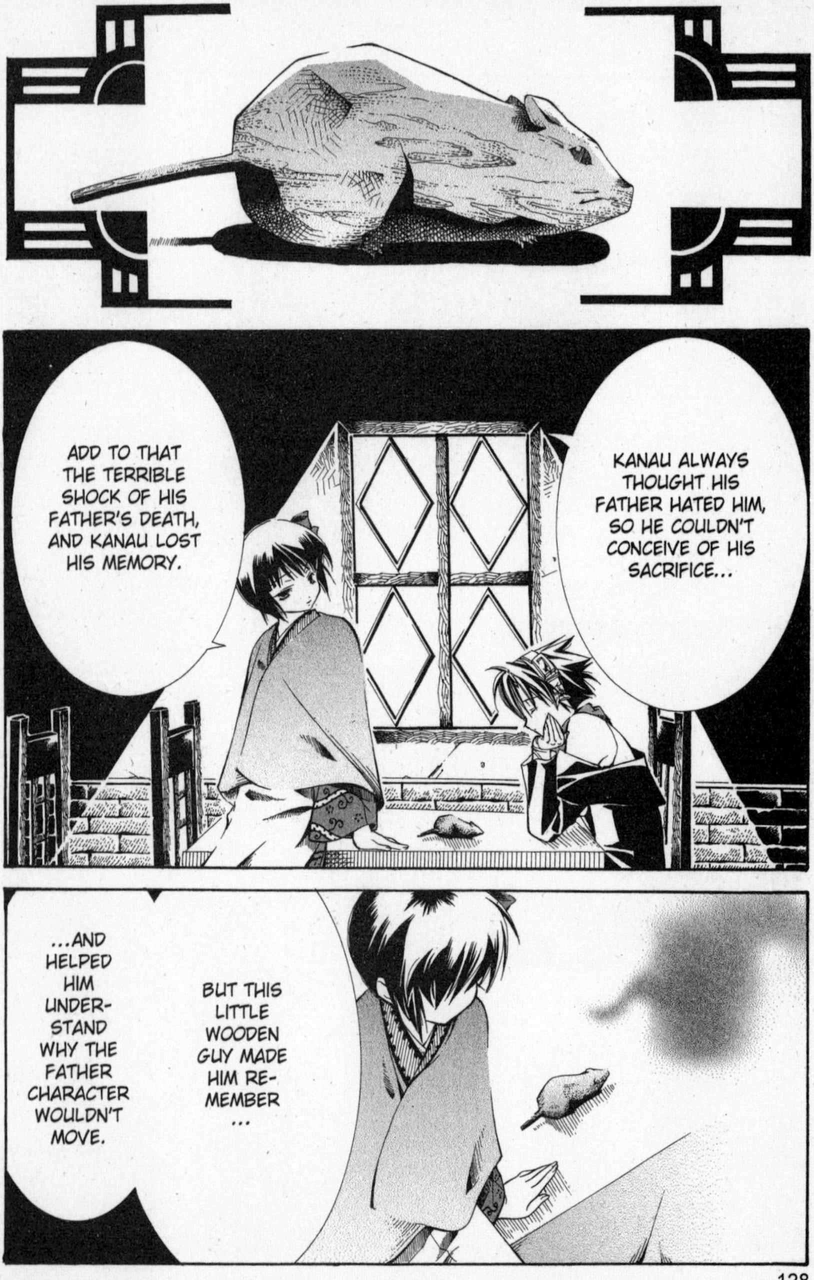
KANAU ALWAYS THOUGHT HIS FATHER HATED HIM, SO HE COULDN'T CONCEIVE OF HIS SACRIFICE...
ADD TO THAT THE TERRIBLE SHOCK OF HIS FATHER'S DEATH, AND KANAU LOST HIS MEMORY.
BUT THIS LITTLE WOODEN GUY MADE HIM RE-MEMBER...
...AND HELPED HIM UNDER-STAND WHY THE FATHER CHARACTER WOULDN'T MOVE.

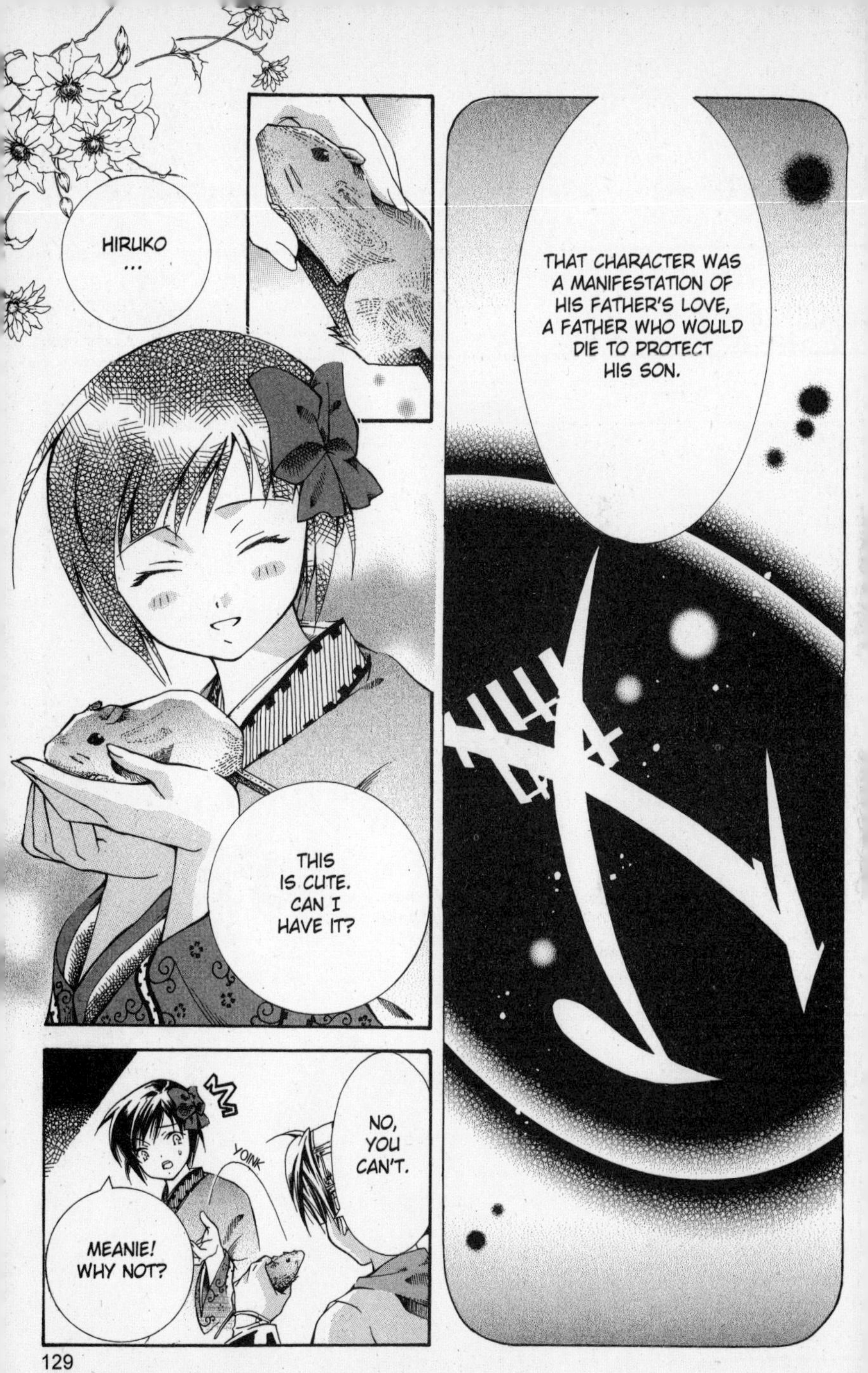
THAT CHARACTER WAS A MANIFESTATION OF HIS FATHER'S LOVE, A FATHER WHO WOULD DIE TO PROTECT HIS SON.
HIRUKO ...
THIS IS CUTE. CAN I HAVE IT?
NO, YOU CAN'T.
YOINK
MEANIE! WHY NOT?

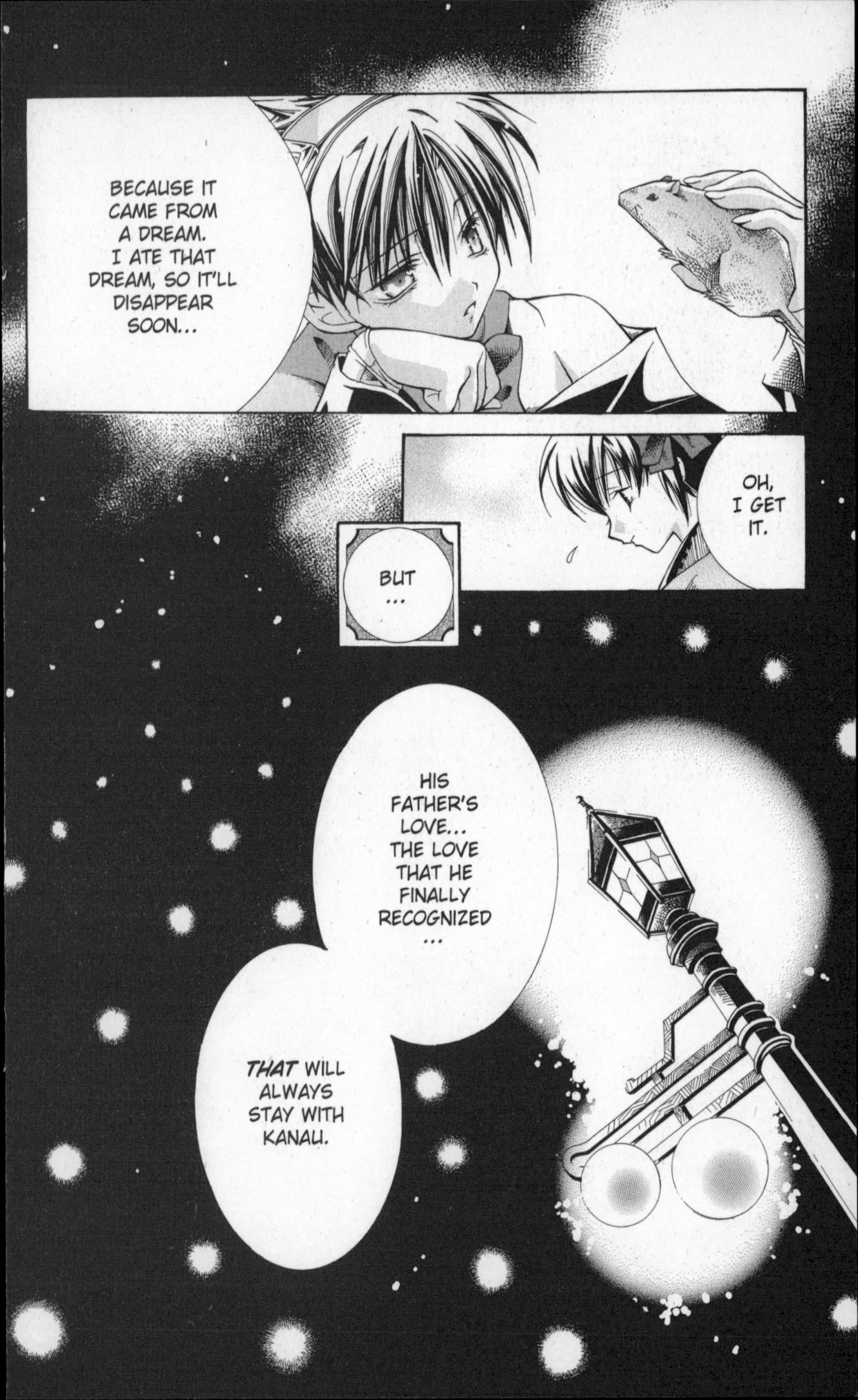
BECAUSE IT CAME FROM A DREAM. I ATE THAT DREAM, SO IT'LL DISAPPEAR SOON...
OH, I GET IT.
BUT ...
HIS FATHER'S LOVE... THE LOVE THAT HE FINALLY RECOGNIZED ...
THAT WILL ALWAYS STAY WITH KANAU.

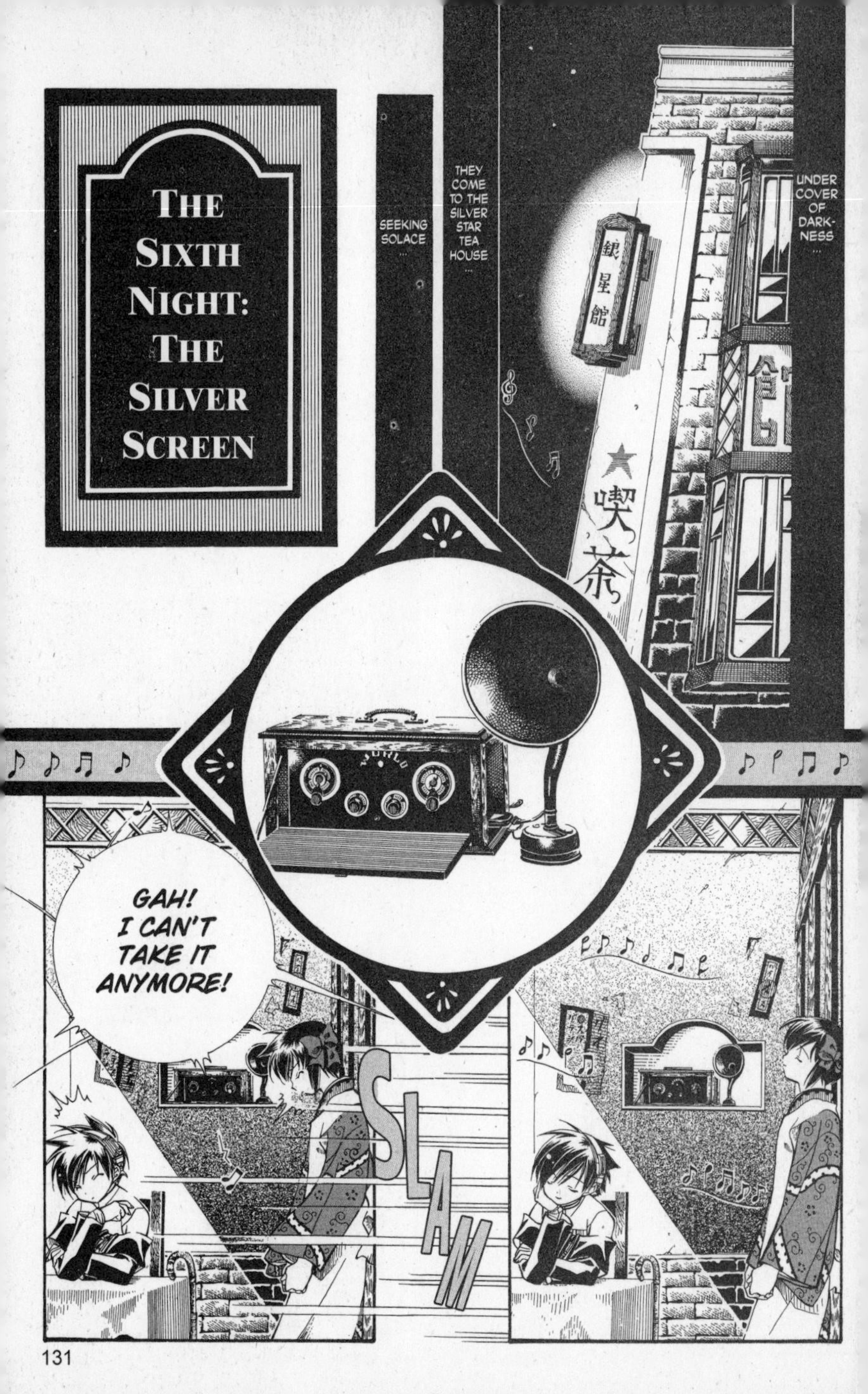
UNDER COVER OF DARKNESS...
銀星館
喫茶
THEY COME TO THE SILVER STAR TEA HOUSE...
SEEKING SOLACE...
THE SIXTH NIGHT: THE SILVER SCREEN
WORLD
GAH! I CAN'T TAKE IT ANYMORE!
SLAM

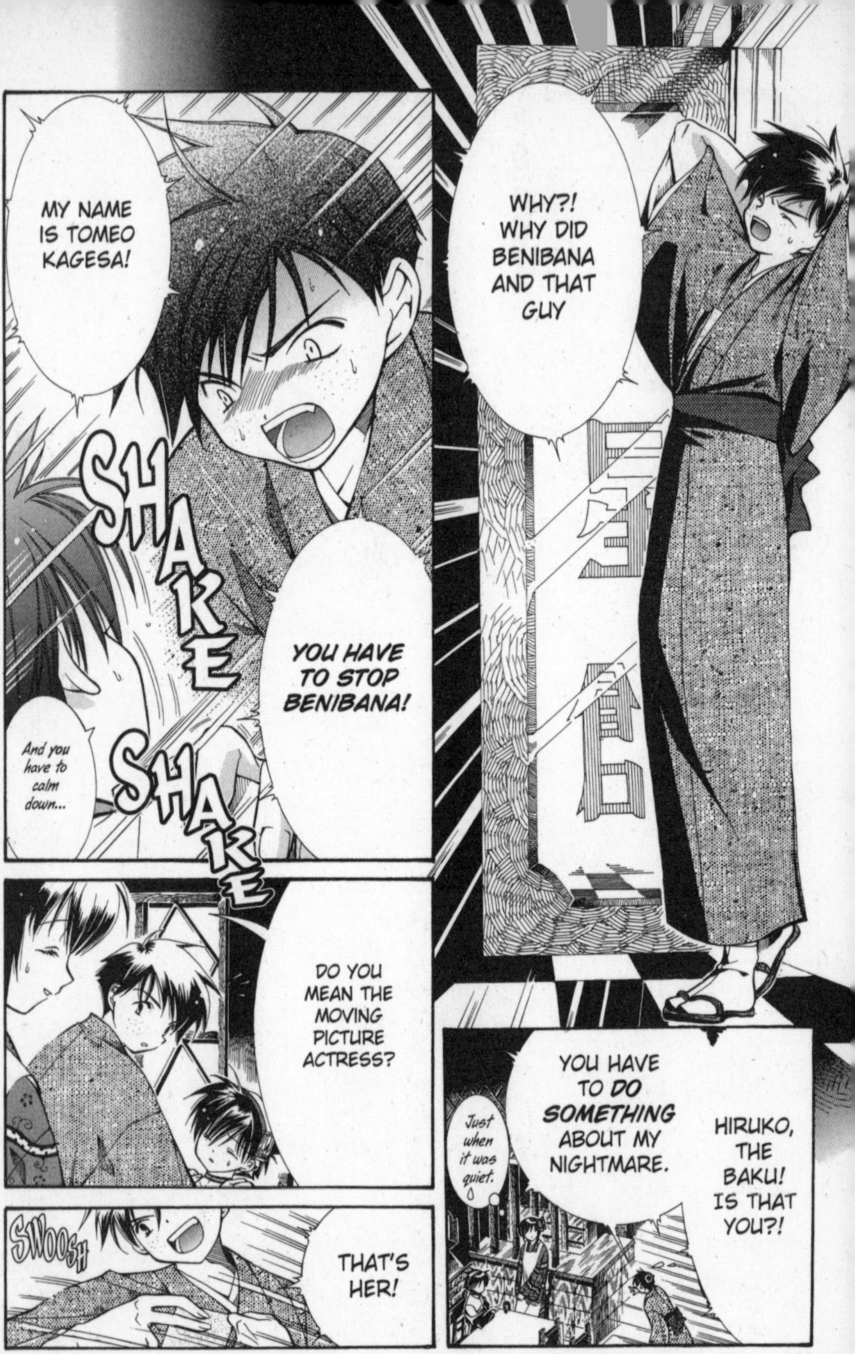
WHY?! WHY DID BENIBANA AND THAT GUY
MY NAME IS TOMEO KAGESA!
SHAKE SHAKE
YOU HAVE TO STOP BENIBANA!
SHAKE
And you have to calm down...
DO YOU MEAN THE MOVING PICTURE ACTRESS?
HIRUKO, THE BAKU! IS THAT YOU?!
YOU HAVE TO DO SOMETHING ABOUT MY NIGHTMARE.
Just when it was quiet.
SWOOSH
THAT'S HER!

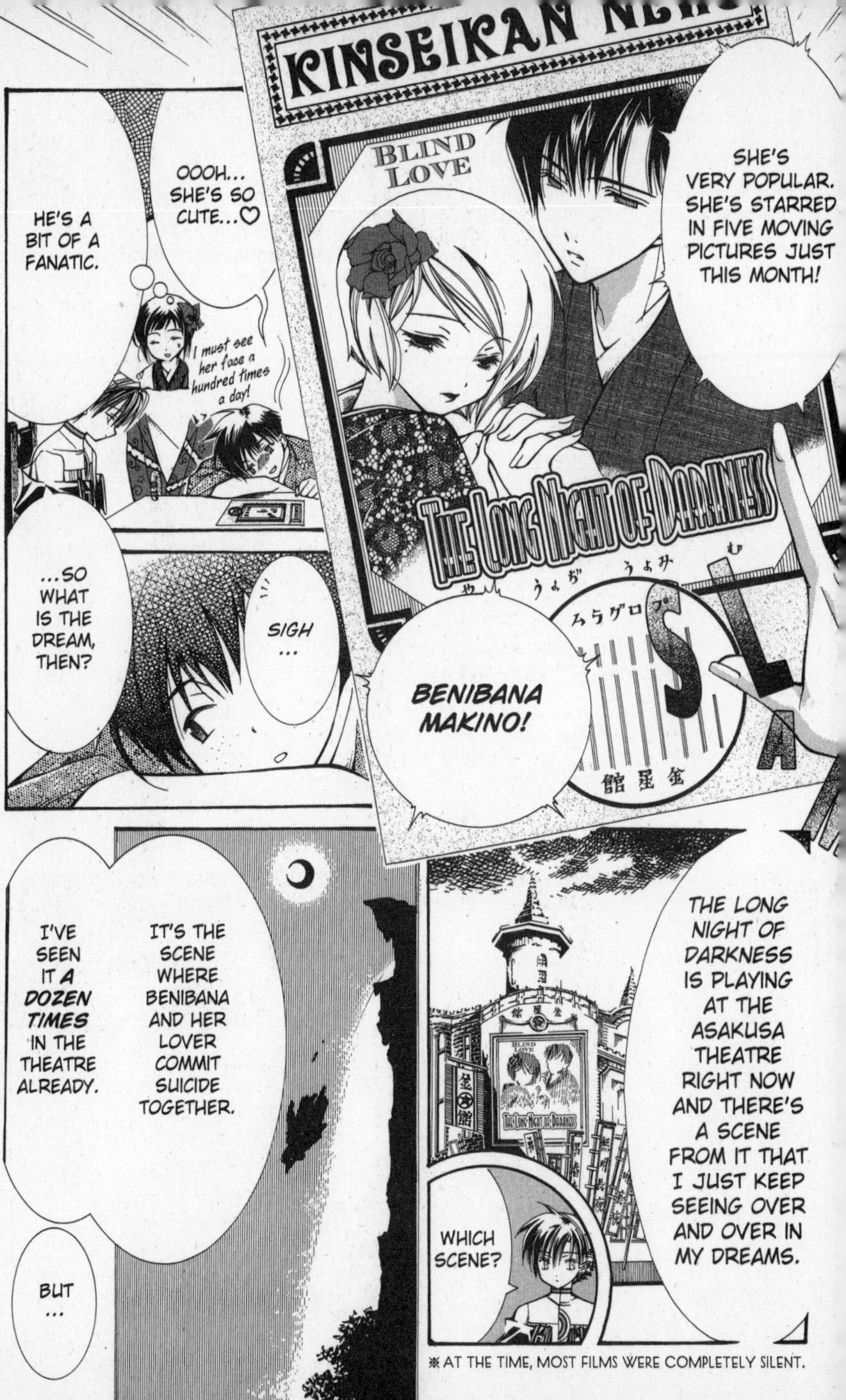
KINSEIKAN
BLIND LOVE
SHE'S VERY POPULAR. SHE'S STARRED IN FIVE MOVING PICTURES JUST THIS MONTH!
THE LONG NIGHT OF DARKNESS
BENIBANA MAKINO!
OOOH... SHE'S SO CUTE...♡
HE'S A BIT OF A FANATIC.
I must see her face a hundred times a day!
SIGH ...
...SO WHAT IS THE DREAM, THEN?
THE LONG NIGHT OF DARKNESS IS PLAYING AT THE ASAKUSA THEATRE RIGHT NOW AND THERE'S A SCENE FROM IT THAT I JUST KEEP SEEING OVER AND OVER IN MY DREAMS.
BLIND LOVE
THE LONG NIGHT OF DARKNESS
WHICH SCENE?
IT'S THE SCENE WHERE BENIBANA AND HER LOVER COMMIT SUICIDE TOGETHER.
I'VE SEEN IT A DOZEN TIMES IN THE THEATRE ALREADY.
BUT ...

※ AT THE TIME, MOST FILMS WERE COMPLETELY SILENT.

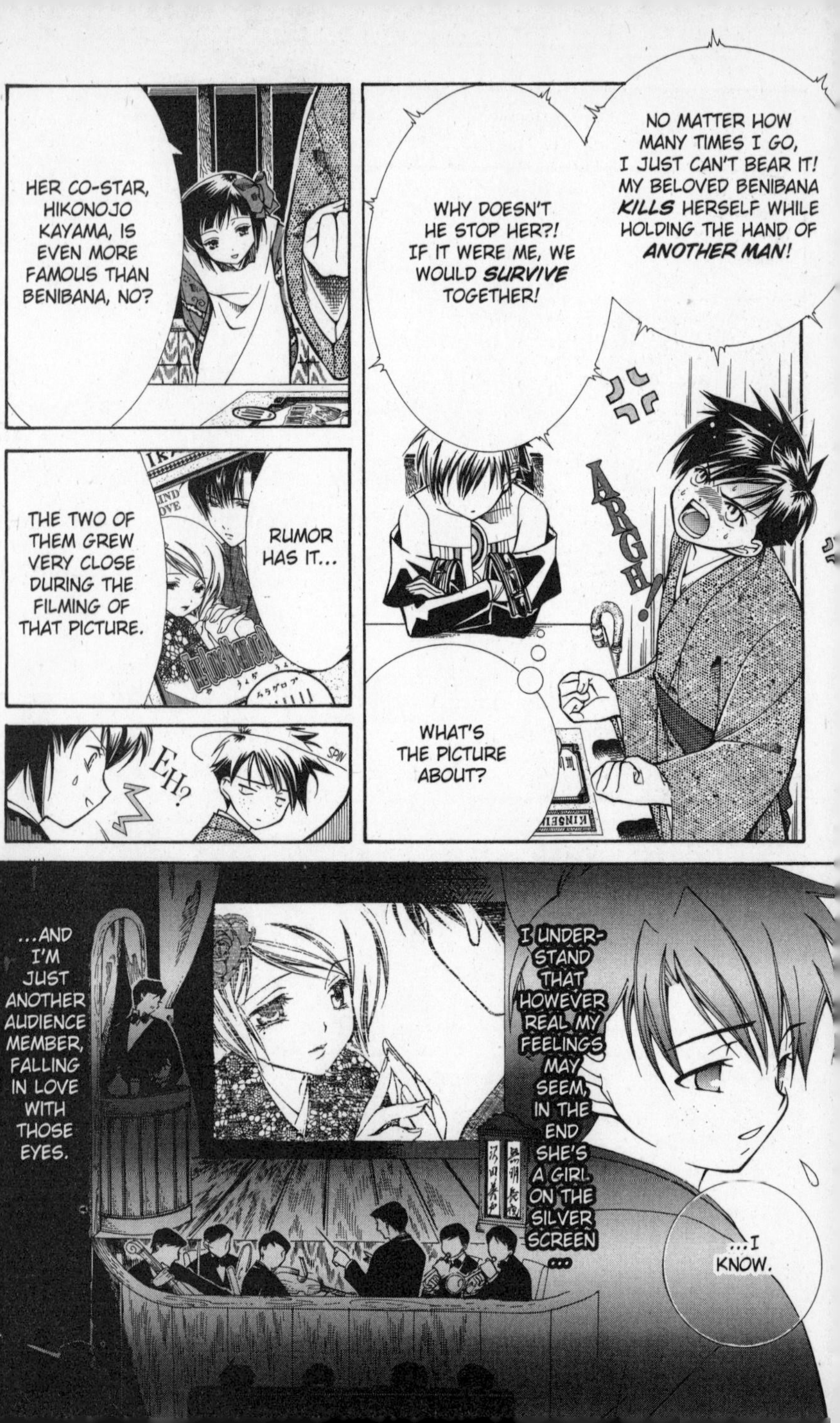
NO MATTER HOW MANY TIMES I GO, I JUST CAN'T BEAR IT! MY BELOVED BENIBANA **KILLS** HERSELF WHILE HOLDING THE HAND OF **ANOTHER MAN**!
WHY DOESN'T HE STOP HER?! IF IT WERE ME, WE WOULD **SURVIVE** TOGETHER!
ARGH!
WHAT'S THE PICTURE ABOUT?
HER CO-STAR, HIKONOJO KAYAMA, IS EVEN MORE FAMOUS THAN BENIBANA, NO?
RUMOR HAS IT...
THE TWO OF THEM GREW VERY CLOSE DURING THE FILMING OF THAT PICTURE.
SPIN
EH?
...I KNOW.
I UNDER-STAND THAT HOWEVER REAL MY FEELINGS MAY SEEM, IN THE END SHE'S A GIRL ON THE SILVER SCREEN...
...AND I'M JUST ANOTHER AUDIENCE MEMBER, FALLING IN LOVE WITH THOSE EYES.

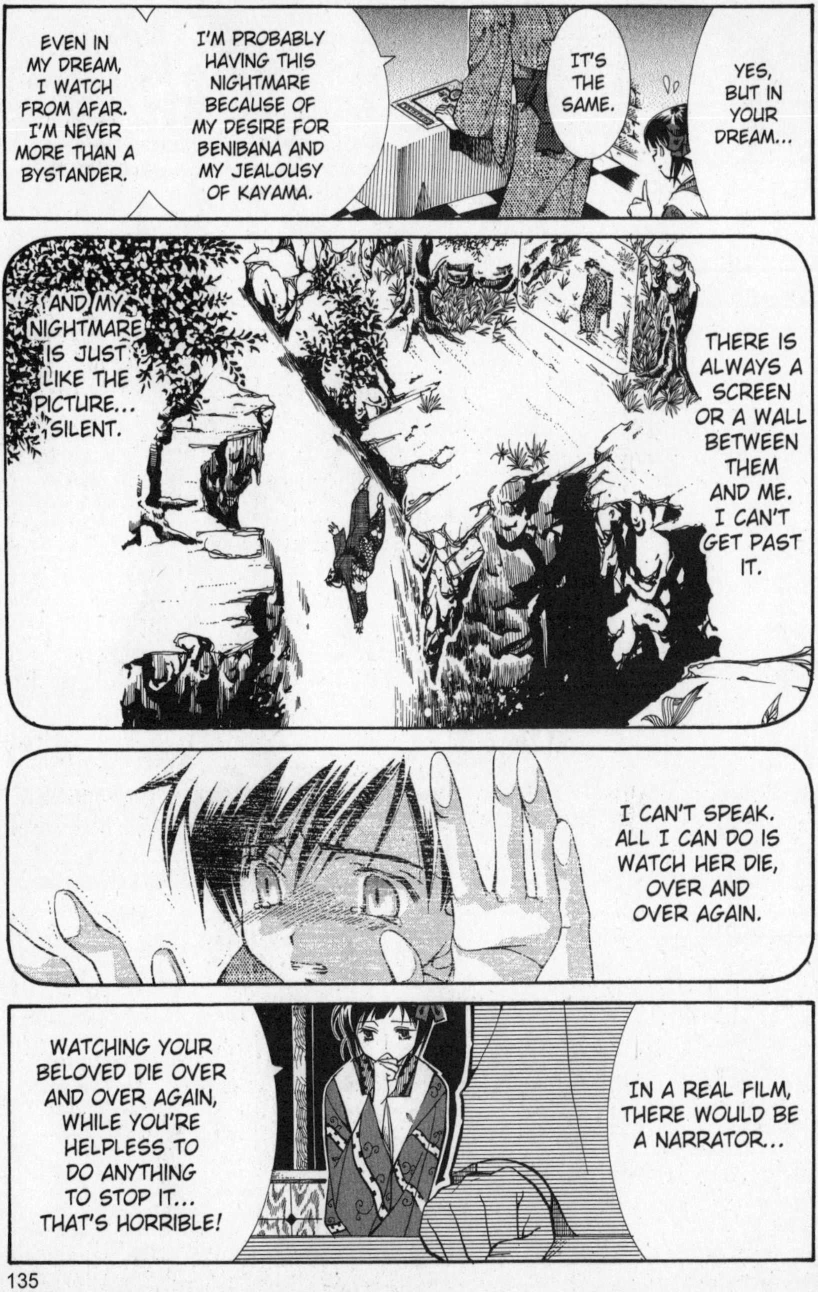
YES, BUT IN YOUR DREAM...
IT'S THE SAME.
I'M PROBABLY HAVING THIS NIGHTMARE BECAUSE OF MY DESIRE FOR BENIBANA AND MY JEALOUSY OF KAYAMA.
EVEN IN MY DREAM, I WATCH FROM AFAR. I'M NEVER MORE THAN A BYSTANDER.
THERE IS ALWAYS A SCREEN OR A WALL BETWEEN THEM AND ME. I CAN'T GET PAST IT.
AND MY NIGHTMARE IS JUST LIKE THE PICTURE... SILENT.
I CAN'T SPEAK. ALL I CAN DO IS WATCH HER DIE, OVER AND OVER AGAIN.
IN A REAL FILM, THERE WOULD BE A NARRATOR...
WATCHING YOUR BELOVED DIE OVER AND OVER AGAIN, WHILE YOU'RE HELPLESS TO DO ANYTHING TO STOP IT... THAT'S HORRIBLE!

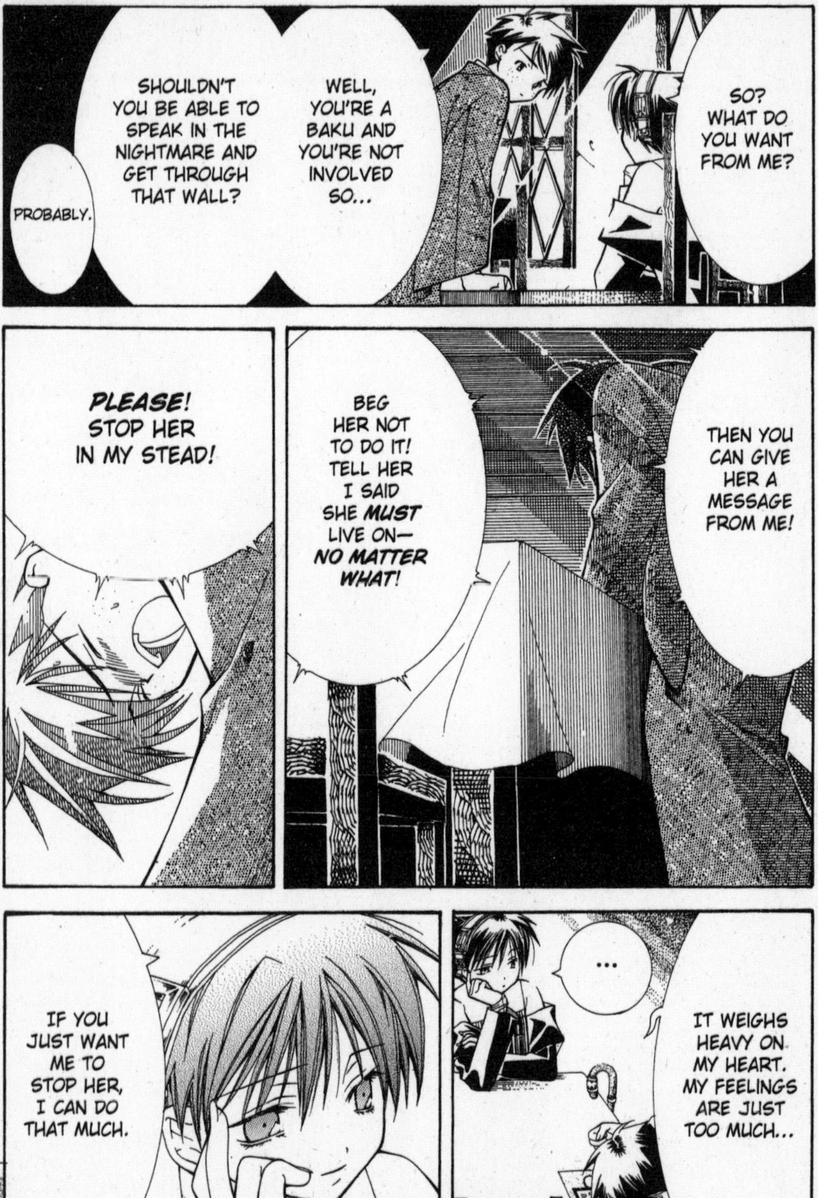
SO? WHAT DO YOU WANT FROM ME?
WELL, YOU'RE A BAKU AND YOU'RE NOT INVOLVED SO...
SHOULDN'T YOU BE ABLE TO SPEAK IN THE NIGHTMARE AND GET THROUGH THAT WALL?
PROBABLY.
THEN YOU CAN GIVE HER A MESSAGE FROM ME!
BEG HER NOT TO DO IT! TELL HER I SAID SHE *MUST* LIVE ON— *NO MATTER WHAT*!
PLEASE! STOP HER IN MY STEAD!
IT WEIGHS HEAVY ON MY HEART. MY FEELINGS ARE JUST TOO MUCH...
...
IF YOU JUST WANT ME TO STOP HER, I CAN DO THAT MUCH.

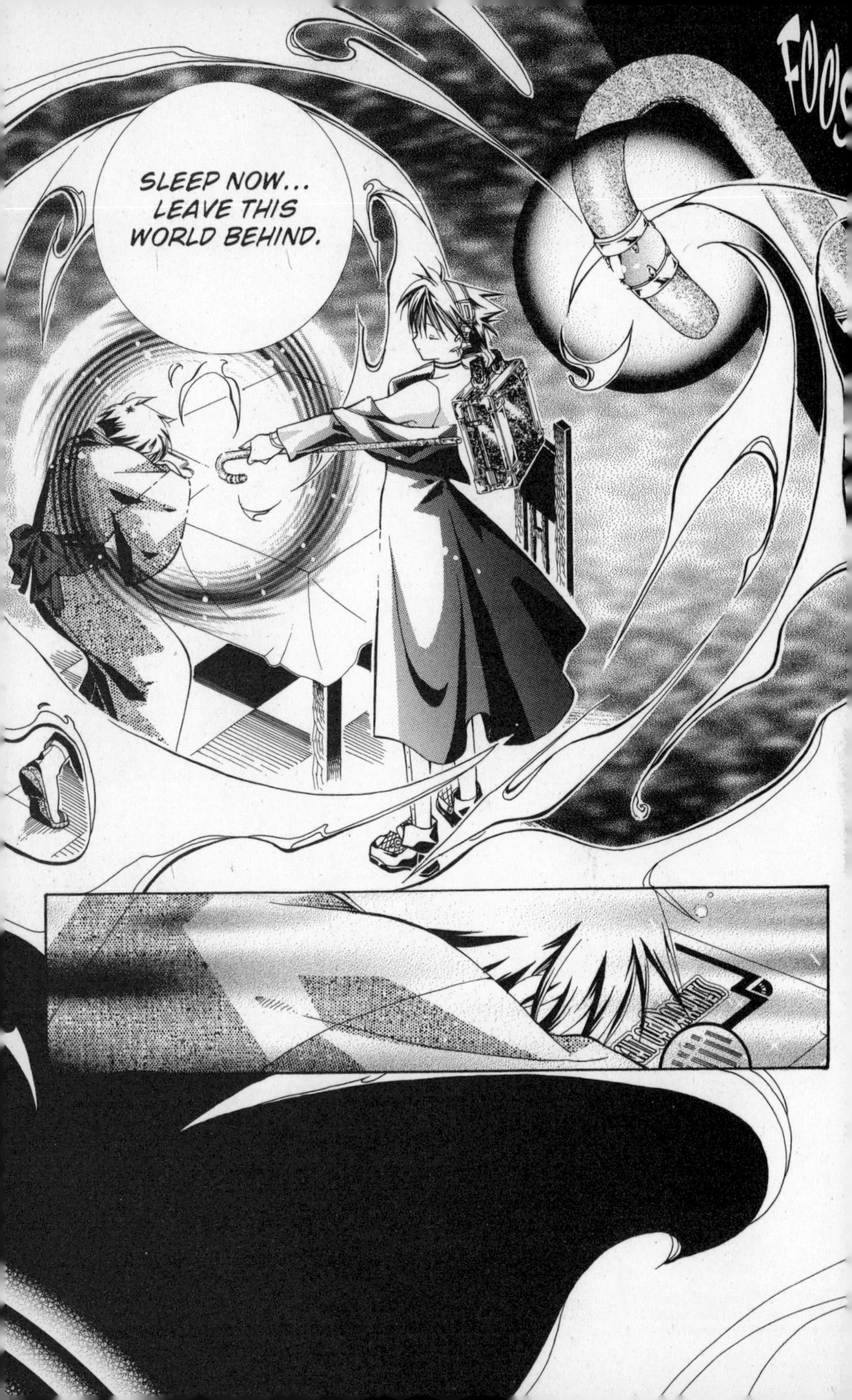
SLEEP NOW... LEAVE THIS WORLD BEHIND.

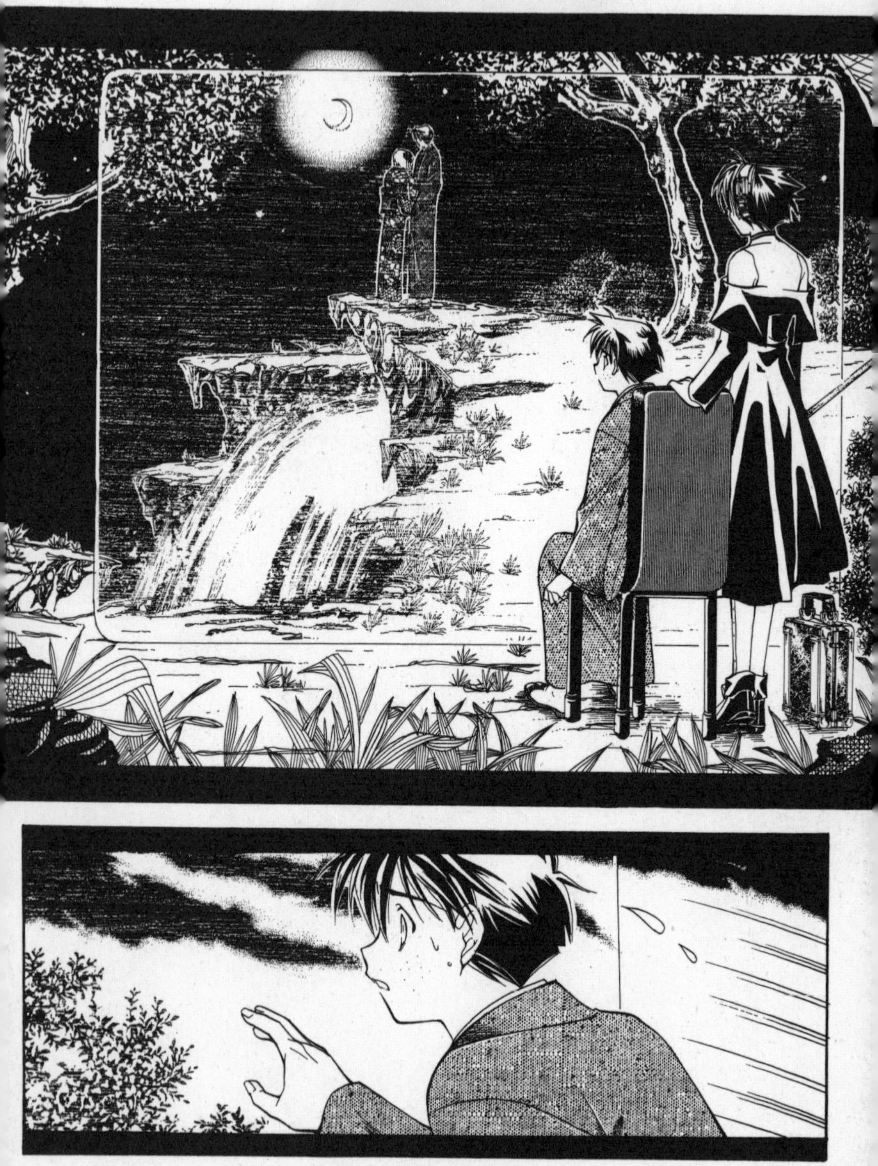

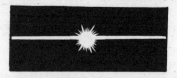

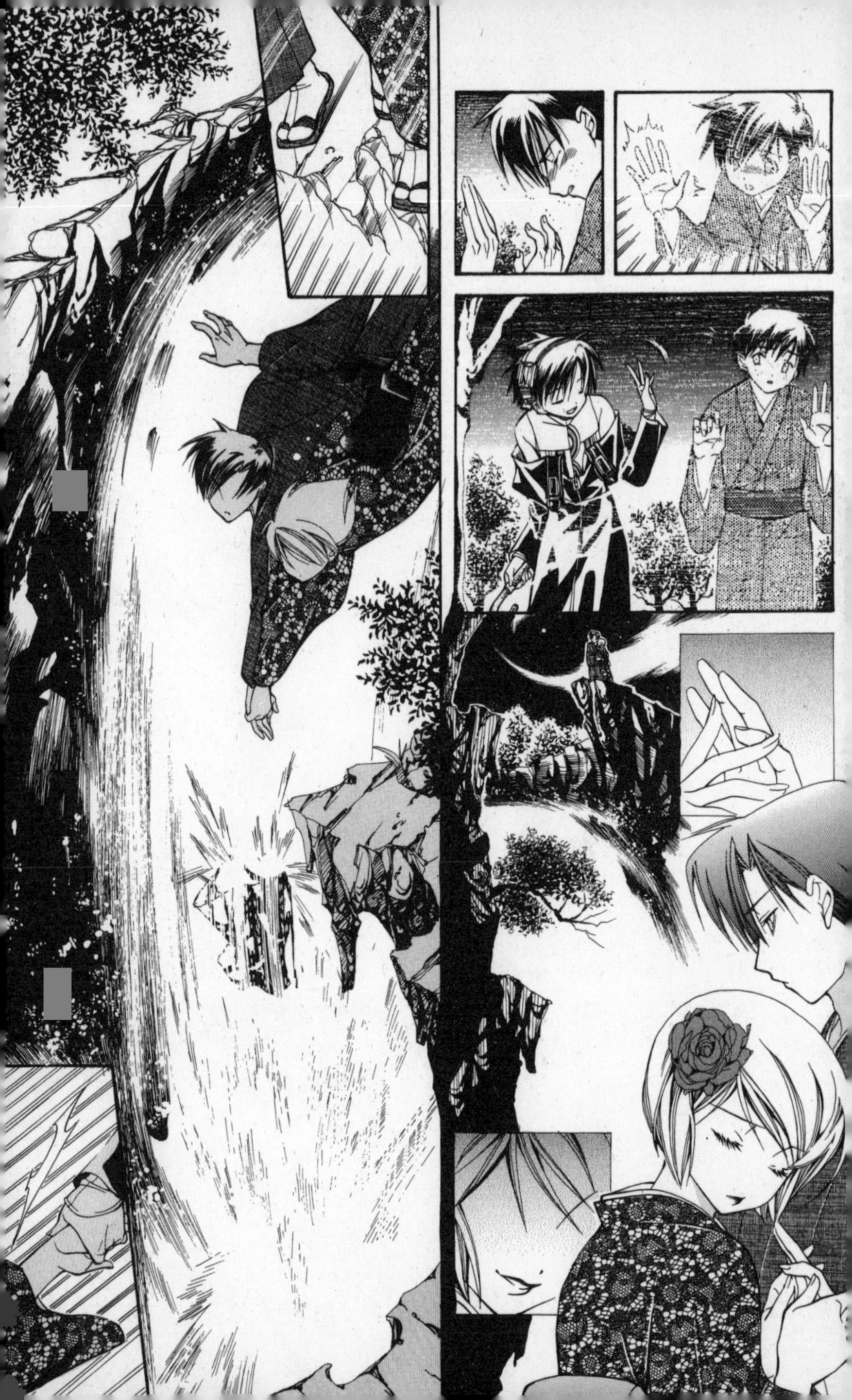

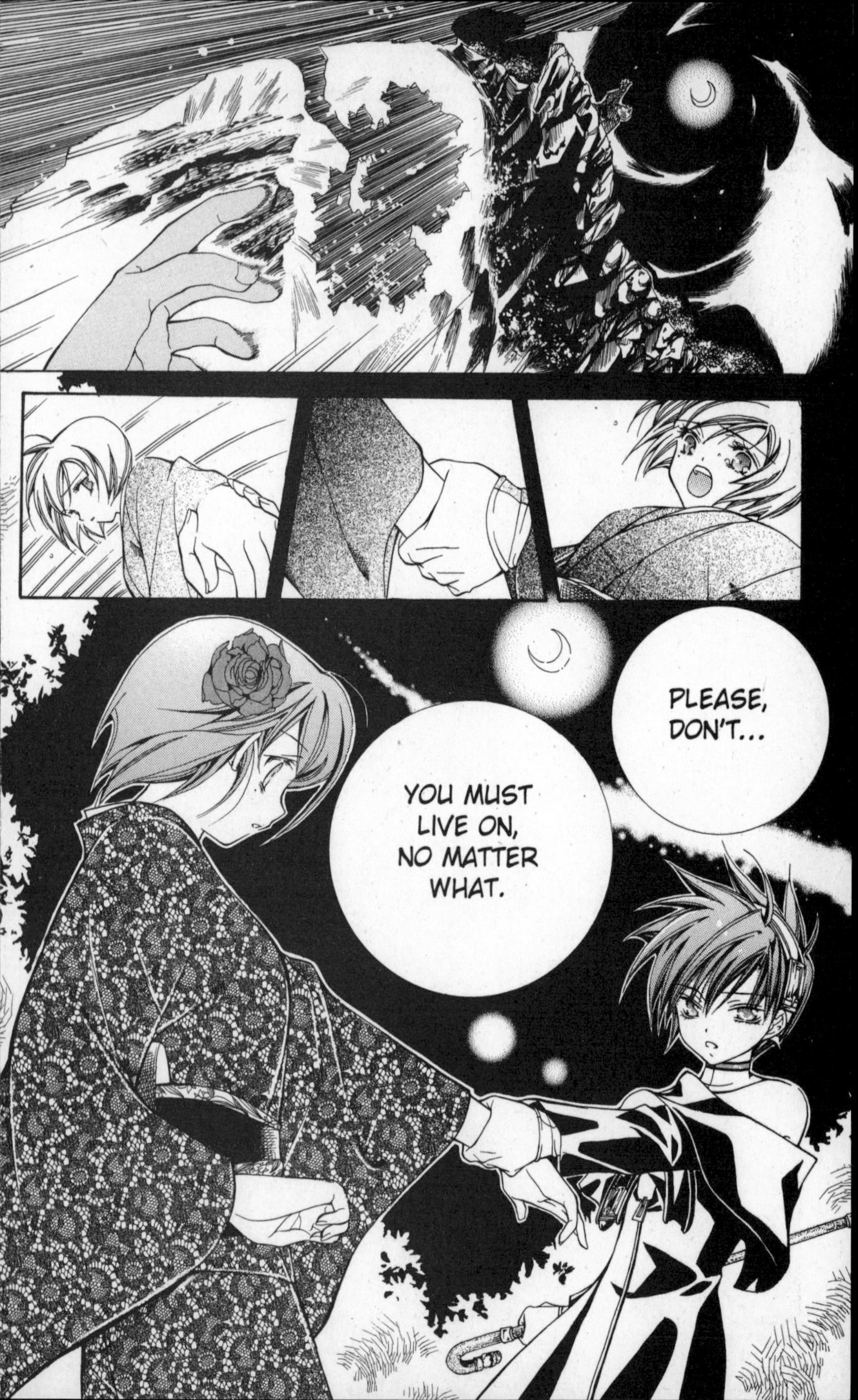
PLEASE, DON'T...
YOU MUST LIVE ON, NO MATTER WHAT.

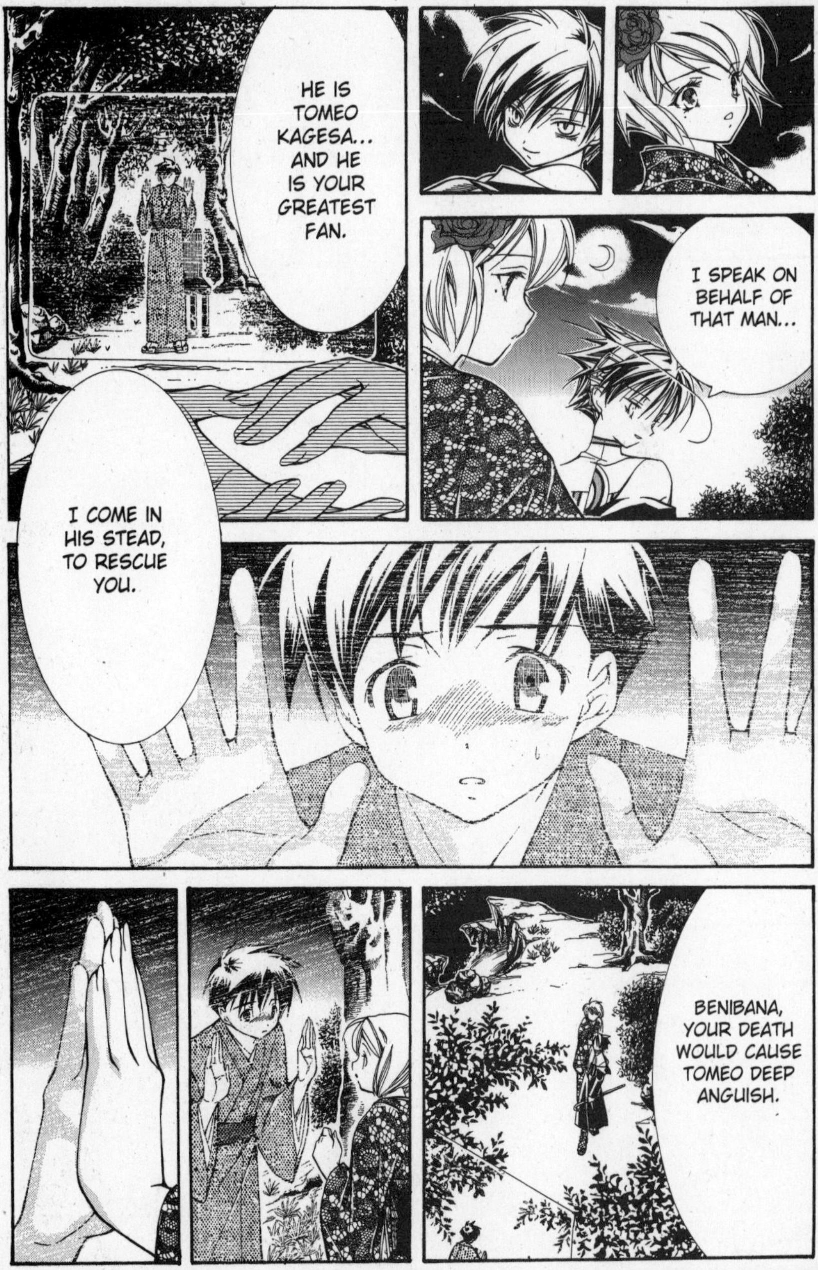
I SPEAK ON BEHALF OF THAT MAN...
HE IS TOMEO KAGESA... AND HE IS YOUR GREATEST FAN.
I COME IN HIS STEAD, TO RESCUE YOU.
BENIBANA, YOUR DEATH WOULD CAUSE TOMEO DEEP ANGUISH.

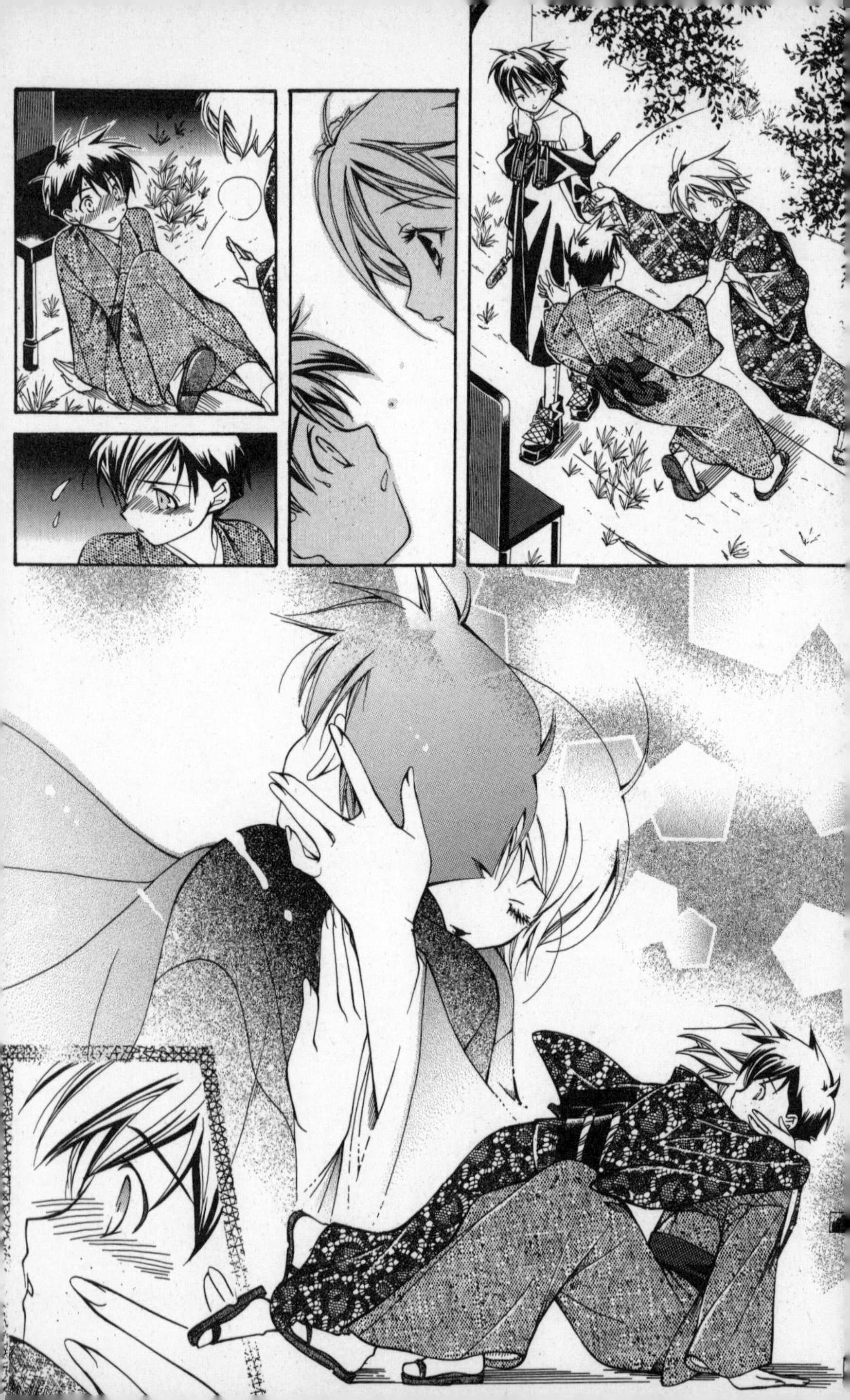

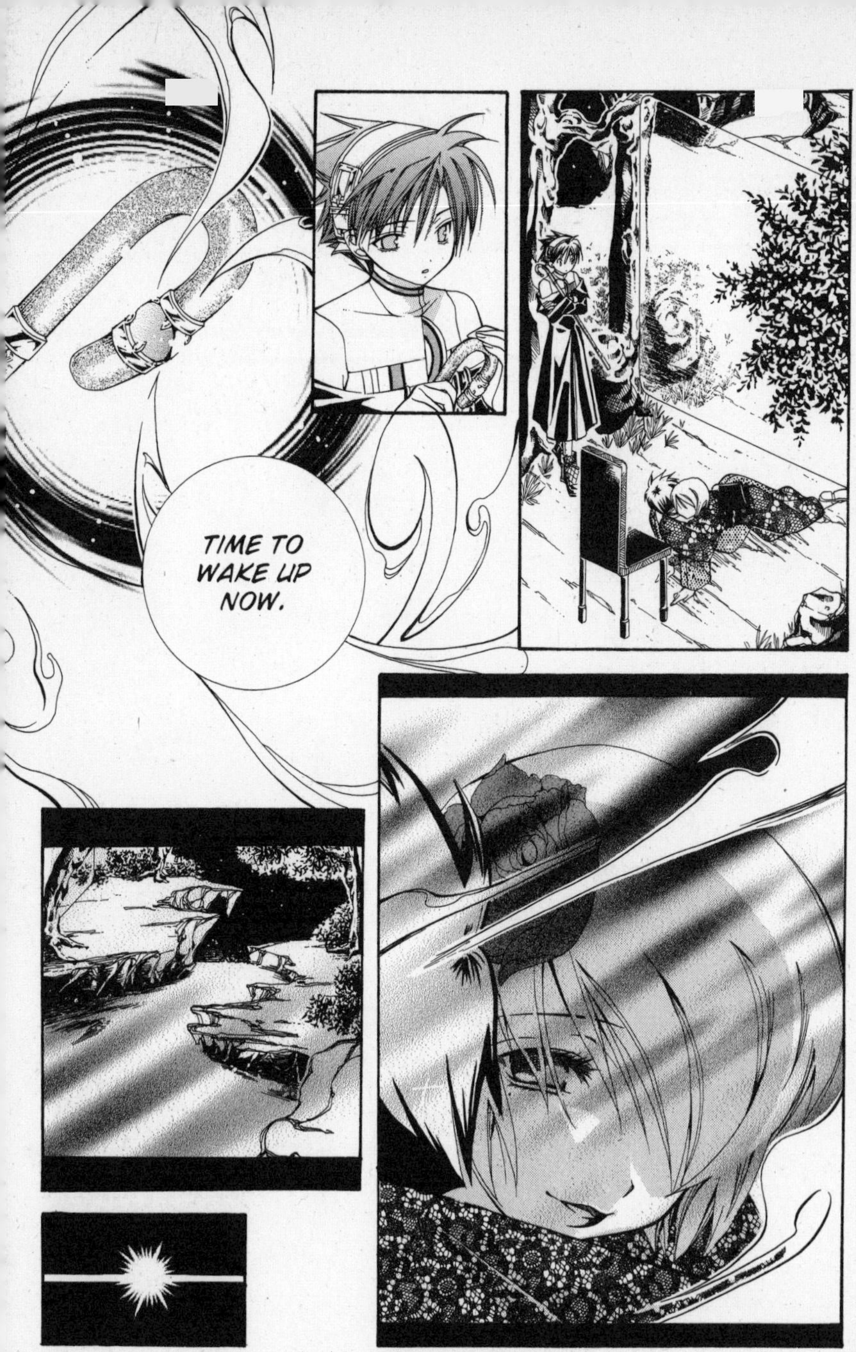
TIME TO WAKE UP NOW.

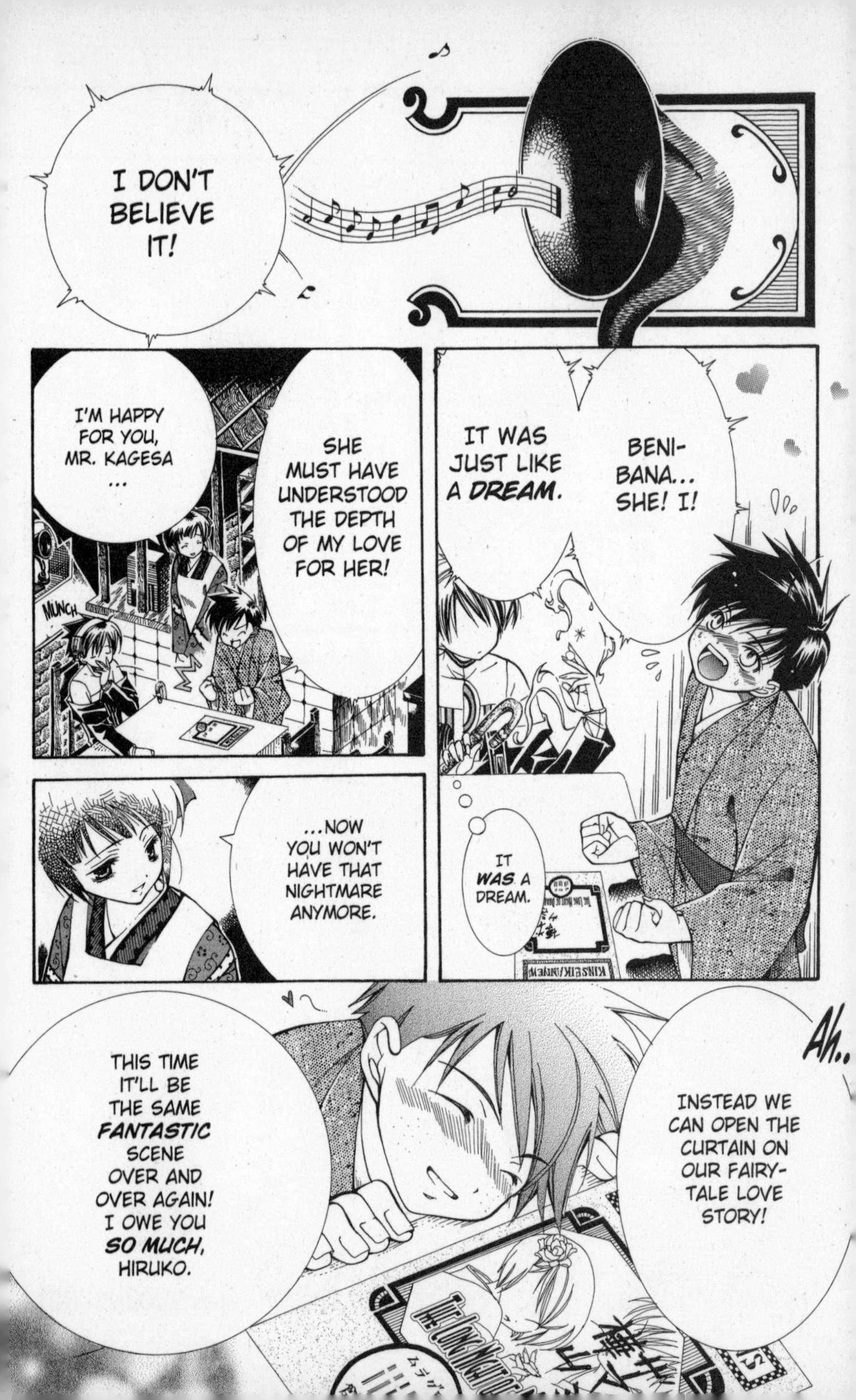
I DON'T BELIEVE IT!
BENI-BANA... SHE! I!
IT WAS JUST LIKE A DREAM.
SHE MUST HAVE UNDERSTOOD THE DEPTH OF MY LOVE FOR HER!
I'M HAPPY FOR YOU, MR. KAGESA...
MUNCH
IT WAS A DREAM.
...NOW YOU WON'T HAVE THAT NIGHTMARE ANYMORE.
Ah..
INSTEAD WE CAN OPEN THE CURTAIN ON OUR FAIRY-TALE LOVE STORY!
THIS TIME IT'LL BE THE SAME FANTASTIC SCENE OVER AND OVER AGAIN! I OWE YOU SO MUCH, HIRUKO.

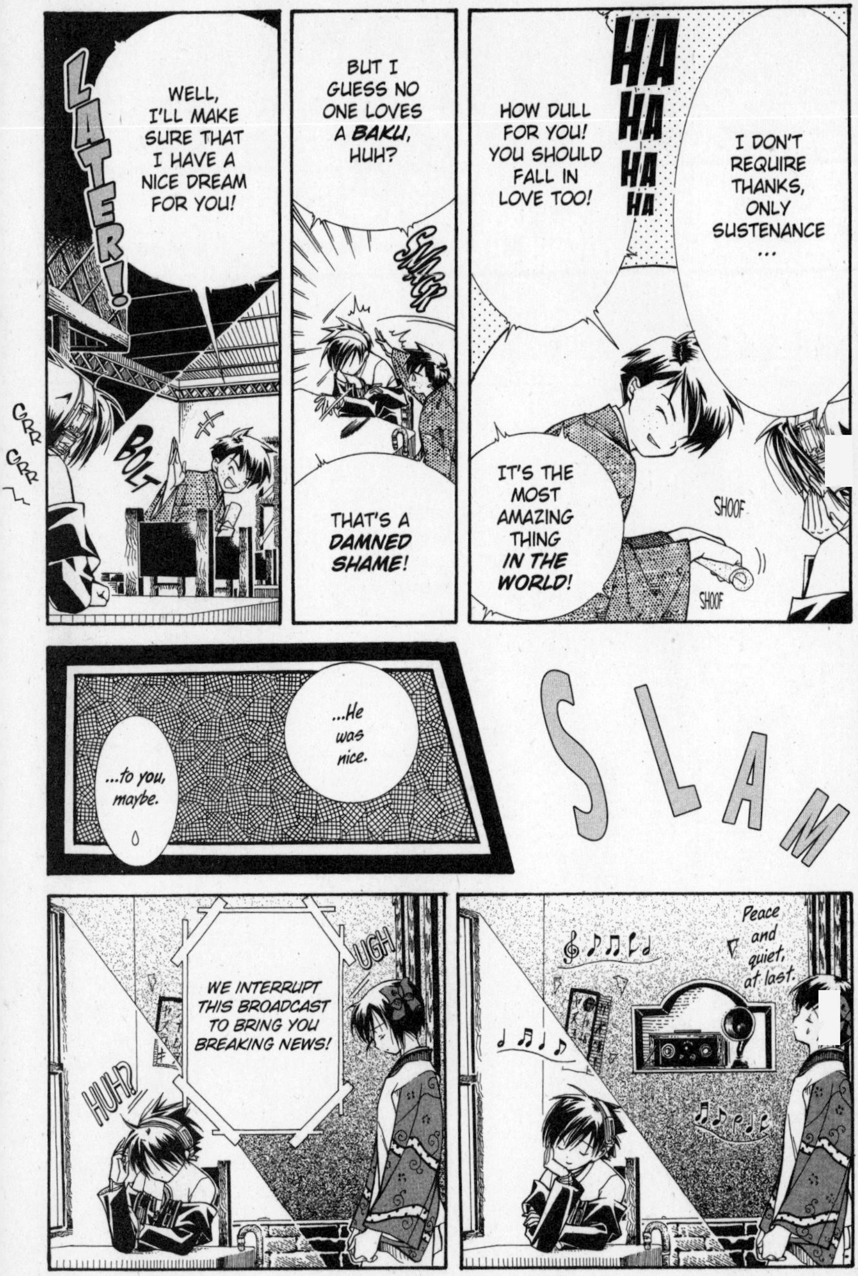
I DON'T REQUIRE THANKS, ONLY SUSTENANCE...
HA HA HA HA HA HA
HOW DULL FOR YOU! YOU SHOULD FALL IN LOVE TOO!
IT'S THE MOST AMAZING THING *IN THE WORLD*!
SHOOF
SHOOF
BUT I GUESS NO ONE LOVES A *BAKU*, HUH?
SMACK
THAT'S A *DAMNED SHAME*!
WELL, I'LL MAKE SURE THAT I HAVE A NICE DREAM FOR YOU!
LATER!
BOLT
GRR
GRR
SLAM
...He was nice.
...to you, maybe.
Peace and quiet, at last.
UGH
WE INTERRUPT THIS BROADCAST TO BRING YOU BREAKING NEWS!
HUH?

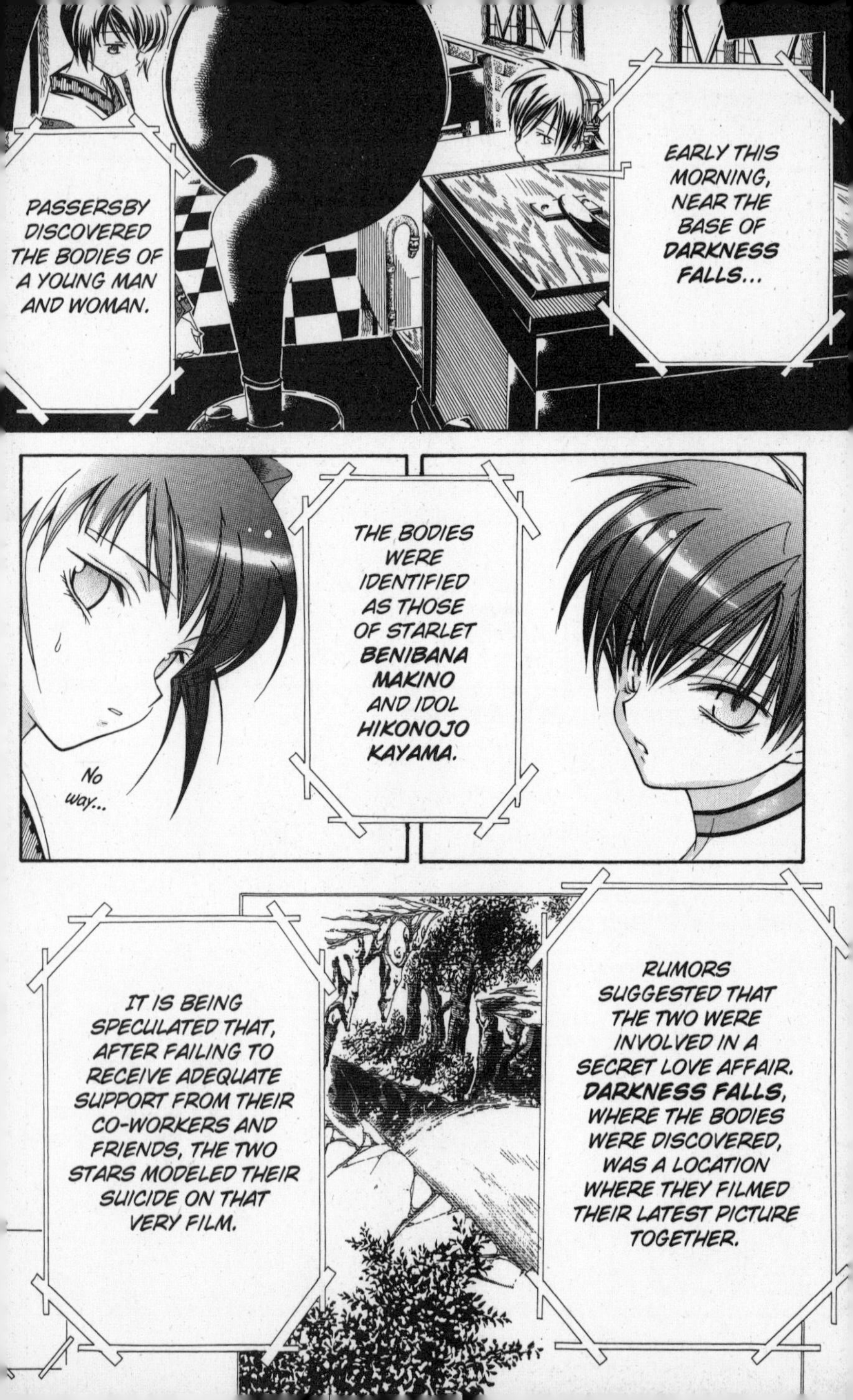
EARLY THIS MORNING, NEAR THE BASE OF DARKNESS FALLS...
PASSERSBY DISCOVERED THE BODIES OF A YOUNG MAN AND WOMAN.
THE BODIES WERE IDENTIFIED AS THOSE OF STARLET BENIBANA MAKINO AND IDOL HIKONOJO KAYAMA.
No way...
RUMORS SUGGESTED THAT THE TWO WERE INVOLVED IN A SECRET LOVE AFFAIR. DARKNESS FALLS, WHERE THE BODIES WERE DISCOVERED, WAS A LOCATION WHERE THEY FILMED THEIR LATEST PICTURE TOGETHER.
IT IS BEING SPECULATED THAT, AFTER FAILING TO RECEIVE ADEQUATE SUPPORT FROM THEIR CO-WORKERS AND FRIENDS, THE TWO STARS MODELED THEIR SUICIDE ON THAT VERY FILM.

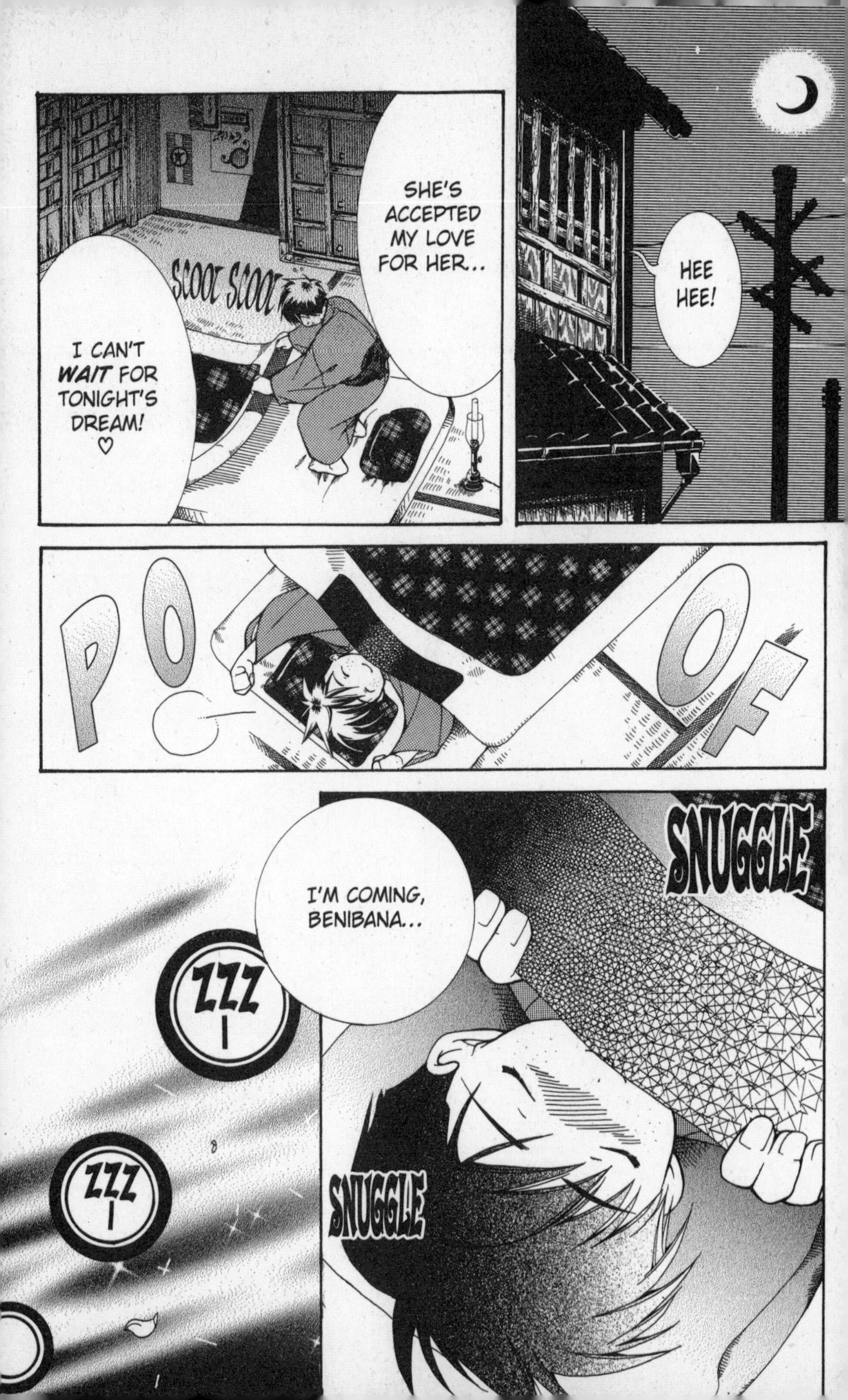

HEE HEE!
SHE'S ACCEPTED MY LOVE FOR HER...
SCOOT SCOOT
I CAN'T WAIT FOR TONIGHT'S DREAM! ♡
POOF
SNUGGLE
I'M COMING, BENIBANA...
SNUGGLE
ZZZ
ZZZ

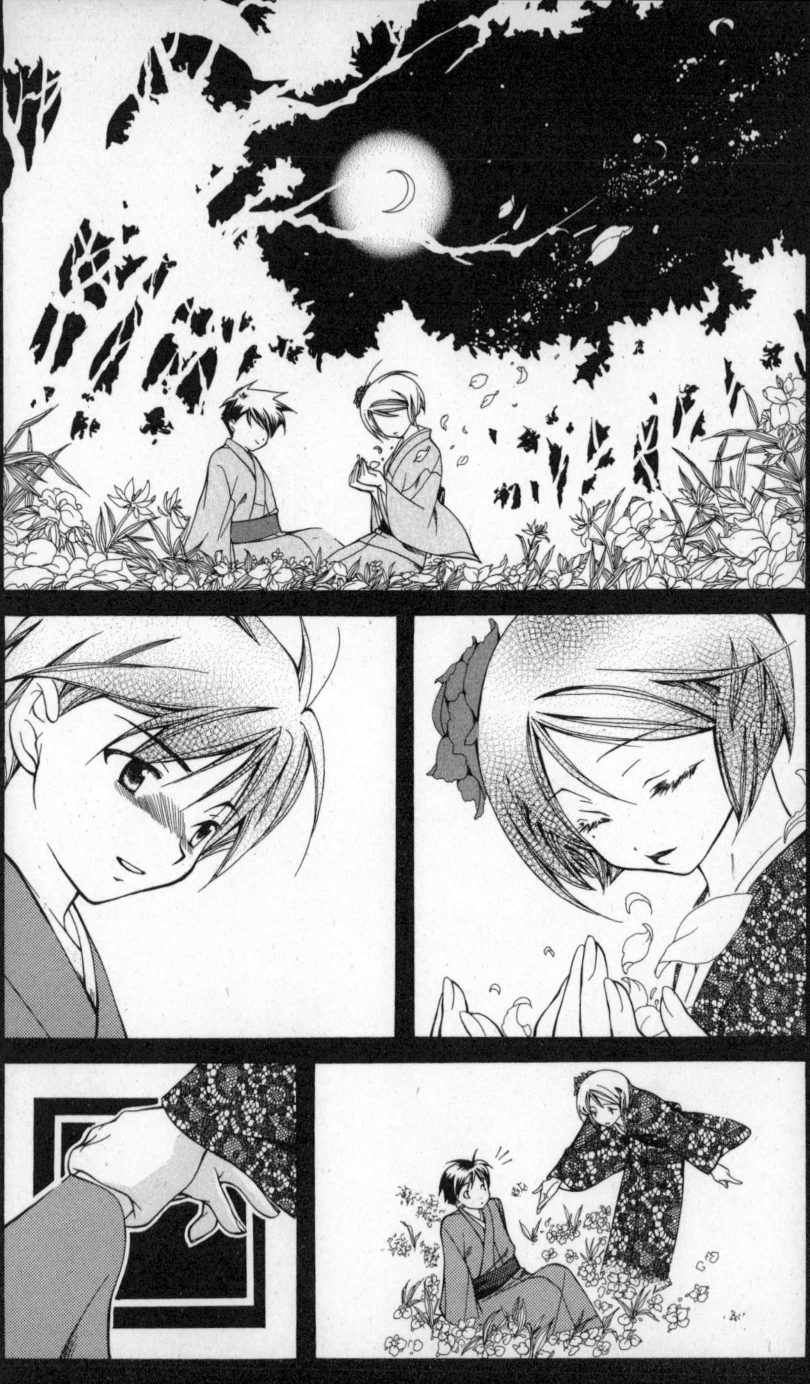

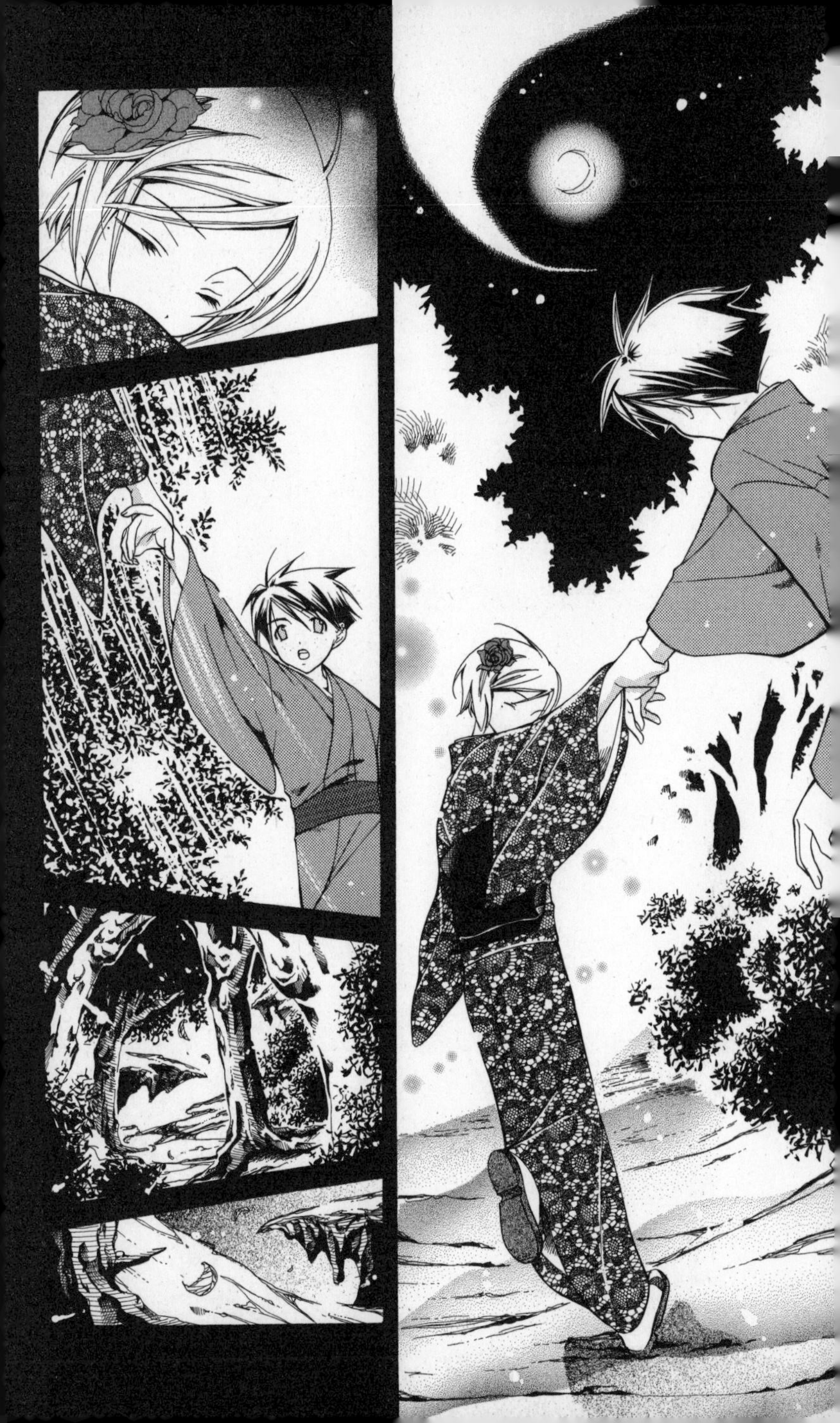

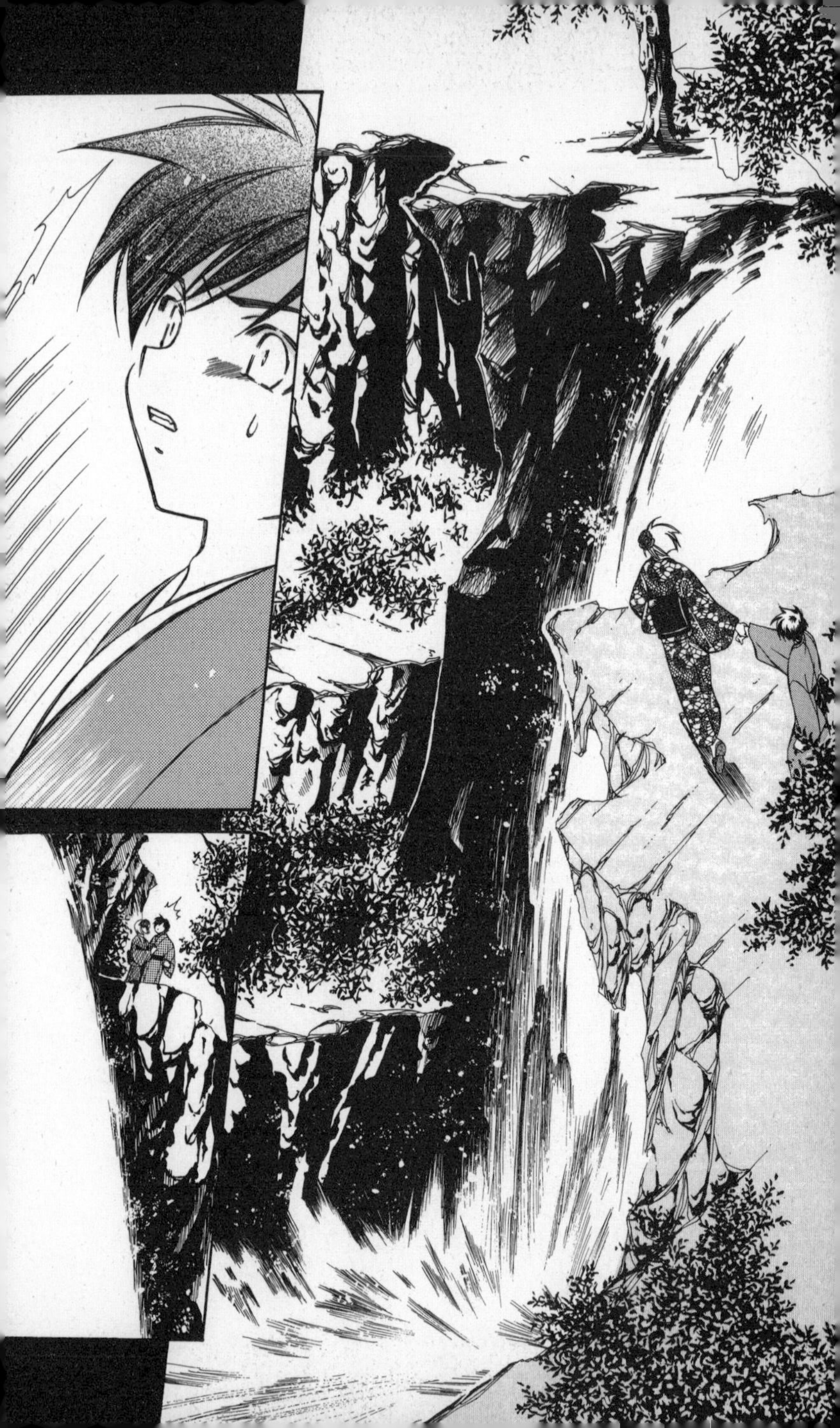

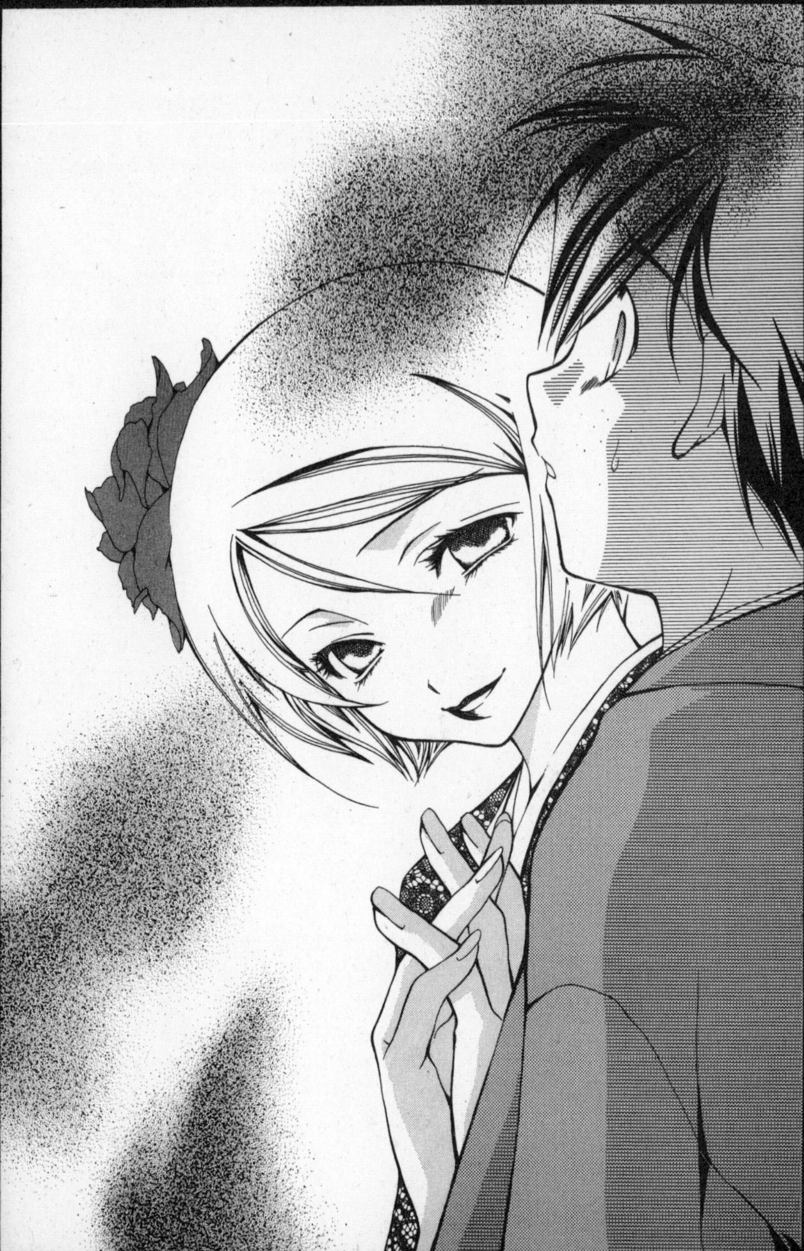

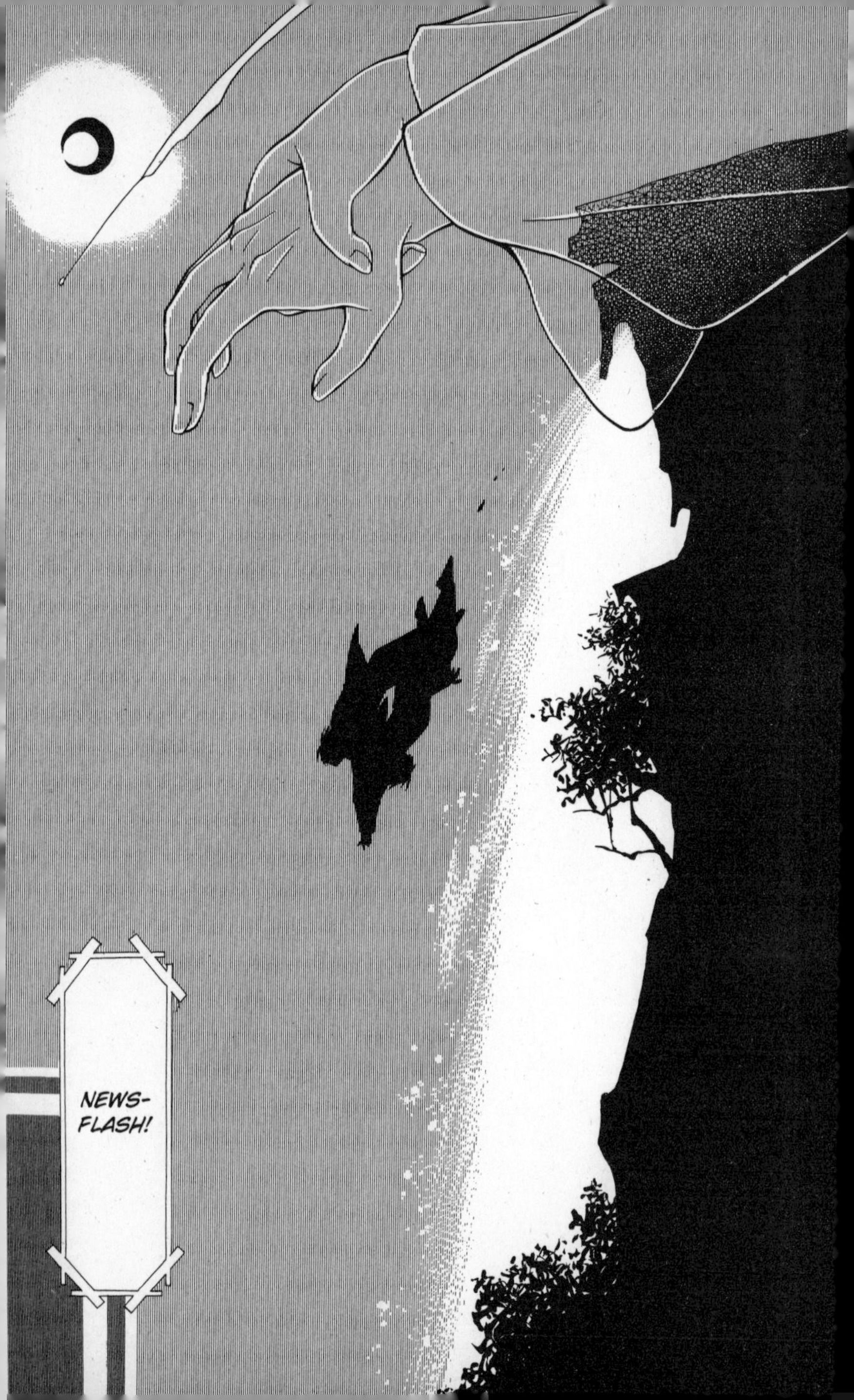
NEWS-
FLASH!

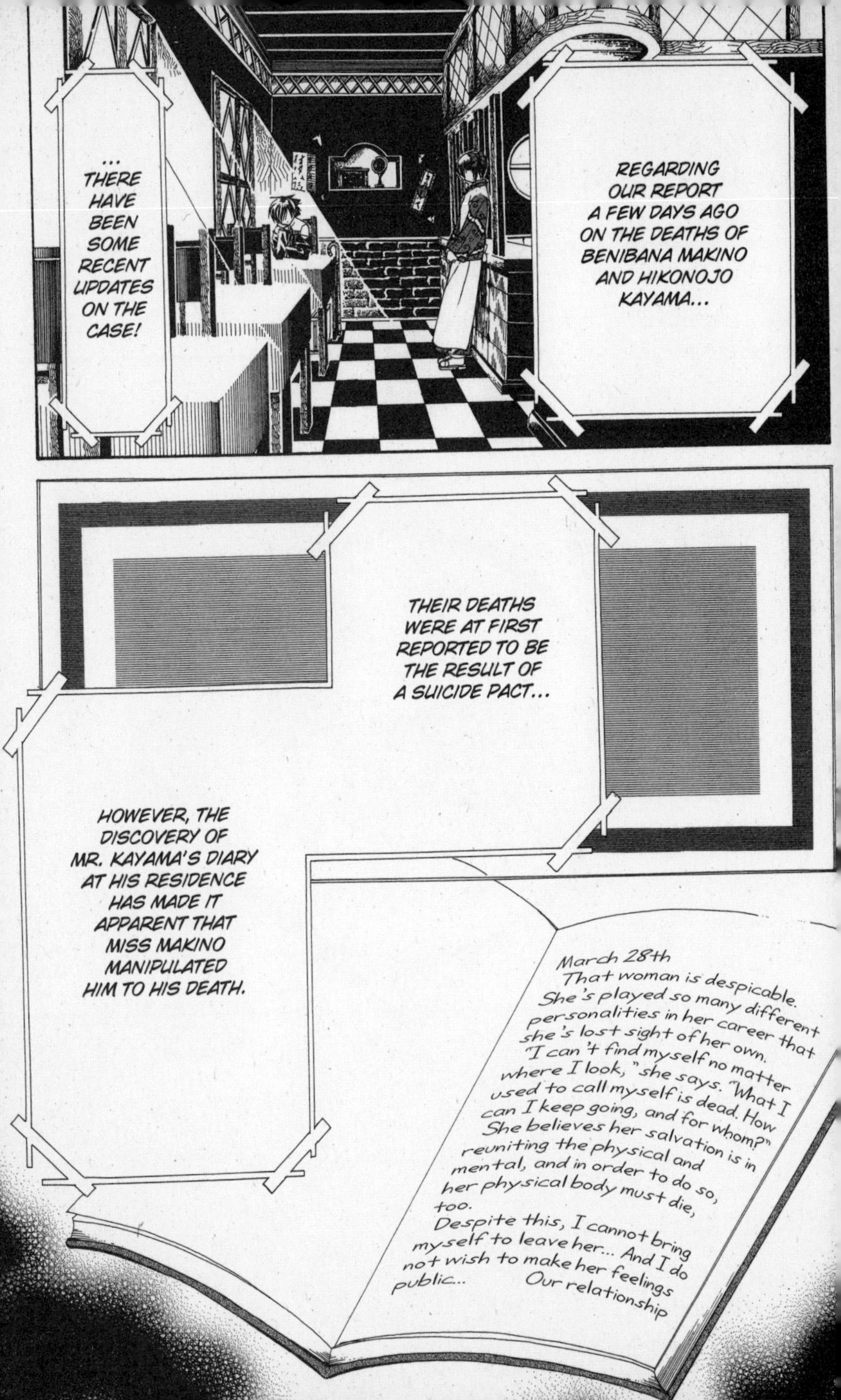
REGARDING OUR REPORT A FEW DAYS AGO ON THE DEATHS OF BENIBANA MAKINO AND HIKONOJO KAYAMA...
... THERE HAVE BEEN SOME RECENT UPDATES ON THE CASE!
THEIR DEATHS WERE AT FIRST REPORTED TO BE THE RESULT OF A SUICIDE PACT...
HOWEVER, THE DISCOVERY OF MR. KAYAMA'S DIARY AT HIS RESIDENCE HAS MADE IT APPARENT THAT MISS MAKINO MANIPULATED HIM TO HIS DEATH.
March 28th
That woman is despicable. She's played so many different personalities in her career that she's lost sight of her own. "I can't find myself no matter where I look," she says. "What I used to call myself is dead. How can I keep going, and for whom?" She believes her salvation is in reuniting the physical and mental, and in order to do so, her physical body must die, too.
Despite this, I cannot bring myself to leave her... And I do not wish to make her feelings public... Our relationship

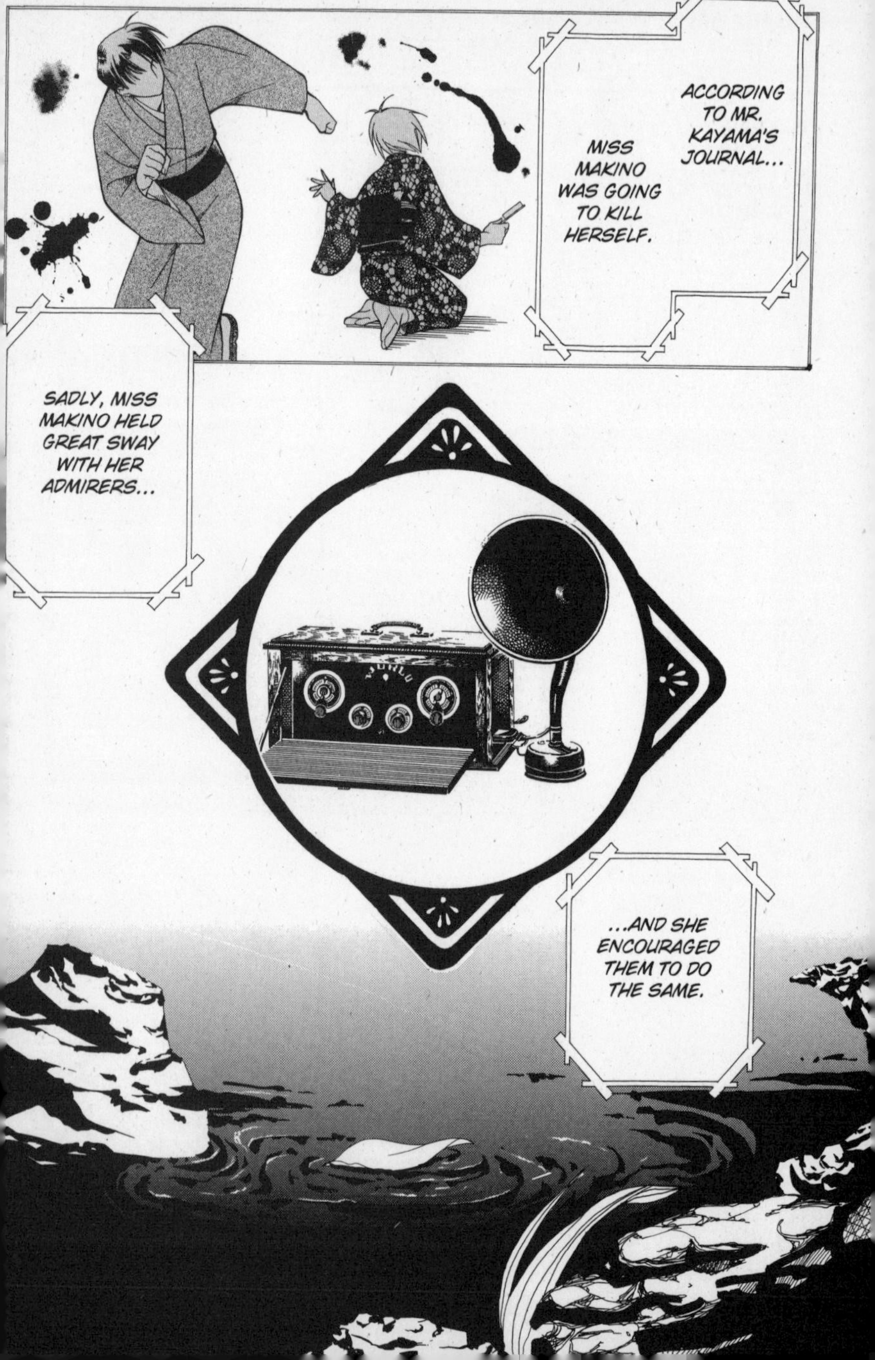
ACCORDING TO MR. KAYAMA'S JOURNAL...
MISS MAKINO WAS GOING TO KILL HERSELF.
SADLY, MISS MAKINO HELD GREAT SWAY WITH HER ADMIRERS...
...AND SHE ENCOURAGED THEM TO DO THE SAME.

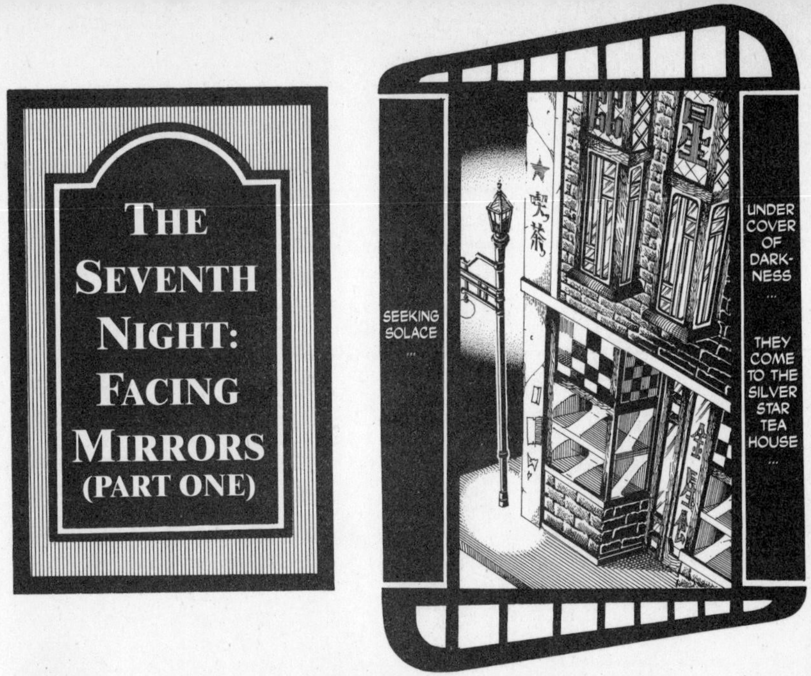
UNDER COVER OF DARKNESS ...
THEY COME TO THE SILVER STAR TEA HOUSE ...
SEEKING SOLACE ...

The Seventh Night: Facing Mirrors (Part One)

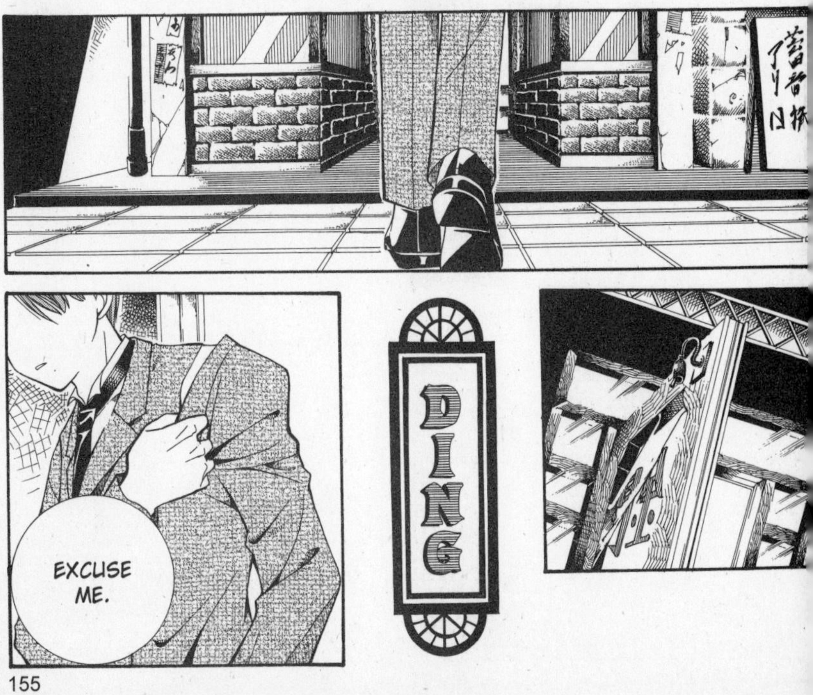
DING
EXCUSE ME.

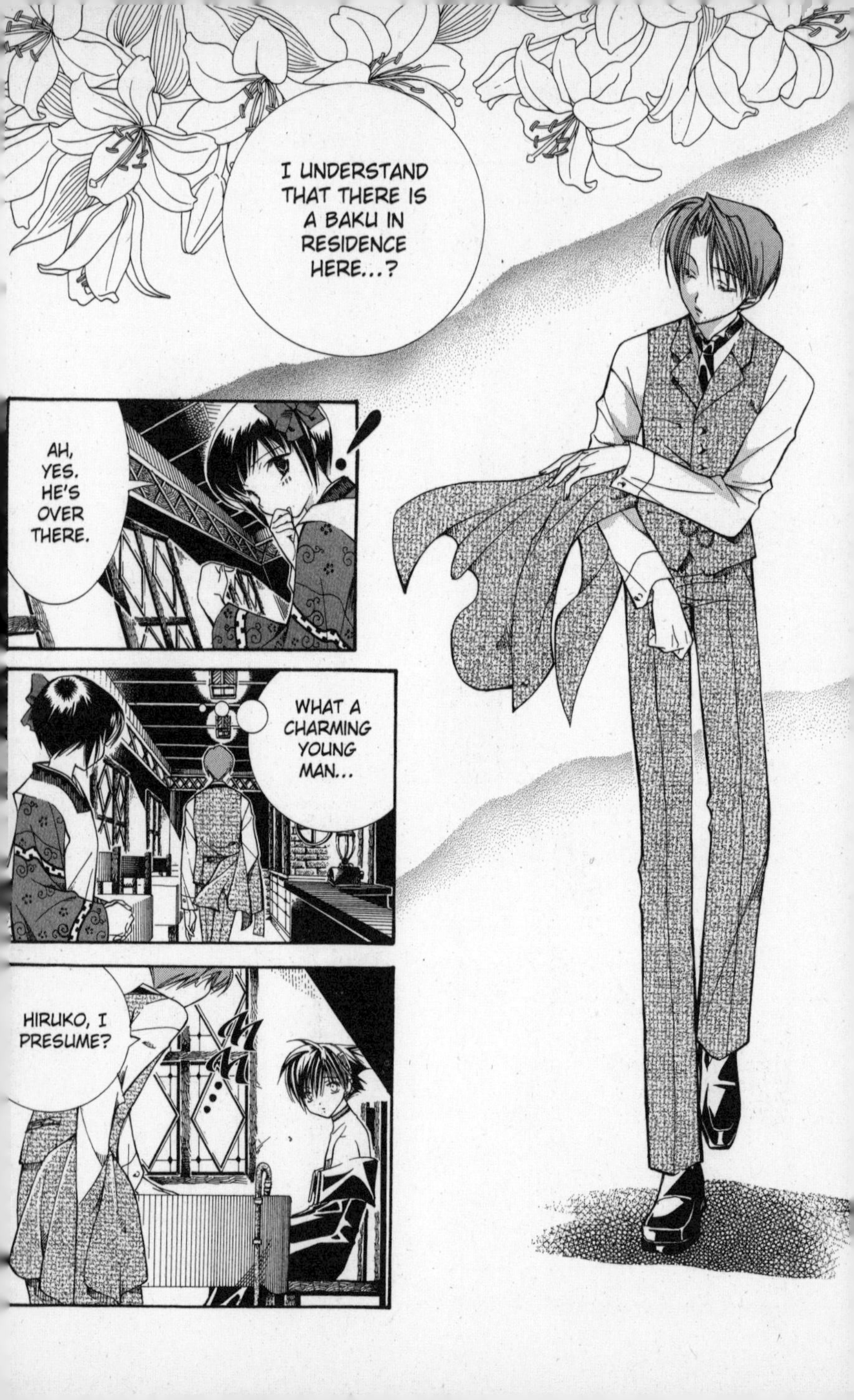
I UNDERSTAND THAT THERE IS A BAKU IN RESIDENCE HERE...?
AH, YES. HE'S OVER THERE.
WHAT A CHARMING YOUNG MAN...
HIRUKO, I PRESUME?

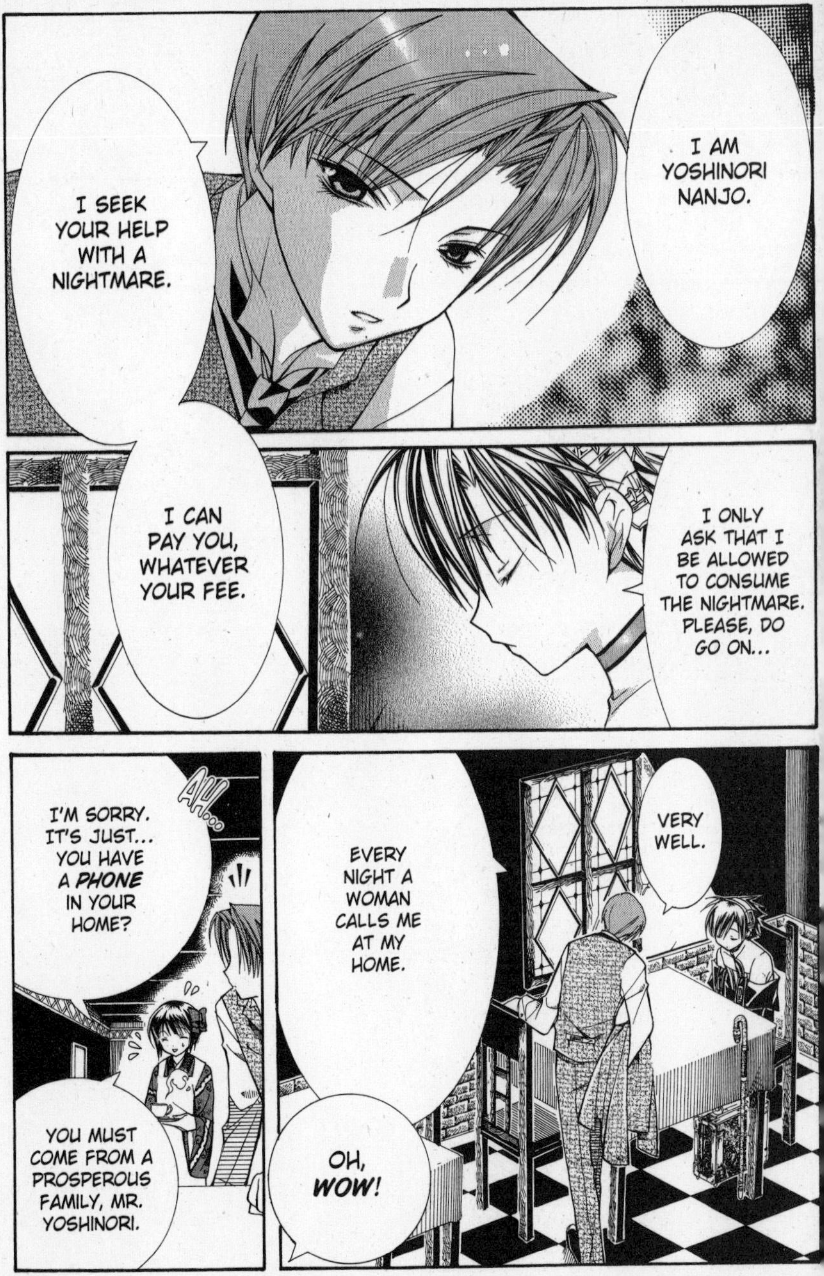
I AM YOSHINORI NANJO.
I SEEK YOUR HELP WITH A NIGHTMARE.
I CAN PAY YOU, WHATEVER YOUR FEE.
I ONLY ASK THAT I BE ALLOWED TO CONSUME THE NIGHTMARE. PLEASE, DO GO ON...
VERY WELL.
EVERY NIGHT A WOMAN CALLS ME AT MY HOME.
OH, *WOW*!
AH...
I'M SORRY. IT'S JUST... YOU HAVE A *PHONE* IN YOUR HOME?
YOU MUST COME FROM A PROSPEROUS FAMILY, MR. YOSHINORI.

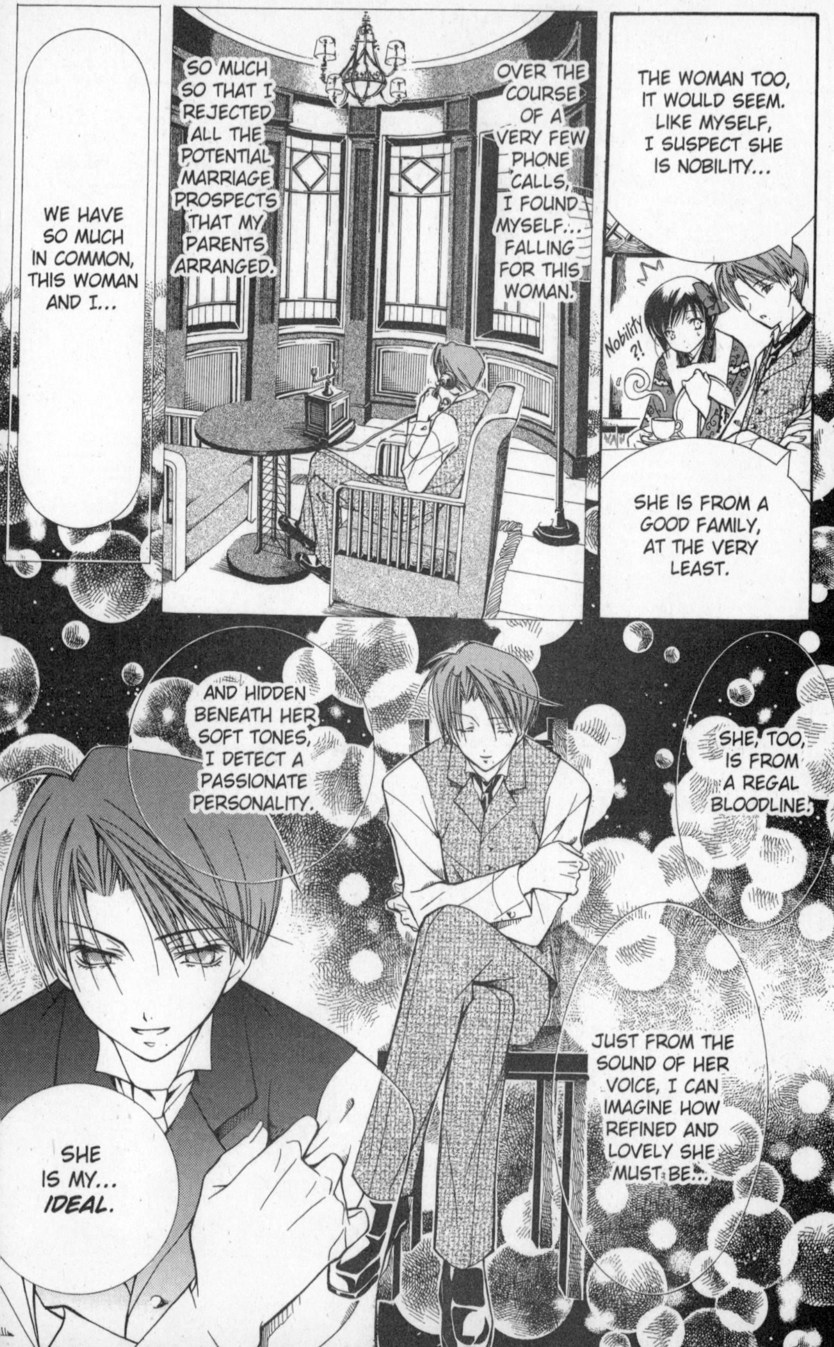
THE WOMAN TOO, IT WOULD SEEM. LIKE MYSELF, I SUSPECT SHE IS NOBILITY...
Nobility ?!
SHE IS FROM A GOOD FAMILY, AT THE VERY LEAST.
OVER THE COURSE OF A VERY FEW PHONE CALLS, I FOUND MYSELF... FALLING FOR THIS WOMAN.
SO MUCH SO THAT I REJECTED ALL THE POTENTIAL MARRIAGE PROSPECTS THAT MY PARENTS ARRANGED.
WE HAVE SO MUCH IN COMMON, THIS WOMAN AND I...
SHE, TOO, IS FROM A REGAL BLOODLINE.
AND HIDDEN BENEATH HER SOFT TONES, I DETECT A PASSIONATE PERSONALITY.
JUST FROM THE SOUND OF HER VOICE, I CAN IMAGINE HOW REFINED AND LOVELY SHE MUST BE...
SHE IS MY... *IDEAL*.

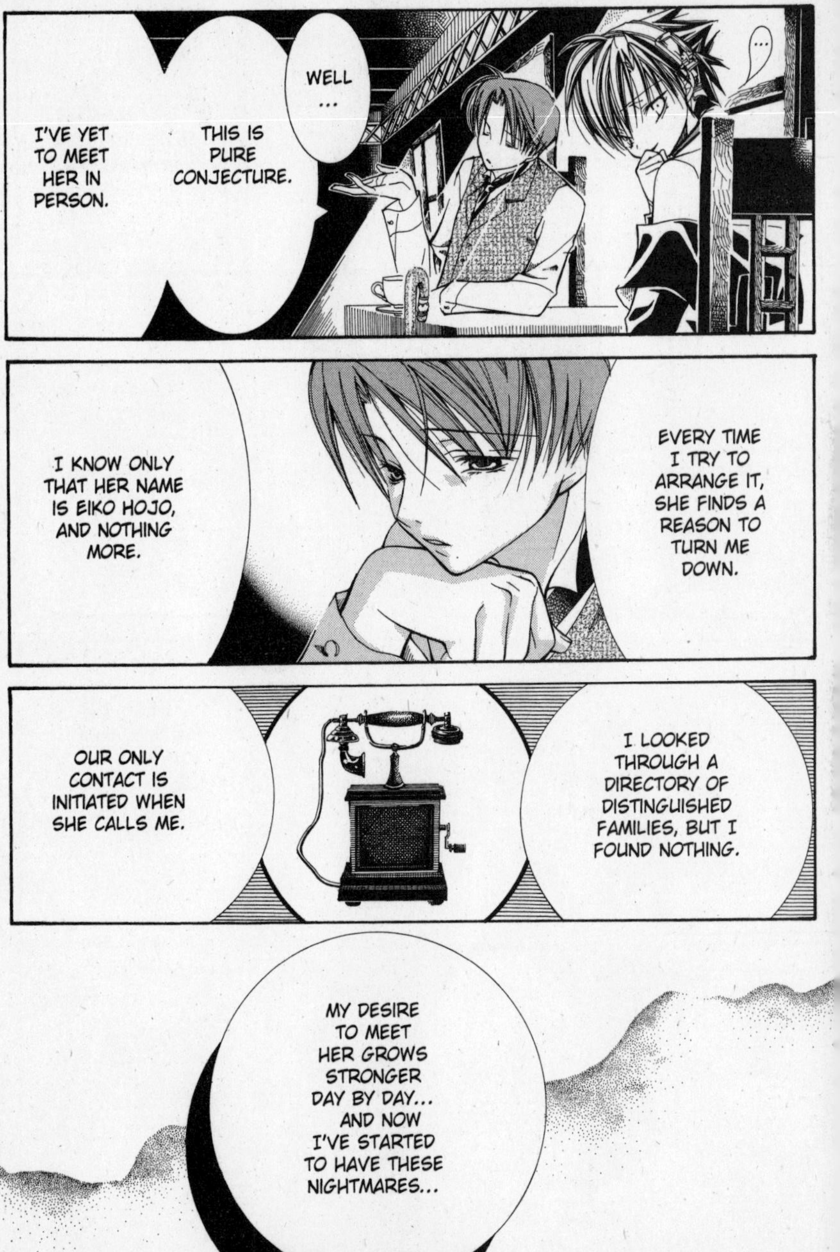
...
WELL ...
THIS IS PURE CONJECTURE.
I'VE YET TO MEET HER IN PERSON.
EVERY TIME I TRY TO ARRANGE IT, SHE FINDS A REASON TO TURN ME DOWN.
I KNOW ONLY THAT HER NAME IS EIKO HOJO, AND NOTHING MORE.
I LOOKED THROUGH A DIRECTORY OF DISTINGUISHED FAMILIES, BUT I FOUND NOTHING.
OUR ONLY CONTACT IS INITIATED WHEN SHE CALLS ME.
MY DESIRE TO MEET HER GROWS STRONGER DAY BY DAY... AND NOW I'VE STARTED TO HAVE THESE NIGHTMARES...

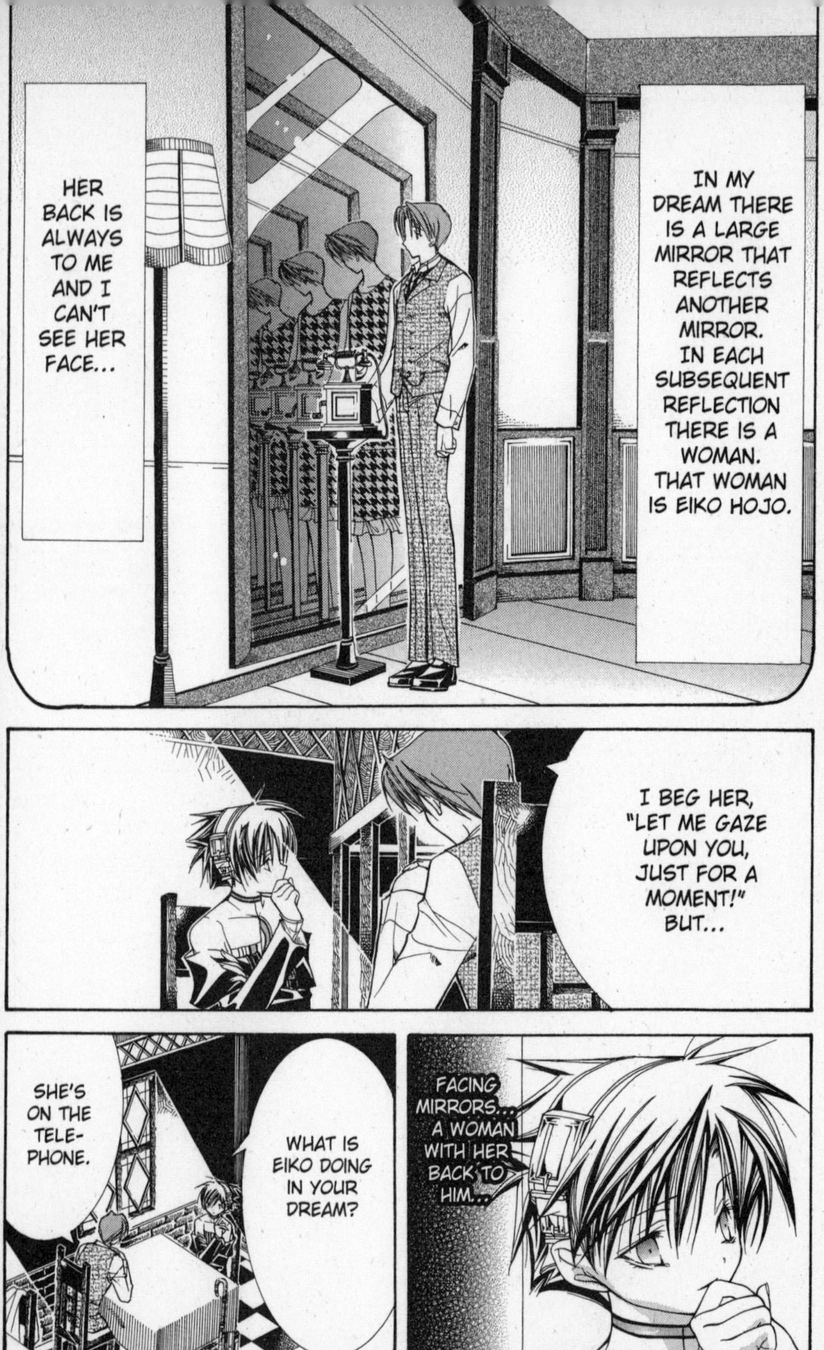
IN MY DREAM THERE IS A LARGE MIRROR THAT REFLECTS ANOTHER MIRROR. IN EACH SUBSEQUENT REFLECTION THERE IS A WOMAN. THAT WOMAN IS EIKO HOJO.
HER BACK IS ALWAYS TO ME AND I CAN'T SEE HER FACE...
I BEG HER, "LET ME GAZE UPON YOU, JUST FOR A MOMENT!" BUT...
FACING MIRRORS... A WOMAN WITH HER BACK TO HIM...
WHAT IS EIKO DOING IN YOUR DREAM?
SHE'S ON THE TELE-PHONE.

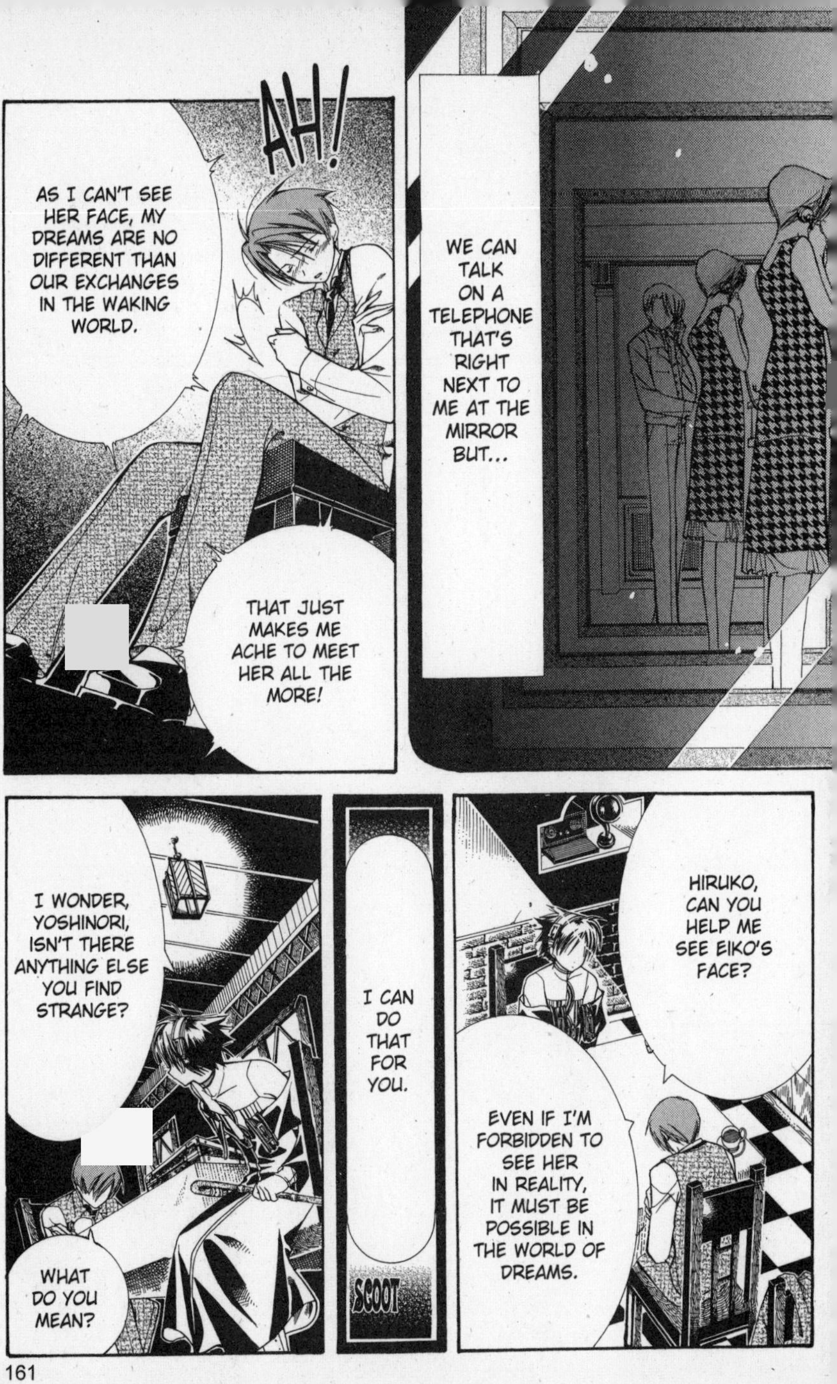
WE CAN TALK ON A TELEPHONE THAT'S RIGHT NEXT TO ME AT THE MIRROR BUT...
AH!
AS I CAN'T SEE HER FACE, MY DREAMS ARE NO DIFFERENT THAN OUR EXCHANGES IN THE WAKING WORLD.
THAT JUST MAKES ME ACHE TO MEET HER ALL THE MORE!
HIRUKO, CAN YOU HELP ME SEE EIKO'S FACE?
EVEN IF I'M FORBIDDEN TO SEE HER IN REALITY, IT MUST BE POSSIBLE IN THE WORLD OF DREAMS.
I CAN DO THAT FOR YOU.
SCOOT
I WONDER, YOSHINORI, ISN'T THERE ANYTHING ELSE YOU FIND STRANGE?
WHAT DO YOU MEAN?

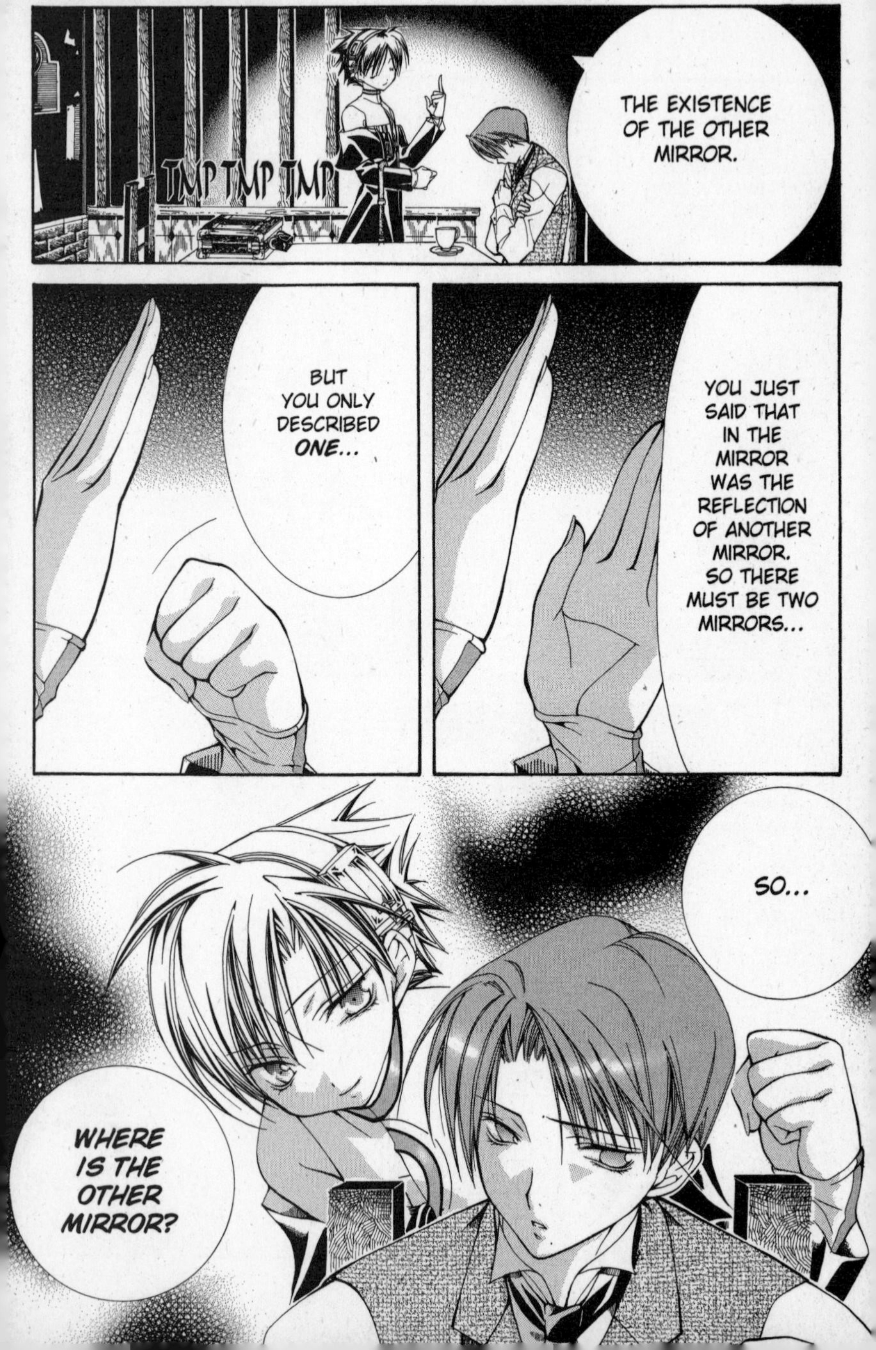
THE EXISTENCE OF THE OTHER MIRROR.
TMP TMP TMP
YOU JUST SAID THAT IN THE MIRROR WAS THE REFLECTION OF ANOTHER MIRROR. SO THERE MUST BE TWO MIRRORS...
BUT YOU ONLY DESCRIBED ONE...
SO...
WHERE IS THE OTHER MIRROR?

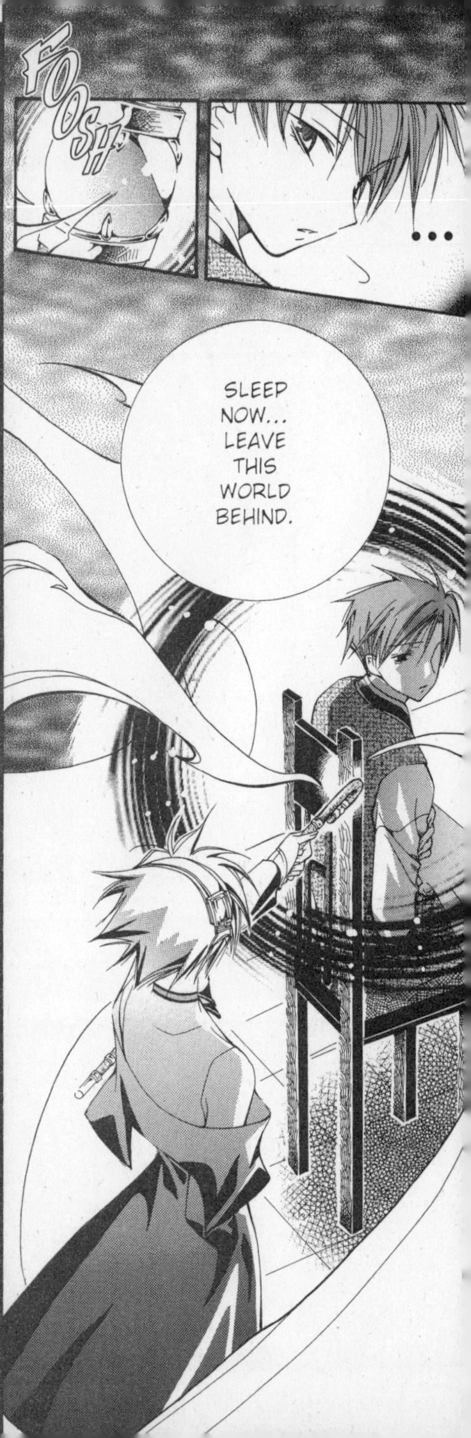
...
FOOSH
SLEEP NOW... LEAVE THIS WORLD BEHIND.
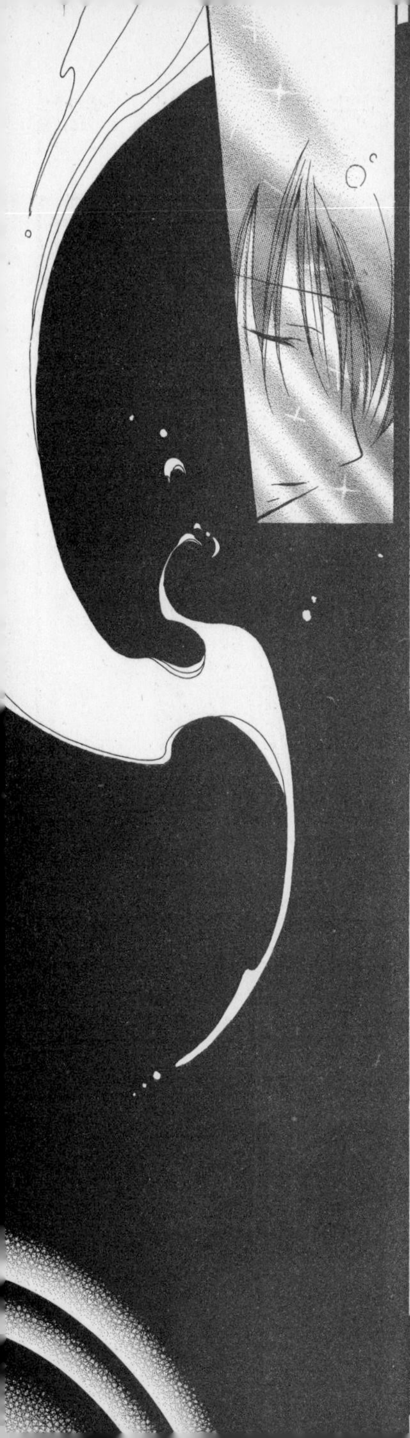

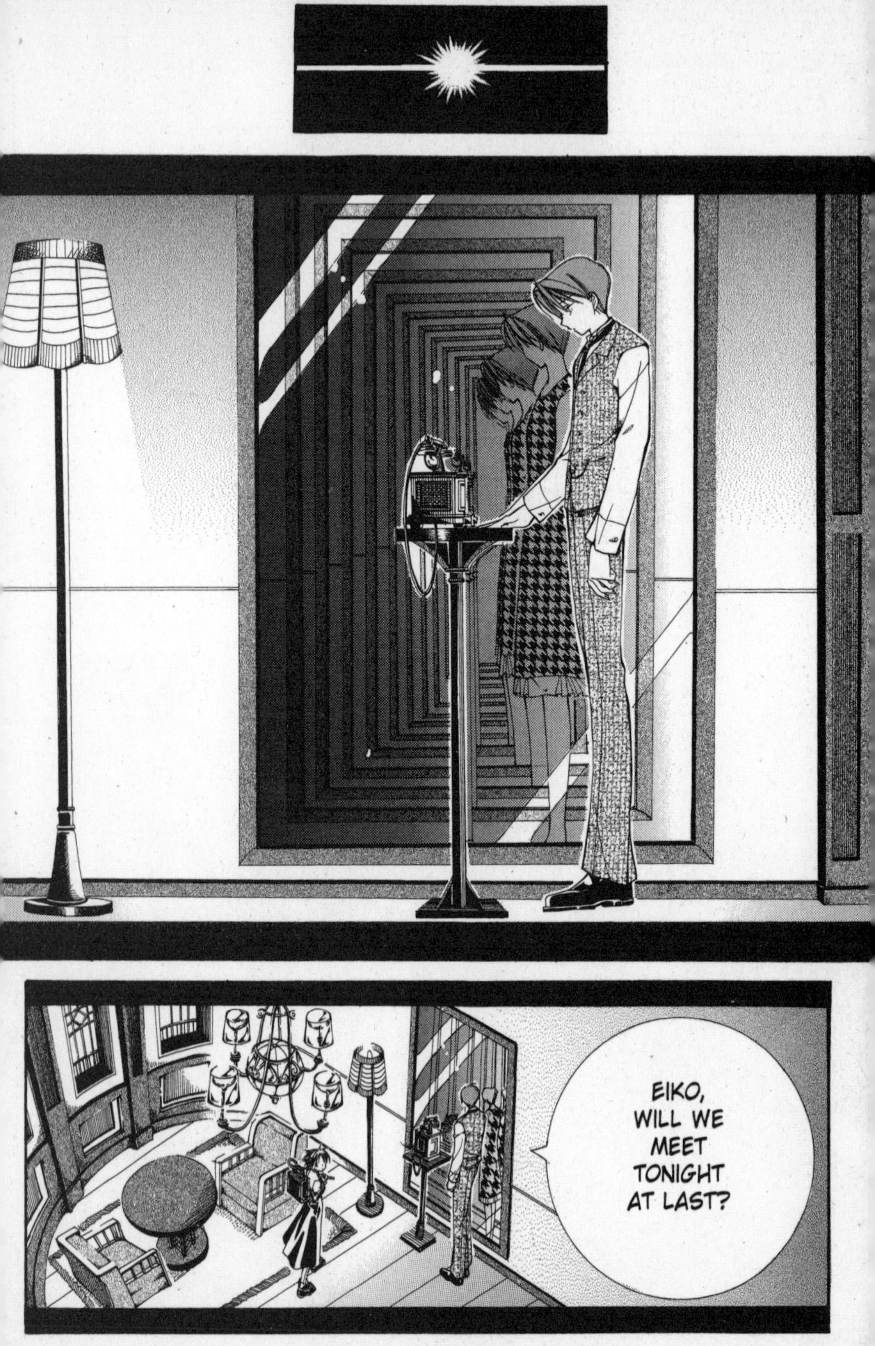
EIKO, WILL WE MEET TONIGHT AT LAST?

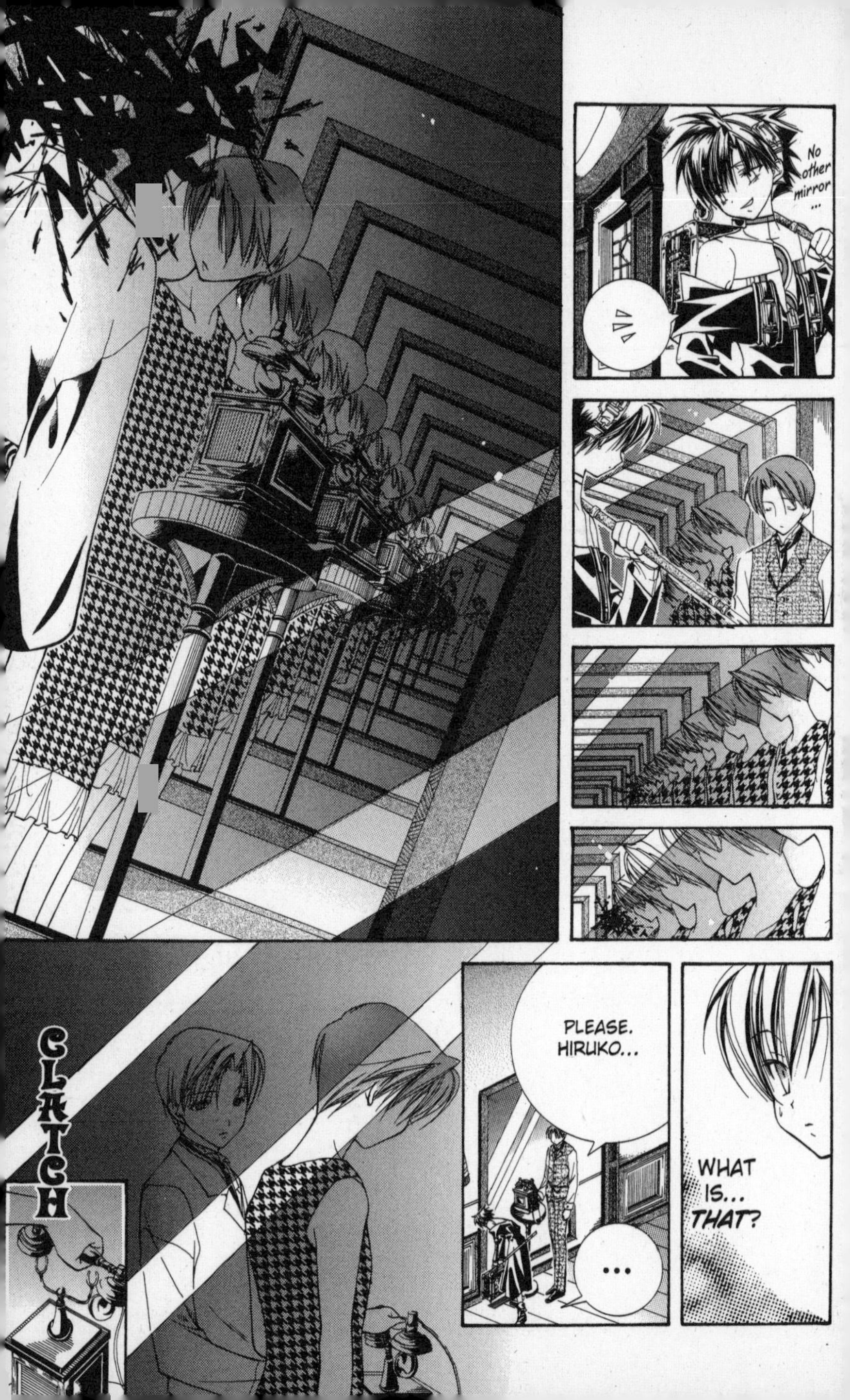
No other mirror ...
WHAT IS... THAT?
PLEASE. HIRUKO...
...
CLATCH

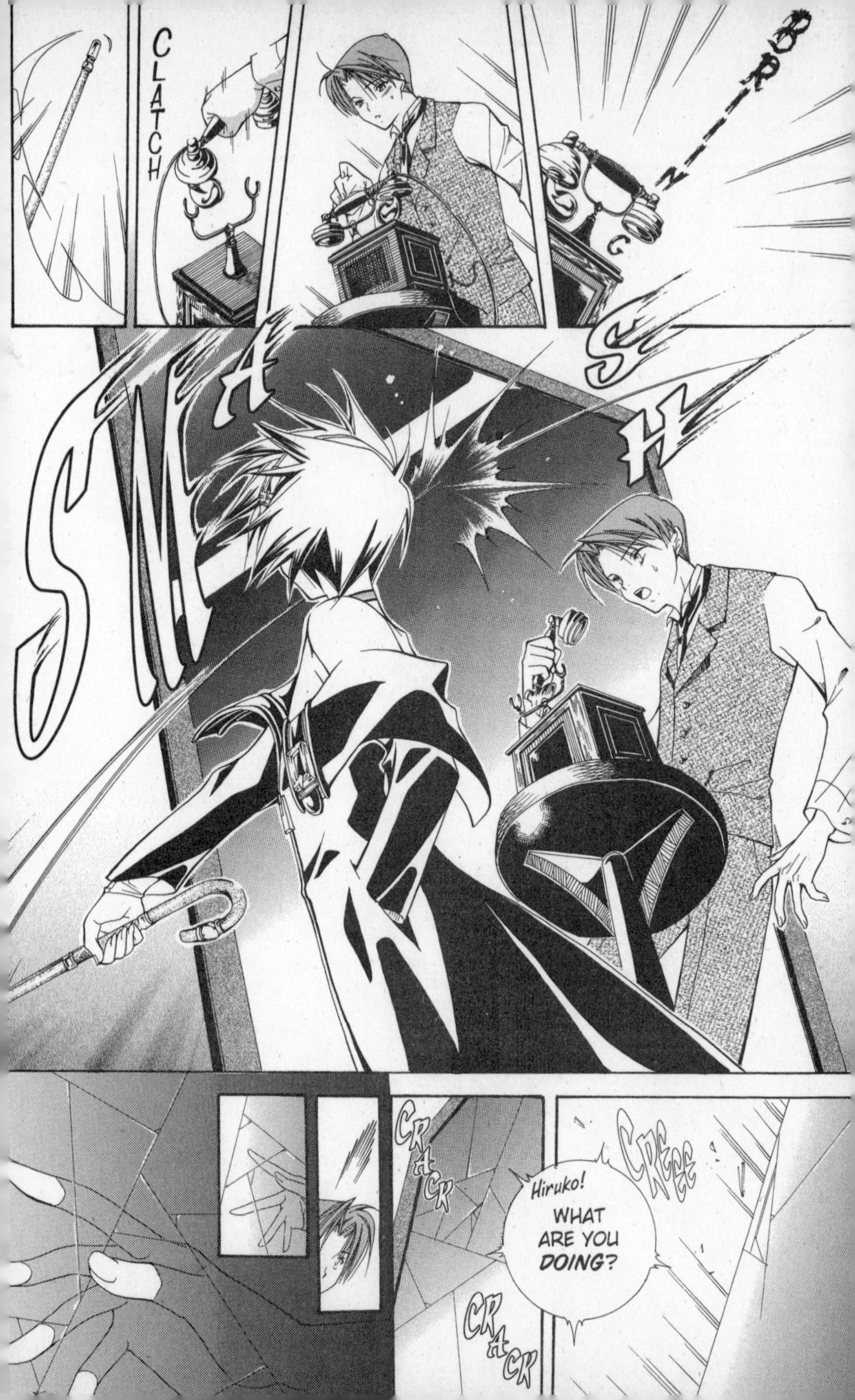
BRIIING
CLATCH
SMASH
CREEE
Hiruko!
WHAT ARE YOU DOING?
CRACK
CRACK

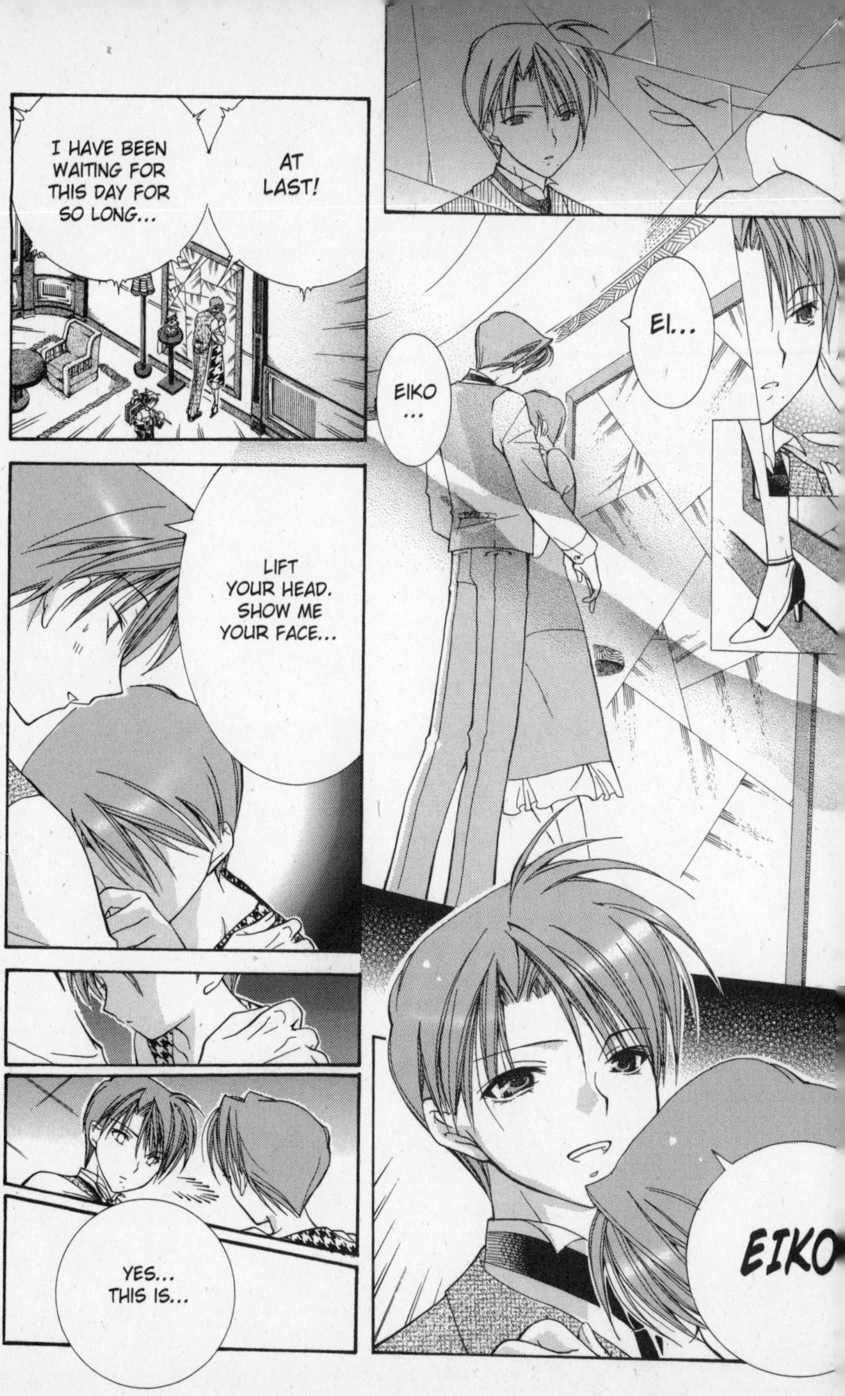
AT LAST!
I HAVE BEEN WAITING FOR THIS DAY FOR SO LONG...
EI...
EIKO ...
LIFT YOUR HEAD. SHOW ME YOUR FACE...
YES... THIS IS...
EIKO

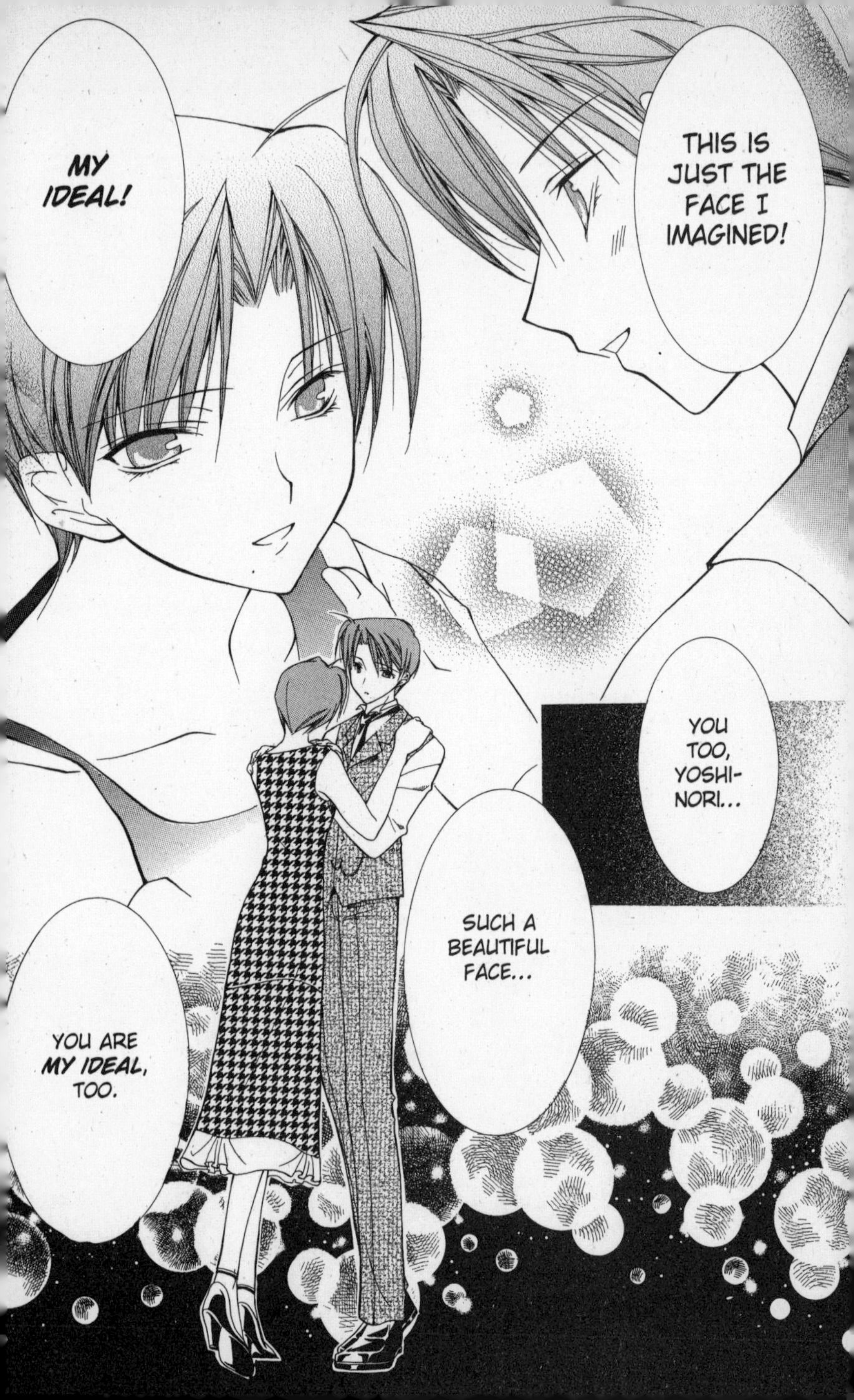
THIS IS JUST THE FACE I IMAGINED!
MY IDEAL!
YOU TOO, YOSHI-NORI...
SUCH A BEAUTIFUL FACE...
YOU ARE *MY IDEAL,* TOO.

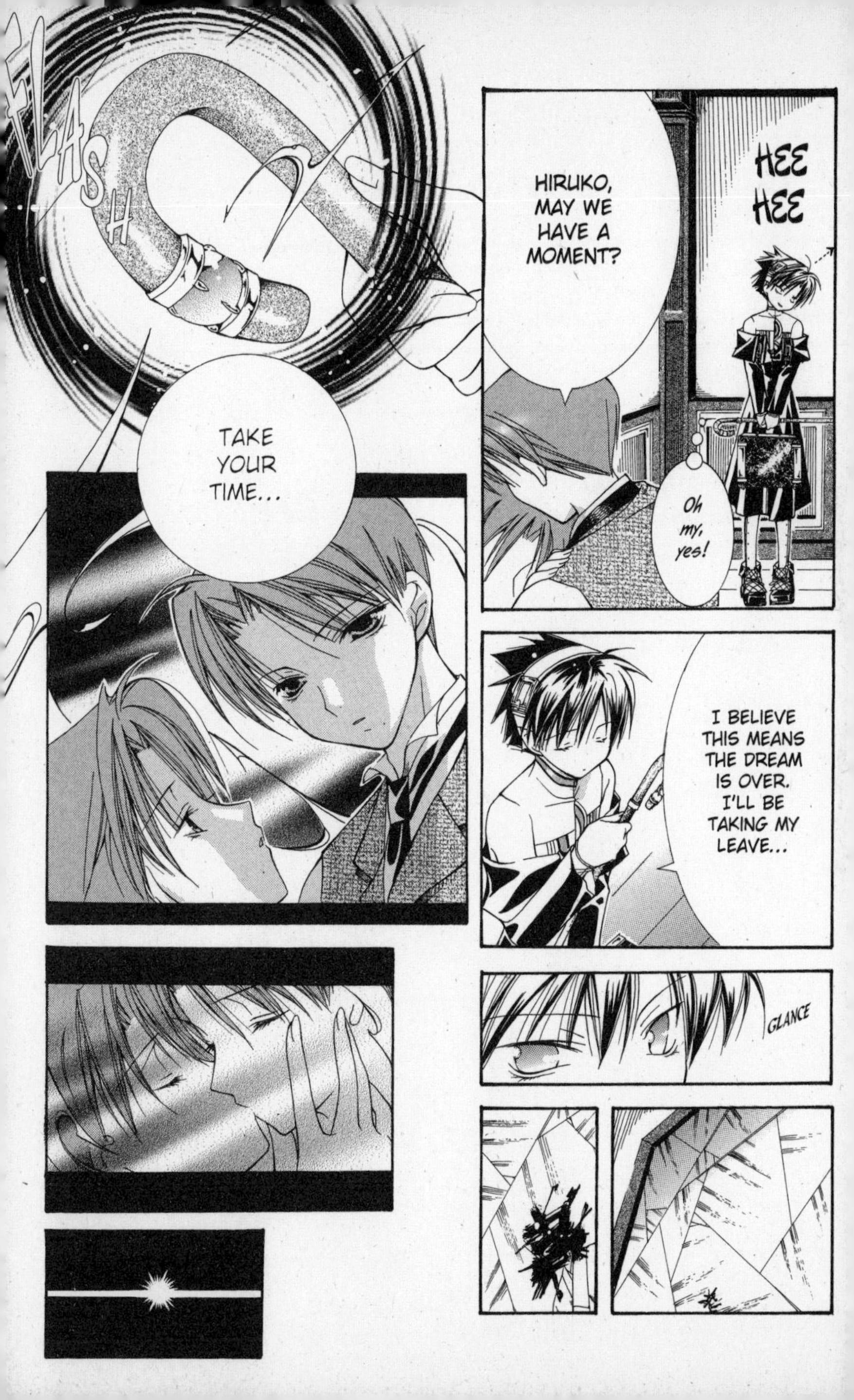
HIRUKO, MAY WE HAVE A MOMENT?
HEE HEE
Oh my, yes!
FLASH
TAKE YOUR TIME...
I BELIEVE THIS MEANS THE DREAM IS OVER. I'LL BE TAKING MY LEAVE...
GLANCE

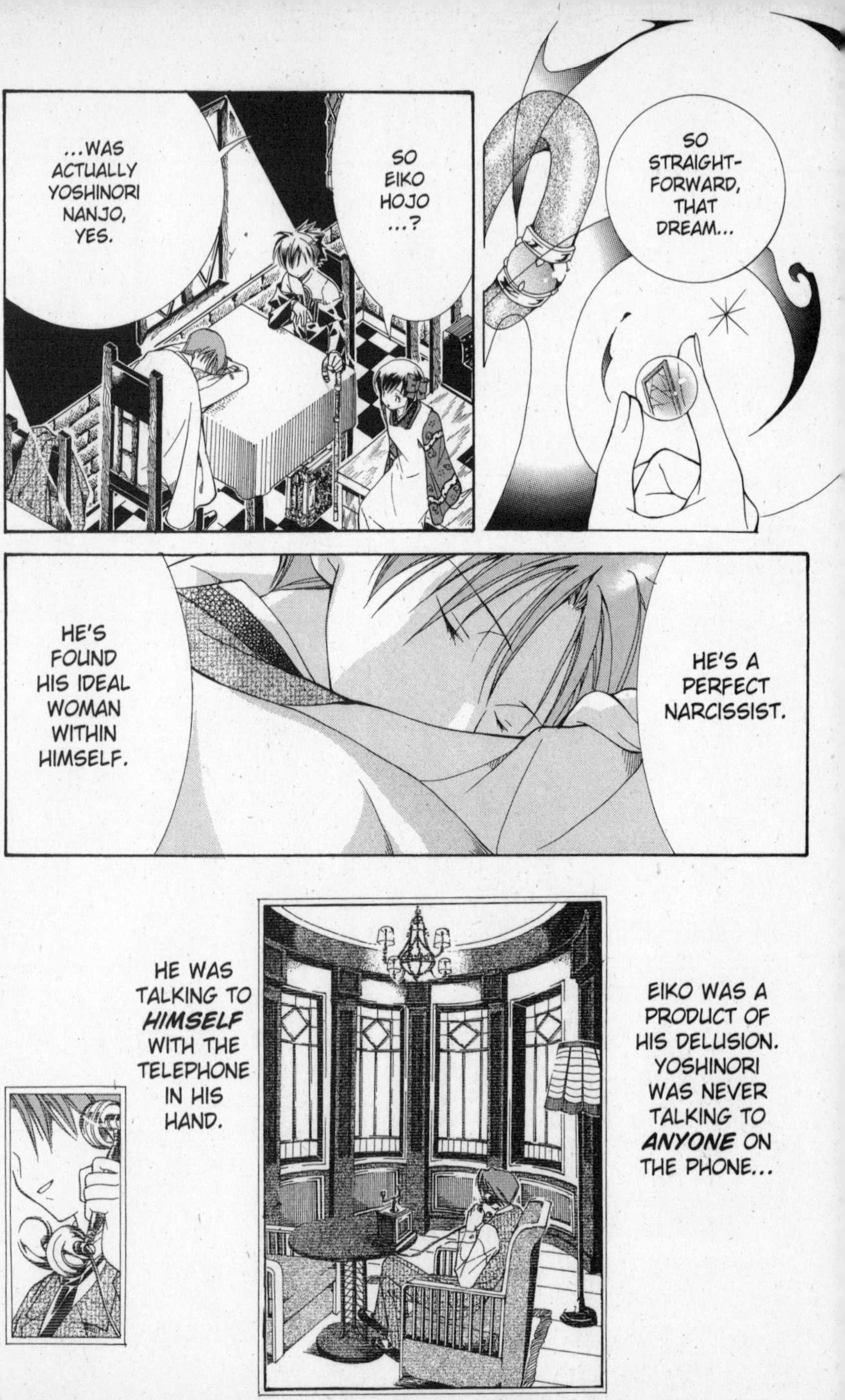
SO STRAIGHT-FORWARD, THAT DREAM...
SO EIKO HOJO ...?
...WAS ACTUALLY YOSHINORI NANJO, YES.
HE'S A PERFECT NARCISSIST.
HE'S FOUND HIS IDEAL WOMAN WITHIN HIMSELF.
EIKO WAS A PRODUCT OF HIS DELUSION. YOSHINORI WAS NEVER TALKING TO *ANYONE* ON THE PHONE...
HE WAS TALKING TO *HIMSELF* WITH THE TELEPHONE IN HIS HAND.

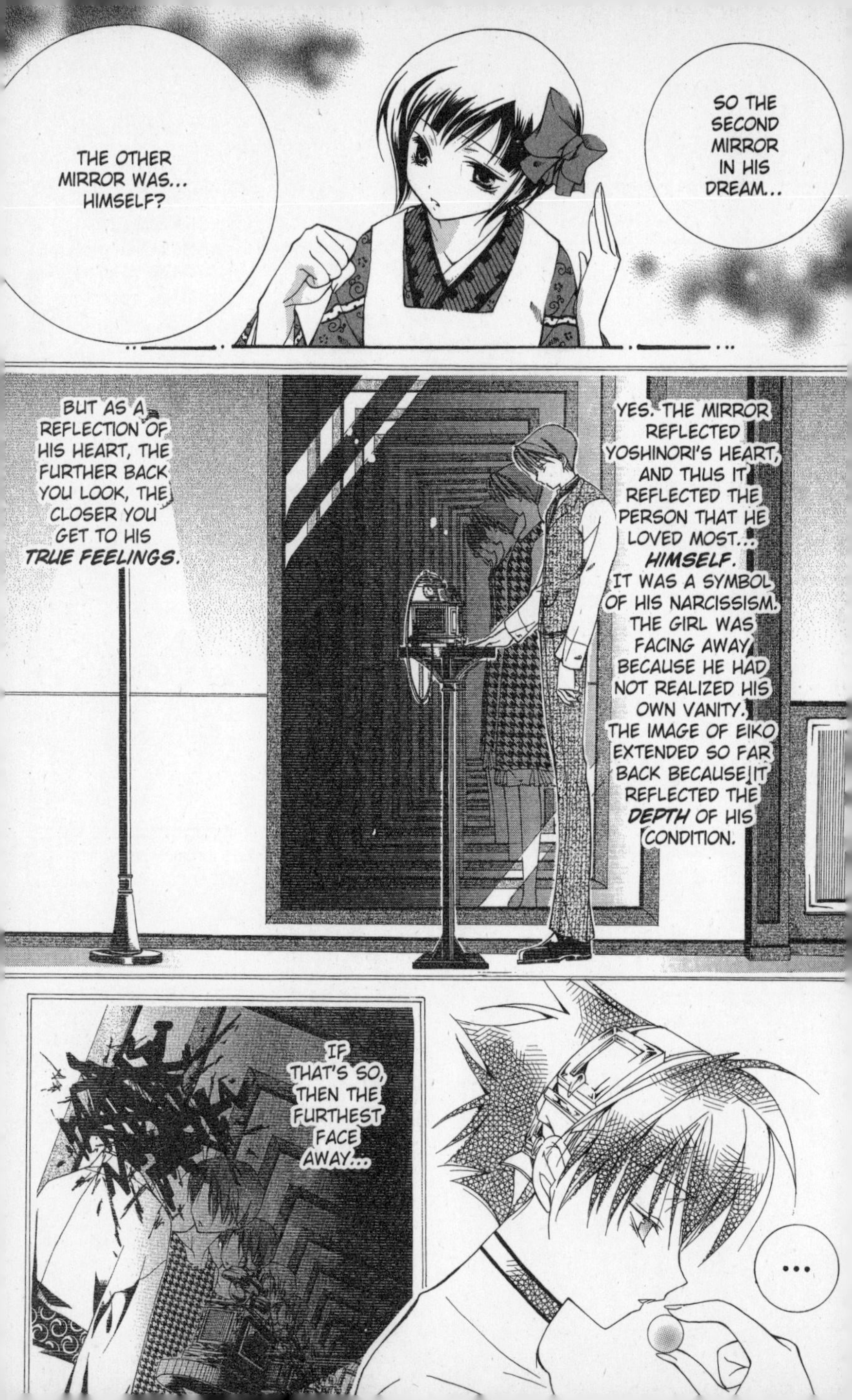
SO THE SECOND MIRROR IN HIS DREAM...
THE OTHER MIRROR WAS... HIMSELF?
YES. THE MIRROR REFLECTED YOSHINORI'S HEART, AND THUS IT REFLECTED THE PERSON THAT HE LOVED MOST... **HIMSELF.** IT WAS A SYMBOL OF HIS NARCISSISM. THE GIRL WAS FACING AWAY BECAUSE HE HAD NOT REALIZED HIS OWN VANITY. THE IMAGE OF EIKO EXTENDED SO FAR BACK BECAUSE IT REFLECTED THE ***DEPTH*** OF HIS CONDITION.
BUT AS A REFLECTION OF HIS HEART, THE FURTHER BACK YOU LOOK, THE CLOSER YOU GET TO HIS ***TRUE FEELINGS.***
...
IF THAT'S SO, THEN THE FURTHEST FACE AWAY...

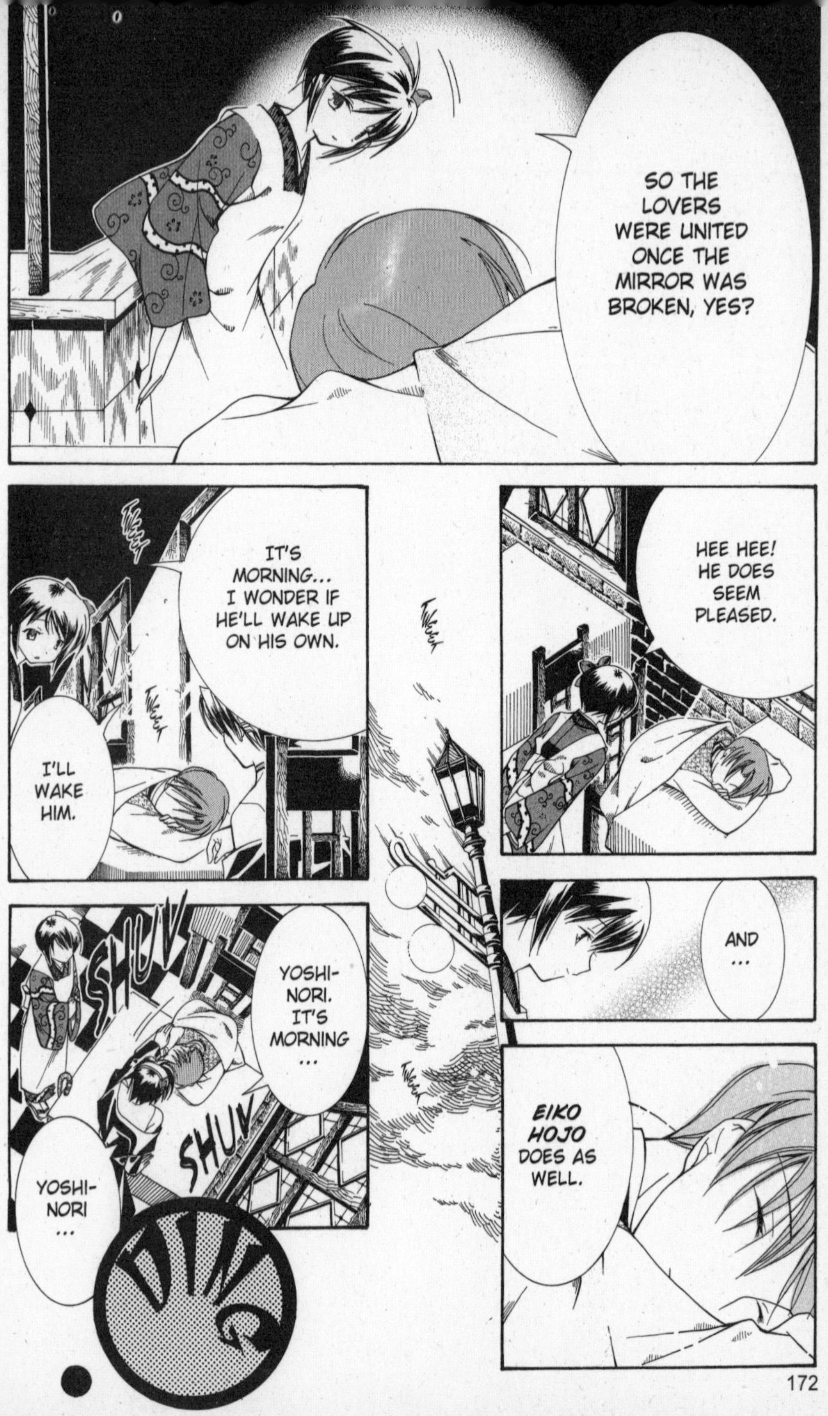
SO THE LOVERS WERE UNITED ONCE THE MIRROR WAS BROKEN, YES?
HEE HEE! HE DOES SEEM PLEASED.
IT'S MORNING... I WONDER IF HE'LL WAKE UP ON HIS OWN.
I'LL WAKE HIM.
AND ...
EIKO HOJO DOES AS WELL.
YOSHI-NORI. IT'S MORNING ...
SHUV
SHUV
YOSHI-NORI ...
DING

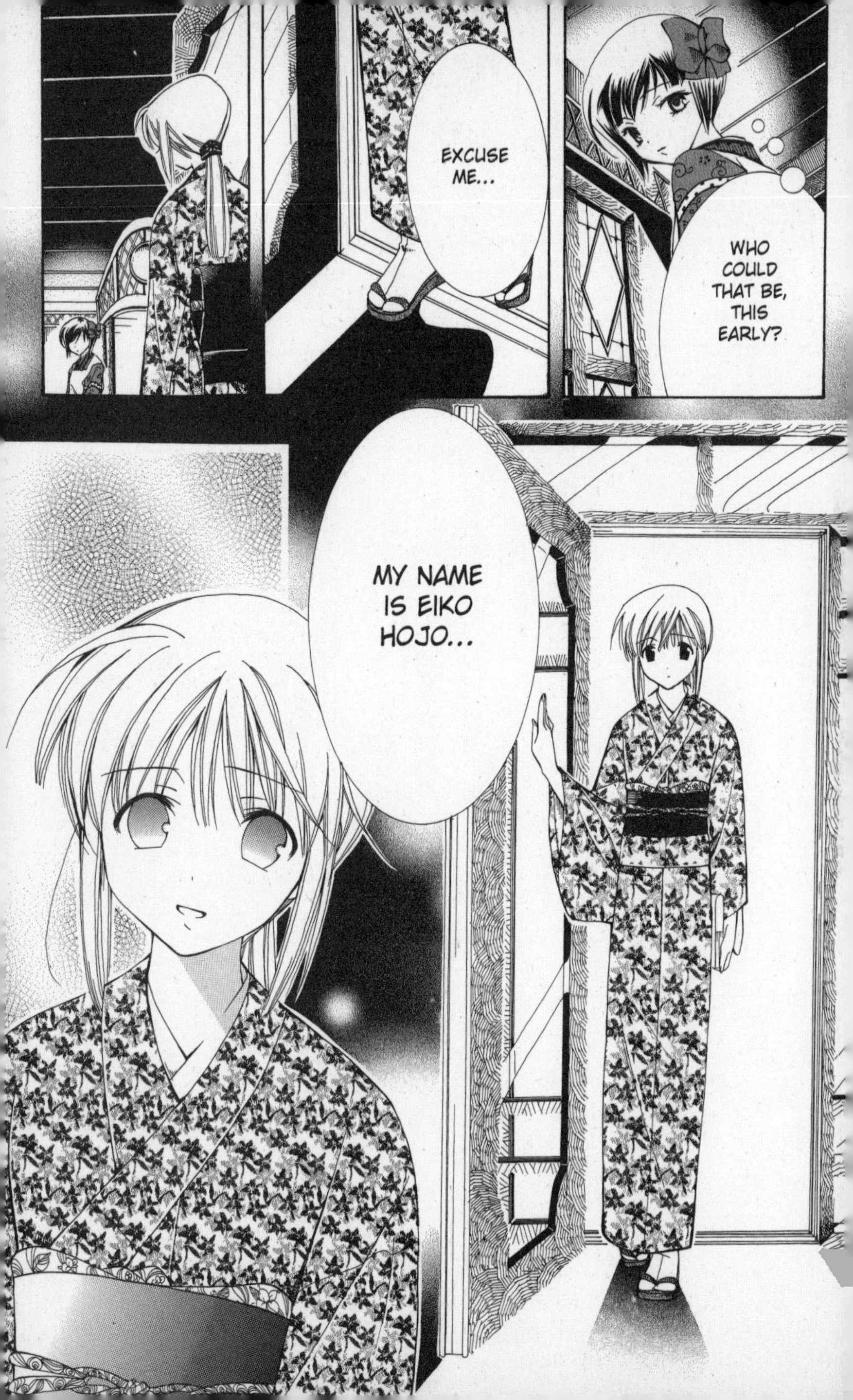
WHO COULD THAT BE, THIS EARLY?
EXCUSE ME...
MY NAME IS EIKO HOJO...

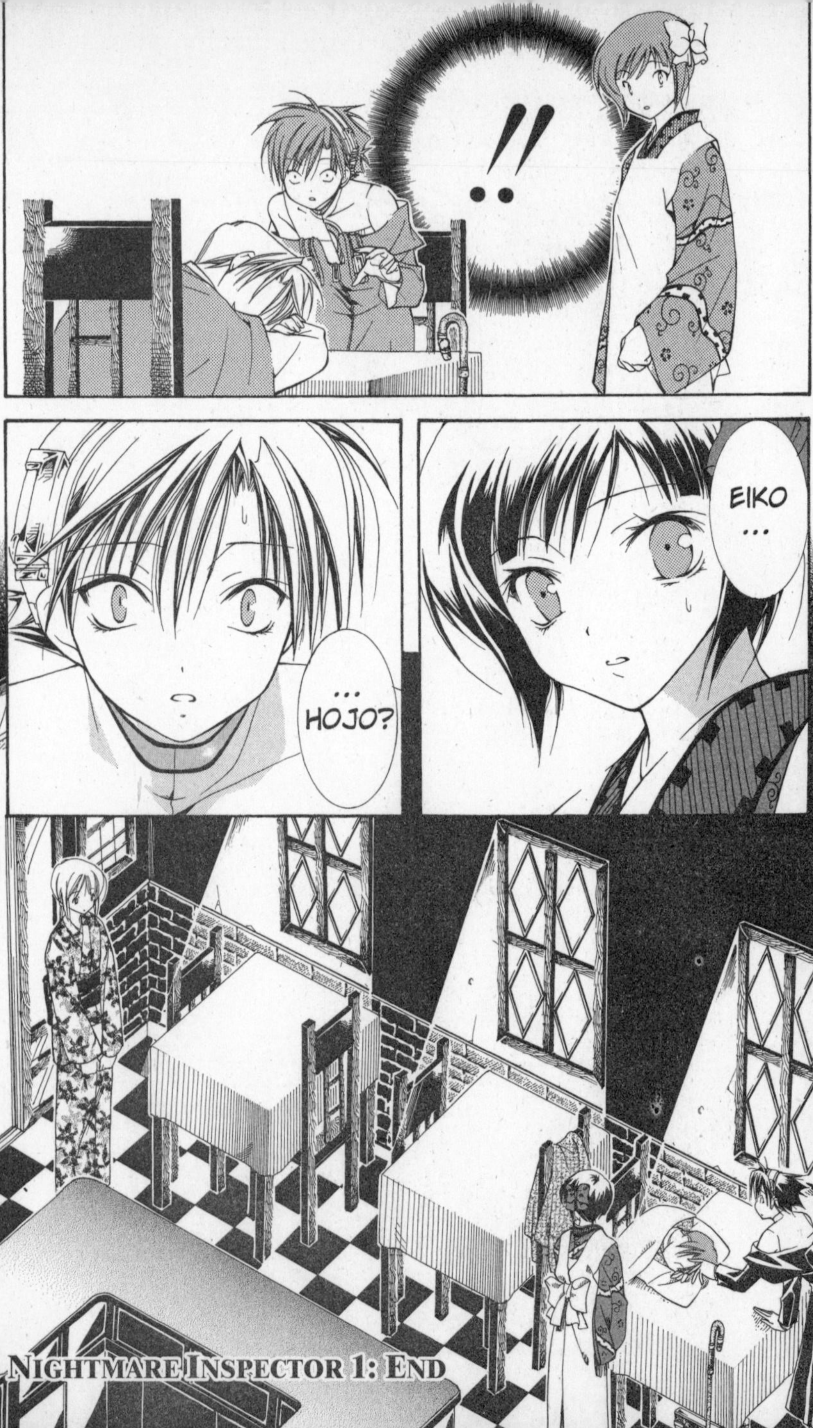
!!
EIKO ...
... HOJO?
NIGHTMARE INSPECTOR 1: END

あとがき AFTERWORD

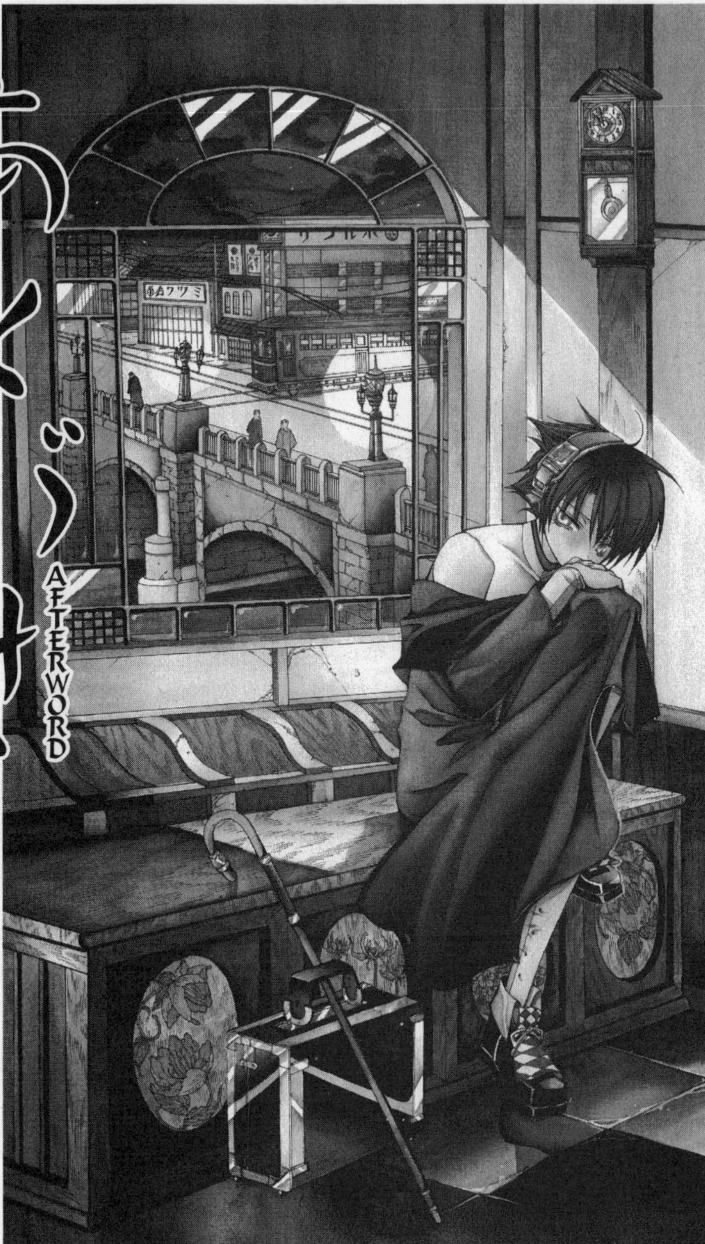

Hello, everybody, this is Shin Mashiba. First, I want to thank you for buying this book. Thank you from the bottom of my heart! I didn't have any experience with serialization before this project and I'd be remiss if I didn't also thank my gracious editor who kindly directed me when I had no idea what I was doing. And finally, I offer a very special thanks to all the readers who have followed my young career from the start.

I really enjoyed drawing the backgrounds to Nightmare Inspector. Really, my only regret about the book thus far is that name of the waitress at the Silver Star Tea House is never mentioned. Well, that and the fact that there is no conclusion to chapter seven just yet...

Wanwan Shiroi has been such a great help to me, that I asked him to do a guest feature in this volume. It's like he's drunk some magic potion that makes it all seem real.

★初代担当様
Chief Editor.
二代目 俳人 松下正孝様
The poet, Masataka Matsushita
三代目 佐伯有希様
Yuki Saeki
★アシスタント 白井わんわん様
Assistant: Wanwan Shiroi
タケっち様
Takecchi
★情報担当 MOAI様
Information: MOAI
マミー様
Mami

Thank you all so much!

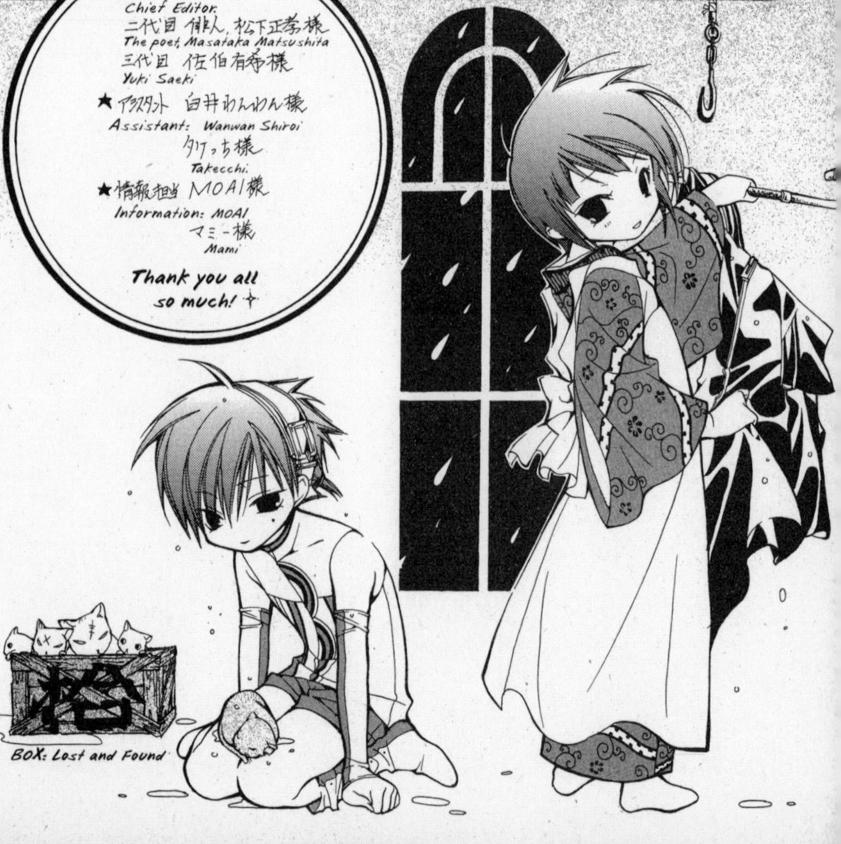
BOX: Lost and Found

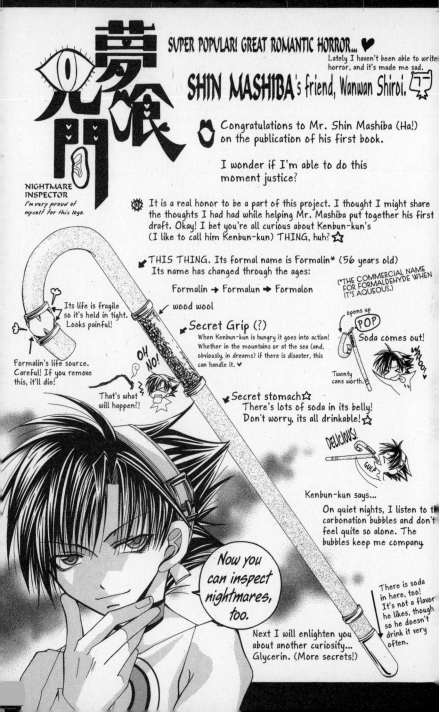

夢 喰 見 聞

NIGHTMARE INSPECTOR

I'm very proud of myself for this logo.

SUPER POPULAR! GREAT ROMANTIC HORROR... ♥

Lately I haven't been able to write horror, and it's made me sad.

SHIN MASHIBA's friend, Wanwan Shiroi.

👄 Congratulations to Mr. Shin Mashiba (Ha!) on the publication of his first book.

I wonder if I'm able to do this moment justice?

It is a real honor to be a part of this project. I thought I might share the thoughts I had had while helping Mr. Mashiba put together his first draft. Okay! I bet you're all curious about Kenbun-kun's (I like to call him Kenbun-kun) THING, huh? ☆

THIS THING. Its formal name is Formalin* (56 years old)
Its name has changed through the ages:

Formalin → Formalun → Formalon

(*THE COMMERCIAL NAME FOR FORMALDEHYDE WHEN IT'S AQUEOUS.)

wood wool

Its life is fragile so it's held in tight. Looks painful!

Formalin's life source. Careful! If you remove this, it'll die!

OH NO!

That's what will happen?!

▶ **Secret Grip (?)**
When Kenbun-kun is hungry it goes into action! Whether in the mountains or at the sea (and, obviously, in dreams) if there is disaster, this can handle it. ♥

opens up

POP

Soda comes out!

WAHOO!

Twenty cans worth.

▶ **Secret stomach** ☆
There's lots of soda in its belly! Don't worry, its all drinkable! ☆

DELICIOUS!

GULP

Kenbun-kun says...

On quiet nights, I listen to the carbonation bubbles and don't feel quite so alone. The bubbles keep me company.

Now you can inspect nightmares, too.

Next I will enlighten you about another curiosity... Glycerin. (More secrets!)

There is soda in here, too! It's not a flavor he likes, though so he doesn't drink it very often.

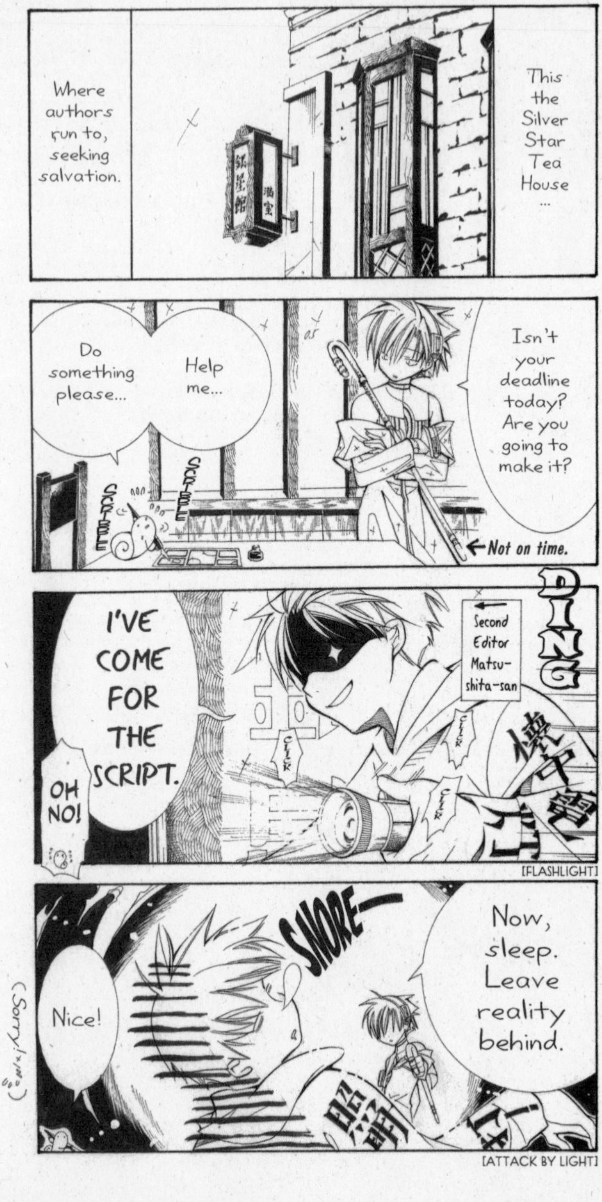
This the Silver Star Tea House ...
Where authors run to, seeking salvation.
Isn't your deadline today? Are you going to make it?
← Not on time.
Help me...
Do something please...
SCRIBBLE
SCRIBBLE
DING
← Second Editor Matsushita-san
CLICK
CLICK
CLICK
I'VE COME FOR THE SCRIPT.
OH NO!
[FLASHLIGHT]
Now, sleep. Leave reality behind.
SNORE—
Nice!
[ATTACK BY LIGHT]
(Sorry!)

COMING NEXT VOLUME

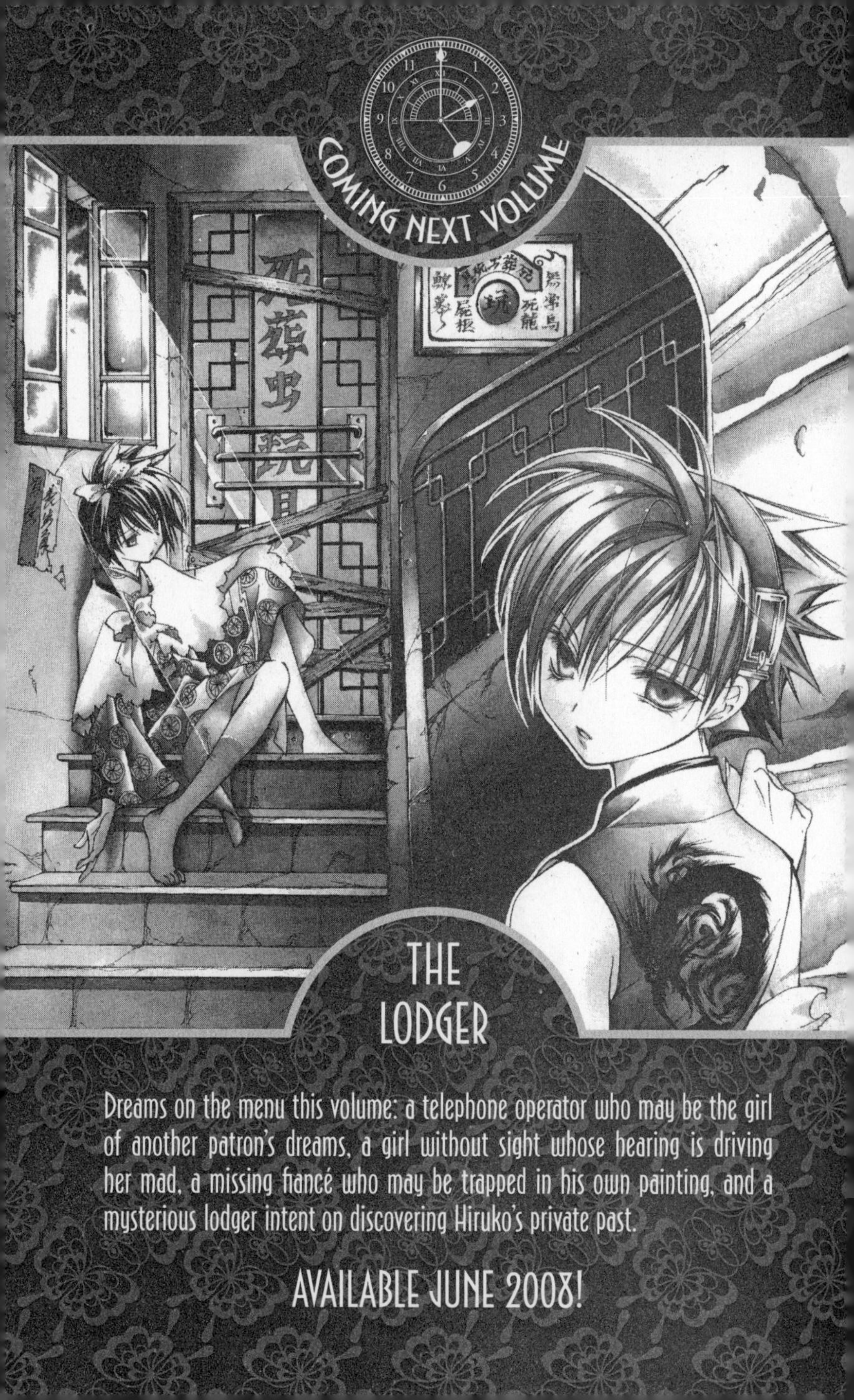

THE LODGER

Dreams on the menu this volume: a telephone operator who may be the girl of another patron's dreams, a girl without sight whose hearing is driving her mad, a missing fiancé who may be trapped in his own painting, and a mysterious lodger intent on discovering Hiruko's private past.

AVAILABLE JUNE 2008!

SHIN MASHIBA

I'm very nervous about my first book. When I was drawing this manga I was wondering about how a nightmare might taste exactly. I suppose because you see a dream inside your head, maybe it would taste like brains?

Shin Mashiba's first manga, *Yumekui Kenbun* (Nightmare Inspector), premiered in *Monthly Stencile*, a shojo magazine, in December 2001 and was then serialized in *Monthly G Fantasy* from 2003 to 2007. Mashiba-san's own nightmares include being forced to eat 50 living slugs and being chased by time.

YUMEKUI KENBUN
NIGHTMARE INSPECTOR

YUMEKUI KENBUN: NIGHTMARE INSPECTOR
VOL. 1
The VIZ Media Edition

STORY AND ART BY
SHIN MASHIBA

Translation/Gemma Collinge
English Adaptation/Kelly Sue DeConnick
Touch-up Art & Lettering/James Gaubatz
Design/Sam Elzway
Editor/Joel Enos

Editor in Chief, Books/Alvin Lu
Editor in Chief, Magazines/Marc Weidenbaum
VP of Publishing Licensing/Rika Inouye
VP of Sales/Gonzalo Ferreyra
Sr. VP of Marketing/Liza Coppola
Publisher/Hyoe Narita

Printed in the U.S.A.

Published by VIZ Media, LLC
P.O. Box 77010
San Francisco, CA 94107

VIZ Media Edition
10 9 8 7 6 5 4 3 2 1
First printing, April 2008

store.viz.com

www.viz.com

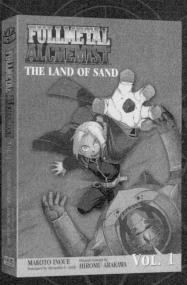

LOVE MANGA?
LET US KNOW WHAT YOU THINK!

OUR MANGA SURVEY IS NOW
AVAILABLE ONLINE. PLEASE VISIT:
VIZ.COM/MANGASURVEY

HELP US MAKE THE MANGA
YOU LOVE BETTER!